Alice,
with my love
Mildred
Christmas 1939

FROM ANOTHER WORLD

THE AUTOBIOGRAPHY OF
LOUIS UNTERMEYER

From Another World

THE AUTOBIOGRAPHY OF

LOUIS UNTERMEYER

HARCOURT, BRACE AND COMPANY, NEW YORK

Typography by Robert Josephy

PRINTED IN THE UNITED STATES OF AMERICA
BY QUINN & BODEN COMPANY, INC., RAHWAY, N. J.

To My Sons
JOHN, LAUREN, *and* JOSEPH

FOREWORD BY LETTER

My dear sons:

There are many things I would like to say, many stories to tell, many thoughts to exchange with you. But there is such a gap in time. You, at about eleven, are so young, and I, at about fifty-three, am, alas, so old. By the time you are ready to read this, if you ever read it at all, we will be (figuratively and, perhaps, literally) in different worlds.

The three worlds I have lived in were as dissimilar as imaginable. There was the world of security and some serenity, of creative excitement, serious play, and happy conflict; a world that ended in 1917. This was followed by the world of distorted rumor and daily nightmare, of the World War and the false peace. And there is the world in which we are now living, the world of undeclared wars and methodical violence, of political aggression and moral disintegration, a world of fear which has exchanged the forces of security for the security of force.

I cannot hazard a guess as to what the next world will be like. Already the world in which I grew up has assumed an unreal detachment. The outlines blur; causes and movements lose meaning; it is hard to recognize the patterns which were once our faith. Many of the men and women I knew have become not only famous but fictional; some of them have taken on mythical proportions. Time has subtly softened the line between the real and the legendary.

I would like to trace that line. Before it becomes too vague

7

I would like to plot the curious curves it has made. To do this I must attempt something between a history of a period and an autobiography. The emphasis will be strongly on the former, for there will be little of my "inner" self, less of my own work, and nothing (if I can help it) of my emotional maladjustments. I did not (like some of my contemporaries) instigate "movements," inspire schools, or direct the lives and times of my friends. In such an account as this I see myself not at all as hero nor deus ex machina nor even as the machine itself, but merely as the contact point which sets the mechanism going. The motor of memory gets increasingly untrustworthy with age, and I do not wish to wait until it balks or runs down entirely.

This, then, is my letter to you, a book-length letter, wordier than any father has a right to inflict on any son. You may examine it, if books are not all burned or "purged," to find out what your father was like. (Thank Heaven, you won't succeed in this.) Or you may turn the pages with a mixture of amusement and boredom. Or you may flatly refuse to believe in most of the people herein chronicled. Perhaps you will be right. But, like Longfellow's "Life," they were real and ever so earnest. At least they were real enough to me.

Elizabethtown
  New York
    1939

CONTENTS

FROM ANOTHER WORLD

THE DIVIDED COUNTRY

THE HOME of my New York City childhood was a divided country. I was twelve years old in 1898 and Admiral Dewey's fleet had sunk the Spanish ships at Manila. Yet, more than a quarter of a century after the Civil War, my father advanced over every foot of ground won by the Union troops at Chattanooga, and my mother triumphed with Stonewall Jackson in the Shenandoah Valley. Actually my parents knew little about the details and less about the causes of the war they kept on fighting, but they argued campaign tactics only less feverishly than they challenged each other's systems at the card table. The engagements fought by Grant and Lee are still confused in my mind with the battles over Hoyle and Elwell.

My father lost every encounter. He was a baffled and laconic (or possibly outtalked) Yankee who never understood the inexhaustible Southerner he had married. She was many years his junior, socially and intellectually his superior; he was both jealous and afraid of her. His people were commoners; there were no traditions in the family. My paternal grandfather, who proudly bore the redundant name of Meyer Untermeyer, had emigrated from Bavaria and had been a butcher in the town of Waldoboro, Maine, before he bought out a larger market in Boston, where my father was born. There were four brothers (to say nothing of several sporadic sisters), David, Henry, Samuel, and Emanuel—I always wondered how a frivolous and secular Henry got in

13

that sternly Biblical list—and my father was the last. Youngest of the four, Emanuel, my father docilely grew up into whatever business his older brothers entered. First it was meat in Maine; then the market in Boston became a small general store; then the brothers traveled with a "line" of watches; finally a watch-chain factory was acquired, and David, Henry, and my father moved to that jewelry district of New York incongruously named Maiden Lane. Only Samuel escaped, or, according to my aunts, ruined himself by running off to be an actor. Alas, for the righteousness of the aunts. Samuel became the close friend and business associate of Charles Frohman, the theatre's first mogul; he was the personal manager of the favorite actress of her day, and his funeral was attended by the Great Ones of the stage. But, apart from Samuel, the Untermeyers were a homely, humdrum lot.

It was my mother's family that had all the glamor. The legend of my mother's father, after whom I had been named, compensated for the conspicuous lack of romantic Untermeyers. Louis Michael could never have been the hero which the memories of childhood enshrined, but I remember nothing commonplace about him or his children. All his daughters were beautiful and accomplished in the arts—my mother played Chopin desperately and my aunt Sallie made *petit point* chair-seats. All his sons lived exciting lives (one of them continued to own slaves in Texas five years after the Emancipation Proclamation), contracted irregular marriages and strange diseases (the handsomest had leprosy in Astoria), and died interesting deaths. Louis Michael was French (at least Alsatian), and his Latin Orientalism acquired a deeper color when he moved to New Orleans, where my mother was born, and where he "converted" cotton on Poydras Street. In Galveston, where mother lived until she came North, he ran (unsuccessfully) for Mayor, and in Houston, where he had much to do with horses—I forget whether he bred them or merely had them branded—he was known as Judge Michael, for lawyers (so my mother implied) were not only incompetent and immaterial but irrelevant in Texas.

It was decided, long before I was ten, what was to become of me. To be on the safe (Untermeyer) side, I was to be a businessman; to uphold the cultural (Michael) strain I was to be an accomplished musician. I gave no thought to the former, but I struggled grimly through Czerny's *School of Velocity*, for I was in love with Mr. Baer. Mr. Baer came Tuesdays and Thursdays, and he romped through Moszkowski, galloped over Chopin, and stormed the ramparts of Liszt with his ten steel-shod fingers. Mendelssohn's lingering "Songs Without Words" were merely a series of brisk setting-up exercises for Mr. Baer. I remember the patronizing contempt when my mother told him she thought I, at fifteen, was ready for Herman Epstein.

"Epstein!" he snorted, or he may have only sniffed. "Epstein is a Schumann-player. *I* play Liszt!"

II

I remember my thirteenth birthday, for on that day I received my first bicycle and wrote my first poem. It was a patriotic poem and it stirred me deeply. The warring loyalties for North and South had merged in one noble and concentrated fury against Spain. Not stopping to consider the relative sizes and chances of the countries involved, I waved my country's flag and defied the Spanish "invader" through sixteen flaming verses. They began:

> *'Twas in Havana harbor*
> *As silent lay the "Maine,"*
> *Not dreaming of a fearful plot*
> *Laid well by treacherous Spain.*
>
> *The sailors in their berths they slept*
> *The sleep that knows no waking*
> *But woke to hear, 'midst shot and shell,*
> *The sound of iron plates breaking.*
>
> *They woke to die, that noble band,*
> *In all the smoke and fire.*
> *What though they found a watery grave,*
> *Their souls ascended higher!*

That is all I remember, but the ballad rose from one vigorous climax to another; and I, on wings of flame and song, rose with it. Too proud to commit the ringing lines to apathetic paper, and fearful of my ever-prying brother and sister, I chanted the lines to myself like a bard or a ballad-singer, intoned them dramatically before an awe-struck mirror, and flung them forth in the privacy of the bath-tub. I was a poet, a patriot, an undeniable mover and shaker. I coddled my secret and exulted with it; I was, I think, a little afraid of myself. It is something of an occasion when you walk into your teens and into a new world at the same time.

The shock back to ordinary existence came within forty-eight hours, and in the rudest possible way. Pauline and Martin, my younger brother and sister, spent their childhood attached to key-holes. Listening to my rapt declamations the little fiends had achieved a horrid jumble of the inspired verses. These they delivered loudly at dinner during one of the rare visits of Uncle Samuel.

" 'Twas in Savannah harbor" the two terrors began, and I hated them as no relatives have ever been hated, partly because they had dared to learn my sacred singing lines, partly because they had learned them wrong. It was only after I had beaten up Pauline and taken Martin's magic-lantern set that I spoke to them again.

It was at about fourteen that I fell in love in earnest. This time it was simultaneously with Heinrich Heine and Maude Adams. A German governess had prepared me for the simpler verses in the *Buch der Lieder,* and Herman Epstein, via Schumann and Schubert, had revealed the contrasting glories of the romantic *Dichterliebe* and the sterner *Doppelgänger.* I, too, yearned elaborately and took to sighing under the street-lamps; I saw my life twinned with Heine's, a succession of ghostly trysts in faery woods, where the lotus-flower bared her bosom to the unfaithful moon, and the rose was hopelessly in love with the nightingale. I, too, wrote brief self-poisoned lyrics, translated my unsuspecting, unoffending aunts into devouring dragons, and felt my heart torn with unreal but immedicable woes. Yet I was not happy in my misery. For one thing, I was too healthy, and, for the most part, too hungry; there was no grief at fourteen that could not be assuaged by a chocolate ice-cream soda. For another thing, I suspected there were depths to which I had not plunged, and that Heine may have had experiences he was not sharing with me.

But if my passion for the dead poet was not reciprocated,

my devotion to the leading actress of her day was returned
to the full. Maude Adams was playing in *The Little Minister*
—this was in the days before actresses insisted that authors
change the names of their plays so they could star in the
title-rôle—and, since my Uncle Samuel was her personal manager, I saw Barrie's first dramatic success a hundred or more
times. At least I saw the end of the play that often, for on
matinées I would go straight from class, pedaling rapidly
from the Boys' High School on Thirteenth Street, to the
theatre on Fortieth and Broadway. There I would watch the
metamorphosis of the whimsical Lady Babbie into the irre-
sistible gypsy, and vice versa. The great lady first met me
formally at a children's party, where I showed proper disdain for the youthful companions who had been forced upon
me, got used to seeing me pop up behind a property bush
between the acts, and finally visited me in my own house. It
is true that, on this occasion, she was also having dinner with
the family—and all the aunts—but I knew she understood! It
is also true that she addressed none of her conversation to
me; but she was a shy person and afraid of men. Besides,
between two artists, despite a difference of age, there was no
need of words. She spoke casually to the others, told them
about the queer little Scotchman, half genius, half journalist,
who was writing another drama for her—*Quality Street,* if I
remember correctly—and said he was going to make a sort of
a play out of his book *The Little White Bird.* "He's thinking of calling it after one of the characters, Peter Pan, and
it's to be a little like poetry and a little like pantomime.
You children will love it."

I flushed. It was the first remark she had addressed to my
end of the table. But "You children!" You children, indeed!

Then, looking at the adored face, I was reassured. Of course she had meant Pauline and Martin, grade school pupils, who knew nothing about poetry and pain and who did not bicycle from high school every Wednesday just to see her. I gave my inamorata a swift and intense look; she smiled back. I was glad that mother had let me wear my first long trousers.

III

Pain and poetry were accentuated by Miss Adams's growing repertoire. To celebrate my fifteenth birthday I was permitted to attend my first opening night. My heroine was to inaugurate the fall season at the Knickerbocker Theatre, famous for its "carriage trade," in a translation of Rostand's new play, *L'Aiglon*. This was another metamorphosis, and it was a little hard for me to reconcile the beloved woman with the fragile but still masculine son of Napoleon. Nevertheless, the power of poetry triumphed; disbelief was held in willing suspension. I was not only captivated and convinced, I was transformed. I, too, identified myself with the sick eaglet, dreaming, with wings clipped, of wild horizons, feeling the imperial blood pound in his pulse, pining away on a luxurious eyrie. Comfort became suddenly repugnant to me; I looked upon our elegant front room, full of the period's best gold and velour, with esthetic pleasure but with spiritual loathing. What right had I to dawdle in a house that had a carved brownstone front with two sandstone caryatids and a stoop with fifteen stairs when the world was calling for action and St. Helena was waiting to be avenged! Though I could not claim to be of royal blood, there was a racial tie—

had not my grandfather been a Frenchman, at least an Alsatian? Our home on Lexington Avenue became Schönbrunn. My mother, busy with her Settlement sewing-circle, was the frivolous Archduchess Maria Louisa; and my father, the preoccupied little jewelry salesman, was the fond but tyrannical Emperor Francis of Austria, by whose will I was kept a prisoner. I rattled my chains while I was supposed to be studying physics, wrote secret documents in invisible ink—a chemistry set had been a birthday present—and learned all the purple patches in Louis N. Parker's version of the play. Possibly I was not quite as charming as Maude Adams, but I was more devastatingly ironic in the speech beginning:

> Good Lord, I'm not a prisoner—"but"—That's all!
> "But"—not a prisoner, "but"—That is the word!

I was thoroughly the chained soul and completely myself as I thundered:
> —It is my soul! It is my name!
> That mighty name which throbs with guns and bells,
> Clashes and thunders, ceaselessly reproaches,
> Against my languor with its bells and guns!

I was brave and wistful and ever-so-pathetic when I declared:

> Then I, who have no power, no throne, no title,
> I, who am but a memory in a phantom—

But it was at the end of Act Three that I was at my best. This was the scene in which the sinister Metternich tries to prove to Napoleon's son his unfitness by showing him in a mirror the weak Austrian features inherited from his mother.

L'Aiglon, torn by half-acknowledged fear and outright fury, twists the chandelier out of the hands of his tormentor, hurls it into the mirror, shattering the glass and the images. I always "gave" this scene to a rapt audience of two; my brother and sister suffered the rest of the rhetoric for the physical denouement. Since the scene was complicated, I played three parts: L'Aiglon, Metternich, and the property-man. It was a protean rôle, and Pauline and Martin were gratifyingly breathless. I was chillingly suave as Metternich, pitiful and heroic as L'Aiglon, but overwhelming as the property-man. At the crucial moment, just as the tortured Duke cries:

'Tis shattered! Not one remains! Not one!

I hurled a bit of window-pane or a broken tumbler against the metal andirons. The effect was tremendous and my audience always cheered. Maude Adams had only one advantage. Her curtain came down, while I had to clear up the glass.

IV

Meanwhile, I was fighting my way through algebra. It was only after a long struggle in Public School No. 6 that I had mastered—well, co-operated with—addition, multiplication, subtraction, and division. But anything more complicated was beyond me, and no matter how often Mr. Berry demonstrated the simplest algebraic problems, x to me was not only an unknown but an unknowable quantity. When we—that is, Mr. Berry and the rest of the class—reached geometrical formulas I was baffled, bewildered, and completely befogged; I could not even appreciate the standard pun about "plane" and "plain" geometry.

I remember the day when I finally rebelled against the absurdity of re-proving what had been proved countless times centuries ago. I was at the blackboard sweating blood and breaking chalk over what seemed a hopelessly confused set of angles. When none of the figures jibed and nothing seemed to make sense and Mr. Berry's pencil-tapping sounded like an infuriated woodpecker, I cried, "It can't be done. There's no way of solving it."

"I don't like to disagree with you, Untermeyer," said Mr. Berry with (I suppose) justifiable sarcasm, "but Euclid proved it fairly satisfactorily."

"Well," I retorted desperately, "if Euclid proved it, that's good enough for me. Why should I have to check up on him?" As a reply to my rhetorical question, I was suspended for the rest of the week.

It was then that Mr. Berry learned, somehow, that I played the piano. Mr. Berry had studied composition and, for a short time, had taught harmony in a freshwater college. For years he had been assembling data to prove the close relation between mathematics and music. He tried to rescue me not so much from failing in the final exams as from failing to appreciate the beauty and definiteness of the connection.

"Look, Untermeyer," he would say, "as one who loves music, you should be able to appreciate the similarity, a similarity of impulse and effect. What difference is there between a proposition in Euclid and a sonata by Mozart? Both are the finest possible examples of form. And *pure* form! Sublimated feeling—depersonalized, abstract thought! One is in terms of sound, the other is in terms of space. But both are as colossal in concept as they are delicate in detail, exquisite in structure, pieces of airy architecture. They go further than the emotions roused by words, they touch sublimity. And why? Because they are beyond emotion, beyond matter. They are bodiless, yes, spiritual; abstractions without the blemish of the senses. Of course you *hear* music—and in a way that is something against it, for it becomes confused with sensations, stories, ideas. But when a score is *read*—when it is heard with the inner ear—then it attains its greatest glory, for then is heard the true music of the spheres, the music of numbers."

"But Debussy," I interrupted, seizing the most modern name I knew, "in Debussy there are—"

"Gregorian chants!" Mr. Berry excitedly exclaimed, pulling his sandy Vandyke beard. "Perfectly balanced systems of numbers—as orderly as the law of dynamics, a set of pure deductions. No music in mathematics? My God! Show me a finer, more awe-inspiring example of compactness and balance, of axioms and equations—of pure and applied mathematical form—than a Bach fugue!"

From theory to practice or, rather, to play. With Epstein as teacher, I had attacked the left-hand parts of the Mendelssohn overtures, the Wagner potpourris, and the Beethoven symphonies. Mr. Berry showed me a stranger musical terrain, the brave new world of the Frenchmen and the Russians. In spite of his preoccupation with pure form, Mr. Berry's admiration for Bach and his sons was controlled; it was with respect rather than with love that he illustrated his points with "The Well-Tempered Clavichord." His quick if unmathematical passion was for the exotic, the loudly languorous and the inordinately rich, and we were soon pounding out four-handed arrangements of "Prince Igor," "L'Apprenti Sorcier," "Scheherazade," "Marche Slav," and "Symphonie

Pathétique." It was glorious, and at sixteen, all true gold.
It was years before I detected the inflated theatricalism of
Tschaikowsky and discovered how prettily Rimsky-Korsakow
had "refined" Moussorgsky. For two school terms Mr. Berry
and I luxuriated in Russian folk-songs wrapped in tinsel and
Weltschmerz trailing clouds of rhetoric. Nevertheless, with
all of Mr. Berry's pianistic energy and his persuasive enthusiasm, I failed twice in geometry. To save me the humiliation of being inefficient in only one subject, I was "conditioned" in history, physics, and Latin, and only a horribly
realistic drawing of a dissected frog (*rana temporaria*) saved
me from failing in zoology.

There was still a chance to redeem myself. One of the
ways we were taught poetry was by paraphrasing it. "Tell
what the author means, using your own words." So we
brightly reduced poem after poem ("the best words in the
best order") to the worst words in the greatest possible confusion. I became adept at this game: "What Coleridge means
to say is . . ." "What Longfellow is trying to tell us is . . ."
"*The Vision of Sir Launfal* teaches us that . . ." And so I
was made Athletics Reporter for the school paper.

My first assignment was a football game between our team
and the Boys' High of Brooklyn. On the Saturday which was
to decide the long-contested championship there was a light
drizzle; by noon there was a brisk shower. It never occurred
to me that (a) football could be played in the rain and (b)
that it might be clear in Brooklyn. So I went to another
Maude Adams matinée. This ended my career as a journalist.

It also ended my days in high school. Dr. Buchanan, the
principal, called in *both* my parents—he was weary of seeing them separately—and asked them what, in the light of my

progressively disheartening report-cards, they had to suggest. My mother wept and suggested Columbia University. Dr. Buchanan tried not to sniff; he merely reminded her that there were entrance examinations, requirements which were hopelessly beyond me. My father, trying to look disappointed, suggested the jewelry business in which the only opposition would be my uncles who had sons of their own. Dr. Buchanan smiled. He was so relieved that he failed to look distressed, and, forgetting about my mathematical shortcomings, he insisted that the life of trade was just what I needed. There followed a fervent duet between my father and Dr. Buchanan in which they played variations on leading themes: "golden opportunities," "self-made captains of industry," "carving your own destiny." But I was deaf to the inspiring phrases; I was thinking happily that, instead of the weekly allowance of fifty cents, I would get, as my youngest cousin was getting, a *salary*—a salary of three dollars per week and supper-money when we worked overtime.

So, at sixteen, I entered the jewelry firm which was already supporting my father, two uncles, and five cousins. I stayed in it, somehow, for twenty-two years.

FIRST FUSION

NOW I began to lead a double life in earnest. Between the hours of nine and five I learned how to card link-buttons and brooches, decipher price-codes, deliver packages, twist burning sealing wax so it dripped neatly beneath the copper seal instead of on my clothes, detect the difference between Roman and English finish on gold, put the minimum amount of rouge on the polishing chamois, and boast of my non-existent love-affairs to the boys in the shipping-room. Because of no particular ability I became a salesman, then assistant buyer, then (because of a slight talent for drawing) a designer of engraved lockets and "art nouveau" lavallières. I stopped eating the twenty-five cent lunch (baked beans, Boston brown bread, heavily encased apple dumpling) at Naethings and graduated to the soft clams at Libby's Oyster House and the higher orgies of the sixty cent French dinner (with an occasional carafon of cheap but ostentatious wine) at the Fulton Street Mouquin.

But these occupations did not concern me after five o'clock. After hours I dreamed about being America's leading composer and the world's greatest pianist. Of course I did nothing to bring the dream into the harsh realm of reality. I improvised when I should have been practicing, and deceived myself with violent imitations of MacDowell's worst fumblings when I should have been preparing my counterpoint. Nevertheless, the dream went on with all a dream's illogical logic, and it was no surprise to me when I found myself in the dressing-room of Vladimir de Pachmann. I knew that de Pachmann was considered the greatest interpreter of Chopin, even though James Huneker, the *enfant terrible* among the music critics, had referred to the pianist as "That Chopinzee!" I also knew that de Pachmann had a reputation for eccentricity, even for carefully rehearsed eccentricity. I had heard him end Schumann's "Vogel als Prophet," or rather not end it, by omitting the final notes. Instead of the bird's vanishing phrase, de Pachmann fluttered his hands high above the keyboard, rose from the piano bench, the hands still winging their way through the air, and tiptoed toward the proscenium, whispering, *"Der Vogel ist fort! De bird iss gone!"*

So here I was, face to face with the Pole who had all the preludes, the mazurkas, the nocturnes, the very multiple soul of Chopin in his fingertips.

"And vat are you playing for me—eh?" inquired de Pachmann, motioning me to the stool.

"Chopin," I replied with the magnificent aplomb of youth. And then I added, fearing perhaps that de Pachmann might not recognize it, "Valse Brillante, opus 34. The waltz," I obligingly translated, "the famous one in A minor."

I had not gone beyond the sixteenth bar of the hackneyed "parlor piece"—a meal of marshmallows with whipped cream—when I struck three false notes. By the time I had arrived at the sentimental sostenuto and the change of key I had managed to hit a half-dozen more.

"Bravo!" cried de Pachmann. *"Sehr original!* Jus' like me! Madame," he bowed to my mother, "you have a genius. He has listened well to me! Don't let any teacher spoil him! What an ear! But he mustn't practice—no! A genius—*ja!"*

I could not tell whether this was another instance of egotism or eccentricity, of simple sincerity or Polish sarcasm.
But, even though I made a semi-professional debut at Mendelssohn Hall, I knew I would never be a concert pianist. I
resigned myself to music for pleasure and to the jewelry business for profit. With the quick adaptability of youth I grew
scornful of "professionals" and made speeches about the exploitation of art. "Pianists! Penny-in-the-slot performers!
Spoiled organ-grinders, using composers for monkeys! Self-
oiling machines turning out passion for pay!"

I was too noble for words and too lazy for technique. I
resolved to be an originator, not an interpreter; to be the
creative amateur who would also be the spontaneous composer. I fell in love with the image; my head was full of
grandiose musical schemes. Rejecting anything of less than
major dimensions, I projected two sets of song-cycles around
the lyrics of Poe and the Rossettis, a Celtic "melodrama"
based on an otherworldly prose poem by the nebulous Fiona
Macleod, a heroic sonata "suggested" by the Prophetic Books
of Blake—or, rather, suggested by the strange drawings, for I
had no notion what the words were prophesying—and a
choral symphony to be entitled "The Canterbury Pilgrims,"
of which I had read only the Prologue and the bawdy Wife
of Bath's tale. I sketched out themes, imagined vast development passages, and "heard" overpowering climaxes in that
limbo of consciousness between excited sleeplessness and con-
tented sleep. Need I add that not one of these monumental
works ever got itself down to paper?

When, many years later, I finally made my one appearance as a published composer, it was with two small songs;
one was set to a gay little narrative by Charles E. Carryl,

and the other used the grave nonsense of Lewis Carroll as a
text. To the dreaming youth of nineteen this would have
been an act tantamount to betrayal, prostitution, and suicide
of the soul. It was not until I was twenty-one that I realized
my disjointed melodies and harmonic ribbons were rags from
the shrouds of Schumann and the lesser romantics; that, to
paraphrase Gilbert, I had not been composing but decom-
posing.

II

The irony did not crush me for, before that revealing moment, I had become a part-time poet. The century turned
just after I became fourteen; at seventeen I decided to do
something about it. Possibly there were others who observed
the end of 1899 turn into the beginning of 1900—there may
have been an editorial or two—but two years passed before I
was willing to commit myself on the subject. Once I got
around to it, however, I wrote a ponderous and convincing
essay about the phenomenon. I remember it began with a
casual examination into the nature of time. This led to a
consideration of the calendar, the nebular hypothesis, the
probable age of the earth, the place of man in the universal
scheme, and so down (or up) to the dawn of the Twentieth
Century. The piece was many paragraphs in length, and in
it I embodied two verses which I quoted from Ronald Mac-
Fie, one of the least known of the lesser poets—a poet who
might have been a blood brother (or, to be more exact, a
bloodless brother) of Max Beerbohm's Enoch Soames. The
apostrophe to the new century began with this grand fan-
fare:

Upon a grave your cradle stands,
  Lo, Life and Death,
  Commingling breath,
  Wedded their hands,
As in the lap of Time you lay,
And the Old Century passed away.

  The young and old,
  The warm and cold,
  The quick and dead,
All strangely in your soul are wed.

I would have sent the essay and its embalmed verses to
St. Nicholas had I known that most American geniuses of
my time would some day write how they had received their
start in the Young Contributors' Column of *St. Nicholas*.
But I was not in the least clairvoyant. Foolishly enough, I
sent the piece to a magazine that had nothing whatsoever to
do with the renaissance of American literature. I think its
name was *Helpful Thoughts*. The editor accepted my contribution—that is, he kept part of it. Discarding my exhaustive prose, he printed MacFie's hortatory rhymes and
signed my name to them. I was delighted. This showed how
easy it was for poets to get published. In a way, that is how
I became a poet.

Between my fifteenth and eighteenth years I feasted impartially on the richly spiced fare of Keats, the solid chunks of
Browning, the cooling draughts of Burns, the hot wine of
Shelley, the red-blooded beef and beer of Kipling, the prettily poisoned sweetmeats of the Naughty Nineties. My discrimination was limited, but my appetite was large—and di-
gestion was a word that did not enter my vocabulary until I

was forty. I gorged myself on strong rhythms and rebounding rhymes; on swiftly rising inflections and beautifully dying falls; on all that suggested or simulated music.

III

Then I happened to see Alla Nazimova in *Hedda Gabler* and *A Doll's House.* She had come from Russia, had not yet mastered English, and she brought to her performance of the Scandinavian heroine an exotic fire which would have shocked Ibsen with its Slavic intensity. I had never seen anything like it, nor have I seen anything to equal it since. I was literally swept off my feet; at the very least I was weak in the knees. It was the first time I had been so struck—so stage-struck—since Maude Adams captivated her Gavin in *The Little Minister.* That night I wrote a sonnet to the actress and mailed it, without stopping to correct the punctuation, to the *Theatre Magazine.*

Strangely enough, the lines were accepted and, in little more than a month, were spread out over a full page decorated with pictures of Mme. Nazimova in a stunning variety of rôles and poses. Again I was bowled over. This time, however, I was more impressed by my own performance than by my heroine's. I was a poet, an acknowledged creator, a public word-musician. A musician? Yes, and more—a magician! Only eighteen and, by a sudden sleight-of-phrase, occupying an entire page in a leading magazine! Fame was at hand; prosperity was perching on my fountain-pen; I felt as God must have felt when he discovered that in the beginning was the Word! People would speak of me enviously from coast to coast; celebrities would invite me to their homes, hoping to have future sonnets dedicated to them; editors would seek me out with their hats in one hand and checks in the other.

They never did. A long time later I realized that the sonnet to Nazimova was a particularly bad example of its kind, and that it had been printed only as an excuse for the alluring photographs of the lady. Before I discovered this disillusioning fact, I had launched myself as an author—at the same time prudently remaining close to the jewelry establishment. It was well that I took that unromantic precaution, for if I had had to live by poetry alone I would have ceased to stay alive. Between the ages of eighteen and twenty-three I wrote about four hundred poems, and not more than twelve of them appeared in print. My first volume (a long-drawn-out sigh of self-dramatization called *First Love*, full of the sickliest echoes of Heine and Henley) was printed in my twenty-fifth year, and with it I was committed to the literary life. But it was still as an amateur that I entered the publishers' lists. Though poetry yielded me more pleasure than any other form of expression, between the ages of eighteen and thirty it yielded me less than five hundred dollars, or about forty-two dollars a year.

I began to feel more cordial toward my uncles; I made my first deposit in the Chatham National Bank.

Utterly unself-critical about my own imitative verse, I was free with criticism of my betters. I began a monthly page of book-reviews smirkingly headed "Pierian Hand-Springs," changed it to "—and Other Poems," and a year later joined Joyce Kilmer on the youthful magazine which

gravely called itself *Moods*. Since Joyce determined to review both prose and verse, I nonchalantly turned to music
criticism and, in "Chords and Discords," disposed of Mahler,
Madame Louise Homer, and, in one devastating article, the
entire Manhattan Opera House. Meanwhile, in the throes of
love, I was writing the sort of verse which the *Houston Post*
acclaimed as "exquisite, far better than Meredith's 'Lucille,'
the kind that a young man will bring with joy to the little
girl-woman just starting out with him on life's roadway."
At nineteen I announced my secret engagement to "the little
girl-woman" who had admired my piano playing; I took out
life insurance, and entered the bourgeoisie. It was with a
noble resignation that I rejoined the middle class, unaware
that I had never left it.

My mother was not inclined to take my engagement seriously; even my marriage, at twenty-one, seemed a frivolous
gesture and an affront to her. Defeated in her few attempts
to make an intellectual companion of my father, she had
fastened upon me, her first-born, with ardent possessiveness.
I was to express in action, or some sort of creation, her own
frustrated dreams. Indiscriminate in her love of music, she
sang agreeably but self-consciously—so I was to write her unwritten songs. She paraphrased the novels of Mrs. Humphry
Ward and S. Weir Mitchell for a small circle interested
chiefly in her huge afternoon *Kaffeeklatsch*—so I was to complete the works she scarcely could begin. To all this my
father never once objected; he was satisfied with any "extra-
curricular" study for me. He made only two conditions: I
was to regard the jewelry factory as my true goal, and he
was to keep his Thursday nights for pinochle. Since my

father nodded unconcernedly through every opera except "Carmen" I was my mother's companion at the Metropolitan before I was in my teens; by the time I was twelve she had taught me all the *leitmotifs* in Wagner's "Ring." She supervised my reading and, after I had graduated from the historical fictions of G. A. Henty, censored the volumes I chose for gifts or brought home from the library. She loathed anything that challenged sentiment, platitudes, and the *status quo*. When, inevitably, I discovered the works of George Bernard Shaw, she, with equal inevitability, refused to allow his books in the house. I read *Three Plays for Puritans* by stealth; I devoured *Man and Superman* including "The Revolutionist's Handbook" while sitting up with my grandmother's body the night before the funeral. My mother refused to speak to me for a week when I went to the disturbing first night of *Mrs. Warren's Profession,* although the version was bowdlerized and although I was engaged to be married at the time. For years she said "Shaw!" as though she were repeating a dirty word, and she considered every girl I met a combination of the pursuing Ann Whitefield, the designing Raina, and the unspeakable Mrs. Warren herself. Hers may have been a dubious, even a destructive, attitude, but it was a consistent one. She looked upon my first wife as a deliberate challenge; she scorned my second as an impertinent intrusion; and only age and weariness reconciled her finally to my third. She fought stubbornly, stupidly, for my love, and, after every crisis, she commanded it. When my first son was born I was unready to be a father; I was still her perpetual child. I was not even ashamed of referring to myself as a Peter Pantheist.

I V

Maturity for me was a long and unpleasant process; I evaded its implications whenever I could. For several years I escaped responsibilities by letting my parents assume them; enjoying a bifurcated existence, I was serious neither about business nor art. Even my "escape" was petty. I played with pretty tunes; appeared in F.P.A.'s columns under a fancy pseudonym; wrote dozens of "exercises" in the French forms; prided myself on a mechanical technique, and paraphrased the first stirrings of revolt in glib stanzas. I came to many conclusions without real conviction; I had passions but no purposes. Nothing had happened to fuse them.

Suddenly, when I was about twenty-five, unity came by accident. Through Herman Epstein I had become intimate with an illustrator, Seymour Stone (originally Sigmund Stein), who taught me how to use a palette knife and look like an artist. The latter was accomplished by wearing a Windsor tie when I visited among the Bohemians. Actually the studios on Fifty-Ninth Street were occupied by hard-pressed and rather prosaic men and women, but I, fresh from Puccini's opera, saw them all as irresponsible, roistering companions right out of the first act of *La Bohème*. Among the more industrious of Seymour's acquaintances were Charles Winter and his wife, Alice Beach Winter. They had been one of the little group influenced by Howard Pyle—the group some of us superior souls used to call the Haemorrhoids; their work was stern in subject but soft in treatment. Charles Winter's paintings were especially vague, as though, after planning an arresting mural, he had redesigned it for a magazine cover and then washed the outlines down in mist. I still remember one composition which looked as though it had been painted in syrup. It consisted of a neatly organized mob of semi-nude figures in a twilight zone, smooth young men with burning eyes, lovely mothers and idyllic babies, a soulful lot, while from the lower right-hand corner hands were upthrust, evil hands holding jewels and croziers and money-bags, symbols of power. The fake classicism cried out of every inch, yet something else, blurred in utterance, cried out, too. I sensed the mangled revolutionary spirit before I saw the "motto" which Winter had attached to the drawing. It was this verse from Shelley's "The Mask of Anarchy":

> *Rise like lions after slumber*
> *In unvanquishable number—*
> *Shake your chains to earth like dew,*
> *Which in sleep had fallen on you.*
> *Ye are many—they are few.*

Here was the first realization of the tie which bound art and youth together. The lines of the poem and the lines of the drawing established a relation between reading and dreaming. This is what I had half-heard, re-echoing and unrecognized, in Shelley and Schumann, Byron and Shaw, Burns and Tschaikowsky, Heine and Beethoven—a mixed chorus, anti-Philistine, decisive, arrogant and just. The meaning was clear even though the method was not. The good and the beautiful (Had I heard it in Emerson?) were one; sentiment and purpose could be—must be—united. It would be pretentious to say that, for me, this marked the birth of a social conscience, but it was the beginning of a social consciousness.

EACH AGE IS A DREAM

IT WAS through the Winters that I got to know Piet Vlag. Vlag was a Dutchman almost to the point of caricature: great in appetite and argument, serious and fearfully stubborn, seemingly lethargic, but, under a cover of indifference, intensely alive. Superficial unconcern was the mark of his trade —he had been a waiter—but his passion for justice was second only to his passion for good food. As a cook he was severely chauvinistic. Vlag's revolutionary ardor blends in my memory with *Aalsoep,* a spiced eel soup which Vlag said was one of Holland's great national dishes; *Hutspot met Klapstuck,* an ancient hodge-podge of soup-meat, carrots, potatoes, leeks, onions, and cabbage; *Haringsla,* characterized by the uncooked herring and the addition of apples and beets to the potato salad; *Jan in den Zak,* which I remember because of its whimsical name, literally "John in the Sack," a heavy flour and raisin pudding. Vlag boasted of his plebeian taste with the pride of a patrician. I still see him (falsely perhaps) as Ragueneau struggling with Robespierre.

When I first met him, in 1910, Piet was "managing" the restaurant in the basement of the Rand School of Social Science, a gathering-place of all the utopians, muckrakers, young intellectuals and elderly malcontents south of Forty-Second Street. His home was as close a replica of the Rand School restaurant as he could make it. As a concession to Winter's accompanying Americans, there always appeared toward midnight a hugely heaped platter of gargantuan sand-

37

wiches. Vlag talked to everyone at once; plate in hand he held forth.

"Art?" he challenged through a mouthful of stockfish. "Sure, we need art. But not art that's for the few—not art that lives in pretty ivory towers built on golden quicksands. What's the use of making paintings and poems and putting up museums on top of a"—he waved a fork and changed his metaphor—"a volcano. Do you want it all to go up—pouf!— in smoke? Art must live with the people—in the streets, in the slums. It must work and sweat; it must stand up and fight. Every artist is a fighter, a rebel. Here, in America, he must be twice a rebel. Why? Because he must throw off Europe and the dead hand and his own snobbery. And how is he going to do it? Socialism. The artist can only be his real self if he forgets about himself, his oh-so-precious self. Romantic notions—*pfui!* What about his social responsibility? Why be afraid of it? Everything is breaking up. All the old ideas—all the old forms. Why should art stand outside, afraid of the changes in human society? Listen to what an English poet said, a poet who was always fighting—fighting his surroundings and his disease:

> *Bury me with clenched hands*
> *And eyes opened wide;*
> *For in storm and struggle I lived,*
> *And in struggle and storm I died."*

"But," I interrupted, confused by the impact of Vlag's rush of words, "the world of the imagination must have peace, serenity; at least" (I finished lamely) "some sort of harmony. The artist," I continued sententiously, "can't rise higher or sink lower than his own image of himself."

"He can rise above his wish to run away," said Vlag, reaching for a sandwich, "to run away from the struggle—from himself. Look here, at Horatio Winslow"—he pointed to the end of the table, to a young fellow with the build of a trained athlete and the face of a careless boy—"Horatio is a professional humorist; you've seen his pieces in *Puck* and *Judge*. Well, read this article Horatio has written for our magazine."

Soon I, too, could call it "our" magazine. It was *The Masses*, not the vivid, insurrectionary publication it became a year or so later, but a tentative monthly full of elevating ideas, sentimental drawings, and dull doctrine. I contributed occasional verse which tried to graft the loose vigor of Henley on the tight moralizing of Tennyson; I borrowed Chesterton's unorthodox idiom, his paradoxology, to prove uncontested truisms; I compiled statistics about co-operative stores and composed inflammatory and (I thought) convincing appeals for the brotherhood of man.

I I

In early 1912 *The Masses* was gaily teetering, if not in full swing. Piet Vlag was on the masthead as Editor-in-Chief; Eugene Wood (father of the actress Peggy Wood) was President; Inez Haynes Gillmore, the novelist, was Fiction Editor, although we scrupulously published little fiction; Horatio Winslow and I were Assistant Editors. The May issue opened with a drawing by Alexander Popini depicting an unusually depressing slum interior, and I was chosen to "point" the picture. It was my first special assignment since I had failed to cover the Boys' High School football game in Brooklyn and I was proud of this, my first propagandist prose. All I remember of Popini is his sartorial elegance and his monocle, which then seemed to me a perfect symbol of cynicism. I recall another of our artists more vividly. This was William Washburn Nutting; he is in my memory not so much for his art as for his story. He was essentially a sportsman. After drawing for *The Masses* he became editor of—it scarcely seems possible—*Motor-Boating;* he sailed small craft across the Atlantic. In the early 1920s he started to look for a new route north; he was heard of near Iceland; after that he was never seen again.

Late in 1912 a few of us met to expand the magazine or abandon it entirely. Piet was losing faith in his dream of cooperatives; our "angel," an insurance man who played with experimental economics, lost interest. It was a gloomy meeting.

Then Max Eastman came into the editorial "offices" which consisted of a chair and a second-hand roll-top desk in a small room on Nassau Street, two blocks from my father's and uncles' jewelry establishment. Piet had told me that Eastman might make the magazine more literary as well as more class-conscious. I could understand how he might accomplish the latter purpose, for the name suggested "Monk" Eastman, the monosyllabic king of New York's underworld. Piet had told me nothing about Max's backgrounds—it was months before I learned that Max's mother as well as his father had preached for years in upstate New York pulpits—and that Max had been assistant professor in philosophy at Columbia. My first sight of him was discomfiting. For here, instead of the East Side plug-ugly I had somehow pictured, was one of the most civilized and most sensitive faces I had ever seen.

The face was long but not gaunt; the features were young but already sharply sculptured; the head was covered with such a trim cap of hair as to appear crowned with feathers— an eagle's feathers, it seemed to me, as I thought of Shelley in my first enthusiasm. There was a line of pedantry across the brow, as though the professor were at war with the poet, but it was the poet that had conquered. Years later I was to recognize the same incongruous combination in the face of another poet, the Californian George Sterling. But if Sterling resembled a Roman Emperor on a coin run over by an American steam-roller, Eastman looked like a startled Bellerophon just after the gadfly had stung his Pegasus. Even at our first meeting there was that mixture of surprise and imperturbability, of security and veiled suspicion, which I saw in him hundreds of times when he faced small groups and large gatherings. It was a mixture which confused his opponents, who were misled by his fixed fancies and his chuckling reasonableness. Even his friends rarely knew when they were talking to the pure poet or being addressed by the skilled persuader, the professional charmer—and I was not yet his friend.

But that first meeting was enough to convince me that Max Eastman was a delegate from Destiny. The artists wanted to change the character of *The Masses* into a broadly satirical publication, a sort of Americanized *Jugend* and *Simplicissimus* combined; the writers wanted a magazine in which they could print the naked transcripts of reality which the commercial monthlies would not consider. Max, with his training in philosophic compromise, was the very man to effect the fusion. Several of us sat down to draft a letter which would state all our ideas, reasons, and requirements.

After we had spent several hours shaping and re-shaping cumbersome and contradictory paragraphs, John Sloan and I composed what the others considered a masterpiece. It ran: "Dear Eastman: We have just elected you editor of *The Masses* at no salary per annum." Everyone signed it.

About a year after its foundation, the office of *The Masses* was moved from the fringe of the downtown jewelry district to 91 Greenwich Avenue, in the very heart of Greenwich Village. At that time the Village had not been exploited as a combination of the Quaint, the Queer, and the Clandestine. Uptown was practicing the Uplift in its own exclusive way; it had not yet invaded the lower depths to rub shoulders with organized Bohemia. Misunderstood wives had not discovered repressed desires and submerged creative impulses dragging them from Riverside Drive to put up easels in Washington Square and renovate their adjectives along Minetta Lane. High school teachers from Brooklyn and the Bronx had not yet hailed the squalid alleys around Macdougal Street as the Promised Land of Happy Perdition. Instead of the fake swashbuckling fantasy of *The Pirate's Den* and *The Purple Pig,* there were a few cheap Italian restaurants and even cheaper bakeries. Instead of a sensation-seeking mob of out-of-town department store buyers, college sophomores, and rakish Babbitts drinking illicit liquor and hunting well-advertised "free love" (invariably a contradiction in both terms), there were many immigrant laborers, few geniuses, and little groups of hard-working painters and writers. Greenwich Village, before the war, was neither an exotic escape nor an erotic utopia; it was a casual, a commercial, convenience. It was easily accessible, midway between the canyons of lower Broadway and the flats of West

End Avenue. Rents were comparatively low; the mixture of races had prevented a stiffening of convention; and the region, with its tangled lanes and streets that crossed themselves, still retained something of the character which gave it its name—a village somehow tucked away in the midst of a metropolis.

I I I

The Masses had its habitat in the Village, but it was not a part of it; it considered itself neither barbarian nor bohemian. It was—and remained until it dissolved into *The Liberator* and was absorbed in the *New Masses*—socialistic, definitely co-operative, indefinitely cultural. In the exodus from Nassau Street we had lost Piet Vlag; there was no longer the semblance of an Editor-in-Chief. There were now two groups of allied editors who represented various tendencies but no one school. Sometimes the rapport was close, sometimes the two groups glowered distrustfully at each other, reconciled at the end of the evening only by Max and beer. The literary staff comprised the benevolent Eugene Wood; energetic, intense, and unpredictable John Reed; Horatio Winslow; the intransigent Mary Heaton Vorse, that quiet firebrand; Robert Carlton Brown, who turned from experimental writing to the practical prose of cook-books; Howard Brubaker, whose caustic paragraphs differed only in degree from his columns twenty years later in *The New Yorker;* Ellis O. Jones, who worked as editor of *Life,* then a fairly comic weekly, while he planned revolutions; the dialectician William English Walling; Max Eastman, and myself. The art editors were that benign spirit and bitter cartoonist, Arthur (Art) Young; John Sloan, the most uncompromising realist of the "New York School"; the savagely independent Stuart Davis; the little-known Cornelia Barnes, who said nothing in words and everything in line; the decorative and kindly Winters; and the slow-moving, emotional Maurice Becker, whose work was sternly proletarian long before "proletarian art" became a Marxist slogan. Sloan, the veteran villager and inveterate fighter, was "foreman of the composing room," and, though (theoretically) no editor had more power than any other editor, someone had to see that the paper was physically put together, pasted up, printed, proofread, and bound.

Max Eastman attended to these prosaic but necessary details. Gradually Max became the editor in fact, if not in name. It was a responsibility partly given, partly assumed, and it led to many small frictions and a few disastrous flare-ups. It was Max who raised most of the funds to pay the printer, who went out and cajoled poor artists into helping "the cause" and frightened wealthy clubwomen into protecting themselves against the Day of Revolution. It was Max who organized the make-up meetings; it was Max who urged the greatest latitude in taste and argument; and it was he who, when differences could not be ameliorated, made the final decisions. For this he received practically no salary, little praise, and even less thanks.

I remember one meeting when the discussion grew particularly acrimonious. We were skeptical of all panaceas, as skeptical as only the young *intelligentsia* can be, but that did not prevent us from trying to make the world over every second Thursday at 8 P.M. It was our habit to pass upon contributions (for which, having no money, we paid nothing) without the restraint of mercy. It had been an evening full

of fine quarrels and far-flung irrelevances; we were anticipating the peace which always came with the beer and cheese
when one last drawing was submitted. It was unsigned—even
the editors submitted their work anonymously—but, though
we pretended to judge abstractly, everyone recognized the
drawing as Stuart Davis's. No one but Davis could have expressed himself so fiercely, so flatly. The picture consisted
of two girls, one shown in slant-jawed profile, the other staring full face; two of the scrawniest, most lackluster, loose-
lipped, dead-eyed, badly jointed wenches ever drawn. They
wore no softening ornaments. There was no mollifying background. It was "Stew" Davis's naked protest against over-
romanticized, overworked "glamor," the commercialized pret-
tiness of the period, and (apparently) against our own fondness for the sweet and slick redeemed by a sharp caption.
There was a spontaneous tribute, an immediate outcry.
Everyone caught the purposeful ugliness; only a few caught
the point. The cheese was brought on, but we ignored it;
the beer grew stale. But still we wrangled. After the words
"beauty" and "bunk" had been angrily exchanged and heat-
edly, repeatedly, redefined the meeting broke up. This worried us. It may have worried Max, also, but it did not deter
him. Two of the editors had threatened to resign if the drawing ever appeared in the magazine; Max, a practical casuist
as well as a good compromiser, took them literally. The
drawing did not appear *in* the magazine; it appeared full
size in all its challenging sordidness on the front cover.
There, printed in an evil green and black, hideously effective among the languorous pink-and-cream bathing beauties,
it leered from the news-stands above the caption: "Gee, Mag,
think of us bein' on a Magazine Cover!"

It was Max who fought for revaluation all along the line. Art Young, George Bellows, Cornelia Barnes, and John Sloan were rousing national comment with their black-and-white "brutal flings at the social order"; John Reed, Horatio Winslow, and Howard Brubaker were satirizing the smugly complacent in etched prose; Max was promoting the class struggle in his editorials which quietly but consistently called for the conquest of power by those who did not hold it. The artists were more provocative; they were causing a much greater stir than the writers. The writers were accepted with little controversy; the artists were vigorously applauded or violently condemned. Sometimes the condemnation came from our "liberal" friends who feared we were growing too insurrectionary; sometimes it came from those who felt *The Masses* was become too "art-conscious" and insufficiently class conscious. Someone put the latter criticism into a jingle that Jack Reed maliciously loved to quote:

> *They draw nude women for* The Masses,
> *Thick, ungainly, ugly lasses.*
> *How does that help the working classes?*

Again it was Max who directed the course. The others tacked and veered, but he steered straight for the difficult goal which would unite art and propaganda—or, rather, which would express propaganda *as* art—an art which combined the free play of the painter and writer with the purpose of the reappraiser. It was not that we had infallible systems and cure-alls ready to shake out of our sleeves. We agreed that the artist's function may well be to correct, but it is, first of all, to conceive, to quicken sensibility so that life takes on a more vivid character, a more active color and energy. We felt that the writer's power could not be defined by passion or limited by propaganda; it could reach, by virtue of its very flexibility, from one to the other; it could exhort as well as exalt. The end of art, we maintained, was not primarily to recommend but to reveal. That we fell short of our program sometimes occurred to us, but it did not deter us from taking on the Philistine world with every issue. Once a month we persuaded ourselves that this time emotion and imagination would be fused, the truth would be recognized, and the creative will would be roused. "Each age is a dream that is dying," we echoed O'Shaughnessy, "or one that is coming to birth."

A month after Davis's "green girls" had outraged the newsstands and most of our subscribers, another drawing by Davis appeared, this time on the back cover. It was a typical sordid scene: girls walking under the Sixth Avenue Elevated railroad, an empty lot behind broken hoardings, a sputtering arc light disputing the murky red of the setting. It illustrated a poem I had just written about a prostitute. I felt (and still feel) that the picture was far better than the poem, but Max cheered me up. He wrote:

I've read your poem in the July *Masses* again and again. . . . If anybody now says that our graphic art excels the art of that poem he's a damned fool. That poem justifies our aim.

"Our aim" was expressed in the manifesto which declared our principles in unalterable ink: "This magazine is owned and published co-operatively by its editors. It has no dividends to pay; nobody is trying to make money out of it. A revolutionary and not a reform magazine—a magazine with a sense of humor and no respect for the respectable. Frank,

arrogant, impertinent, searching for the true causes. A magazine directed against rigidity and dogma wherever it is
found; printing whatever is too naked or true for a money-
making press; a magazine whose final policy is to do as it
pleases and conciliate nobody—not even its readers."

Toward the end of the year Floyd Dell came on from
Chicago, and the magazine became more determinedly cultural. Floyd had edited the nationally known literary supplement of the *Chicago Evening Post,* and, though I had
never met him, we had already had a long correspondence.
I had been writing a weekly column of poetry reviews for
him and for his predecessor, Francis Hackett, and, after
Floyd began sharing with Max the ungrateful duties of acting editor of *The Masses,* I began a similar department for
our co-operative venture. Our editorial line-up shifted, our
pages became increasingly controversial, our meetings grew
more and more belligerent. Determined to "conciliate nobody," not even its editors, *The Masses* grappled with abstract injustice and personal prejudice, dealing direct blows
to confused enemies and even more confounded friends; the
life of the magazine was a record of resignations, reconsidera-
tions, new contributors, postal suppressions and conflicts
with the federal authorities. As though our indiscriminate
onslaughts were not bloody enough, we often invited guests
to our make-up meetings, and they, suddenly inspired with
the lust of battle, joined issue on every point.

I will never forget the evening when one of our guests
was Hippolyte Havel, the gentlest anarchist who ever threw
an expostulation. Hippolyte suffered through a long descriptive poem commending nature for various effects, and furnished a climax of his own. He exploded, "Nature! Moun-

tains! Scenery! What have they got to do with economic determinism!"

The rest of us howled. In those days we considered any regimentation of ideas a humorous absurdity. And it was Hippolyte who objected to a work of art being put to a vote—least of all to a vote determined by "the oppressive bourgeois majority."

"But," Floyd argued, "even anarchists must decide things by some sort of democratic method."

"Sure—sure," replied Hippolyte. "We anarchists make decisions. But we don't abide by them!"

I V

A few weeks after Floyd joined *The Masses* our letter-heads designated him Managing Editor and Max was officially Editor, which, in practice, he had always been. The meetings, however, went on; the anonymity of each contribution was still attempted; votes were scrupulously counted; but Floyd and Max "managed" the paper in an almost literal sense. Their basic philosophic differences in attitude and technique did not develop until much later. But even then, with Floyd as lookout and with Max as helmsman, our strangely assorted crew was in for adventurous if not smooth sailing. Max had ideas for new departments, schemes for surprises, plans for everyone. My correspondence was enriched by hurried demands, imperative scribbles. Here are two of the few that were not destroyed:

This is fine. Why not add a piece about the new volume of "Jean Christophe"? That would help the sales department, for it would be a fine book to sell. I'd rather sell it than read it myself—although I don't know why a man shouldn't go on writing the same book all his life instead of writing a lot of different ones. Note: Idea for a new literary form! You could change your mind in each yearly installment—(But that's not new, either; Walling does it!)—and then you could have the end agree with the beginning. This would give the desired "unity" to the work—and also show the folly of writing it at all.

Max

Floyd's away, and I'm alone with the October number. Help! Won't you write me another book review? I need it.

Louis, why don't you review your own poems? Dante used to—and you look like Dante. I think it would be fun, and more than just fun. You could give yourself hell in your own inimitable way and so convince everyone of your greatness. Let me know. The final date is September 16.

I'm enjoying Heine and you simultaneously.

Max

Floyd Dell's activities on *The Masses* became rapidly more important. Since the burden of raising funds to keep the magazine alive was allowed to fall on Max's shoulders, the editorial duties were permitted to rest on Floyd's. My correspondence files are crammed with brief notes and bulky envelopes from Floyd, but most of them are undated and many of them refer to events I cannot recall and items I cannot explain. There is a long letter about "our" poem which Floyd hopes to have illustrated by Boardman Robinson. There is a longer outline suggesting collaboration on a critical selection of "escapist" poetry, the crux of which was to be the false freedom of Carman and Hovey's *Vagabondia* verses—Floyd quotes with approval a pun I seem to have made about "vagabondage." I remember nothing concerning either partnership. But I remember vividly our conversations and subsequent correspondence about the eternal paradox of law and liberty. I had speculated on the contradiction of natural conformity and natural instinct, and I had hung my speculations on the figure of Moses. Moses, it seemed to me, was a perfect example of the universal spirit, the divided soul, for he was both liberator and law-giver. More than that, he was not only the law-maker but the law-breaker; I saw the smiting of the rock and the smashing of the tablets as closely related and significant symbols. In my version Moses was not punished and forbidden to enter the Promised Land. On the contrary, he knew (half realist, half philosophical anarchist as I saw him) that the law, like the Kingdom of Heaven is within you, and that Canaan, like Palestine, is the Promised Land only as it remains a promise. Many years later I said all this at length—to the length of almost four hundred pages—in a five-part novel, a reconstructed pentateuch, stressing the self-divided human being called "Moses." But, at the time, I was trying to say it in a poem of about one hundred rhetorical lines. Floyd wrote to me about it with his usual keenness and candor:

Dear Louis: Max doesn't like your "Moses" poem. He most particularly *doesn't* like it, I'm sorry to say.

Under the circumstances I'd like to say that I particularly do and have threatened to resign, etc. But I must painfully confess that I myself don't feel enthusiastic about it. It has, however, set me thinking about Moses; it has made me think about him for the first time as a real person. I like it for that, and I suppose that ought to be enough. But, damn it all, I just can't conceive

Moses—or any man born earlier than 1880—writing any line of this except the first:

Once more my solitudes—

That is Mosaic, or archaic, or sufficiently in what used to be called "the grand manner." It is a line that Michelangelo's Moses—for so I must visualize him—might say. The rest—the style of it chiefly—is Louis Untermeyer, and not (I should say) at his maturest. Moses—here's my thought, conventional if you like— is a Miltonic sort of person. And he's a Jew! Well, if Moses is (as you picture him) sad or angry or prophetic, I expect a vast sadness, a terrible anger, a cosmic prophecy: even in the ratiocination I expect an overwhelming passionateness. Put a beard on your Heine, leave out most of the jokes, and underline the eloquence, and I'd accept him (almost) for a Moses. The tempestuous power of Heine seems to me to be a part of the Moses-Solomon-Isaiah-Jesus tradition. "Thou shalt not have none other Gods before me." "Babylon the great is fallen, is fallen." (That isn't Isaiah, but an echo of him.) "Woman, what have I to do with thee?" "Kiss me with the kisses of thy mouth, for thy love is sweeter than wine." . . . The quality, the tempo, the flavor of that utterance, that kind of rhetoric, is (it seems to me) at the other pale from:

The sun's concern, the smoothing little winds;
The green and silent sympathy of trees.

Maybe I'm wrong. I'd like to print the poem, because, though I don't feel it's equal to the subject—or to you—I do like it. Especially for what you suggest. But . . .

Faithfully,

Floyd

Evocative of Floyd's brisk badinage is a letter about an ironic poem I seem to have sent *The Masses* from Maine, where I spent most of my pre-war vacations. The date, August 27, 1914, scarcely helps me to "place" the unfortunate piece, but Floyd's note reconstructs the mixture of perspiration and ennui which characterized the summer meetings of the editorial board.

Dear Louis: I still think these lines are among your best. God damn me if I don't. They are brisk and bitter and—in the way that Heine was both vulgar and moving—beautiful. The whole poem is fine and, at the same time, funny. But when it percolated into the limp ardor and congealed languor of the meeting the other night, it— Well, it got a laugh from M.J. who was lying on a shelf in the back of the room, but that was all. Becker smiled, but not at the poem; he was looking at Art Young, who was trying to sleep and fight a persistent fly at the same time. I *think* I read the lines well, but evidently not with sufficient humor and persuasion. The waters of sobriety closed over the piece without a ripple. I didn't even press for a vote. Well, its place will be taken by an editorial disquisition on the philosophic aspects of the economic shift in the humanitarian view of the consequences of war. So all will be well. Damn!

Faithfully,
Floyd

Such letters have no epochal significance, but they give the lie to those critics—and, a year or two later, the prosecuting attorneys—who pictured the editors of *The Masses* as a group of grim conspirators, hatching revolution in a gun-lined, bomb-proof cellar. Purposeful we were, but purpose did not negate play. Floyd had not yet conceived his seemingly flippant but basically searching *Were You Ever a Child?* and Max did not suspect that some day he would write not merely an Outline but an exhaustive Analysis of

Laughter. Yet our foolishly high hopes for the betterment of human society were expressed through spirits that were equally high and (alas!) equally foolish. We alternately harangued and joked, raged and teased, mocked our readers and ourselves. The tone is found in another note from Floyd:

Dear Louis: I learn by *The Dial* that you are "officially" one of the Greenwich Village set. Now I understand. What I thought was a delightful sparkle and levity in you, well befitting the American Heine, is really a slackening of spiritual fiber such as comes from spending your days and nights in that loose and trifling company. It must be so. Anyone who is connected, even by hearsay, with Greenwich Village is

(1) wasting his time
(2) doing little work
(3) doing poor work
(4) doing subversive work
(5) deteriorating spiritually
(6) etc.,
(7) etc., etc.,
(8) etc., etc., etc. . . .

What have you to say for yourself?

Ever yours, but sadly,

Floyd

The point of Floyd's note is not that it was obviously ironic, but that I should ever have been listed as a Greenwich Villager. True, I had lunched at Polly Holladay's with Horace Traubel, Whitman's Camden Boswell; and I had attended rehearsals of the plays given under the auspices of the Liberal Club, that circle of Lost Souls (often referred to as sons-of-habitués) incongruously founded by a high school teacher, Henrietta Rodman. But I lived in the respectable West Nineties, notoriously (if sometimes uncomfortably) bourgeois; a jewelry manufacturer by day, a writer (and, infrequently, a poet) by night. I am afraid I was not conscious of the dichotomy, and my visits to Greenwich Village never seemed the "escape" claimed for that locality by the neighborhood psychoanalysts, restaurant proprietors, and real estate agents. But it was flattering to be part of a legend—and Floyd, one of the more liberal spirits of the Liberal Club, alternately mocked and fostered it.

Another undated note from Floyd displays his shrewd directness.

Dear Louis: Another appeal—and a peremptory one. We need a poem and we'd *like* another book-review. I've just been reading Willard Huntington Wright's much-touted "novel," *A Man of Promise*. My Gawd! My Gawd! Take a look at it, old sport. Not a drop, not a ray, not a shred, not an iota, not a gleam, not a jot, not even a tittle of an idea to redeem it. Not a hint of the art of fiction about it. It might have been written by a statistician, a professor, a Pinkerton detective—or all three in collaboration. If you'll review it for us I'll be grateful. You might do better—you might psychoanalyze it.

Yours ever,

Floyd

Floyd's literary judgments were often tricky, but they were usually convincing and sometimes clairvoyant. At the time Willard Huntington Wright was unknown as a writer, yet Floyd's summary was not only pungent but prophetic. After Wright had edited *The Smart Set,* conducted a daily column, and offered to revise the *Encyclopaedia Britannica,* he changed his name and, as S. S. Van Dine, wrote a series of murder mysteries, in which the central figure is the painfully erudite Philo Vance, "a statistician, a professor, a Pinkerton detective—or all three in collaboration."

Although he was trying his hand at a quasi-autobiographical novel—it turned out to be the highly successful *Moon Calf*—Floyd was still grieving over his early demise as a poet. He sent me scraps of his verse, ranging from pseudo-Elizabethan sonnets (crammed with capitals that pretended to be allegorical) to irregular psychoanalytic verse that succeeded in being free; complained about Max's "tasteless enthusiasms and willful energy" in refusing to frame a poetic policy for the magazine; praised my own contributions as an esthete and attacked them as a member of the Party. When I made my first tentative outline for an anthology of modern poetry, Floyd and I spent many lunch hours in a Fourteenth Street saloon considering the proportionate representation of Bliss Carman and William Vaughn Moody (Floyd's favorites) against Robert Frost and E. A. Robinson (my first choices) over the beer and *sauerbraten*.

This preoccupation with poetry was not strange, for it is the writer's deepest concern. The best prose aims at, struggles toward, and lifts itself into poetry; it might almost be said that prose is what one writes after one has failed to write verse. The first books by many of my non-poetical contemporaries were books of poems: H. L. Mencken, that anti-poetic pundit, author of some thirty collections of essays, linguistic studies, and bewildering prose prejudices, began with a volume coyly entitled *Ventures into Verse;* Willa Cather, Pulitzer prize novelist, preceded her many fictions with the idyllic *April Twilights;* the gently professorial Irwin Edman, to whom philosophy is both a pursuit and an escape, made his debut with the lilting *Measures of the Moment;* the mature James Branch Cabell turned violently against the young poet he started out to be, but overcompensated for his revulsion by inventing (in *From the Hidden Way*) a whole galaxy of poets who never lived except in Cabell's "translations," and perfected a highly colored prose which attempted to disguise poorly concealed rhymes, runaway rhythms, and even artful hexameters.

V

But the most ardent revolutionary and the most consistent poet of those days was John Reed. (I write John for the record, but he was never, not even by his detractors, called anything but Jack.) At twenty-five Jack was a big-boned, broad-shouldered, handsome, semi-theatrical figure. In appearance he was midway between the frankly melodramatic defier-of-lightnings, which Art Young depicted in a drawing entitled "Storm Boy," and the grim young hero shown in Robert Hallowell's painting at Harvard. He was only a few years out of the college, where he was, even as an undergraduate, "unassimilable." He had been rejected by the socially exclusive campus clubs, and he was the intimate of such insurgents as Lee Simonson (who began, not as an artist or scenic designer, but as a brilliant epigrammatic essayist); Walter Lippmann, who became president of the undergraduate Socialist Club and who was to write his penetrating *A Preface to Politics* at twenty-four; Edward Hunt, who emulated Reed in everything from schoolboy jokes to journalism; the artist Robert Hallowell; and the poets John Hall Wheelock, Alan Seeger, and Conrad Aiken. Superficially Jack seemed the playboy *in excelsis*—friends recalled how he and another undergraduate visited Mt. Auburn cemetery leaving a dozen calling cards on which he had written "Sorry you were out when we called," and dashed through the streets of Lexington crying, "Hurry! The British are coming!" Jack fostered this devil-may-care picture of himself—he was, as Max testified, the spoiled child of *The Masses* meetings—and it is no wonder that most of his acquaintances regarded him as a predetermined gypsy masquerading as a gentleman-adventurer, a *sans culotte* assailing the walls of tradition with a pamphlet in one hand and a bladder in the other, a combination of Jack London, Peck's Bad Boy, Don Giovanni, Don Quixote, and The Playboy of the Western World.

Some knew him as the political reporter, the unforgiving foe of chicanery, contributor to the *American Magazine* (which, with nonchalant inconsistency, attacked the evils of the "system" and glorified the successful exponents of it), diagnostician of National Conventions, and, later, as the best war-correspondent in America. Only a few of us knew the slowly maturing man. This was the other Jack Reed, the sensitive young night-wanderer, the interpreter of Bowery dives and bread-lines, who wrote, "It didn't come to me from my books that the workers produced all the wealth of the world, which went to those who did not earn it." This was the probing realist, the disciple of Lincoln Steffens, who gave Jack his first assignment on a periodical with a national circulation; it was the propagandist off-guard, the recorder of heroic defeats, the poet.

It was as a poet that I first knew Jack. At twenty-five he had published *The Day in Bohemia,* a helter-skelter collection of verses lightly caricaturing "our foibles, weaknesses and shortcomings." It included some account of the life led by "Geniuses in Manhattan's *Quartier* Latin," a teasing-tender tribute to Greenwich Village, a scattered set of parodies showing how Shelley, Keats, Whitman and Maeterlinck would have apostrophized "The Tenement Clothes-Line," and ended with a devastating burlesque of the self-advertised wickedness of George Sylvester Viereck, a resuscitated hangover from the Eighteen Nineties:

> *O let us humbly bow the neck*
> *To George Syl-ves-ter Vi-er-eck,*
> *Who trolled us a merry little Continental stave*
> *Concerning the Belly and the Phallus and the Grave—*

My copy bears a mocking but not altogether disingenuous inscription: "To Louis, who promised to review this; but my affection for whom antedated the promise. Inscribed by [in enormous capitals] The Author, John Reed."

Two other books of verse by Jack appeared in the same year: *Everymagazine, An Immorality Play* and *Sangar*. The first was written for the Dutch Treat Club, a gathering of commercial editors, columnists, and artists. Its tone was that of musical comedy, but, beneath the banter, there was caustic satire on the muckraking *McClure's*, the spinsterly *Century*, the senescent *Scribner's*, the cheaply sensational *Cosmopolitan*, and the whole "kept" press. The second was in a totally different *genre;* a romantic allegory in which the soldier-hero attempts to pacify both sides, is denounced by the militant priest and slain, as a traitor, by his own son. *Sangar* represented, though Jack could not have foreseen it, the contemporary tragedy of the liberal, torn between the

desire to battle against injustice and the conviction that
there never has been a "good" or even conclusive war. The
poem, traditional in technique like all Jack's verse, had a
genuine resonance and a rousing vitality. Before he published "Tamburlaine" four years later, he was turning away
from pretty rhymes of private malaises, from an art which
was only "an esthetic enjoyment to a few highly sensitized
minds."

Jack and I, among others, had a mutual distrust of a de-
humanized, fastidious, and hermetic art, an art beyond good
and evil. But we had something stronger in common: a love
of bad poetry. We agreed that there were only two kinds of
poetry worth remembering: unfathomably great poems and
unforgettably bad ones. We flung Shelley and "The Sweet
Singer of Michigan" at each other, interrupted conversation
with snatches from Swinburne to prove he was not quite as
good—or bad—as James Byron Elmore, "The Bard of
Alamo." We listed dozens of entries for an anthology to be
entitled: "The World's Worst Poetry," a collection I have
been making most of my life and which occupies two shelves
of my studio, but which is still unready for the printer. Set
to winnowing the fast-accumulating sheaves of verse for *The
Masses,* Jack and I howled with delight whenever we discovered some particularly gaudy gem. We would leave notes
for each other on the editorial desk which we shared with
Floyd, calling attention to some of the choicest dithyrambs.
For God knows what reason Jack must have kept several of
my notes to him, for one of them is quoted in Granville
Hicks's excellent biography. I have found only two or three
of the notes Jack left for me, but I have recovered several
of the submitted poems which (evidently because of failure

to enclose stamps) never went back to their creators. On the
bottom of the manuscripts I find a few scribbled lines: "My
God! This is the true afflatus! The finest thing of its kind
since Whitman and Ella Wheeler Wilcox!" "I felt you *must*
see this—spelling and all intact. It's too good for print—or
for the author. You're the only one who deserves it." A
poem entitled "Where Is the Boy I Used to Be?" ends:

> *Come to me, boy that I used to be;*
> *Come back to me, little child!*
> *O make me happy and gay and free,*
> *Innocent, undefiled!*

And Jack wrote under it "O, all right!" Whenever the question of women's rights came up at our meetings, one of us
would quote from a treasured manuscript "The Hand That
Rocks the Cradle Rules the Big Wide World":

> *Read Ida Tarbell's words; all noble deeds record;*
> *Learn of Dr. E. B. Davis, in New York at Bedford.*
> *God in His great wisdom, His truly wondrous plan,*
> *Created not one woman to act like any man.*

Restless and resistless, Jack had a genius for inspiring affection. Before he met Louise Bryant, the "wild, brave and
straight creature" who gave him the emotional center he had
been seeking, he had been engaged, broken off the engagement, had become the idol of an intelligent, rich and neurotic woman who has since become famous for a more than
usually revealing set of intimate memories, and had been
arrested during the strike of the silk mill-workers at Pater-
son. He went as war-correspondent to Mexico, where, at
twenty-six, he was compared to Richard Harding Davis,

Stephen Crane, and Rudyard Kipling, and where he became
a close friend of Pancho Villa, who was (according to what
paper you read) a Mexican Robin Hood, protector of the
poor, or a bloody bandit who threatened America's—and
chiefly William Randolph Hearst's—investments.

That was the Jack Reed I knew—at least that was part of
him. The boisterousness and the quiet passion for truth, the
insurgency and the integrity, never quite fused until his last
phase (the real, not the romantic, revolutionist) when he
wrote his masterpiece *Ten Days That Shook the World.* He
died, stricken with typhus, in Russia at thirty-three, already
a legendary figure. When, some years later, a group of young
radicals honored his memory by organizing the John Reed
Club I naturally joined it. For this I was put down in *The
Red Network* and, subsequently, blacklisted by several expensive forums. I suppose I am a little vain about this, for
The Red Network, a preposterous compilation prepared by
a silly, hysterical clubwoman, shows me in the nefarious
rôle of writing for *The Liberator* and *The New Republic,*
and lists me among such "enemies of the country" as Jane
Addams, founder of that great humanitarian institution Hull
House, Felix Frankfurter of the United States Supreme
Court, and Mrs. President Franklin D. Roosevelt.

But that came afterwards. Something else came first. Something united the disunited elements on *The Masses.* The
artists and the writers were at loggerheads; each group
claimed the other was interested only in gay irresponsibility.
It was the most serious of our customary crises. The artists,
headed by John Sloan, claimed Max was a dictatorial doc-
trinaire; the writers, represented by Max, analyzed the situation as the inevitable conflict between Socialism and Bo-

hemianism. After a verbal feud that threatened to disrupt the magazine, several of the artists mutinied. ("How can they mutiny?" cried Floyd. "They've never been paid!") We feared the worst. We got it, though not as we had expected it. We got the war.

WORLD-LOSERS
AND WORLD-FORSAKERS

WAR ABROAD united the editors of *The Masses* more effectively than any local issue. *The Masses* had announced several articles of faith, but it was going along without a central credo. Spreading itself in many directions, it had impartially championed woman suffrage, free thought (and, by implication, free love), socialism, birth-control, and the art of beautiful letters. But it was most characteristic when it attacked. It fought against easy conventions and the prevalent standards, commercial success, against the banality of contemporary taste and the hardening cynicism of a corrupt press. Yet, though the attacks were conducted with gaiety and gusto, our battles were negative. We had vigorous onslaughts, but no discernible victories; high-hearted convictions, but no real conquests.

One effrontery had already caused *The Masses* to be interdicted by various public libraries and news-stands; our mailing privileges had been revoked by the Dominion of Canada; the *Associated Press* had sued us for libel. But, with America's entrance into the World War, we found a common integrating policy and new trouble. Long before Wilson had been re-elected on the strength of the slogan "He kept us out of war," *The Masses* had been consistently pacifist. We believed with Jack Reed, who had seen fighting on five fronts, that this was a commercial conflict and that, unless a decent policy were announced in time, a bad war would be followed by a worse peace. It was an unpopular opinion and (since we maintained it in poems, stories, editorials, and cartoons) a dangerous one.

The war hysteria was worst in America, where, unlike Europe, we had little to fear and less to lose. It prohibited the songs of Schumann and the music-dramas of Wagner—a form of cultural censorship brought to final perfection twenty years later by the Nazis—it raged from the churches, where the mild God of Love was invoked as an old tribal ally, to the colleges, where the boys with the finest records were prepared for the very best trenches. Besides my general concern, I felt an immediate responsibility for a few of these boys. A group of undergraduates at Columbia University invited me to address them on two occasions, and their enthusiasm for my opinions gratified me as only the praise of the young can please an old man—the undergraduates were in their beginning twenties and I was thirty. To even the score, they paid me the compliment of founding a magazine of protest and naming it for a volume I had recently published, *Challenge*. Among the group were Morrie Ryskind, who divides his time in Hollywood between turning poor plays into effective movies, devising less method and more madness for the Marx Brothers, and writing satirical skits for *The Nation;* the biographer M. R. Werner; Irwin Edman, now sufficiently ancient to indulge in the reminiscences of *Professor's Holiday;* George Sokolsky, who, after an insurrectionary and even anarchistic youth, became the St. George of the *status quo,* glorifier of cosmetic advertising—"beauty, swank, the joy of living, every girl a queen; these are the realizable ideals of the American woman"—and the paid apostle of the American Association of Manufacturers; Larry Hart, the lyrical partner of Rodgers and Hart; Howard Dietz, the shy "Freckles" of F.P.A.'s column, who made a fortune or two as publicity expert for Samuel Goldwyn; Ilo Orleans, who traded lyrics for law; Charles Phillips, who went straight from a revolution in Mexico to write for *The Wall Street Journal;* M. Lincoln Schuster, who, attached to a couple of Simons, founded the well-known publishing firm that started with a lead pencil and a puzzle-book; James Marshall, son of a modest great man, who, even more modestly, became president of the Board of Education.

Most of the group of Columbia insurgents took their rebelliousness with a liberal dash of literature; Morrie took it seriously. His outspoken objection to the war and his equally frank criticism of Nicholas Murray Butler, Columbia University's President and space-consumer in *Who's Who,* were such that he was expelled from the university a few weeks before he would have been awarded his degree. Morrie must have smiled some years later when the very qualities which so offended Butler so pleased the Pulitzer Prize Committee—a Committee with its headquarters at Columbia. The Committee awarded the prize for the best play of the year to *Of Thee I Sing,* a critical anti-militarist musical satire which Morrie wrote in collaboration with George S. Kaufman to the memorable music of George Gershwin.

II

The Masses met the war head on—or, rather, the U. S. Post Office crashed into us without even putting out its hand. There had been rumblings of censorship and threats

of suppression; the Associated Press, fulfilling our predictions and the predilections of its owners, had howled for our
heads. Merrill Rogers, business manager of *The Masses,* had
taken one of our issues to George Creel, presumably the
national censor, and Creel had assured him that there was
nothing in the magazine in violation of the law, as far as he
could interpret it. Nevertheless, and without further parley,
the post office refused to allow the use of the mails to the
August, 1918, issue. We took counsel with two eminent
jurists, two cousins poetically (and, we thought, significantly) named Learned Hand and August Hand. Judge
Learned Hand granted an injunction, which was stayed by
an appeal on the part of the post office. Under the influence
of the judicial decision in our favor we brought out two
other issues. The post office struck back through the Federal
Government, and we were suddenly faced with an indictment on two counts: (1) that we had "conspired to effect
insubordination or mutiny in the armed and naval forces of
the United States" and (2) that we had "conspired to ob-
struct enlistment and recruiting."

At first we took the charges lightly. We sent postcards to
each other: "We expect you for the—ssh!—weekly sedition.
Object: Overthrow of the Government. Don't tell a soul."
Art Young drew a form letter which we circulated freely:
"Dear Bill: Come to the conspiracy Tuesday night. Yours,
The Conspirators." This seemed grotesque enough; it never
occurred to us that we were, as a prosecuting attorney
charged, "all the more dangerous because these are intelligent young men." We thought the situation fantastic; but
something far more grotesque was to come.

On a bright April day we found ourselves in the unhealthy confines of the United States District Court, Southern District of New York, faced by a black-gowned Judge and three gentlemen with bulging portfolios from the United States Attorney's office. There was also a jury-box with twelve of our "peers," according to the fiction of the Constitution, for the jury panel consisted mostly of retired bankers, salesmen, foremen, and professional talesmen, unblemished by wageworkers or members of the "lower classes." It was inconceivable. It was, as Floyd Dell wrote in his story of the trial, "like a scene from *Alice in Wonderland* rewritten by Dostoievsky." It was a staged nightmare produced by hysterical fears and mass-suspicions, by fear of the truth, distrust of independent thinking, and opposition to the minority. As Floyd summarized it, "we did not agree with other people about a lot of things. We did not even agree with each other about many things. And when the war came we were found still saying what we individually thought about everything—including war. No two of us thought quite alike about it. But none of us said what the morning papers were saying."

I echo Floyd by saying "we," for we all felt we were defending primary public principle: the maintenance of a free press and constitutional rights even in war time. Although we were all in court, actually only five of the suspects faced prison: Art Young, Floyd Dell, Max Eastman, Merrill Rogers, and Josephine Bell—an artist, an author, a poet-editor, a business man, and a youngish woman who had contributed a single poem to the magazine and whom not one of us had seen until the day we were arraigned. It was hard to feel the reality of the proceedings. We felt a little sorry for our lawyers, Morris Hillquit and Dudley Field Malone,

who took it so seriously. But a Liberty Bond band was playing patriotic airs in adjoining City Hall Square; the newspapers were screaming for action against conscientious objectors; and we were confronted with the crime of not only
violating, but *conspiring* to violate, the Espionage Act.
After some argument, Judge August Hand sustained a motion to dismiss the first count of the indictment, wherein it
was charged we had conspired to get the army and navy to
mutiny against the Government, but he denied the motion
on the second count wherein we supposedly conspired to
prevent young men from Joining the Navy and seeing the
world or Joining the Army and seeing the next world.

The prosecution put eleven witnesses on the stand—clerks,
printers, salesmen, bookbinders, stenographers in the employ of the magazine, officials in the employ of the Government. The prosecution proved that *The Masses* had been
written, printed, sold (we were tempted to cheer at the un-
solicited advertisement) and circulated, but they proved
nothing else. Once more our lawyer moved to dismiss the
indictment on the remaining count on the ground that the
Government had not made a case of conspiracy against any
of the defendants. No evidence had been offered to show
mutual agreement upon anything or that we had any con-
certed action apart from being both owners and contributors
to a magazine which published our work. Judge Hand ruled
that the fact that we were associated on a common enterprise
might not be conclusive evidence but was sufficient to go to a
jury. Even here he had to make an exception in the case of
Josephine Bell. Although humor is not necessarily part of a
jurist's equipment, it must have seemed a little comic to
Judge Hand to hold as co-defendant in a conspiracy a per-

son who had never met her co-conspirators. Shades of the prison-house no longer closed about Josephine Bell. The rest breathed more lightly—all except Art Young, who was breathing far more heavily. He was asleep.

Later Art excused himself for disgracing us. Half apologetically, half defiantly, he claimed that a court atmosphere was the ideal place for slumber. The slow parading of irrelevant matter first irritated, then wearied, then soothed him, he maintained. "An artist eliminates detail; a lawyer piles it up. You can't go home and forget it; so nothing can save you but a quiet little nap. I am not recommending it to other criminals," concluded Art, "but it put me *en rapport* with the higher law where every case goes at last." When Art was wakened he made a pencil sketch of himself as he imagined he had looked during his short but complete oblivion. There he was, slumped down against the back of a chair, his arms dangling, his mouth slack, his nose obviously and audibly snoring. Above the drawing he had scribbled "Art Young on Trial for his Life."

I I I

As the trial went on it was evident that the indictment was a legal subterfuge and that what really was on trial was the issue of a free press. Actually the Government was contending that in a time of war—and the totalitarian states have extended the idea to include times of peace—there can be no criticism, no minorities, no expression of the free individual. We of *The Masses* naturally contended that, even in war time, a critical minority was not only permissible but necessary, that no conflict could be brought to a successful end except by a fully informed people, and that the true aims of a war must be understood before terms of peace are imposed. (This was the attitude, subsequently adopted by President Wilson, of "no annexations, no indemnities, and self-determination of all peoples.") How idealistic and pathetically academic these aims seem as I am writing this, twenty years later. Today, in the midst of a world where nations have repudiated international agreements, where Fascist laws, instead of protecting the citizen, exist only to subjugate him, and where the least murmur against a dictator is high treason against the State, such phrases seem the dream-babblings of Utopians in secure ivory towers. But either we were other people or it was—as I am tempted to believe—another world. Max Eastman spent almost three days testifying to the difference between an inherent love of liberty and the acquired "ritual of patriotism." Floyd Dell, less eloquently and more unconcernedly, confirmed the heretical truth. Art Young, the dormouse at this mad tea-party, was prodded awake by his fellow-conspirators; but he gave, I fear, a poor performance of an agent of sedition. He testified that, as an artist, he was not always aware what his cartoons might mean to others because, he added simply, they did not always mean the same thing to the other editors. He was not disturbed about the possibility of twenty years in prison, for he could not even imagine himself on trial for treason, and, he concluded with his characteristic irrelevance and benign grin, he was always happy as long as he had a pencil in his hand.

The prosecuting attorney was not to be put off by Art Young's ingenuousness; he scented some dark "intent" and kept after Art like an irate weasel (which he much resembled) sniffing a plump and sleepy mole.

"And what," he insisted, "did you mean by Exhibit F?"

Exhibit F was a drawing entitled "Having Their Fling." It showed a war-maddened crowd of men who represented the press, politics, pulpit, and what we used to call "the vested interests." The throng was dancing to an orchestra which played on cannons instead of trombones, guns instead of flutes, rifles instead of oboes.

"And the Devil is leading the orchestra!" shouted the prosecuting attorney. "What do you mean by that?"

"Well," Art drawled, "it wasn't my idea in the first place."

"No?" mocked the prosecuting attorney. "Some other pacifist's?"

"Yes. General Grant's," said Art. "Grant said—oh, you know. And if war *is* Hell, it seems to me that the Devil should be the conductor of the band."

Just before the lawyers summed up the case on the ninth day of the trial, I was called to the stand. I had hoped, vaingloriously, that Prosecutor Barnes might attack one of my poems, although none of them had been mentioned in the indictment—an omission which, it seemed to me, pointed to a singularly insensitive Government. I was either followed or preceded by Howard Brubaker, now the sustaining ironist of *The New Yorker,* and we both testified briefly to our diversity of opinion on political and esthetic matters—a diversity which we shared with our fellow editors—to our continual relationship with the magazine, and to our belief in unpopular views. I think (mistakenly, perhaps) that I made the more impressive witness. A noble bearing was on Brubaker's side, and I never looked the way a poet is expected to look. But the firm of Untermeyer, Robbins & Company had invested heavily in Liberty Bonds, and our Newark jewelry factory had become an "essential industry" by manufacturing surgical knives.

The evidence was in. It established the fact that *The Masses* was a radical magazine in which various contributors exercised their (then lawful) expressions of opinion. The Government was unable to prove conspiratorial intent. It was, we learned later, a close call. Only one juror voted for our acquittal. The other eleven wrangled over shades of opinion and what constituted "evidence." The result of the disagreement was that the jury was unable to arrive at a verdict; the Court had to dismiss the jury and declare a mistrial. For us this was as good as an acquittal; it was—we wore the phrase out—a moral victory. That was in April, 1918. The feeling of triumph lasted until October.

IV

Possibly because it was an anticlimax, my memory of the second *Masses* trial is far less clear than my recollection of the first. It is refreshed by letters, passages in Art Young's *On My Way,* and Jack Reed's report in the December, 1918, issue of *The Liberator.* During the first trial Jack had been in Russia, witnessing Kerensky's defeat and the rise of the proletariat under Lenin, maturing with the revolt of the Bolsheviki, and gathering material for his accurate and impassioned *Ten Days That Shook the World.*

Once again the Liberty Loan Band was blaring out military marches underneath the window of the courtroom; the prosecuting attorney sat behind formidable portfolios of accumulated ammunition; the patriotics accompanying the Fourth Liberty Loan drive mounted with increasing virulence; the jury panel was conspicuously blue-blooded. Our counsel, Seymour Steadman, who had taken the place of Hillquit and Malone, asked an especially portly juror if he had any prejudice against Socialism.

"I don't know what it is," said the gentleman, who had given his business as "Wall Street," "but I'm opposed to it."

In spite of the forbidding atmosphere, our attitude in the second trial was different from what it had been in the first. Jack Reed summed it up simply: "Last spring Germany was invading Russia; this fall the United States was invading Russia, and socialists were in a different frame of mind. . . . I think we all felt tranquil, and ready to go to prison if need be. At any rate, we were not going to dissemble what we believed." This attitude, as Jack insisted, had its effect not only on the jury but on the judge. The judge was Martin Manton, and Jack concluded that Manton was fair-minded because he allowed socialism to be mentioned and actually argued in court. It seemed to me that Judge Manton was actuated more by curiosity than by tolerance and that he was reluctant to allow any of the defendants to state their basic philosophies. I was probably more splenetic than Jack, but I was less impressed by the well-swathed judicial temperament. I sent Jack the following quatrain, the only piece I have ever written in the shadow of the bench:

> *How well this figure represents the Law:*
> *This pose of neuter justice, sterile cant;*
> *This Roman Emperor with an iron jaw,*
> *Wrapped in the black silk of a maiden aunt.*

I do not remember much of the proceedings, but I do remember the poetry. The courtroom was full of it. During periods of argument Floyd Dell busied himself composing psychoanalytical free verse. Edna St. Vincent Millay quoted lines from an Elizabethan sonnet and was not too pleased when I asked her, without smiling, when she had written it. Before Jack took the stand he said, "Comfort me with apples —or Elmore. I think I'm going to need it." Whereupon we exchanged two or three lines of the poem by "The Bard of Alamo," entitled "Ode to Sassafras," a poem which we agreed was the greatest medicinal lyric ever written.

> *In the spring of the year*
>   *When the blood is too thick,*
> *There's nothing so good*
>   *As a sassafras stick.*
> *It regulates the liver;*
>   *It livens up the heart;*
> *And to the whole system*
>   *New life doth impart.*
>
> *O sassafras! sweet sassafras!*
>   *Thou art the stuff for me!*
> *And in the spring I love to sing,*
>   *Sweet sassafras, of thee!*

Of the proceeding itself, the only things I vividly recall are Max's three-hour speech, Jack's unequivocal opposition to the war, and Art Young's unexpected interruption of the prosecuting attorney's summing up. Max eloquently took up the Russian question, which previously had been ruled out, championed the cause of the revolutionists, and made

it part of his defense. Jack described what he had seen in the
trenches, described it with such graphic candor that the
courtroom was both horrified and purged of hate. Prosecutor
Barnes came off least well. Steadman and Max had fore-
stalled him, predicting, almost to the inflection, what he
would say. Barnes went on and on, wrapping himself in the
flag, quivering and quavering with the expected theatrics.
"Somewhere in France," concluded Barnes, pulling out the
last tremolo stop, "a man lies dead. He is but one of a
thousand whose voices are not silent. He died for you and
he died for me. He died for Max Eastman. He died for
John Reed. He died for Merrill Rogers. He demands that
these men be punished. . . ."

At this moment Art Young, roused by the ascending pitch,
started from his customary doze.

"What!" exclaimed Art. "Didn't he die for me, too?"

The peroration was ruined, and I suspect that Art's indignant query did as much as the brilliant speeches to bring
about a disagreement. At any rate, the jury disagreed again.
This time eight were for acquittal, and one of the "con-
victing" four later declared that he had sworn never to let
a socialist go if he could ever get his hands on one.

We were never again brought to trial. We had already
changed the name and, to some extent, the nature of *The
Masses*. We now called it *The Liberator,* and the first issue,
which featured Jack's story of the Bolshevik revolution, was
issued (significantly, we thought) on Lincoln's Birthday,
1918.

The aims of *The Liberator* were not new but they were
less revolutionary. The manifesto on the first page spoke
up for the struggle of labor, advocated (long before the CCC

and TVA experiments) the opening of the land to the people, and urged the taking over by the Government of the railroads, the mines, the telegraph and telephone systems, and all public utilities. It stood (with what now seems a charming archaism) for the independence of women. It called for a new method of dealing with crime. Opposed to a rigid scholasticism, it declared (long before the present return to "the humanities") for an educational system with a vivid relation to life. It asserted the social and political equality of all races, and finally endorsed the aims outlined by the Russian people and sounded by President Wilson: a peace without forcible annexations, without punitive indemnities, with general disarmament, and with free development and self-determination for all peoples.

The Liberator was barely in existence when Jack resigned from it. The action was not, as some of us thought, the result of a quarrel with Max and his "personal policy." Jack wrote, "I cannot in these times bring myself to share editorial responsibility for a magazine which exists upon the sufferance of Mr. Burleson." (Burleson was the Postmaster General.) "In the happy day when we can call a spade a spade without tying bunting on it, you will find me as you have in the past. . . ." Nevertheless, Jack continued to contribute to *The Liberator* which flourished (if I may use the enthusiastic verb) for almost six years. But the compromises which Jack resented and which we felt were needed, were too much—or too little—for the magazine. In 1924 it was merged with *The Labor Herald* to form *The Workers' Monthly*. Neither *The Masses* nor *The Liberator* would have recognized its final left-handed—or should I say left-winged?—offspring, *New Masses*.

V

Where, to paraphrase the nostalgic ballade, are the heroes of yesteryear? Where are the music-makers, the dreamers of dreams? Where, by what desolate streams, are the movers and shakers, world-losers and world-forsakers?

Max Eastman has abjured not only the sons of the revolution but their spiritual father, Karl Marx. In a periodical inappropriately named *Liberty* Max has concluded that the Russian Communist group is becoming a Fascist party, and he has thereupon retired from politics, which, like marriage, makes such strange bedfellows. Max has recently added to the gaiety of education with an Outline of Laughter (a popularized combination of Bergson's essay on the same theme and Freud's *Wit and the Unconscious*); he has even (God knows at what cost to himself and his sponsors) been Master of Ceremonies for a radio Question-and-Answer game.

Art Young, who once plunged traditionally bloated capitalists through limbos unknown to Doré in Art Young's own *Inferno,* is a quiet country gentleman, cultivating his potatoes and pruning his hedges near Danbury, Connecticut.

Floyd Dell, once the apostle of free love and the white hope of the literary insurrectionists, is a placid landowner respectably married, raising a family, and writing salable novels for the once-despised bourgeoisie. The conspirator who was accused of trying to disrupt the Government was recently brought to Washington to help the Federal Writers Project.

Judge Martin Manton, before whom the conspiracy

charges were tried, was charged with violation of Federal
Statutes early in 1939. He resigned under fire, and was subsequently indicted on three counts—counts of conspiracy.
A few months later he was tried and convicted of "selling
justice"—selling it at exorbitant rates.

Jack Reed lies in Russia, buried in the Kremlin.

And I travel about these states lecturing on "New Frontiers
in American Culture," teaching teachers what not to teach,
or sit here in the Adirondack Mountains, raising Eskimo
puppies, letting my wife run the farm, and coddling my
memory. I try to be neither sentimental nor satirical about
it, but . . .

ROOTS AND SKYSCRAPERS

BEFORE *The Masses* had failed to live up to its hope of being *The Liberator,* I was an active member of another magazine so short-lived that it died within the year of its birth. It was a brisk and exciting venture, and I had thought that, after its demise toward the end of 1917, all but a few of us had forgotten it. Yet twenty-one years after *The Seven Arts* had ceased to exist, it came to life again in *New York Panorama,* the liveliest and most brilliant of the guidebooks prepared by the Federal Writers Project. This comprehensive and often breath-taking collation delighted me with its vigor and definiteness: "While the Midwest was engaged in discovering itself, New York writers were about to embark upon another and more ambitious voyage of exploration, their objective being nothing less than the discovery of America, of the continent's soul and the meaning of its vast sprawling civilization. . . . Out of this was to grow one of the best, if shortest-lived, literary magazines that the country has known, *The Seven Arts,* which numbered among its editors and contributors Waldo Frank, James Oppenheim, Randolph Bourne, Van Wyck Brooks, Louis Untermeyer, and others. . . . The fostering impulse behind *The Seven Arts* was one of 'back to our native roots'—the same impulse that was to find expression, some years later in Hart Crane's poem 'The Bridge,' and that eventually was to degenerate into a sterile cult of the skyscraper, of a skyscraper civilization and its 'Lively Arts.' Combined with the expression of this impulse was a new note of social liberalism. . . ."

These phrases bring with them a swift association. They re-create the nightlong argument when James Oppenheim and I juggled pieces of paper, chewed pencils, and ransacked literature, art, and Bartlett's *Familiar Quotations* to choose a name for a magazine which had, at the moment, nothing more than a mothering sponsor and two editorial godfathers. I remember I wanted to call it something loose and all-inclusive like *The Open Book* or *The New World*. Jimmie held out for something more dramatic; he (and, I think, Waldo Frank) favored *The Frontier* or, as a compliment to a forthcoming collection of my poems of the same title, *These Times*. Among other titles we considered and discarded were *Roots, "America Singing," The Modern Arena, The Forge, Today and Tomorrow, The Trend, The New Pioneer, Native Soil*. We rejected all of these as being too flaccid or too florid, too prosy or too poetic, too ambitious or just too hard to remember. Out of weariness rather than inspiration we finally decided upon *The Seven Arts*, perhaps the most innocuous and ambiguous title possible, but one which allowed the widest latitude.

My intimacy with James Oppenheim was as deeply grounded as it was old. He was the first literary person I had known. More than that, he was the first living writer to influence me. I think it was his personality even more than his prose and poetry which awoke in me a strong sense of the contemporary scene. When I first met Jimmie, I was fashioning pretty little lyrics which I attempted to set to even prettier music, while he was not only writing about actual, if slightly super-heroic, people against an industrial background, but selling his stories to the more popular magazines. He was also writing a new kind of poetry—at least it seemed new to me. It was regular, even lilting, in rhythm, and conventional, if sometimes inaccurate, in rhyme. But the sense was unorthodox, the phrasing was fresh, and the spirit rather than the form was free. I was spinning fancies; Jimmie was writing about *things*. Even in my stubborn early twenties I appreciated the difference; I drew closer to what was a real and fertile source; and, although Jimmie was little more than three years older than I, he became my first preceptor.

For a while, I followed Jimmie with a blind allegiance; I was beguiled not only by his writing but by his Messianic panaceas. There was a time when I dispensed with my eyeglasses; for Jimmie, persuaded by a current healer, convinced me that chronic astigmatism could easily be cured by exercise and good thoughts. This was during Jimmie's social settlement phase. From Jane Addams to Jung and the *Psychology of the Unconscious* was a long step, but Jimmie and I took it in our stride. Our family circles drew ever closer; our wives exchanged gossip and recipes; Jimmie's two gifted sons were models for my then only child. When Jimmie turned from couplets and quatrains to a polyrhythmical set of cadences, I tried to write free verse. In this I was even less successful than my attempt to do without eyeglasses. My natural impulse was toward a pronounced pattern; in poetry, as in music, I delighted in expressions free in spirit but fixed in form. My ear craved all the sensual properties of traditional verse, the alternating caress and clang of rhythm, the little bells of rhyme. Yet I could not help but admire the ease with which Jimmie rolled out his loose cadences, and I envied him when he collected them and dared to call the volume *Songs for the New Age.* These poems, and those he wrote subsequently, were psalms rather than songs. They were fragments of David, Isaiah, and the Book of Job in terms of the Twentieth Century; they were the Bible retranslated by Walt Whitman in collaboration with Dr. Freud.

II

It was Freud, "elevated" by Jung and paraphrased by Beatrice Hinkle, who was responsible for *The Seven Arts.* In the clash of conflicting maladjustments Jimmie had found another Healer; for a while he simultaneously underwent psychoanalysis and practiced it. Dr. Hinkle, the authorized translator of *Wandlungen und Symbole der Libido,* had another patient. Like Jimmie, Mrs. Rankine was seeking a new message of health, "a new light upon the meaning of life." Her wealth had insufficient therapeutic value; she wanted an occupation. We wanted a magazine. Dr. Hinkle acted in the dual rôles of marriage-broker and midwife, and in November, 1916, our child was born.

The staff of *The Seven Arts* consisted of James Oppenheim, editor, Waldo Frank, associate editor, and an advisory board which included Van Wyck Brooks, Robert Edmond Jones, Robert Frost, Edna Kenton, and—I never discovered how or why—Kahlil Gibran, whose vogue was tremendous and whose art was a soothing blend of William Blake, Rabindranath Tagore, and Maxfield Parrish. I was also one of the advisory board, but, though I contributed regularly, the actual work was done by Jimmie, Waldo, and Van Wyck. Jimmie had published his challenging *War and Laughter;* Van Wyck had just fluttered the Brahmins with

America's Coming-of-Age, which was to have so rich an efflorescence in *The Flowering of New England;* Waldo had not yet written *City Block* nor *Our America,* which were to mingle native comment with cosmic prophecy. Four of us divided the literary responsibility. Jimmie wrote the editorials; Waldo superintended the fiction and introduced such writers as Sherwood Anderson and John Dos Passos; Van Wyck took charge of the essays, and I the poetry. We all collaborated on the opening manifesto: "It is our faith and the faith of many that we are living in the first days of a renascent period, a time which means for America the coming of that national self-consciousness which is the beginning of greatness. In all such epochs the arts cease to be private matters; they become not only the expression of the national life, but a means to its enhancement."

Such a paragraph, read today, may need the excuse of youth to explain its pretentious chauvinism—Jimmie, the oldest, was thirty-four, and Waldo, the youngest, was twenty-seven. Yet the first few issues contained such important prose and verse as "America and the Arts" by Romain Rolland, "The Bonfire" by Robert Frost, "Queer" and "Mother" by Sherwood Anderson, "Aesthetic Form" by Willard Huntington Wright, "The Splinter of Ice" by Van Wyck Brooks, "A Way Out," the only published play by Robert Frost, "The Thimble" by D. H. Lawrence, and the famous little "Grass" by Carl Sandburg. Meanwhile in the back of the magazine Van Wyck analyzed culture and criticism; Waldo prefigured the pattern of an emerging national greatness; Paul Rosenfeld turned monthly handsprings for the newest names in music; and I, as usual, contributed verse and criticized poetry.

III

In the April, 1917, issue there appeared an article, "The Puritan's Will to Power," by Randolph Bourne. There was little new in what Bourne had to say; but the way of saying it was so keen and yet so casual, so profound without being at all pompous, that it had the air of novelty. The name, too, was new to me. It was some time before I met Bourne; he was unusually deformed and, not unnaturally, morbidly shy. A hunchback and lame, he made his twisted body seem more grotesque by shrouding it in a thick black cape. He hobbled awkwardly into the restaurant on Eighth Street where Jimmie and I were to meet him; but as soon as he was seated a transformation took place, a transformation recalling the tales of princes bewitched and betrayed. You forgot the misshapen dwarf with the long wooden face, the mangled ear and the torn mouth, as the fine eyes flashed and the small hands punctuated some particularly devastating criticism. There was not only a noble fire in what Bourne said, there was an exquisite courtesy in his manner. I only saw Bourne twice, and I have no idea what we discussed, but I remember his being, the essence of the man, more vividly than I remember hundreds of older and longer acquaintances. If there has ever been an actual inner flame, Bourne burned with it. He lived by it and died of it.

Later issues of *The Seven Arts* were to contain Bourne's dramatic but dignified "The War and the Intellectual," the sadly prophetic "Below the Battle," the uncannily accurate "The Collapse of American Strategy," and the half despairing, half defiant "Twilight of Idols," which ended, "It is the creative desire more than the creative intelligence that we shall need if we are ever to fly." These essays have more than historic value, they have a prevision and vitality which represent the liberal at his highest. Bourne was critical and clairvoyant; imprisoned in that distorted frame there lived a courageous spirit that was both realistic and visionary. The words he wrote more than twenty years ago might serve as an illuminated credo today: "In the midst of the sternest practicalities the radical finds blossoming those activities and personalities which the unbelieving have told him were impossible in this human world. . . . In his camp he finds all those writers and leaders who sway men's minds today and make their life, all unconscious as they are of the revolutionary character of the message, more rich and dynamic. To live this life of his vision practically, here in the present, is the exceeding great reward of radical youth. And this life, so patent and glowing amongst the crude malignity of modern life, fortifies and stimulates him, and gives him the surety, which is sturdier than any dream or hope, of the coming time when this life will permeate and pervade all society instead of only a part."

Some months after this was written, the war stopped Bourne's eloquence; the magazines which had courted him turned to the glib patriotics of the moment. He was quoted, not as a prophet and a promise, but as a vicious example. A few years later he was prematurely dead, a victim of the frail child's body over which the mature mind had only briefly triumphed.

Later issues of *The Seven Arts* contained "The Song of Ariel" by S. N. Behrman, soon to be known as one of America's wittiest playwrights, then put down in our notes as "a beginner in the field of fiction, attending courses at Columbia University"; "In a Time of National Hesitation" by John Dewey, which began "Were I a poet this should be, even at the dangerous risk of comparisons invited, an ode"; "Tomorrow," a long short story never republished by the author, who later was awarded the Nobel prize and who then called himself Eugene G. O'Neill; Lee Simonson's brilliant "The Painters' Ark," an attack on academies as asylums; D. H. Lawrence's intensely moving and intensely Lawrentian story, "The Mortal Coil"; two of the most characteristic poems of the period, Amy Lowell's polyphonic "Guns as Keys: and the Great Gate Swings" and Vachel Lindsay's "The Broncho That Would Not Be Broken of Dancing"; H. L. Mencken's defensive analysis "The Dreiser Bugaboo"; "Farmhands," a curious little portrait by Mabel Dodge; segments of Horace Traubel's revealing conversations "With Walt Whitman in Camden."

I V

Either because of its youth or its inclusiveness *The Seven Arts* was mocked and imitated, hailed and condemned. The first issue of *Secession* made its bow "to the adventurous" with this paragraph: "*Secession* exists for those writers who are preoccupied with researches for new forms. It hopes that there is ready for it an American public which has advanced beyond the fiction of Sinclair Lewis and Sherwood Anderson and the criticism of Paul Rosenfeld and Louis Untermeyer." A heterogeneous school of little magazines swam in the wake; the early twenties spawned such curious fish as *Gargoyle, Tambour, The Quill, Pagan, The Little Review, Contact,*

*Exile, Close Up, The Glebe, The Double Dealer, This
Quarter, Broom, Secession,* and *transition.* Some of these
were hatched in Greenwich Village; some swam as far
abroad as the favorable exchange would permit them to go;
some turned proudly expatriate. Many of them exhaled a
passionate loathing for everything American, from the midwestern prairies to the eastern skyscrapers; a few were actually put together on the marble-topped tables of the Café
du Dôme. They were variously cynical, impudent, precious,
outspoken, outrageous, unconsciously eccentric and purposely irrational; united in nothing but their gusto and
belligerence. They quarreled not only with the general opposition but among themselves; their manifestoes were loud
with rival claims, vigorous and self-contradictory credos,
virulent "discoveries."

Secession in many ways was the most consistently inconsistent of the lot. Its element was surprise. It discussed the
dualism of Paul Elmer More and anticipated the surrealists
by cutting up, rearranging, and distorting its material. One
of its editors, Gorham Munson, was a dialectician; another
editor, Matthew Josephson, was a dadaist. A little later
Munson accused Josephson of being a "literary opportunist
and an intellectual faker"; Josephson countered by challenging Munson's intelligence and daring him to fight it out
physically. One of Josephson's more spectacular feats of editing was cutting down a hundred-line poem which Munson
had accepted. Abetted by Malcolm Cowley, an associate
editor, Josephson calmly deleted ninety-seven lines and published the remainder as a three-line aphorism.

A detailed and far too sober account of the movement is
given by Munson in *The Fledgling Years: 1916-1924;* an-

other, and even more serio-comic, phase is presented in Cowley's *Exile's Return*. But the future historian will (alas for him) have to read all the multicolored ephemera of the times if he is to obtain a composite picture of the period— and then he will be tempted to doubt his findings.

I did not meet most of the rebels until they returned to the America they had repudiated. But long before that time, even before the founders of *Secession* had threatened to secede, I had encountered one of them. Or, rather, he had encountered me. It happened, of all places, at the factory I was superintending in New Jersey.

The jewelry-manufacturing plants in New York had been fairly well organized, but Newark was a "backward" region —backward, at least, from the standpoint of the Union delegates. This was because the jewelry workers in Newark considered themselves the aristocracy of the trade; they were paid high wages, the work was steady, even in the slack season they were well taken care of. Our own establishment, a factory of about one hundred and fifty workers, was run on an almost paternalistic basis. Many of the men owned their own homes, others were buying them on Building and Loan shares for which we advanced the money, and all of them enjoyed a reasonable degree of security. The idea of unionizing troubled and displeased them. There was a strike in New York, and, somehow, it spread to Newark. The men came to me perplexed.

"Those delegates!" said Kastner, who had been foreman of the factory when I was still in knee-breeches. "They've got a few of the younger fellows. Koenig's with them and Kress, the die-cutter, said he's going to join. What should we do?"

"Why don't you all join?" I asked him by way of answer. "You'll have to sooner or later."

"Unionize the whole shop!" exclaimed Kastner, scandalized. "Why, Mr. Untermeyer, that's socialism!"

"It may be," I said, sorry that he could not appreciate the irony of the situation. "But I'd rather bargain with one representative than with one hundred and fifty. Besides, I don't see anything wrong with shorter hours. It will be good for the men and it won't hurt the manufacturers if all of them are on the same weekly schedule."

"Good for the men! Shorter hours!" Kastner was aghast. "What will we do with our spare time!"

I was unable to persuade the shop to unionize itself. But a strike was averted and I reduced the working period to forty-four hours a week, the first time this had been done in the industry. There was a great deal of comment, most of it adverse; my New York partners considered I had betrayed them. The telephone buzzed continually.

At the height of the controversy, Miss Autz, my secretary, came into the office at Mulberry Street in a state of excitement. This alarmed me, for I had never believed that anything could disturb Miss Autz's placidity, Miss Autz having been conceived (so I thought) out of a Greek column by a German stone-mason.

"It's a reporter from the *Newark Ledger*." Miss Autz was breathless, as though to apologize for her emotion. "He says he's got to see you."

So far we had escaped publicity, but evidently there was no way of concealing anything from the omniscient press. "Tell him to come in."

He came in; a thin, not unpleasant young fellow, even

though he seemed to be carrying a few more chips than his shoulders would support.

"I suppose you want to talk to me about the strike," I said.

"No," he replied, "I want to talk to you about Ezra Pound."

We talked. It was his first newspaper job, and one of his associates (also just out of college) was helping to run the paper. This friend, H. R. Knickerbocker, suggested that the idea of a poet being a "business magnate" might make a feature story. I think my interviewer did most of the talking. He was not (then) interested in industry, but he let me know he was a champion of advance guard poetry and challenged some remarks I had made about T. S. Eliot and other expatriates. It was an animated hour and, although there was no bloodshed, arrows (probably poisoned) flew and reputations fell as we constituted ourselves generals of the unyielding opposition. I felt that I was contending with Young Anarchy, while he was convinced he was doing battle with Old Fogey Himself. When he left he told me his name was Matthew Josephson.

Today I rather think Josephson was right—right, at least, in his championship of youth and its will to play, no matter how recklessly. Then I respected nothing so much as tradition; now I relish experiment. Instead of asking the young creator to venerate tradition, we should urge him to struggle against it. Tradition, like the poor, is always with us. It does not have to be sought after; it seeks us, holds us by a thousand remote and intricate associations. Unless we free ourselves, it absorbs us into an old and perfectly established anonymity.

This does not mean that experiment is to be worshiped as an end in itself or that experiment should be confused with accomplishment. The revolutionary of one generation is the reactionary of the next. T. S. Eliot is, perhaps, the outstanding exponent of this swiftness of change. Hailed as revelation of the new freedom by the young insurgents of the twenties his philosophy has been repudiated by the rebels of the thirties. I have grown to admire Eliot's combination of flat statement and rich rhetoric, of power and triviality; but when his early poems appeared I attacked them in print. I attacked them (I see now) not from a poetic but from a personal standpoint. I was a confirmed yea-sayer, full of the social fervor of *The Masses* and the liberalism of *The Seven Arts*. I believed in the possibility of man's salvation, if only through art and education. Eliot seemed to me a voice crying all too effectively in a literary cactus-land. A fairly young and outraged disciple of affirmation, I flew at Eliot as at an apostle of everything that was negative and disillusioned. Looking back now, I think the uncritical praise provoked me more than the poetry; the group sometimes known as "the younger ineffectuals" triumphantly hailed the poems as a gospel of defeat.

Curiously enough, Eliot half agreed with me. When I went abroad for the first time, we had lunch in the City near Lloyd's Bank where he was then a clerk. The handsome native of St. Louis, who had been living only a few years in London and who had not yet renounced his American citizenship, already looked as British as the House of Lords. Remembering my critical reservations, I wavered between taking a truculent and an apologetic attitude. In the end

I did neither; Eliot, the younger man, managed to put me gravely but completely at my ease.

"I think you overlooked most of the poetic implications," he said. "But I could not object to your attacking the work on moral grounds."

After reading Eliot's later, definitely religious plays and poems, the sentence seems almost prophetic. Much though I relish the strange diction and powerful imagery of his work, Eliot has always seemed to me a self-divided person and a literary paradox. He became the archetype of all that is advanced in poetry, and yet he is an anachronism in that he is both futurist and fin de siècle, a poet of protest and yet a poet of the library. No one, as far as I know, has compared him to the esthetes of the nineties; yet his course and theirs are not unlike. They mixed Anglican intellect and Parnassian impressionism; he combined academic erudition and French symbolism. They found their own times ugly, and retreated into the comfortably remote and spectacularly exotic; he, equally horrified by his world, pitted a beautiful past against an evil present, and explored an unreal limbo where even the brutal was bizarre. When they—Lionel Johnson, Oscar Wilde, Aubrey Beardsley, Ernest Dowson, among others—could no longer face their own distortions, they turned to the Catholic church, which supplied them with a new impetus; when Eliot found it impossible to dwell in his wasteland, with its nightmares of vulgarity, he sought an Anglo-Catholic haven, which gave him another kind of subsistence as well as fresh subject-matter. Their desperate audacities marked the end of the century; his confused disillusions marked the end of an epoch.

No creative artist has ever better expressed his own para-

dox than Eliot. "The Love Song of J. Alfred Prufrock" and
the satirical poems which immediately succeeded it are biting yet pathetic in their study of feebleness and futility;
"The Waste Land" and its sequential "The Hollow Men"
brought frustration to an impasse; the poet could descend
no further into boredom, emptiness, pervasive drought. The
religious hope in "Ash Wednesday" pointed the way out;
the moving "A Song for Simeon," the churchly pageant
"Murder in the Cathedral" and the even more intense "The
Family Reunion" defined the escape. The early work may
have been technically the more brilliant, but it was self-
limited by its romanticized tone as well as by its technique.
At its best, it remained a mordant light verse, a kind of
verse rare in English but not uncommon in French. The
amalgam of accents, the wit and purposeful banality, "the
boredom and the glory," the juxtaposition of lines vividly
his own and lines lifted from other poets without benefit
of quotation marks, made Eliot not a major poet, as his
admirers claimed, but a new kind of minor poet—a minor
poet in the grand manner.

V

The epoch shifted alignments; it dissolved personal al-
legiances in party factions and changed revolts into revul-
sions. The irresponsible dadaists of the early twenties became the social economists of the late thirties. Cowley assumed with holy zeal the rôle of radical editor on *The New
Republic,* that courageous weekly which made a conspicuous
success of being a moderate failure. Josephson rediscovered
the American scene and drew full-length pitiless portraits

of the exploiters in *The Robber Barons,* who spoke little
and did much, and *The Politicos,* who spoke much and did
as little as possible.

The Seven Arts never reached the twenties. Like *The
Masses* it was a war casualty. We offended the Government;
worse, we offended our sponsor. Mrs. Rankine was an ardent
patriot; she believed that President Wilson was to be hailed
for keeping us out of war and also for plunging us into war
in order to end the war. Equally convinced that kings (not
Kaisers) could do no wrong, she was distressed by the anti-
war articles that crept into the magazine; she was especially
offended by the leading article in the August, 1917, issue,
Jack Reed's "This Unpopular War." The magazine had
tried to remain a literary periodical; it hoped to continue
to tap the hidden wealth of young American talent and express "a richer life, a flowering of mature and seasoned personalities." But the war could not be ignored. We found
that everything the magazine stood for was bound up with
this new action.

An irreconcilable difference arose. Our sponsor refused
to continue her subsidy unless we avoided the issues of the
war; although faced with the loss of financial backing, we
could not surrender editorial freedom. We appealed to some
of our affluent well-wishers. One of them, Amy Lowell, had
been a sympathizer as well as a contributor. But she, too,
was helping win the war with a furious patriotism. She had
warned me that we of *The Seven Arts,* and particularly
Randolph Bourne, might be included among the "enemies
within" unless we mended our ways. Now she volunteered to
help support the magazine—on condition that we pledge
ourselves to abandon criticism of the administration and to

omit discussion of the war. "If you believe, as I do," she wrote Oppenheim, "in the saving grace of the arts, and poetry in particular, you will not allow any desire to express your personal opinions upon subjects outside of this scope to interfere with your mission of keeping alive the spirit of poetry and of beauty in this sorely tried country." Jimmie replied that such a pledge would be tyranny, and that he could not dictate to his contributors. "If," he answered, "Bourne writes about the breakdown of pragmatism and the need of the poetic vision instead, it is necessary for him to show the moment of breakdown; namely, the application of pragmatism to the war technique." It was an impasse; we could advance no further.

The October, 1917, number contained a plea which was also a protest against "the overmastering national obsession of the war." There were many responses but insufficient practical results. The October number had come head on against the popular policy; it was, in both senses, the last issue.

(Can a world change back and forth so completely in twenty-odd years? I know that A. E. Housman, that blithe singer of black disillusion, has written:

> *The troubles of our proud and angry dust*
> *Are to eternity, and shall not fail.*

But "our proud and angry dust" once had time to be troubled by happy trivialities, absurd gaiety, lively philosophies that covered everything and proved nothing; there was time, even in the struggle for our deepest convictions, for teapot tempests about technique. Is it the age or merely my age that makes me think that the very language of communication has altered? Digging through letters from James Oppenheim I find two other communications in the file under O. One is from John Myers O'Hara, whose adaptations of Sappho and whose "Pagan Sonnets" I seem to have praised sometime in 1913. O'Hara ends a letter of thanks in the grand manner: "Some day, in the near future, we must meet, and pledge the Muse—perchance, in a Bohemian environment, with myself as host—Mouquin's, for instance—for I love music and table-cheer when I make an excursion into the rare Parnassian realm." The Muse . . . Bohemia . . . Parnassus . . . Did anyone say these things seriously? . . . And here, also under O, is a letter of 1916 which asks my opinion of a group of four poems whose first lines run "I saw him naked on a hill above a world of gold." "Fair body, flower not in vain," "Sleep, little poppy, and rest from thy play," and "As I came over the April hills." Can my correspondent have been pulling my leg? Can the author have been, if his signature is to be trusted, the perennial editor of the Annual Best Short Stories, Edward J. O'Brien? . . . Was it in this world?)

I return to Oppenheim and *The Seven Arts,* which was his pinnacle. After the downfall of the magazine he did not cease writing, but his fortunes fell with his journal. There are earnest probing and some clairvoyance in *The Book of Self* and the more outspokenly autobiographical *The Mystic Warrior;* but there are also effort and a painful self-consciousness. His career dwindled. He tried to train himself to hackwork; he prepared two oversimplified handbooks on psychoanalysis. But he was not born to be a popularizer, and the made-to-order books soon passed out of circulation. There were marital misadventures; he became ill. His two young sons did what they could; one of them helped support him by writing for pulp magazines. Small personal differences alienated us for a while. We met occasionally; but the warm intimacy, the quick understanding, the easy give-and-take, had gone. He always accepted criticism with good humor if not with nonchalance; now he became abnormally sensitive to the slightest reservation. A hurt letter late in 1930 begins, "Dear Louis: An attention-caller has just brought to my notice the latest edition of your *Modern American Poetry,* I suppose to annoy me with your downward revision concerning my work. Quite aside from the merits of my poetry, I know you quite too well to believe that you are correct." It ends, "Do you remember a man named Stedman who was the L. U. of his day? If you will get out one of his anthologies, you will see how wrong *he* was about some of our best native talent. Well, Louis . . ."

The letter saddened me, the more so since I had praised Jimmie's poetry more consistently and more continuously than any American critic. My sadness was increased by a report that he had willfully chosen obscurity but was unhappy in it. The mystic warrior was no longer giving battle, not even to himself. I wrote suggesting a visit, but nothing came of it; I was living in the mountains three hundred miles from the city and he had buried himself in Greenwich Village. I was writing to him again one August day in 1932 when the afternoon paper arrived. It told me that, after a severe illness, he had died. There was nothing more to say then. There is nothing now.

STORM CENTER
IN BROOKLINE

THAT was a strange evening the first time I visited Amy Lowell. It was strange that I should have been there at all. A year or two before this I had reviewed her first book, and reviewed it most unfavorably. It had come to my desk with several other pleasantly competent volumes, from which it differed in no distinguishable way. It seemed the conventional "slender sheaf" full of apostrophes to dead romantic poets, second-rate imitations of Robert Louis Stevenson, and a lengthy tribute to the Boston Athenaeum whose spirit dominated the book; everything about it was familiar except the author's name. Not being a Bostonian, and unaware of any august relationship, I had pictured the author as a young female Laocoön struggling, not too strenuously, in the coils of poetic stereotype. I had resolved to read her a lesson. My review must have been insufferably patronizing —she told me later it was one of the few reviews that had ever made her weep—and I remember that I concluded the offensive paragraph by saying that the only good line in the book was the title, *A Dome of Many-Colored Glass,* and that was taken from Shelley. Less than two years after I had disposed of the sentimental disciple of Tennyson and Keats, I had to change my tune. Another Amy Lowell had confronted me with *Sword Blades and Poppy Seed*. It was an experimental and far more belligerent poet who exhibited a new individuality and range, who expressed herself with equal determination in precise cameos of verse and rough-hewn masses of polyphonic prose. I was astonished at the transmogrification, and I said so in print.

And now I was waiting for her to descend the great staircase of the famous house, which, according to rumor, was occupied only by herself, a companion, and a retinue of servants—a house fronted by its own park and backed by a fabulous garden, a house where the mirrors were always draped in black, whose every door-knob was of sterling, and in which the owner lived in a kind of shrouded battlement on the top floor of her castle. I had even heard that, like the legendary princess, she slept on a bed made of eighteen pillows because ordinary sheets were too coarse for her. Like Caesar, she was reputed to keep two secretaries continually at work. She ignored the clock, and her world waited until she woke and the sleeping palace accommodatingly came to life.

I waited. I had been summoned to appear at seven in the evening. I learned later that all new guests, obviously on probation, were put through an ordeal not of fire but of patience. I did not know it then—so I waited. Sometime between thirty minutes and an hour after my arrival Miss Lowell appeared. It was easy for her. Her routine was the opposite of everyone's. A wealthy woman, she could indulge herself not only in her fancies but in her hours. She slept all day and worked all night, claiming that in this way she was free from the telephone, the importunities of friends and tradesmen, and all the countless interruptions of the day. She awoke about three in the afternoon, planned the details for the following day with her housekeeper over a four o'clock breakfast, and came down to dinner, her first real meal of the day, at eight. After dinner there were friends, concerts or other diversions. This lasted until midnight. Then she began to work, to write new poems and revise old ones. At five in the morning she sustained herself with a light lunch, arranged the manuscripts for the secretaries, and so to bed. Nothing could interrupt, no one could intrude upon her. It was a system much to be recommended —for those who could afford it.

Miss Lowell came down the stairs. She waved no plumes and rattled no sabers, but she seemed to be advancing at the head of a victorious army. There was gunfire in the air; I thought I heard bugles. She endeavored to put me, a stranger, at my ease. She offered me a cigarette, pulling out a drawer which seemed to contain the contents of the United Cigar Stores, Incorporated.

"No, thank you," I said, "I do not smoke."

"I hope you don't mind that I do," said she, taking up a rich-looking cigar. "My doctor tells me the paper in cigarettes is injurious. Besides, I prefer tobacco wrapped in its own leaf."

The shock was only for a moment. I had heard of Hungarian duchesses who smoked cigars imperturbably and, years later, I was to know a Viennese grand dame who cherished a meerschaum pipe. But I was unprepared to watch a Lowell, the sister of Harvard University, knocking the ash from a colorado claro. (She had a supply of ten thousand.) The apparition seemed the more grotesque because of Miss Lowell's size. I do not know what she weighed at the time, but, although she was forty, it must have been well over two hundred pounds. To make the effect still more incongruous, she preferred high-collared dresses sprinkled with beads and lavishly trimmed with passementerie. Some glandular defect made the heavy body seem more swollen and the short frame more stunted than it really was. ("Lord," she would say, "I'm a walking side-show.") Yet the rakish cigar and the abnormal stoutness were forgotten five minutes after she had seated herself. One noticed only the marvelous neatness, the fine hands and delicate ankles, the small mobile mouth, the coolly modulated voice, the quick-appraising but not unkind eyes, the fine features and almost transparent skin. One saw a woman who was not only intelligent but—there is no other word for it—pretty. The most implacable adversary, more masculine than most males, she could also be the most charming feminine persuader. I capitulated. I think I apologized for not smoking. Then we went in to dinner.

It was a good, even a grand, dinner. But I was not comfortable. There were six or eight celebrities at the table; but it was not the guests or the service that undid me. It was the dogs. They were English sheepdogs, immense longhaired creatures, and there seemed to be a ferocious flock of them. They sat around the dining-room in a semicircle, their mouths dribbling with hungry anticipation. As the meal progressed their eyes grew larger and larger, like the magic dogs in Hans Christian Andersen's tale, and I felt more and more like a frightened bone.

Dinner over, the guests, led by Ada Dwyer Russell, who served as Amy Lowell's companion, confessor, wailing wall and buffer state, trailed into the imposing library. I had barely begun to examine the famous collection of volumes with Keats's own annotations when I was motioned to a chair. The other guests were seated; they knew the ritual which was to ensue. We were grouped about a fireplace large enough to roast an ox or a critic. One maid entered with the coffee. Another followed with a huge pile of bath towels.

"Thank you very much," I said, trying to cover my bewilderment with a poor facetiousness, "but I had my bath this morning, and I rarely spill the coffee."

"Don't be absurd," Miss Lowell replied. "It's for the dogs."

"Surely, you're not going to bathe them here?"

"Nonsense." She made a moue. "The darlings don't need a bath, either. But they are so companionable, and their hair is so long, and they *do* dribble after food, and they like to put their heads in your lap."

So there we sat with towels across our knees, while the seven dogs—there seemed to be seventeen—alternately guzzled their food and nuzzled us, and the conversation grew increasingly animated.

But my contretemps with Amy Lowell's pet monsters was nothing compared to the misadventure suffered by another poet. Maxwell Bodenheim was expected to arrive at about seven one evening. Amy sent her huge Pierce Arrow (with tires deflated for luxurious driving) for the more important guests; the others arrived by the blue Chestnut Hill street car. Bodenheim was not one of the favored; he was intransigent and his clothes were shabby. He got off at Heath Street and walked up the curving driveway to the entrance of Sevenels. There was a sign: "Motors be careful not to run over the dogs." Ordinarily the dogs were put in their kennels before strange visitors arrived; but Bodenheim, fearful of being late, arrived much too early. The seven oversize dogs spied him. They wanted to play. Barking, they sprang about—and on—him. Bodenheim misunderstood their motives. He dodged behind a tree.

"Aha!" thought the dogs. "Here is a new diversion. Here is a bone that runs." Immediately a thousand pounds of dog leaped to the chase. Bodenheim zigzagged desperately, trying to throw them off the scent. But they surrounded him, barking all the more furiously. He reached the house, spent and bespattered, guided but not helped by the stone statue of Flora which stood, apathetically, above the doorway. He had just strength enough to ring the bell. A maid, incongruously small, appeared.

"Shoo!" she cried. Bodenheim did not know whether to be grateful or offended. Then he realized she was talking to the dogs.

"Shoo!" she said a second time, stamping her little foot. The monstrous seven, the worst watch-dogs in the world, dropped their tails and fell over each other in an awkward rush to escape.

A similar mishap occurred to Randolph Bourne. Bourne, as I have said in the preceding chapter, was a hunchback, physically weak and easily frightened. He was sure that the dogs had viciously attacked him, and he was so terrified that he could not rise to his hostess's sallies during dinner. Amy, in turn, despised the "weakling." Her repulsion extended even to his writing; in a talk with James Oppenheim and me she insisted that his deformity showed itself in his "tortured style and twisted mentality." Oppenheim told me she returned to the false charge at another session with him.

"Everything he writes," she repeated, "shows he is a cripple."

Intending nothing more than a sententious generality Oppenheim said, "Aren't we all cripples?"

Amy's aggressiveness fell away from her. "Yes," she said, surveying her enormous girth. "Look at me. I'm nothing but a disease."

II

At the time I knew little about Amy Lowell's militancy. It was not until later that I heard (and saw) how she invaded editorial offices, bore down upon the heads of magazines and publishing offices, treated editors as if they were office boys, and brought every kind of armament into play—wealth, charm, political astuteness, family background, good-fellowship, and dictatorial commands—to forward her powerful offensive. Every new book was a new campaign, and never has there been a more determined general. "I am as bad as Napoleon," she wrote unashamedly to the editor of *The New York Tribune*. "I believe in my star."

I remember one of her sorties into what she considered enemy territory. She descended upon New York, accompanied by the faithful Mrs. Russell, and put up at the Hotel St. Regis, from which she sent out her summonses. I shall never forget that "receiving room." As in her own home, the mirrors were concealed behind black cloths. One table held a dozen pitchers of ice-water; another table was precariously balanced with scores of the latest books; a third table was a litter of clippings, letters, telegrams, memoranda. During dinner, which was served in her rooms, Amy discharged a battery of dicta; gave orders over the telephone to obviously cowed listeners; alternately blandished and bullied the waiters—"Here! put all my vegetables on one plate.

I don't want them sitting around in little bird-baths"—
and kept her guests in a state of amusement and apprehension. Joyce Kilmer told me she had "made" him interview
her on the subject of the new poetry. What is more (such
was her power) she got him to send her his manuscript and
permitted him to print it in *The New York Times* only after
she had approved it.

Later she attempted to bring a weightier influence to bear
upon the newspapers. "You advertise so much in the *Times*,"
she wrote to her publishers, "that you ought to force them
into a somewhat less hostile attitude." She believed in controversy, not only for its own sake but for its advertising
value. I mocked her once by saying, "Sweet are the uses of
publicity," and she did not resent it. She wrote to Ezra
Pound, "I consider you an uncommonly fine poet. You ought
to have an impresario—your knowledge of how to 'get yourself over,' as we say in this little country, is *nil*."

It was Ezra Pound who told me how Amy had "captured"
the Imagist movement. Pound, born in Hailey, Idaho, had
progressively exiled himself in England, France, and Italy,
from which vantage points he had discharged a series of
public broadsides and private diatribes against his native
country. Some of us (I, among others) had replied. We had
even made counter-charges, claiming that Pound, in spite of
his immense erudition, suffered from a lassitude of the creative faculties and a decadence which appraised all the values
in terms of esthetic values. There had been a short and bitter
correspondence between us, savagely conducted by Pound
in his characteristically abbreviated Saxon style. Yet when I,
one of his numerous "enemies," came to Rapallo there was
a note at my hotel. "The fact that your taste in poetry is

execrable shouldn't prevent us from having a vermouth to-gether."

During the week that I explored the Ligurian coast, Pound told me his side of Amy's historic invasion and victory. In London in 1912 Pound and one or two others, chiefly T. E. Hulme, revolted against the current "morbid romantic atti-tude and outworn false generalities." Seeking, most of all, a cure for the stock allusions and general vagueness, they hit upon the *image* as a clear and definite objective. To express this definiteness Pound and his coadjutors, organizing them-selves into a group, drew up a manifesto which declared for "the hard, definite word. Each word," they continued, "must be an image seen, not a counter or cliché. Images in verse are not mere decorations, but the very essence of an intuitive language." Endeavoring to use no word that did not con-tribute to the presentation of the image, the group was led by Pound to challenge the critics with *Imagisme*. Pound says he invented the term "to avoid vain gabble as to the nature of poetry." He wrote me during the brief period fol-lowing my Italian sojourn when we seemed to be friends, "I have no objection to the pleasure others have had in ex-ploiting the label and offering cheap imitations, but I regret the loss of critical distinction between poetry which uses no word which does not contribute to the presentation—and verbosity (more or less rhythmic)." Pound attracted and re-pelled disciples; one of them, Hilda Doolittle, born in Beth-lehem, Pennsylvania, began signing her Tanagra-like poems "H. D., Imagiste." While the movement was gaining mo-mentum, Amy Lowell arrived in London with a letter of in-troduction to Pound. The two, born doctrinaires and dicta-tors, met head on. A few months later Amy returned to

America at the head of an Imagist movement of her own. Her group consisted of three Englishmen: D. H. Lawrence, Richard Aldington, and F. S. Flint; and three Americans: H. D., John Gould Fletcher, and herself. Pound's anthology, *Des Imagistes,* was published in 1914; Amy's collections, *Some Imagist Poets,* appeared in 1915, 1916, and 1917. Pound repudiated any connection with the American wing which he always referred to as "the Amygist movement."

Pound made light of the defection when he told me about it as we sat in the *Giardino Pubblico* looking toward Sestri. But there must have been a day when he threatened suit, for, in November, 1914, Amy wrote to him, "So far as I know you have not copyrighted the name 'Imagiste.' I never heard of a school of poetry being copyrighted; I doubt if it could be done. But if you should feel inclined to sue, I should be exceedingly delighted, as then they would put new jackets on the book, which I should greatly prefer. Also, it would be a good advertisement." Imperturbable and magnificent Amy! Anything for "a good advertisement." Lowell or no, she would have made an independent fortune as a promoter of bond issues or the head of a public relations firm.

Never has there been a leadership like Amy's. She used every form of persuasion, every kind of weapon. She fought alone and with badgered recruits; she stormed every battlement of convention. As a determined Imagist she not only laid siege to Poetry, she invaded it. Since much of the work was written in unrhymed lines with "cadence" instead of a regular rhythm, Imagism became (falsely) synonymous with free verse, that contradiction in terms. The emancipated champions of *vers libre* were maliciously ticketed as "vers-libertines." Free verse, more challengingly than free love, became a fighting phrase, and Amy exulted in the conflict. "By Jove!" she ended one of her letters to me in the midst of the controversy. "We are pushing the Philistines to the wall!"

Pound could never have done it; Pound, she wrote in one of the first letters I received from her, "would have ruined the movement, important though it was, as he has ruined everything he has touched. You are quite right in implying that bitterness has upset his brain. The only thing I object to in your article is your saying that it was under his leadership 'that the Imagists became not only a group, but a fighting protest.' It was not. The Imagists during the year and a half in which he headed the movement were unknown and jeered at, when they were not absolutely ignored. It was not until *I* entered the arena, and Ezra dropped out, that Imagism began to be considered seriously. I feel sure that if I had not done all I did and worked hard to prove the value of the movement, the thing would never have achieved the recognition it now has. . . . The name is his; the idea was wide-spread; but changing the whole public attitude from derision to consideration came from my work." This was Amy *in excelsis*.

At this time her letters were variations on the theme. She evidently kept carbon copies of every letter she wrote, for I read excerpts in Foster Damon's comprehensive biography, quoting from letters whose originals I must have destroyed. Yet in 1916 alone I find more than twenty epistles, all on the chaste and businesslike letterhead: "Miss A. Lowell, Heath Street, Brookline, Mass." Her very first communication was a reproach for not being sufficiently enthusiastic about the new gospel. After thanking me for a *causerie* in which I praised her, she wrote, "I think perhaps you are a little hard on the Imagists. Don't you think you are reading into them characteristics which perhaps they have not got? One of the things which they represent to my mind, is the ascendancy of the purely imaginative impulse. It is this quality of imagination which has seemed so hard to get America to fitly understand. It frightens them, worries them, repels them."

It was the form, rather than the imagination itself, which worried the critics. Amy herself continually violated the Imagist manifesto and extended her work far beyond its tenets; but she, too, confused the form with the substance. It was not until much later that she was able to separate the true "inwardness" of the poem from the outer technique. She was (at least in the flush of her Imagist triumph) so convinced that *vers libre* was the only possible contemporary form that she extended her prejudice into the past. She intimated that even translations of the classics should be "cadenced"; in the midst of a highly complimentary review of my Heine versions she wrote, "Why, O why, has Mr. Untermeyer chosen to follow Heine in his tight little rhythms and mathematically cut stanzas?" At about this time Keith Preston, then writing a lively column in Chicago, sent me a paraphrase of his much-quoted quatrain:

> *A toast to Amy Lowell,*
> *That most incredible She,*
> *And all the little magazines*
> *That died to make verse free.*

Amy would have relished it. She enjoyed the quick thrust and parry; she did not disdain puns. (Referring to my Michigan lectures at Ann Arbor she hoped I had been pleasantly entertained by the "Ann Arborigines.") It was only in (and about) her work that she lacked a sense of humor. I remember once, when we were discussing the Imagist credo, she insisted that words could render not only the exact nuances of music but record the most minute differences of color. "But," she added, "it takes an unusually trained vision to apprehend and register the shades of difference. For example, you must have noticed how the color of a country road is changed when seen through the spokes of a fast-moving car. What color would you say it was?"

"Well," I hazarded, trying to play the game, "earth-color. Or dull brown. Or dusty tan. Or . . ."

"Cinnamon!" she shouted triumphantly. "Use your eyes!"

Although she herself was not precious as a person, she pushed theory into preciosity. She claimed so much for her pet project that she rated Emily Dickinson as a precursor of the Imagists. ("It is an odd story," she wrote, "this history of Imagism, and perhaps the oddest and saddest moment in it is comprised in the struggle of this one brave, fearful, and unflinching woman.") She went further; she insisted that Emily Dickinson would have been a better poet had she written in *vers libre;* "a knowledge of the principles of unitary verse (that is, verse based upon a unit of time instead of a unit of accent) would have liberated Emily Dickinson from the bonds against which she chafed." She pushed her theory so far in this instance that she completely misread and misunderstood the poet to whom she was paying tribute. "She (Emily Dickinson) made use of what I have called elsewhere the 'unrelated' method; that is, the describing of a thing *by its appearance only.*" Misapprehension can go no further than the italicized phrase (the italics are mine), for no poet dealt less with "appearance only" than Emily Dickinson. Her descriptions, startlingly vivid and exact though they were, were backgrounds for the play of the restless mind; the outer and inner world surpassed appearance to form "the landscape of the soul."

III

The effect of the new poetry was explosive, and Amy laid much of the dynamite. Although her illness was aggravated by an umbilical hernia that necessitated four operations within three years, she stormed about the country, horrified the pedants, made enemies in order to fight them, and shocked her audiences into feverish debate. She was continually traveling "for the cause," although train trips were a torture to her, for her blood pressure compelled her to sit at open windows no matter how much other passengers complained. Once she broke a glass pane in a sleeping-car to get air. The hotels rarely had the accommodations she required; she was never satisfied with a suite of less than four rooms— a whole floor in the smaller hotels—clocks had to be stopped, mirrors covered, meals served in the middle of the night. The lecture halls were never right; the lecterns had the wrong slant, and the lights were such that she always carried her own reading lamp with her. This led to a curious mishap at the University of Michigan. When her lamp was plugged in, it blew a fuse and the hall was in a dark confusion while chairmen and the heads of various departments fumbled for the janitor who was groping for them. Wherever she went she astounded the naïve and sophisticates alike; a storm center in Brookline and a cyclone on the warpath. She was not merely a lecturer, she was an event, a national phenomenon, a freak of nature, a dynamo on the loose.

In personal relationships she was the kindest of friends and the warmest of defenders. She fought until the experiments of John Gould Fletcher were acknowledged and H. D. was established. Yet her most admiring friends could not help but resent her assumption of power, even when it was exercised in their behalf. Upon my first return from Europe, H. D. wrote me from Switzerland, "Do let me know how Amy is now. I expect you to give her tactful messages from me, for I do wish the best in the world for her. My only objection is: she will NOT leave other people alone." Fletcher had less cause to complain; he realized she was "chiefly responsible for the furor caused in academic circles by the new poetry." But he, too, was indignant at her high-handedness, yet had not the temerity to gainsay her. In his autobiography, *Life Is My Song*, Fletcher complains, "She spoke enthusiastically of capturing Louis Untermeyer. . . . The thought of Untermeyer as a potential ally made me doubtful. I knew nothing of him except that, as a poet, he had been a staunch champion of the Whitmanian, cosmic, 'social brotherhood' type of verse. He had defended the poets of this type long ago in the columns of Harold Monro's magazine in England. He was also a writer of clever parodies of other poets. I felt that, on all three counts, he was a person to mistrust."

Later Fletcher relates how he resisted "to the end" Amy's

attempt to include my first wife's poetry in a forthcoming volume of *Imagist Poets*. Moreover, he was offended at Amy's request that he should be especially nice to me. "I resented this suggestion that my behavior was something that could be turned on and off for the benefit of any new friends of hers, and I determined to be on my guard." Fletcher "on his guard" was something memorable; at least *he* remembered it. He tells how he got into the car which Amy had sent for him and which was already occupied by the Untermeyers, how he condescended to nothing more than "a gruff handshake," and then sat silent, "deciding that it was up to the Untermeyers to do the talking."

It seems I did talk. It seems, moreover, I flattered Fletcher and was otherwise not at my best. It appears that I asked him why he wrote in Japanese hokkus, and Fletcher replied that only the other day he had written a hokku about hockey. According to him, "a gasp of astonishment, followed by a gleam of appreciation, came to Untermeyer's face. That I could combine 'hockey' and 'hokku' in the same sentence made me a person of some importance in his eyes. During the dinner that followed he did not attempt to attack either me or my poetry."

Apart from my lack of desire to "attack" Fletcher or his poetry, and apart from the pun (which sounds less like Fletcher and more like me at my worst), I do not recognize the "gasp of astonishment." An unregenerate paronomasian myself, I have relished all degrees of verbal play from the devastating double meanings of Heine to the mad ambiguities of the Marx Brothers. But I doubt that such a pun as "hokku" and "hockey" ever knocked the breath out of my body.

Nor, I confess, do I recognize the physical picture of me which Fletcher has drawn with so fine a flourish: "A glance at the male member of the family revealed a young man resplendently handsome in a swallow-tailed coat, white waistcoat, finely starched shirt-front decked with a row of diamond studs, white gloves, and tie." I admit there is a dim familiarity about the portrait, even though it seems to resemble a cross between a tailor's dummy and a neon light. I once did own a swallow-tailed coat and, presumably, there were white gloves, tie, and "finely starched shirt-front" to match. But, in spite of the profitable jewelry business, that "row" of diamond studs was a single mother-of-pearl affair harboring a none too perfect one-sixteenth of a carat stone. I may even have been a young man at the time—but "resplendently handsome"! No, no; this is none of I.

It is Fletcher's animadversions against the parodies that cause me to believe he really means me, and here he has uttered (unconsciously, perhaps) something of a libel. I have always believed that parody is not a kind of cheap burlesque, an exhibition of buffoonery, but one of the lesser arts, a light-handed exposure, a combination of compliment and criticism. I was fond of quoting Chesterton's "Parody is the critic's half-holiday" and Disraeli's "Far from degrading truth by ridicule, parody will only strike at what is chimerical and false"—possibly because, for many years, I practiced this sort of literary surgery and was somewhat vain about it. Amy played upon my vanity in this regard. When my first collection of parodies appeared she quoted from them in public and praised them in private. She wrote in an unguarded moment:

Those parodies are far more than parodies—the more I read them the greater is my wonder that anyone could have got into the skin of the men who were writing so as to reproduce them and yet retain his own personality enough to criticize them all the way. I think that they will live as long as the poets themselves are read, and will take rank with the great parodies of literature.

I don't know which are the best—Robinson and Yeats, Frost and Lindsay, Masters and Hodgson, and, perhaps best of all, Ezra Pound. . . . And I blush to say that there are parts of your parody on me I wish I had written. I shall never get over your "drunken Pierrot spilling the stars from his too-long sleeves." It is *exactly* like me. Why didn't I write it!

I V

It was Amy's own delight in parody and masquerade that made her publish *A Critical Fable* anonymously. But she did more than that. To insure secrecy she misled almost everyone concerned in the publication. Even if a literary detective had had access to her publisher's files, he would have found that the author was William Williams John—who happened to be the husband of one of her secretaries. The work itself was a heterogeneous picture-gallery of the leading living American poets, somewhat in the manner of her distant dead relative, James Russell Lowell. To increase the confusion Amy subtly and mendaciously spread reports that various poets were responsible. She wrote blandly to John Farrar, then editor of *The Bookman,* "Have you seen *A Critical Fable?* I must say I find it immensely amusing in spite of not particularly enjoying the part about myself. . . . I wonder who wrote it? Louis Untermeyer guessed me, and

I guessed him; and then we agreed to cry quits on the
strength of each other's denial and find a third person. Sara
Teasdale says it is Gamaliel Bradford; Gamaliel Bradford
says it is Leonard Bacon; who Leonard Bacon says I do not
know. . . ."

From the beginning I was certain that Amy was the author, partly because the critical estimates generally agreed
with those she had so often expressed, partly because of the
hit-and-miss rhythms and the wretched rhymes. I was not at
all complimented when Amy insisted that she recognized my
touch throughout. Purist that I was in the matter of rhyme,
my teeth were continually set on edge by such awkward
pairings as "grand-aren't," "absurdities-acerbities," "Piano-
and so," "clearly-really," "Olympus-impasse," "goddess-prog-
ress," "parley-finale." Yet I could not help but be flattered
by the pleasant pages she devoted to me in the volume, and
her letter of disclaimer was as disarming as it was disingenuous. She wrote in part:

My dear Louis, You are mad if you think I wrote it; I wish
to God I had. And permit me to offer my congratulations on your
excellent *bluff!* From the first moment I opened the book, I said
to myself: Louis is the *only* person who would have been likely
to write this book—and now you hastily forestall me by suggesting that I have done it, which is one of the neatest little side-
steppings I have ever seen. Oh, Louis, Louis! So you were not
going to do that sort of thing again, weren't you. *Heavens* was
to be your last skit! And all the time you had this up your sleeve.
All I can say is I envy you in the way you have got us all off and
the neatness of your versification. [*Sic! L. U.*] Oh, but don't I recognize that neatness: I chuckled again when I read your "Roast
Leviathan." How anybody, after reading that poem, can think

it was not written by the same man who wrote *A Critical Fable*
I do not see. I think it is a bully book, and you have hit the
people off wonderfully. If nothing else gave it away, your remarks about my "thunderous" quality would have done it.

By the time I had finished the letter and had received
other congratulations (prompted by Amy) I was almost ready
to believe that I *had* written the book. I was beginning to
see new virtues in it; in another month I would have convinced myself that the rhymes were as daring as Emily Dickinson's. However, it never came to that. Amy could never
keep a secret from her public; she enjoyed herself—and her
public—too much.

I will never forget the pleasure she took in one of the
most curious public functions I have ever attended. It was a
Civic Forum dinner given at the Hotel Astor for a group
of poets. Ten of us were guests of honor—three English and
seven American poets—and its chief reason was a hail-and-
farewell to John Masefield, who had been in America as "an
ambassador of good will." I was seated at the speaker's table
between Amy and a tall southerner whose name I had not
caught.

"But we have met," he said. "Not in the flesh, but in the
newspaper columns—in one of your reviews."

"That's gratifying," I smiled. "I hope I said something
more than ordinarily pleasant."

"On the contrary," he replied without a smile. "You were
extraordinarily *un*pleasant. You began your attack with the
title of your review and ended it with a gratuitous insult.
You quoted my worst lines, including the typographical errors, and you turned my most serious phrases into shoddy
flippancies. You ridiculed my tragedies; you—"

"There is only one living poet I ever treated like that," I interrupted, still trying to hold a smile. "And that was—years ago—Cale Young Rice."

"I," he echoed grimly, "am Cale Young Rice."

Since, at that time, the Hotel Astor did not offer alcoholic comfort, I spent the rest of the dinner talking to Amy Lowell. At the end of it she said, "Louis, I've never heard you talk so much and so badly. I haven't the faintest idea what you've been saying—and I don't think you have either."

It was not only my discomfiture she enjoyed, but her eminence. Each of the guests of honor read, spoke, or mumbled. Next to Masefield, Amy received the most applause. But she raised her hand and asked them to stop. "Just to make me feel at home," she said, "please add a few hisses. I'm not used to speaking without them." Later, when she attacked some of the enshrined poets of the past, the hissing was renewed—and this time the audience meant it.

(A newspaper cut is before me as I write. There we are: "American Poets Gathered at Farewell Dinner." Amy is in the center, seated on a Louis Quinze couch much too frail for her. She is clad in a magnificently unbecoming dress with half-length sleeves and a yoke calculated to increase her width, strewn with a maze of gold beadwork. She is clutching a purse and a program, her head cocked, daring the world to come to blows. Seated next to her is the only other woman; birdlike, bright-eyed Josephine Dodge Daskam Bacon, with the smile of a canary that has just swallowed the cat. The rest of us are grouped about Amy. Reading from the traditional left to right, they are Laurence Housman, brother of A. E. Housman, bearded, dark-browed, staring into eternity like a bashful, even a benevolent,

Mephistopheles; Witter Bynner, tall, immaculate, and aloof; Percy MacKaye, his arm about Bynner's shoulder, smiling archly at the camera; Edwin Markham, looking like a slightly blurred composite photograph of four Hebrew prophets and all the New England poets; Cale Young Rice, trying to forget he was the husband of *Mrs. Wiggs of the Cabbage Patch*; I, a cross between a frightened rabbit and a complacent ant-eater; Vachel Lindsay, his head tilted back dangerously as though he were about to explode in a chant; Alfred Noyes, doggedly facing his inquisitors and desperately clutching one of his own books; and John Masefield, quizzical and vague, like a benign but slightly befuddled leprechaun.)

V

In 1920 some six of us American poets decided to start a biennial *Miscellany of American Poetry*. The plan was frankly imitative; it undertook to do for American readers what the collections of *Georgian Poetry* had done for the English public. The dissimilarities of temperament, range, and choice of subject were manifest. But the outstanding difference was this: *Georgian Poetry* had an editor, and the poems it contained reflected that editor's highly personal taste. *The Miscellany* was to be collected and controlled by a *group* of editors so that no particular school or tendency would be stressed. The program was inspiring; the performance fell far short of our aim. The poets included (Frost, Sandburg, Lindsay, Oppenheim, Aiken, Eliot, Jeffers, Teasdale, and others) contributed hitherto unpublished poems and appeared together by mutual accord: "it is as if a dozen unacademic painters, separated by temperament and distance, were to arrange to have an exhibition every two years of their latest work." Amy, having accomplished something similar with the Imagist group, volunteered to collaborate in the venture, and, though the actual editing fell on my shoulders, she almost succeeded in managing us. When the question of new contributors came up Amy was both dogmatic and evasive. She yielded grudgingly to my desire to include Edna St. Vincent Millay "since your heart is set on her. Personally, I am not at all sure that she will count in the long run. . . . I think Millay's real claim to inclusion in the *Miscellany* rests not so much upon her lyrics as upon her remarkable 'Aria da Capo.'" Amy was even more doubtful about Elinor Wylie. Even after I had won over the others to recognize the newcomer, Amy wrote me a long letter which was almost a dissent. I quote the most revealing passages:

I think the collections should contain *only* the work of established poets, and that they are not the proper place for airing the work of new writers. I quite agree that Eleanor [*sic!*] Wylie's work is remarkable. I admire it, but it is a fact that it is not as good as her prototype, Emily Dickinson's. It lacks the sheer originality and spring of Emily Dickinson's work, and it is not the first of its kind; though, for neatness, deftness, and charm, it is far in advance of the rhymed lyrics of other people, even your beloved Edna St. Vincent Millay. . . . I do not feel at all certain as to Eleanor Wylie's future. She is thirty-six years old, I understand, if not more, and this is her first book. Now I am the last person to quarrel with an author beginning late in life. I myself was thirty-eight when my first book came out and my first book was not in the same class as hers—as *you* know only too well. But the thing that makes a reputation in the end, the thing that really makes a poet, is not the first book, but the last book, and all the books between. It is the power of a poet to go on and develop and constantly pass himself. A minor poet may throw off an excellent poem or two, an excellent thirty poems, as Eleanor Wylie has done. A major poet may have a lot of bad verse to his name, as Keats has; but the major poet makes a very large ten-strike on occasion, and what he does contains this curious power of vitality and growth. It is not static, but constantly rebounding and progressing. Now Eleanor Wylie's work is at the moment static. These little poems of hers are all built to a pattern. She has learned her pattern perfectly, but I see no reason to suppose she can ever vary it. She may be able to; but from what I know of her she will lack industry and perseverance.

Poor Amy! So well-intentioned and so wrong; so canny as a craftsman, so undependable as a critic. Recent judgment has questioned the power of Edna St. Vincent Millay's dramatic and "conversational" work, but her lyrics (and some of her sonnets) are established. Far from "lacking industry and perseverance," no poet ever showed more ability to persist and grow than Elinor Wylie; her last book "and all the books between" reveal a poet maturing from brilliance to permanence, from quick versatility to a quiet nobility.

But Amy declared herself most characteristically toward the end of the letter in which she broadly intimated that even a book of poetry cannot live by poetry alone. "If you publish a new *Miscellany* you *must* have a preface; it is absolutely imperative to make the book understandable. You told me you did not know what to say in such a preface, but perhaps sometime when I am in New York we might pound out one together, if you like. That will give the book a point."

Amy was even more anxious about the third *Miscellany,* but consultation was difficult. At the time I was living in Vienna, and Amy was deep in her Keats biography: "Keats is nearly killing me. I have completed six hundred and thirty pages and have three hundred and seventy left to do. I think I shall never want to undertake so long a job again."

The last sentence was prophetic. If Keats was killed by the critics, Amy, by the same exaggeration, was killed by Keats. She had been a sick woman for more than ten years; her first letter to me in 1915 ends: "Do try and get here as early as possible before they have quite minced me to pieces and swept me up in the dustpan." Her labors on the Keats material, of which she owned one of the largest collections in existence, and the almost vituperative English reviews, aggravated her ailment. She was as unaffectedly in love with Keats as Elinor Wylie was with Shelley; and when such presumably friendly critics as J. C. Squire and Robert Lynd questioned her conclusions, they seemed to be suddenly striking at her and exposing a wound so vulnerable as to be vital. For Keats she spent interminable nights puzzling over his manuscripts, tracking down his annotations, and retracing the worn pencil-scrawls; for Keats she suffered uncounted pains in head and groin and ruptured the small blood-vessels of her eyes. Into the dead poet she poured her life-blood, and after the transfusion she died.

Perhaps this is not altogether exact. She also poured her life-blood into her poetry; her vivacity invigorated it, her gusty personality gave it color and warmth. After her death the blood went out of it. The color seemed superficially applied, the warmth simulated; with the exception of some seven or eight poems the verse was suddenly lifeless. Robert

Frost once said that she never touched the deep emotions because she did not know where to look for them, and D. H. Lawrence wrote, "If it doesn't come out of your own heart, real Amy Lowell, it is no good, however many colors it may have. . . . How much nicer, finer, bigger you are, intrinsically, than your poetry is."

This much seems apparent: Amy too often wrote to fit a theory, to mold her work in the fashion of the moment; she cast herself in the rôle of public poet. Instead of being urged by the quiet subconscious self, she continually prodded the conscious will. She sacrificed a slow searching for quick brilliance, and exchanged a broad understanding for narrow contemporaneousness. Her amazing range of subject and variety of techniques—the adaptations of Indian folklore, extensions of Peruvian myths, translations from the French, melodramas in New England dialect, verbal imitations of Stravinsky, Japanese lacquer prints, Chinese legends, exotic impressionism, homespun couplets—no longer hide the central poverty. She had energy, enthusiasm, power, skill, "everything," as one poet, paraphrasing Goethe, said of her, "everything except genius." It might be truer to say that she had genius—genius for everything except the thing she wanted most: permanence as a poet. Yet how could she have attained it? She had many pleasures, few ecstasies; she wept because of little griefs, never touched by immedicable woes. "It is hard," Malcolm Cowley wrote, "to write true poems when one is rich, blanketed with four-percent debentures and rocked to sleep in a cradle of sound common stocks."

She died an isolated patrician, antagonistic to radicals, suspicious of liberals, and scornful of "the ignorant proletariat." It sometimes seems a pity she determined to be a poet at all;

she would have been so much happier as the Senator from Massachusetts.

Her poems, shrunk to a repeated few, still find their way into the anthologies. But her memorial is the collection she bequeathed to the Widener Library at Harvard. The Poetry Room contains not only her invaluable Keats letters, rare manuscripts, first drafts and first editions, but holograph manuscripts and volumes by almost every modern poet, a record of private influence and public accomplishment. Here is Amy's great mausoleum, a library, once the setting for what seemed the controversial battles of the century.

Several years after her death I stood there, in the Poetry Room of the Harvard College Library, waiting for her ghost. Except for the pale young custodian and myself, the room was empty. It remained unvisited during the time I rummaged about the unresponsive shelves and investigated the sacred vault. Not a sound penetrated, not a specter raised its reminiscent head. After an hour of silent loneliness I thought I detected a murmur. I was not wrong. The murmur grew to a hum, a rumble, a roar. The undergraduates were now underneath the window, loudly returning from the stadium. They went by, and the room was quieter than ever. The shadows did not stir. Even the past refused to speak.

RHYMES FOR BREAD

WHEN the afternoon newspaper announced that Vachel Lindsay had died at fifty-two, giving neither the cause nor the manner of his death, I could not believe it. No man I knew had such indomitable energy, such a steadfast, skylarking, overbrimming sense of life. Only a few months before, I remembered, he had proposed a new scheme for righting the world's wrongs and redeeming America in verse; it was a scheme that called for a collaboration of politicians and poets to fulfill the "gutter dream," the golden vision of democracy.

But of all the vivid meetings during a long friendship with Vachel none came back more immediately than an evening at the Metropolitan Opera House. He had just written *The Golden Book of Springfield,* a pathetic mishmash of prophecy and an almost incoherent translation of Plato's *Republic* to the year 2018. It was a melodramatic apotheosis in which a "flower town," blossoming with Village Improvement Parades, and dotted with such pleasure resorts as Kilmer Square, the Edgar Lee Masters Tower, and Untermeyer Park, was populated by prophet-singers and hero-kings. Vachel (he had just sloughed off the prefatory Nicholas) was my guest; the Opera was *Coq d'Or.* Intoxicated with more than alcohol, which he never touched, Vachel sat open-mouthed. The exotic prolog had set the mood for wild folk-stuff, for witches that rode about in iron kettles and huts that walked on hen's legs. High plucked strings performed eerie glissandos or joined with a glassy celesta to evoke a light that never was except on the foam of perilous seas and fairylands forlorn. Then the legend blossomed for the eye as well as for the ear. Screaming reds and strident yellows fought for domination; fury was piled on fantasy; a ballet emphasized crescendos of strangeness, while two green satin giants swung their way through the singers and dancers as though they were mowing to music.

Vachel gasped and leaned forward.

"I'm *for* it!" he boomed in what he imagined was a whisper but which effectively drowned Rimsky-Korsakow's brasses. "I'm *for* it, Louis! That's what I want Springfield to be!"

There was about the ejaculation something incongruous, even grotesque, but there was also something grand. Truly, that was what he wanted Springfield (his unappreciative and often hostile Springfield, Illinois) to be: an ever-living adventure, a creative excitement, a local legend in spicy music, swift color, heightened awareness. But it was not only Springfield that was to be so happily transmogrified; Vachel wanted to perform the miracle for every commerce-ridden city, every filling-station crossroad. Springfield was far more than the town in which Vachel was born and to which, after many unfortunate wanderings, he returned to die. It was his symbol for a land that never existed, a new Atlantis, an enchanted America, a symbol that served him in the same way that Walt Whitman's "I" served that great yea-sayer as a symbol of a hugely—and, like Vachel's, naïvely—idealized congress and camaraderie of states.

It was to this end that he worked, dreamed, and died.

Vachel became a poet, but he was essentially an evangelist, a combined missionary and minstrel, a rhyming John the Baptist singing to convert the heathen in the hinterlands. In his mid-twenties he took the first of his long tramps, preaching "the gospel of beauty." A true revivalist in spirit, his tent was everywhere; he printed and reprinted an ornate and mystical *Village Magazine* and gave copies for the asking. ("I am a preacher," he said, "and ought to preach until I drop.") He never ceased to be "a propagandist for the preservation of the soul." Until he became a professional lecturer, he wandered up and down in the mixed rôles of poet, priest, and beggar; he never asked for money or goods, but he would exchange an evening's entertainment for a night's lodging. "I come to you penniless and afoot to bring a message," he announced. It was a message of "the new localism," which would unite Greek dancing and the Declaration of Independence, an appreciation of art (borrowed from Ruskin) and Lincoln's Gettysburg address. He slept in barns, Negro cabins, livery stables; hoed corn and split kindling for his breakfast; consorted with harvest hands, hoboes, fortune-telling gypsies, scoundrels and reformers. Literally following the precedent of Tommy Tucker, he sang for his supper; he recited verses to farmers' children and bartered poems for his food. He gave away copies of a pamphlet, "Rhymes to be Traded for Bread," for a meal, if he could get it; if not, he would trade it for a dish of ice-cream, a sandwich, or a chocolate bar.

Vachel was always restless, but he refused to admit it; restlessness was his demon, so he made it into a religious occupation. He was, by turns, Johnny Appleseed and St. Francis.

I want to go wandering. Who shall declare
I will regret if I dare.

Long before the English poet, W. H. Davies, capitalized
himself as a "super-tramp," Vachel prided himself on his
vagrancy; it was not a diversion, it was a dispensation, a call,
a high command. He made many records of his literary-
religious walking tours; he explained them in a *Handy
Guide for Beggars,* in his *Adventures While Preaching the
Gospel of Beauty,* in his diaries, and in hundreds of voluminous letters. In New York he had attempted to become an
artist, a commercial illustrator, a cartoonist; but he had
failed. Although he realized that he could do nothing real
until the esthetic poison of the Eighteen Nineties was out
of him, he continued to draw fourth-rate imitations of
Beardsley—Beardsley "purified" and, at the same time, de-
based. He was glad to take to the road.

Many years ago he sent me an article called "The Man
Under the Yoke." The title was obviously a paraphrase of
Markham's "The Man with the Hoe" and it was subtitled
"An Episode in the Life of a Literary Tramp." "This," he
wrote me with an accompanying letter, "is the account of
my first night's experience—my very first—as a beggar."

It was a Sunday morning in the middle of March when
Vachel started out from Jacksonville, Florida, with five cents
and a sack of peanuts in his pocket. By sunset he was in a
pine forest; there was a house almost a mile ahead. It was
growing dark. Vachel had prepared a speech to be delivered
on the threshold. It was to proceed something like this: "I
am a peddler of dreams. I am the sole living member of the
ancient brotherhood of troubadours. It is against the rules of

our order to receive money. We have the habit of asking a night's lodging in exchange for verses and fairy tales."

I like to picture the startled Florida share-croppers while Vachel declaimed these sentences. But the charming speech was never delivered. As Vachel approached the house the turkeys gawked and gobbled at him, the dogs threw themselves into a fury against the fence, the roadside pig grunted scurrilously, and the man barked him away. ("His tone of voice was such that, to speak in metaphor, he bit me in the throat.") Finally Vachel found a shack in the woods where he was given shelter by a man who had once slept nights in the rain and who swore he would go shares with any stranger if ever he had a roof. The man was gaunt and dirty with a two weeks' beard; "his shirt had not been washed since the flood"; he could not read. The interior included a wife, two babies, and four puppies. Supper consisted of a dish of salt pork "that tasted like a salt mine," a soup of lukewarm water, wilted greens—all served in one deep plate which they shared in common—and cold, half-cooked biscuits. Eight o'clock was bedtime. But before Vachel slept in the corner, looking into the fireplace, he recited pieces from Burns and Lanier, Yeats, and even Milton. The man under the yoke said nothing in response. There was a long silence. Just before he rose he said, "The finest thing in all these woods is a team of ten oxen. Tomorrow I'll put you on the road where you can see half a dozen. If you ever meet a writing-man, have him write them into verses."

Then Vachel slept, one comfort and pillow between him and the floor—it was probably the only pillow and comfort in the house. Far from being discomfited, Vachel was uplifted. The bare floor was sweeter than pastures new; the fire in the grate was the treasure at the end of the rainbow. He rejoiced in it. He said, "This is what I came out in the wilderness to see. This man had nothing, and gave me half of it, and we both had abundance."

II

Vachel was always mixing the ingenuous poet and the industrious pamphleteer; a seeming innocent, he had guile enough to appear guileless. He carried his evangelism over into every field of commerce and culture, from rescuing the South from "carpet-bagging industrialism" to reforming Hollywood. In *The Art of the Moving Picture,* one of the most high-minded and confusing set of chapters ever written, Vachel hailed "this new weapon of men" as a rejuvenator of mankind, a substitute for the saloon (Vachel being a zealous prohibitionist), and an "immemorial wonder" that would change the face of the whole earth. Vachel had often discussed the ideas of the work with me, but they seemed so frenetic and shapeless—Vachel, somehow, managed to drag in *The Masses,* Francis Thompson, the *Imagists,* and eight hundred hieroglyphics—that I demurred. But if I was the devil's disciple, James Oppenheim was on the side of the angels. Vachel remembered the tri-party conferences long after I had forgotten them. On the fly-leaf of *The Art of the Moving Picture* he wrote:

My dear Louis: Indirectly you may find your hand in this book, and in several places. James Oppenheim's suggestion about hieroglyphics is mentioned on page 5; said suggestion was made in your parlor. The Avenging Conscience, described on page 120, was first described to me by you that same evening as an illustration of the principles of that chapter. I saw it here in Springfield long after. . . . Thinking it over, I do myself the honor to hope you will read the whole book, but certain passing suggestions in the chapters "The Intimate Photo-Play," "Painting-in-Motion," and "Progress and Endowment" will perhaps appeal to you most as material in which you can revise the theory or spin it much finer. I will be delighted if you and Oppenheim will do so in private or in print.

As a period piece and as an example of oracular windiness I recommend readers to this book. But the chapter on hieroglyphics has a special significance. Interesting in itself, it is invaluable to anyone who wants to understand Vachel's restlessness and his efforts to find a technique of escape. Vachel was preoccupied with picture-writing; it could not have been otherwise. For one thing, Vachel thought in symbols—he had the metaphoric sense to such a degree that everything reminded him of something else. He saw the state of Illinois as an ear of corn, California as a whale; East and West were united in a hieroglyphic poem called "The Wedding of the Lotus and the Rose"; the moon was forty different objects, from a clown's jumping-hoop to an unmated monk walking the sky, a chalice of silver honey, the northwind's cooky, a griffin's egg, Euclid's circle, a fairy's gong, a jester's mirror, an encyclopaedia of whim and glittering dream. For another thing, Vachel began as an artist; he often recalled his days at the Chase School of Art and his talks with Robert Henri. His diaries tell how, anxious to establish himself as a poet-painter, he hawked his drawings up and down the East Side of New York, in drug stores, delicatessens, fish markets, and Chinese laundries for two cents apiece. From resemblances and similes, from mystical symbolism, he turned naturally to the hieroglyph, a picture which was a word, a design, and a thought in one. He proselyted for an understanding of the power of these pictures, a power which would rebuild his beloved Springfield into the semblance of another Thebes. I was to be one of his chief converts. One Christmas he sent me Murray's *Elementary Egyptian Grammar*. The next Christmas, thinking I was now ready for it, he sent the more advanced *Egyptian Grammar* by Roeder and Mercer, full of beautiful and (to me) incomprehensible "Lesestücke." Whenever he came to New York, Vachel would take me to the Metropolitan Museum of Art, where he would teach me (he hoped) to decipher the signs and their phonetic complements on the tombs and mummy-caskets. He insisted that we should write each other occasional phrases in severe hieroglyphics, work our way into the more fluent hieratic, and finally correspond in the abbreviated demotic script. From Saskatoon, in 1922, he sent me a copy of Akhnaten's *Hymn to the Sun* with English equivalents underneath the drawings. He was a little hurt that I did not reply with a Psalm of David translated into Egyptian.

But Vachel's obsession with hieroglyphics did not rest with mere transcription. With Vachel everything had to be transcended in action; every idea had to be put into a game, a pursuit, a common enterprise, a communal passion. Once he wrote me to collect some of our mutual friends—the publisher Ben Huebsch, the diminutive bombshell Anita Loos, Floyd Dell, the poets Sara Teasdale, James Oppenheim, and one or two others—supply pencils for each, and procure at least a ream of white paper. When Vachel arrived, he added to the mystification by delivering a long talk on "personal hieroglyphics." He did not converse; he lectured.

He said in effect, "We are all poets and painters, if we want to be. Every educator knows that every child begins by making patterns in color, structures in building blocks, music in words. More than that, each child has a way of expressing himself in some particular art—a way that is different than the way of any other child. That way, that difference, is his personal hieroglyphic. We must recover it. We must recapture that creative compulsion, that sense of form and difference, that essential individuality which most of us have lost. We have lost it with education, with experience, with maturity, with living in large centers. We must *will* it back."

"But how?" one of us managed to interrupt.

"By finding your initial impulse; by becoming as a little child. All your creative energies lie in a vast reservoir of desire and memory. These pieces of paper will help us siphon up our own first gropings toward picture-writing, toward the source and symbol of all the arts."

We looked at each other, more puzzled than ever. I distributed the sheets, fifteen or twenty to each person.

"Now," said Vachel. "Write down a short word. Just one word in the center of the sheet. Write it large—and as unconsciously as possible. Something childlike, without stopping to think, something like 'cat,' 'dog,' 'boat,' 'boy,' and so on. It doesn't matter whether your neighbor writes the same word as you do, his handwriting will be different. That's right. Now put that sheet aside. Now write another word on the next sheet. Try to think simple thoughts, kindergarten thoughts, if you have to think of anything. Go on with the next sheet. . . ." After we had gone through our collective orgies of unconsciousness and the piles of paper were assembled, Vachel took the first sheet up and examined it from various angles.

"This, Louis, is the germ of your personal hieroglyphic. It only needs a line or two to complete it. Your first word was 'boat,' and you will notice that all your other words have the same pictorial tendency. Hold it sideways. Look! A stroke here and another stroke there, and you have the symbol which means 'to sail upstream'—surely the symbol of a poet, the courage to 'take arms against a sea of troubles,' as Shakespeare says. Now turn the paper this way, and it looks like a pointed feather. That is the Quill of Thoth, the recorder of the gods, fountain-head of writing and the Egyptian god of letters. See how unconsciously, but how inevitably, you have gone back to the source. . . . Now let's look at yours, Sara. Ah, the word 'snake.' All you have to do is to extend the beginning and end of the word—and there is the snake itself. That's *your* personal hieroglyphic. It's the Egyptian letter 'z,' and one of the most sacred signs we know. Now, James, your word 'water' slants like pointed waves. . . ."

This scarcely clarified matters. But Vachel, serious as ever, swept on.

"It just takes a little practice. Soon you'll be able to arrive at your own idiogram, which is also your own art. A little more practice and you'll be drawing or, if you like, painting. Once you find your own personal hieroglyphic, there's nothing to stop you."

"But," someone objected, "how does that bring us to poetry?"

"That's the next step," said Vachel. "You must proceed with the same childlike simplicity. The greatest poetry is the simplest. It all begins with a half-conscious rhythm, an unsophisticated chant, a sort of glorified nursery rhyme." (Here Vachel was describing, more or less unconsciously, his own poetry.) "What we do next is examine the drawings, the little isotypes, we have just made. Let us take Louis' 'boat' which turned into the Quill of Thoth. Can you think of something to go with this, Louis? Nothing complicated. Just a rhyme, a jingle—anything that comes into your head."

Usually glib, this time I was rhymeless, even wordless. Vachel helped me out.

"Just think of the thing itself—and think in rhythm. How about this?

> *This is the Quill of Thoth,*
> *And this is the feather of truth:*
> *The sword against surfeit and sloth,*
> *The undying challenge of youth.*

"There it is. And I think it sounds very much like you, Louis. Even your favorite word 'challenge' is there. Probably telepathy. One poet often anticipates another."

He turned to a drawing which he had made out of a word submitted by my first wife. The word was "cat." Vachel had tricked out the monosyllable with a bristling mane and a bravely flourishing tail. "This, Jean Starr," said Vachel, "is what might go with it:

> *The kitten has grown*
> *To a lioness,*

Not to a cat.
I am very thankful for that.

"Of course," Vachel said, seeing our blank faces. "You ought to do much better than that as you go on. But that's the fundamental idea. The rhymes are just the mediums with which you tap the abstract sources. Naturally, most of the time you will get nothing but doggerel and nonsense jingles. But once in a while, if you keep on trying—and you may have to do it hundreds of times—a poem, or the skeleton of a poem, will emerge. It is even possible that if you keep on regarding the object in a trance-like state, you might get something great. Didn't Coleridge write 'Kubla Khan' when he was in a trance? A group like this may be the beginning of a new kind of poetry. The interplay of mind upon mind— mind co-operating *with* mind, instead of mind against mind. Each man with his personal signature working toward a communion of spirit, a communal art."

III

The idea of a communal art may have seemed preposterous to others; it was never absurd to Vachel. It was much more than a theory; he carried it continually into practice. Practically all of Vachel's longer poems were partly collaborations. In "The Congo," "The Santa Fe Trail," "The Ghosts of the Buffaloes," "The Kallyope Yell," and half a dozen other poems he perfected a new and intoxicating blend of rhyme, revivalism, and ragtime. Vachel united the old Greek chant, where every line was half-spoken, half-sung, with what he called the Higher Vaudeville.

No one who ever heard Vachel read one of his own chants will ever forget it. He recited other poetry badly, underscoring and overemphasizing it, but he was superb when he rendered his own verse. His head thrown back at a perilous angle, the eyes half-shut or opening suddenly to show only the whites, the arms shooting out like infuriated pistons, Vachel held everyone by his vibrant baritone, his uncanny contrasts in speed, pitch, and volume. He was not all boom and thunder by any means; he startled and charmed, frightened and soothed, in successive breaths. Never have there been such declamations, such swift alternations of shrieking and delicacy, clatter and sweetness, crudity and poignance.

But he was uncertain of his chants in the beginning, distrustful of them in the end. "My new brand of poetry," he wrote as early as 1914, "is just like pink lemonade and firecrackers at the County Fair; a loud noise and a sunset tint." He underrated his originality just as he overrated his sentimental strain, full of tender violets and valentines. He did not need help, but he constantly asked for it. He brought new manuscripts with him whenever he came to New York; he read them to groups of listeners, to friends and strangers, to poets and business men—and he heeded every comment. If Floyd Dell or James Oppenheim or Sara Teasdale disliked a line, or even a passage, out it went. Sometimes other lines were substituted on the spot; sometimes one of us, prodded on by Vachel, offered lines of our own. My letters from Vachel are full of thanks for what any other poet would have considered effrontery; he reminds me often that he has incorporated all the alterations I recommended, no matter how tentatively.

The Macmillan Company brings out *The Chinese Nightingale and Other Poems* next month. It will include several verses that you have helped me write, including the "Nightingale" itself. You and Dell did not notice it afterward, but I took every criticism you offered that midnight I submitted the rough copy to you. And some of them were pretty radical changes. The book also includes "The Ghosts of the Buffaloes" on which you collaborated, if you remember. . . .

It was not excess modesty or servile fear that prompted Vachel to ask for advice, consultation, and correction. It was an integral faith in his fellows, a thoroughgoing belief in the democratic experiment, the collaborative comradeship. We were to make the world over, we brothers in art and industry; we were all to rebuild Springfield into the Golden City, the City of the Dream. Again and again this theme occurs in Vachel's life and letters. Springfield was his final hieroglyph, his symbol for Akhnaten's City-of-the-Sun, the lost Atlantis, Athens and Jerusalem on the green and pleasant soil of Illinois.

I remember a curious offshoot of Vachel's penchant for group-poetry. At one of our more intimate sessions, besides Vachel, there were Robert Frost, Sara Teasdale, and myself; Vachel was always at his best when he was with Sara, his Gloriana, his inaccessible, if not impossible, She. There was some reading of poetry, some criticism that roved far afield, and some good talk on the part of Robert, who, with the possible exception of D. H. Lawrence, was the best talker of my time. Suddenly Vachel proposed that at our next meeting, we should all bring poems written around one theme.

"Nature?" I hazarded. "Or, if Sara won't mind the infringement, Love? Or something more specific?"

"Something more specific, by all means," said Robert. "You name it, Vachel."

"All right," said Vachel promptly. "John L. Sullivan."

We laughed, but it was plain that Vachel was serious. John L. Sullivan was another of Vachel's potent hieroglyphs, a symbol of burly Americanism opposed to the Fauntleroys of his youth and the Boston Brahmins who had patronized Mark Twain. Sullivan was not merely a figure of native strength, he was an ever-living legend, brother of Bryan and Andrew Jackson, one of the old gods, a deity fit to be enshrined when Springfield was rebuilt.

We gasped, and forgot it. Or, rather, we burlesqued it. Sara talked of writing something to entertain Vachel, but the thought of the Muse addressing a tender apostrophe to the champion heavyweight was too much for her. I took it upon myself to write a love song in Sara's manner, but I never showed it to either Sara or Vachel. It began:

> *Corbett kissed me in his stride;*
> *Kilrain in the hall;*
> *But John L. only sighed and sighed,*
> *And never kissed at all.*

I also attempted to parody myself for the occasion. Part of the verses, in the social "urging-surging" style of *Challenge,* ran:

> *God of the ringside, thou who art*
> *No mere protector of the strong,*

Stiffen our sinews; steel our heart;
Preserve us from the final gong.

There was more—including an appeal for Man's Right, to say nothing of his powerful left—but I have forgotten it.

It was Robert Frost who made the most surprising comment, a comment that was both criticism and burlesque. In a letter of February, 1918, which contained neither warning nor explanation, I received the following from Robert. It has never before appeared in print.

JOHN L. SULLIVAN ENTERS HEAVEN

(To be sung to the tune of "Heaven Overarches You and Me")

Sullivan arrived at the very lowest Heaven
Which is sometimes mistaken for the very highest Hell,
Where barkeeps, pugilists, jockeys, and gamblers
And the women corresponding (if there are any) dwell.
They done queer things, but they done 'em on the level,
And thus they escape the jurisdiction of the Devil.

Sullivan felt, and he couldn't find his ticket.
He thought for a moment he would have to go to Hell.
But the gatekeeper told him, "You don't need a ticket:
Everybody knows you: Your name's John L.
There's a lot of fighting characters been setting up waiting
To see if you were up to your mundane rating."

Sullivan asked, "They've been setting up to see me?"
And the gatekeeper answered, "They have like Hell!
They've been setting up to try you, and see if they can lick
*   you,*
And settle who's who in the Fields of Asphodel.

So you may as well be ready to take them all on—
Hercules and Pollux and the whole doggone.

"Fraternity of pluggers, I mean the first-raters
(We send the second-raters to entertain Hell).
I seen Herc's hands all wound with lead and leather
Till they looked like the balls on a great dumb-bell.
  He's mad because the deeds you matched his with
  Were sound printed facts, while his were just myth."

Sullivan burst into Heaven a-roaring.
The devils beyond the board fences of Hell
Put the whites of their eyes to crannies and knotholes
To see who was driving the angels pell-mell.
  They said 'twas the greatest Punch of all times.
  Ring the bells of Heaven! Sound the gladsome chimes!

This, we thought, would be the end of "The Garland for Sullivan." But we were wrong. Vachel could not have taken our skits seriously—he certainly did not take them amiss—but he could not bear to give up the idea. A few months after the rest of us imagined we had laughed the theme to death, in 1918, Vachel wrote me:

My dear Louis: I enclose the Sullivan. I have also sent a carbon to Robert. I am suggesting to him and you that you two send Harriet Monroe your poems. I am asking Harriet to get out a *John L. Sullivan Number,* with a leading editorial on the renaissance of boxing in the camps, the democratic boxing-match versus the cruel and snobbish German duel, and the whole psychology of the antithesis. I hope Robert will be willing to release the skit he sent you, or else write a more serious thing on boxing which may have occurred to him since we met. You will note that my Sullivan is serious enough underneath. I am hoping your

own Sullivan poem is done by now. . . . My heart is yours, you
may be sure. . . . I have gone back to the God of the Hebrews
and the Twenty-third Psalm, and the God and the song saved
my soul yesterday, or at least healed a great sickness of the heart.
I have tried many gods, and Yahveh is the only one that can
heal.

I never quite understood the abrupt transition, for Yahveh
was a queer substitute for the Chinese Buddha whom Vachel
really worshiped. But there was no question that, once
again, Vachel's combination of naïveté and meditation, of
puckish fancy and pugilistic imagination, had produced
another triumph. His "John L. Sullivan, The Strong Boy
of Boston," is one of Vachel's most characteristic expressions. In spite of its theme, it is not bellicose but nostalgic,
even tender. History and muffled histrionics set the key,
from the opening:

> *When I was nine years old, in 1889,*
> *I sent my love a lacy Valentine.*
> *Suffering boys were dressed like Fauntleroys,*
> *While* Judge *and* Puck *in giant humor vied.*
> *The Gibson Girl came shining like a bride—*

to the concluding:

> *And . . .*
> *John L. Sullivan*
> *The strong boy*
> *Of Boston*
> *Fought seventy-five red rounds with Jake Kilrain.*

What is more, to show he bore us no ill will for our failure
to join his pugilistic crusade, when he printed his poem the

generous Vachel added a subtitle: "Inscribed to Louis Untermeyer and Robert Frost."

IV

Springfield transformed; the mighty hieroglyph; communal art—this was the triple *leitmotif* which ran through
everything Vachel thought and wrote. Several letters from
him in late 1917 disclose another variant of the old theme.
In September he tells me he is working on a new long poem
in which commercialism is conquered by culture; rude force,
"the bullock's brawn," is tamed by quiet beauty, "the little
fawn." The poem was to be entitled "The Eyes of Queen
Esther," and it was evident that Esther was also meant to
be Judith and Eve, one more composite tutelary saint of the
new Springfield. "What I want from you," Vachel wrote, "is
any possible suggestion, or modification of the mood of my
allusion to the feast of Purim, and the tribute to the Jewish
race. The preface of your Heine volume came into my mind
as I was writing. You might draw a line through any line
that rang false."

Although I have forgotten what suggestions I made, they
must have been radical, for the verses which finally appeared
in Vachel's *Collected Poems* are scarcely the verses which lie
before me in manuscript. Even the title has been changed.
It is typical of Vachel that he attempted to make his verses
bear a greater significance than they warranted. Just as an
old poem "How I Walked Alone in the Jungle of Heaven"
was re-entitled "How Johnny Appleseed Walked Alone in
the Jungle of Heaven," so the original unpretentious "The
Eyes of Queen Esther" became "A Rhyme for All Zionists."

Another letter from Vachel shows how eager he was for consultation, but it suddenly plunges into deeper waters, into the struggle between the poet and the public and the ever-recurrent Springfield obsession.

My dear Louis. . . . You overestimate this blushing rhymer, but he thanks you. I have accepted every one of your criticisms of "Queen Esther," cut it in half, thrown out the cumbersome argument, brought it near to the Book, which I have carefully re-read, and conveyed what I really meant to say all the time. I *hope* I have conveyed it.

It is obvious to me, as I re-read Esther's story in the Bible, that she had a great and peculiar power over Ahasuerus long before he knew where it came from. It was what we call high breeding, but this in her was synonymous with religion, as in Pavlova it is synonymous with dancing. And going back the other way, whereas religion was synonymous with race, with Esther religion was inseparable from gentility. . . .

The Chinese Nightingale volume has about run its course with the reviewers; its reception has been about the same as *The Congo,* no better and no worse. The hundred million Americans do not yet know that any of us are in existence. As a body— critics and poets, whatever we say about our own factions—we are one faction, about as well known as the Christadelphians or the No-Necktie holiness faction of the Mennonites. And we have about as much political and social leadership. I do not mean I'm all in a sweat for us to become as Bryan, Wilson, or Roosevelt; but I like to look the American people in the face, as a cure for the self-sugaring that comes with reading press-clippings too much. Seventy-five notices make me vain as a peacock and puffy as a frog. Yet Edwin Markham told me last month that he received eight barrels of press-clippings on "The Man with the Hoe," and then his money ran out and he told the bureau to send no more.

He might have run for Mayor of a small town with that much hold on the people, and have almost won the election. . . .

As for my asinine remarks on statesmanship, I have something serious behind them. It is *The Golden Book of Springfield.* It is my forlorn hope, my Thermopylae. I hope locally for it to have as definite effect on the history of the town as any election could have in changing the fabric or policy or mood of the place. . . . I hope I have enough punch to really *make over* five citizens. I am trying to so construct the book that it will transform the civic imagination of those five in such a way that they will slowly make the changes in the mood of the town by the unconscious effect of the book on their minds. . . . Everything I have ever done or written will serve to drive the book deeper into the souls of my five hypothetical converts. Civics is not yet a religion. I hope to make it as much a religion as Healing is a religion in Christian Science, or Undertaking was a religion in Egypt.

I do not want to do it on an ethical or argumentative basis. I hold that men may be transformed by their imaginations. It is not the only basis of transformation; but it is one basis, and *the* one to which I have access. I think this city could be transformed, not by being a bit better or more pious, but simply by dreaming, by dreaming as fervently as one hundred poets you and I know. If a high imagination be once accepted as the first requisite in citizenship, and be made the main fact of citizenship, the rest will follow.

The note occurs again and again. Springfield, as a place and as an allegory, was woven into his fibers. It was his wayward beloved, plunged in adventure and reclaimed in purity. It was his mother, to be cherished and chided, revered and attacked, and ultimately glorified. A long letter received in December, 1920, again sounds the central theme, but this time it is approached in an unusually roundabout way.

Vachel begins by recommending Jack Squire, then editor of the *London Mercury*, to my "care and fine companionship." This was before we had met and before the English poet (and one of the best parodists of the day) became Sir John Collings Squire. Squire was to land in New York early in 1921 and, although Vachel is not too clear in this regard, it is evident that he wanted me not only to entertain and "chaperon" Squire, but to travel with him. Vachel is very earnest about this: "so far as our group is concerned, the capture of Squire means the capture of the field. . . . He is an absolutely open-minded man, stubborn but willing to be shown, and, in final critical independence, so much like yourself that you will be amazed."

Vachel then intimates that I should not only guide Squire about New York, but direct him to and about Springfield. The fact that I had never visited Vachel's home town seemed to be no deterrent. Vachel made this part, at least, plain.

I suggest that you, Louis Untermeyer, become one of my chief councilors in my Springfield policy. To that end, I want you to make an ample visit to this town. How is this for a plan? We will spend the morning reading Floyd Dell's *Moon Calf*. We will spend the rest of the day proving or disproving it on the streets of Springfield. We will spend the next morning reading Masters' *Mitch Miller*. We will spend the rest of the day proving or disproving it on the streets of Springfield. We will spend the next morning reading Sinclair Lewis's *Main Street*. We will spend the rest of the day proving or disproving it on the streets of Springfield. I want you to be my first Springfield critic-visitor. I want you to beat the long parade of Englishmen to this place, to block out the critical path they should follow. I want you to undercut Dell, Masters, Sinclair Lewis, and others in actual first-hand data

on a Middle Western Capital. I counsel you to as judicial an attitude as a Justice of the Supreme Court. We will have long personal conversations with every soul in town that you choose to
interview.

I want you to go back with the fattest note-book and scrap-
book collectible. Above all, I want you to beat the Englishmen
to it. I want you to be prepared to tell them exactly what kind
of a Springfield they should discover.

When all is done, I want the reports to appear where they will
form the American—and Springfield—minds. I will accept your
verdict, if you will look at the evidence.

Unfortunately, I never made the pilgrimage. It was not
until some years after Vachel's death that I visited his far
from Golden City, and then (ironically enough) it was as a
lecturer on "The American Vision." I cannot remember
what evasive excuse I gave Vachel for not blazing the path
for the (alas, unrealized) parade of Englishmen, but he was
not offended. He had still other schemes. He always had. One
of his projects was to "explode" a new and unknown poet
on the world. I was then to attack Vachel's discovery, and a
controversy was to ensue. He informed me, for example, "I
have just written a preface for the poems of Marya Alexan-
drovna Toteana Zaturenska, who sells books in the children's
department in the basement of Brentano's," and he asked me
to do something about it. Again I was remiss, but I am glad
to say I praised the sensitive delicacy of Marya Zaturenska
(later the wife of Horace Gregory) before she was awarded
the Pulitzer Prize in 1938.

Then there was the plan for a long epic on "The American Turkey." Here again we were all to collaborate. "I have
all the data, if I can only make him gobble. The turkey is

more wonderful and beautiful than the griffin, but people only eat him. I am dreaming of turkey-fanciers, who breed him for his beauty like the peacock. Which reminds me of an idea for a book of criticism which I wish you would seriously undertake . . ." and Vachel is off on another fantastic pursuit.

In 1923 he had evolved a fresh and "absolutely fool-proof scheme." This time it was to have my anthologies in all hotels, department stores, and local book-shops at least two weeks before Vachel arrived on his lecture tours. They were to be accompanied by "pictures of all the poets, signed photographs, every form of window display, material for the local papers, etcetera. . . . I want the whole week to be the local Poetry Picnic of the year in every way that can be devised. Then your humble servant appearing in the town on the last day of this Picnic will give a recital of an hour and a half, reading about twelve chosen poems from twelve leading poets. The public is urged to bring their poetry-anthologies and follow the text with their eye, like reading the prayer-book in high church."

Extravagant though this may seem, there was nothing ridiculous in Vachel's intention. It was part of his collaborative, communal philosophy. Besides, he was tiring of reading his popular "jazz" poems over and over again. "I have recited my own work until I am utterly sick of it. If I am to recite, I want to recite the other man's work. I want to get right down now to the man in the street, and pepper him till he is as crazy to go to the bookstore as to the Ford Emporium. Meanwhile, I will have been given a holiday from reciting 'Booth,' 'The Congo,' and 'The Santa Fe Trail,' which will drive me mad if I do them once more. . . . With your help I can at least create a demand for the other man's work and refresh my mind with it while I am planning my own new books."

V

But possibly Vachel's most grandiose scheme, a scheme in which I was to be implicated, if not the prime mover, was a vast assembly and new appraisal of native humor; America in terms of Falstaff. He discussed the plan at length several times, becoming more urgent with each repetition. His letters grew longer and longer; his handwriting was so large that nine or ten lines covered a sheet. Finally he wrote (in part):

I humbly petition that you start out on a new hypothesis, having used Whitman to the limit in your last critical work. Base the serious side of your criticism of poetry with the *tone* of Abraham Lincoln as a touchstone, and the criticism of humor on the *tone* of Mark Twain. You may say that neither of these are poets. Yet I hold that they both have more inspirational "meat" for new poets than any writer of verse. . . . I have said for years that if almost everything that was said in praise of Whitman were rewritten with the names of Johnny Appleseed and Abraham Lincoln alternately substituted, it would be much truer. And most everything said in praise of Thoreau had better be said for Johnny Appleseed, who was one of the great and beautiful and unconscious humorists of his day. He beat the game without knowing it.

But all this as a preliminary to the fundamental suggestion: that you make an Anthology of American Humorous Verse which is really Falstaffian. Like Falstaff it will have good guts, not wit--and you should put in as much comment as verse. The

use of it will be that, hereafter, the young American poet will no
more be afraid to be funny when he pleases. . . . You know
Heine well enough to know how he put depth into humor, and
our friend Horace. . . . I think the great parallels are in the
other arts. Take, for instance, the wonderful "Golden Cockerel"
which you took me to see last spring. The acting was Falstaffian,
the color was Falstaffian, the story was Falstaffian, the music was
Falstaffian, and I have no doubt the libretto was also. Yet there
was not one shallow or trivial phase to the whole performance.
It was the laughter of the gods. It was not merely grotesque or
Oliver Wendell Holmes's polite after-dinner wit. It had some of
the gusto of Huckleberry Finn and the King and the Duke on
the raft.

We *must* have a humorous standard. Above all, young writers
just coming on would be far more liberated than by any "theory
of free verse." They have been offered every kind of freedom by
the critics but this—the freedom to laugh. So the rich wit of the
young is buried in college annuals and cheap humorous sheets,
when they should be taught to laugh with the high gods, not
snicker in corners. . . . I should say that the test of humor is the
same test as that of seriousness: Does it last? Please establish the
classic standard, and save the country.

That was Vachel's cry from the heart, and it was his
tragedy. He urged us all to save the country; himself he
could not save.

He brought a fresh raciness into American literature. He
put the disrupted sounds and stresses of American life into
new syncopated rhythms—and turned away from them. England and America hailed the daring ingenuity, the serenity
and recklessness which could frame the poet's vision in such
popular, even vulgar, music—and Vachel repudiated the very
sound of "jazz." In 1914 he wrote me he would bring with

him "The Santa Fe Trail" ("a hoot with a little balm of
Gilead scattered through—Sara likes it now that I have put
a little bird in it to sort of soften it down"). He warned me
about another wild rhapsody that was forthcoming, "The
Congo," and he described it:

It is equal parts (1) The death of a missionary on the Congo
(2) A cannibal war dance (3) The Springfield, Illinois, race riots
(4) The burnings alive of Negroes in the South (5) The camp-
meetings of half-wild Negroes (6) Bert Williams' Negro Comedy
Company (7) A minstrel show (8) Joseph Conrad's African
sketches (9) Uncle Tom's Cabin (10) The Emancipation Proclamation (11) The songs of Stephen Collins Foster (12) "The Souls
of Black Folk" by W. E. B. Dubois—all boiled down and served
to a ragtime tune.

But a few years later he had forgotten what he wrote. He
was ashamed of the "ragtime tune," the rude vitality which
was the very pulse of the poem. He sought to give it a belated dignity; he tried to foist a spurious classicism on it by
calling it an ode.

They assume that "The Congo" is a new form. It is not. It is
one of the oldest, most orthodox, most stilted and over-conven-
tionalized forms in the English language. I fancy, if you care to
do so, you can find precedents for every line of "The Congo" in
a long line of English odes, which have not failed to remain in
print simply because they were intended to be read aloud. Please,
Louis, do up the conservatives who do not know what an ode is.

Yet in the same letter Vachel inveighs against the very
critics who praised him for his form, "people who assume I
am lost in technical mazes like the Imagists." He admired
Amy Lowell as a person, but he suspected her desire to

found schools and organize tendencies. ("She isn't an Imagist; she's a dogmatist.") He distrusted all theorists, possibly because he was always freeing himself from one theory only to be snared by another. He ends in a burst of inconsistency:

Method is so long behind me that I've forgotten all about method. I suppose technical discussion rages because most poets are twenty-five—which is the technical age. At that period I was full of technical questions of art-school art. I just had to settle them or be unhappy. I vastly appreciate the chapter in your book. I hope there is room for the Standard Dictionary definition of an ode, or such a definition as you would care to concoct. Let us slay all critics by telling them to look up this definition and let us alone till our message or fancy goes wrong.

In the light of what happened later, the last phrase is pathetic. First the message went wrong, then the fancy went altogether. His were loud but quickly passing triumphs; he distrusted his audiences when they applauded; he despised them when he felt he entertained without uplifting them. ("You see, Louis, it is so easy. The house half-full; the check promptly paid; everybody pleasant and nobody giving a damn.") He wanted to reach "the man in the street"; but "the divine average" regarded Vachel as a strange novelty, a crossroads circus in rhyme, a freak who ran his own show. This saddened him and soured the very sweetness of his gift. At the height of his fame he was lonely and distressed, sought after for the thing which he condemned in himself. He needed understanding and quiet responsiveness; what he got was more engagements to "roar in public." The emotional struggles and maladjustments went on year after year. His love for Sara Teasdale was as apparent to his friends as it must have been obvious to Sara from the beginning. Apart from countless letters and courtly gestures, he dedicated several of his books to her, "the golden queen for whom I wrote the best songs of my days."

But this was one more dream which Vachel could not carry over into reality. He was chained to inaction, to a fantasy of life which feared daily responsibility, to a mother whom he loved and hated to the end. Although his mother had fought him "like a wildcat" every time he wrote a poem "till she found Oxford listening," he presented his friends with profiles of his mother and himself on the same photograph. Yet his mother was the demon-angel that held him in a kind of psychic immaturity, that kept him safe from the "lure of the cup and the sin of the flesh." Even after Sara Teasdale married, comfortably, though not too happily, he remained not only celibate but virgin. He, himself, married many years later. His wife, Elizabeth Conner, whom he had met when she was a schoolgirl, was twenty years younger than himself, as capable as she was charming. She accomplished the miracle of adapting herself to his variable moods; there were two beautiful children, Nicholas and Susan. But Vachel was cursed with self-doubt. Imagination had begun to overrun itself; the clouds of despair began to gather. He was tired. Years ago he had confessed, "I feel as though the ground were cut from under me. I stand for no moral issue, no cause, no golden crusade. Perhaps Buddhism as I conceive it has more charm than Christianity. . . . Buddha was not as humble or useful as Christ, but he suffered less, was more impregnable. . . . I am happy when not absolutely in the presence of disaster. And I am most in harmony then, with that stillest room in my inner house that is always cold as the stars, no matter how much noise I may be making. There is a kind of north-star room in my soul—a kind of room of destiny and peace—that I must inhabit."

Now even that room was closed. All the avenues of escape were closing. The audiences that had listened and collaborated with him no longer cared to hear him. He had given himself too freely and too often. He, the most demanded poet-performer of his day, was no longer in demand anywhere. He refused to make new friends and feared to meet old ones. Something in him began to die.

His faith shaken, his following lost, he considered himself a failure. Poverty, which had been an adventure in his youth, was a growing terror for the harassed householder of fifty; he was sinking deeper in debt and despair. He began to have hallucinations. The money that he owed—a few thousand dollars—seemed a quicksand from which he could never extricate himself. He heard voices; he imagined himself persecuted; he fought against actuality. He even turned upon his wife, and yearned to go back to his innocent youth, to begin all over again. He refused to be comforted. He, the rollicking "broncho that would not be broken," was broken at last. On the night of December 5, 1931, he drank a bottle of lysol.

VI

There remain the visions, the evidence of things unseen. Even here the record is confusing. The reader shares Vachel's own uncertainty, unable to draw the line between frank sentiment and affected sentimentality. Often it is impossible to decide when Vachel is celebrating democracy and when he is satirizing it. Floyd Dell, one of Vachel's earliest admirers, even went so far as to say that Vachel's patriotism was a compensation against his fierce Oriental nostalgia. Vachel, according to Floyd, was

a Buddhist Chinaman who happened to be born in Springfield, Illinois, and the only place that he is really at home there is in the Chinese laundry. Observe, in "The Chinese Nightingale," the simple and fond realism of that laundry and that laundryman. What other citizen of Springfield has he drawn so recognizably? Who intrudes even into his anti-saloon campaign? Omar Khayyam! Nicholas Vachel marries the Illinois Rose to the Indian Lotus. He dreams of a time when the U. S. A. will be governed by the Chinese. And it is no accident that "Lepanto," the poem of Chesterton, which gave him his tune, was a poem about Giants and Genii, multiplex of wing and eye whose strong obedience broke the sky when Solomon was king!

Superficially, Floyd is right. But Vachel transcended his sources and transformed his material. The clanging measures of Chesterton's ballad were harshened and syncopated until a new and indigenous rhythm evolved; the fusion of Oriental mysticism and native Evangelism resulted in some of the most peculiarly American poems the country has ever produced. With all his contradictions and influences, Vachel was not merely an original; he was as autochthonous as the ever-present filling-station, that unique and functional American institution which is so often disguised as a Greek temple, a mosque, a pagoda.

Framed variously in clear harmonies and harsh improvisations, Vachel preached his sermon with almost deafening gusto. He preferred singing it to the proverbial lute, but he did not cease to blare it through the stuffed trumpet, the hot saxophone, the steam calliope. "General William Booth

Enters into Heaven" is no less a psalm for being accompanied by the cornet and bass drum of the Salvation Army. "The Chinese Nightingale" takes us from a local laundry to an orchestral Nirvana where music never ceases and spring comes on forever. "The Congo" begins in a barrel-house dive and ends in an African paradise where a million boats with oars of silver sail through a transfigured land, while the voodoo "boomlay, boomlay, boom" is changed to "Hark, ten thousand harps and voices." "The Kallyope Yell" rises from the tanbark of the circus-ring to become the siren singing of a dream-haunted, dream-hunting people. Here, more clearly than ever, Vachel predicts the prophet-singers who will come after him, chanting his song "in softer guise with more delicate surprise."

> *I am but the pioneer*
> *Voice of democracy;*
> *I am the gutter dream,*
> *I am the golden dream.*

Vachel's letters reflect his shifting exaltations and depressions. Even while he was apostrophizing the common man as uncommon hero—Lincoln, Jackson, Twain, Bryan, John L. Sullivan, Johnny Appleseed—he suspected how impossible it was to "blow the proud folk low, humanize the dour and slow." He envisaged every citizen as a driver of chariots with "a steel spring Roman grace." Yet he knew that, as long as lions and demagogs roared, the "popcorn crowd" would rule the town, and his bewildered listeners would worship not only Mammon but Barnum.

His vision was contradictory, but it was his own. "Born of

mobs, born of steam" his energetic genius persists; he still has something persuasive, even powerful, to say to us. I think I know what it is. He is saying:

> *Listen to my golden dream . . .*
> *Listen to my g-o-l-d-e-n d-r-e-a-m . . . !*

SAPPHO, ST. LOUIS,
AND THE DARK SEA

THE FIRST letter I received from Sara Teasdale suggested the long friendship and sounded the note which she was to follow to her death. This was toward the end of 1911. She had published the proverbial first "slender sheaf" of tributary sonnets and tender lyrics some years before. But it was the delicate craftsmanship and definite personality which I praised in a review of her *Helen of Troy and Other Poems* that prompted her letter. After a paragraph of thanks, she wrote in that clear and finely rounded handwriting characteristic of her style: "It is good of you, too, to like my consistently feminine attitude in the love-lyrics. I have a theory that the only way women can hope to make their work compare with men's work, is not by trying to rival what the men say, but by trying to supplement it."

In how many ways is that a voice from the past! What a mixture of condescension and derision such a sentence would provoke were it written by any of the young women poets of our day. Dorothy Parker, whose neat concluding turns owe something to Sara's, would have uttered it in a tone of wry contempt; Sylvia Townsend Warner would have framed it in dexterous malice; Muriel Rukeyser would not have uttered it at all. Only a few of Sara's contemporaries, chiefly her elders, would have approved of it. The ghost of Christina Rossetti, by whom Sara was most influenced before she discovered her own note, would have nodded hesitantly; the then living Lizette Woodworth Reese actually had applauded.

I remember trying to tell Lizette Reese how much Sara appreciated the praise, especially since Sara admired the older woman's crisp lines, simple but not sententious. It happened to be Miss Reese's birthday; she was in her late seventies; I was calling at her home in Baltimore, accompanied by James Whaler, an American poet too little appreciated. I tried to talk about Sara, but Miss Reese took charge of the conversation. She was in one of her admonishing moods, and, with the exception of Harriet Monroe, I had never met a more barbed and prickly matriarch—if an elderly spinster might qualify for the term. An article I had recently written was the cause of her acidity. She scarcely allowed me to be seated before she assailed me. I had to remember that she was almost eighty, that she had been a schoolteacher for years, and that I was her admiring guest.

"There's no use trying to persuade me, Louis"—she pronounced the "s" with what I hoped was not an intentional hiss—"you know you yourself don't like that sort of writing."

"But," I objected, "there are as many mansions in poetry as there are in heaven. I confess I didn't used to like Eliot. I admit I don't understand most of 'A Cooking Egg,' and there are whole areas in 'The Waste Land' where I am lost. But the combination of beautiful rhetoric and purposeful ugliness excites me. It is always surprising and suggestive. After all, poetry does not always have to *mean*—"

"Nonsense!" she interrupted, as if she were addressing a schoolboy who insisted on giving the wrong answers. "It's no use quoting from that poem by MacLeish." She seemed to have read everything, especially the sort of thing she disliked. "It's pretty, but that doesn't stop it from being silly. What's got into the poets, anyway? Why are they so afraid of being understood? Eliot, Pound, and the rest of them—all frustrated, and trying to frustrate everyone else. And then, there's Robinson," she added with an unexpected leap. "What's wrong with him? What worries him so much about other people's marriages? Why doesn't he get married? If he's so afraid of it, why doesn't he just stay single and keep still about it?"

"Maybe being a bachelor is a more difficult occupation than being a spinster," I hazarded at a loss. "Maybe it's an irritating life-work for a man, a project that only a woman could pursue gracefully."

"Don't try to flatter me," she said tartly. "You know what I mean. Stop apologizing for your friends. Don't explain them. Their poetry must say it for them, if it's to be said at all."

"That's just what I'm trying to say," I attempted feebly. "You yourself have shown other women poets an unliterary, distinctly feminine speech—"

"You don't seem to get the point, Louis," and it was obvious she was trying to be patient with me. "You are letting your impulses run one way, your intellect another. A poet shouldn't be bogged down in theories. Take Amy Lowell and her precious Imagists . . ."

I was in my late forties at the time, and even then I preferred to deliver my own monolog. I find that, with rapidly oncoming age, I love to talk and dislike to listen. Robert Frost is the only man who successfully interrupts me. On that day at the end of 1933, I never got to pay the belated tribute from Sara, who died at the beginning of the year.

My roses were still in the hall; Sara's name had barely been mentioned.

I I

Sara, herself, needed neither apology nor explanation. Everything she touched spoke for her—her work, her countless friendly acts, her illuminating letters. Within her self-imposed range, she disclosed herself fully. My correspondence file is by no means complete, yet in 1912 alone I find more than thirty letters and closely written cards from her.

Early in 1912 Sara, then living in St. Louis, where she was born, made one of her many visits to New York. It was there I met her for the first time, at the Hotel Martha Washington, which advertised itself primly as "The Only Hotel in the World Exclusively for Women," and which, until her marriage, Sara always made her headquarters. She was the unexpected fruit of her parents' old age, and this led her to believe that she was lacking in vitality. She was not exactly a hypochondriac; but, even as a young woman, she disliked physical activities, avoided anything that might tax her strength, and generally pampered herself. Somehow, she had been persuaded that she lacked one layer of skin, and this delusion gave her a constant obsession about colds. She liked to wear chiffon (usually gray) in the evening, but this necessitated particular protection; she wore long sleeves to hide the Jaeger underwear, which sometimes failed to remain concealed. If she was not pretty, or exciting, she was always attractive. Her eyes were quietly expressive; her gestures were few but eloquent; her tawny hair, so often celebrated by Vachel Lindsay, was something between a mane and a nimbus. Yet, when only a girl, she seemed destined for spinsterhood; she was maidenly even in her marriage. Reticence walked with her; rudeness of any kind died in her presence.

Still I cannot help but recall the incongruities. The modest Sara learnedly discussed the sexual perversions in Proust: she read Joyce's *Ulysses* over and over and delighted in the concluding monolog of Mrs. Bloom. Although she scarcely specialized in pornography, she was the (unpublished) author of the most scatological quatrain and the lewdest limerick I know. She fancied herself too weak for long sessions, but she conducted telephone conversations of such length that they exhausted most of her hearers. She complained that her throat was feeble, but she had one of the most resonant voices I ever heard, and her laugh was startling.

Because her early songs had an unashamedly sentimental appeal, it was thought that Sara herself was a sentimentalist, devoid of humor and self-criticism. Nothing could be further from the truth. Sara distrusted the insipid and despised the saccharine; quick to puncture pretensions, none of her parodists mocked her early verses more than she did. In February, 1912, while I was still being addressed as "My dear Mr. Untermeyer," she wrote several letters which show how much shrewder were her own estimates than were those of her friends or most of the critics. At that time Edward J. Wheeler was president of the Poetry Society of America and Jessie B. Rittenhouse was its secretary; both praised her more rhetorical lyrics and deprecated the simplest but soundest. "Miss R. seems rather lukewarm about the new ones; you know I told you she didn't like 'When I am dead and over me bright April' "—eight lines which became one of Sara's most memorable poems. "She ought to have liked it a little,

for it is far more musical than most of my other stuff. But
' 'tis brief, my lord,' and I fear it will fall very flatly on the
ears of the Poetry Society. The things that seem most effective when read there are—well—rather ambitious."

Sara's premonition was correct. We attended the Society's
February meeting; her few lyrics were dutifully read and
politely applauded. But Sara was not yet a vogue. Only a few
critics had discovered her deceptive simplicity: the grace
which concealed the canny craftsmanship, the artlessness
which was something of an art. Her volumes were not yet
used as keepsakes and valentines, the co-ed's unfailing companion, and the Bible of every disappointed lover. The
poems which made the most impression at the Poetry Society
were, as she predicted with ironic understatement, "well—
rather ambitious." Besides, the meeting of February twenty-
seventh was mainly devoted to the vital topic for discussion:
"Is modern city life unfavorable to the production of
poetry?"

Another of Sara's letters in February the same year reminds me that we all made a pilgrimage to Staten Island to
surprise Edwin Markham with a (figurative) laurel wreath
and an (actual) frosted cake. "All" included Jessie B. Rittenhouse, whose slender lyrics were attenuations of Sara's, her
mother, and John Myers O'Hara, the determined Bohemian
to whom I have referred in an earlier chapter. I gathered
that O'Hara was courting Sara—she was always on the verge
of a poetic but carefully controlled passion—but Sara did not
take his dramatic attitudes too seriously. "J. M. O. writes
that he is going *if* he is 'in the mood.' You can imagine from
this that he is *very* temperamental. Everybody seems to be,
except two or three of us. Heaven knows what glorious stuff

we'd do if our impulse to write was so terrible that we were forced, like Blanche Shoemaker Wagstaff, to carry around a gold memorandum case and a gold pencil! She says she is never without it. It would be tragic if a great golden thought should come and she were unprepared to record it! . . . As for J. M. O.—I've never seen him in any other mood but one, so I suppose that must be THE one. He is always in the Shadow (the capital is Mrs. W's), and one's whole impulse is to take him by the wrists and pull him into the sun."

I remember little of our pilgrimage to the author of "The Man with the Hoe" except that a great deal of poetry was read and very little was said. We were all too polite to comment on each other's productions, and we were intimidated by our host, the one among us who had achieved fame (and some fortune) as an oracle. Besides, we were tired. There was a long preliminary ride on the 6th Avenue Elevated (Sara met us at the 28th Street Station), and the longer journey on the three o'clock boat at the South Ferry. Then there was the seemingly interminable trolley trip from St. George to Westerleigh Park, in West New Brighton. The bard welcomed us in vatic strophes—or so it seemed—and his silver-haired wife moved with charm and dignity among the teacups. Looking back from the disadvantage point of years, I see him as a deity dispossessed and declining on a suburban Olympus. But he did not seem that way then. Then it was the god who spoke, a god young at 60, and when we heard thunder in the air we knew whose power released the lightnings. The sonorous voice rose; the rain fell. We returned home in storm and silence.

Six weeks later Sara returned to the large house and her doting parents in St. Louis; her notes became more intimate and they bore the embossed family crest, in which a teasel (doubtless a heraldic pun for Teasdale) is rampant. There are passages recalling the poetry evenings at Miss Rittenhouse's, one of which was apparently "For Men Only," where the women were privileged to listen; references to O'Hara, her coy swain; to Mouquin's; and other New York reminiscences. There is a long query about her first publisher who wants to sell her the unbound "remainders" of her first volume, although her parents had paid the "exorbitant" sum of $290.00 for one thousand copies. ("Oh, I was very young and innocent then, and had been sick in bed for months, so that anything I wanted that my parents could possibly get, came to me.") There are pictures of her father, an elder straight out of the Old Testament, with a long, forked white beard and Congress gaiters. There are notes telling of her pleasure in seeing my verse quoted here and there. Then she went abroad.

Although Sara was twenty-eight, nice young women did not go abroad alone, so Sara was accompanied by Jessie B. Rittenhouse ("or Jessica, as she wishes to be called") and an electric stove. Her modesty demanded a companion; her caution warned her that the Hamburg-Amerika Line would not protect her against adventurers and cold drafts. She was delighted with the unknown world, her first escapade. "I have never been happier in my life. Everything, even the electric stove, is perfect." Armed with prudence, the poet could feel bold, even a bit shameless. She sharpened her pencil. "Last night I waked up (or does one say 'woke up') and in a second, splash! came a lot of sea-water into my berth from the open porthole. Things had been perfectly quiet before that; and how that one over-gay wave happened to be so far from the sea, I shall never know. Thereupon, of course, I made a poem, as Dante would say, and said that Poseidon was wooing me. I chid him for not having the generosity and elegance of Zeus, who gave his lady-love gold instead of a cold shower."

Sara made the Grand Tour: Italy, Switzerland, Germany, France. I can trace her excited progress by the spate of picture postcards that followed. It was all of twelve years later that I made the almost identical journey. But at that time Sara seemed to be moving in another universe. Gibraltar, Sorrento, Capri, Perugia, Firenze, Interlaken, Montreux, Heidelberg, Paris—the syllables made music and glowed with a brilliance matched only by the incredibly colored photographs. From Bellagio she wrote: "I spend my time wondering if I am living in a Maxfield Parrish picture or in an A. M. Robinson rispetto." From the Villa Serbelloni facing Isola Comacina, Sara recalled a poem of mine, "God's Youth," and said, "If Lake Como is real, God made it when he was indeed young and exuberant." From Stresa on Lake Maggiore, looking at Isola Bella: "This island is the most unreal thing in the world, and one of the loveliest. It is as exquisite, formal, and artificial as a French verse form." From Florence: "This [a sculptured Madonna and Child] is one of Michelangelo's things, left unfinished like most of his sculptures here. I have a theory that Rodin learned the trick from him." From Como again: "When one sends laurel to a poet, one should accompany it with a graceful triolet or a charming rispetto. I have written the triolet—but it wasn't graceful, and the rispetto—but it wasn't charming. So the leaves must go alone." At Interlaken the electric stove refused to radiate: "We are freezing to death in this hotel-

ridden town. But the Jungfrau is so glittering white that
you forgive the tourist crowds and everything but the cold.
I am reduced to an icicle." In September, after four months
abroad, she was back in America, alternating between the
large house in Kingsbury Place, St. Louis, and the summer
home at Charlevoix, Michigan.

More letters and more visits to New York reveal the
growth of the fluttering girl and the constant writer into
the withdrawn woman and the mature poet. Sara had always
had a deep concern, almost an identification, with Sappho;
for this very reason she had refused to believe that there
was anything abnormal in Sappho's life. At one time, Sara
maintained that Sappho was called a Lesbian only because
she lived on the island of Lesbos. Later she insisted that
Sappho was not merely a poet, but a teacher, a sort of glorified drill-master; and that Anactoria, Erinna, and the other
girl-friends were day-students in a respectable Greek female
seminary. Gradually she accepted Sappho, not only as the
mother of the illegitimate Cleis, but as a woman whose virtue was in her work rather than in her life. After she moved
to New York I never heard her use the words "nice" and
"moral" without a suspicion of distaste. Even in 1912 she
wrote: "My conception of Sappho is undergoing a considerable change. I am beginning to see her not so much as a
woman love-torn (or lovelorn) but as a real priestess of passion. I know the phrase has an unpleasantly Ella Wheeler
Wilcoxian sound; but, in spite of the alliteration, it is what
I mean and what I will try to say." And again: "I have an
idea for another Sappho monologue. I'm going to let it sim-
mer for several months, and in the meanwhile I don't know
whether or not to allow myself to write any songs in the

mood of the new Sappho poem. I think sometimes that an idea that might really amount to something can be exhausted by doing an eight-line stanza that doesn't express more than a thousandth part of what you want to say."

There were at least two versions of the Sappho poem. One came at Christmas ("Here is the Christmas spirit with a vengeance! Sappho and the Leucadian rock on Christmas eve!"), the other in January. The beginning and end of the monolog contain some of Sara's surest lines. It is traditional, yet it is her own spirit and her own musical way with language that make her conclude:

> *It is not for a single god I go.*
> *I have grown weary of the winds of heaven.*
> *I will not be a reed to hold the sound*
> *Of whatsoever breath the gods may blow,*
> *Turning my torment into music for them. . . .*
> *The gods have given life; I gave them song.*
> *The debt is paid, and now I turn to go.*

Travel had not only stimulated Sara, it had infected her. She loved her parents, but she began to hate her surroundings. ("There is no one here I care a straw for.") She saw herself a lonely princess growing old in a crumbling tower, a virgin Sappho chained to the rock of St. Louis. New York became her lodestar, her eventual goal. She compromised on visits to Chicago.

III

Her first letters from Chicago are all exuberance. The lake is superb; the theatre is exciting; the weather is glorious; the parties are superlative. Every prospect pleases and every person is a romance. The literary life whirls, for the first time, around her. Gradually, however, the giddy girl subsides, and the young spinster again takes possession. It is with a queer mixture of pride and priggishness that Sara discloses the Chicago literary background and herself:

Margery lives in a store (called by courtesy a "studio") way over on the south side of town, and her husband lives around the corner in another. . . . Heavens, what a world! You see SEX written over every inch of it. It is fairly screamed at you. Sometimes you can't help feeling a bit apologetic in regard to your own lack of experience. One woman poured an unstemmable tide of violent details into my ears the other night. I had thought of her before as a good-hearted, harmless, and rather romantic creature who had written some passable verse. But suddenly she revealed herself as a lady with not one but many pasts, eager to lay them before me in all their glory! In my desire to be honest I confessed that, to my sorrow, I knew one or two of her secrets. Did that worry her? Not a bit. Utterly against my will I was made the recipient of many more.

All this occurred in a boarding-house bed-room (hers) where she was probably overheard; and in that case if it comes out she will blame me as the guilty one who let out her flaming secrets. Heavens, I was utterly upset when I got home. . . . It is my sense of taste, as well as my conventional bringing up, that is jarred horribly by this. I would make the most terrible fiasco of being "advanced." Well, there is no danger of my ever trying it. . . .

I must tell you something that will amuse you. Margery offered me her studio to live in while she goes away on a visit. Now the joke of this is the contrast of S. T.'s bringing up—and the studio. The latter, as I said, is a small one-story frame store, one of a row of similar buildings, down in the end of nowhere. Male and

female artists live in the stores on either side, and drop into the
one and only room at all hours of the day or night. There is a
sink, but no bath or stationary stand; and, as I said, one room
only, which opens directly on the street. Margery has had a sort
of partition put up to divide the kitchen from the bedroom-
parlor-living-room, all of which is in the front of the store. The
boys who live next door open a door in their backroom—or,
rather, in the back part of their only room—and behold, they are
with you, for the two stores are connected in this way. It is the
most "emancipated" place I ever saw. . . .

Of course Miss Monroe isn't like that lot. She has been a dear
to me—so much gentler and finer than I had thought her in
New York. Here is a tragedy: a woman sensitive and loving, crying out for affection, and yet so repressed and shy that everybody thinks her hard and bitter. . . .

It was the less lovable side of Miss Monroe that I usually
met. She did not seem either hard or bitter, but I must confess she seemed definitely astringent. I admired her purpose
and her pertinacity; I respected the impulse that changed a
society woman into an editor of poetry and a friend of poets.
Yet I cannot claim that I was fond of her. A feud had developed between us. For one thing, I had lampooned her
high-handed manner of handling manuscripts, scribbling
suggestions and penciling annotations over the submitted
sheets. For another, I had intimated that *Poetry: A Magazine
of Verse* was helped, if not made, by the renaissance of poetry
which began when the magazine was founded, whereas she
implied that the excitement about the new poetry was caused
by the magazine. I demurred; she never forgave me. I
should have known better than to have belittled the small
monthly, even by inference. It published some of the most

famous poets and much of the best verse of the period. It was an important outlet and a focus. But my chief mistake was criticizing it because it was Miss Monroe's. It was her unassailably spotless ewe lamb, the virgin's belated child. We quarreled about it at long distance; we argued face to face.

I remember one of our more embarrassing encounters. We were having lunch at *Le Petit Gourmet* in the days when Mrs. Moody was supervising that excellent restaurant. Miss Monroe and I were trying to compromise our differences. She was more gracious than I had ever seen her; the food was delicious; I was practically won over.

"You know," Miss Monroe said, "perhaps our quarrel is not so personal. Perhaps it is only a matter of locale. East versus West. Athens and Sparta."

"Of course," I replied eagerly. "That explains it all. We in the East have taken too much of our culture for granted, while you in Sparta—"

"Sparta!" She froze immediately. "*We* are not Sparta! I assumed you knew that Chicago had become the Athens of America. Even your friend Mencken has been saying that the literary heart of the country is in the Middle West! It isn't just that you in the East lack our physical vitality; you lack—"

And the feud was on again.

(Harriet Monroe and Harriet Moody—what an amazing pair they were. I saw them together at intervals here and there. They were a strange contrast, yet both were definitely challenging, affirmative, Chicagoan. Harriet Moody was the widow of the poet William Vaughn Moody; she had enriched his brief life and made possible his work. After his death, she opened her home unreservedly to all lovers of the art. Once an impecunious painter was asked to dinner and remained three months. In her early years she had been her own housekeeper. Later she had not only learned the art of cookery but its countless nuances; she became a genius in the preparation of food. She organized the Home Delicacies Company, which catered to the most exclusive private houses and the largest department stores. She made a fortune and, because of her trust in untrustworthy subordinates, lost it. She ended, as she began, in poverty. I like to remember her in her days of affluence, the breeziest of hostesses, when she would serve sixteen as easily as six, each at a little table in the circle of her huge living room. Never have soups been so cunningly prepared; never have entrées been such a series of surprises; never have conversations been so brilliantly impromptu. Harriet Moody spiced every dish. She was affectionate but not oversweet; charitable without being ostentatious; witty but never malicious. In her heartiness and humor, as well as in her pervasive charm, she reminded me of Amy Lowell, an Amy Lowell without an ax to grind.)

But it was Harriet Monroe that prompted this digression, and it was Sara who brought me to Harriet Monroe. Sara often ridiculed the parochialism and frequent pretensions of *Poetry: A Magazine of Verse,* but she never made fun of its editor. Once a friendship was established, nothing could shake it for Sara; she was the most instinctively loyal person I knew.

It is evident from Sara's letters that I never was given a chance to appreciate Miss Monroe. "She is not a lovable person on first acquaintance, but, after you know her, she is one of the deepest, tenderest women I ever knew—and she is 'on to' herself as J. B. and a lot of others never could be. In the midst of the emotional vortex of Chicago she was a godsend when I felt as though the whole world were slipping into a Swinburnian hell."

In another letter containing a devastating criticism of Miss Monroe's magazine, she maintains that, in spite of the evidence, "H. M. is fine. She has the gentle art of making enemies down to such an exquisitely fine point that Whistler would have sat at her feet like the man in the Bible at the feet of Gamaliel. She is an unpleasant person on the surface, full of sharp words. But she is waiting to be loved, and you must love her ere to you she will seem worthy of your love, as the bard saith." Because of Harriet Monroe, Sara thought of living in Chicago. But her parents, well over seventy, were still alive and possessive. Besides, Sara was planning longer and more frequent visits to New York. Many of her St. Louis friends had moved to "Gehenna-on-the-Hudson" (Orrick Johns and Zoe Akins, the playwright who began as a poet, had established themselves there), and she had begun a long friendship with John Hall Wheelock, a poet who wrote sonorous lyrics, looked like a young E. A. Robinson, and lived in New York.

Her attitude to Wheelock was by turns sentimental and detached. She respected his reserve, but his impersonality piqued her. She would not say she was in love with him, yet she did not want platonism. Her concern for him and his poetry was confused: "I fear nobody can do anything with him—least of all I. I do not understand him. From my standpoint he is doing the wrong thing for the development of his art, but he is so serious about it that all the angels couldn't convince him to the contrary. He has been an enigma to me—and his letters are equally beyond my understanding." Sara tried to be romantic and aloof at the same time, and Wheelock did nothing to change the situation. Then Vachel Lindsay came bounding into her life.

I V

Sara and I already had argued about Lindsay's mettlesome poetry before we knew him. She was bothered by Lindsay's incongruities of style, but she was fascinated by his new rhythms, and both of us were enthusiastic about the rich and burly tone of the verse. Admiring the poet, we speculated about the man. Sara met him first.

A review of *General Booth Enters into Heaven* prompted her first description of him. On February 28, 1914, she wrote excitedly from St. Louis:

The review of Lindsay is great! I've this second finished it, and I've got to tell you that I'm wild about it. You have put down the *man* as well as the poet. I've not written since he came to see me, have I? He is a real man—full of eccentricities—aggressively himself. He is about middle height, blond, with eager, keen blue-gray eyes full of humor; a good talker—almost a monologist if he gets on a familiar and favorite train of thought. His voice is good, but too loud much of the time and *very* Middle West. When he reads his own poetry (recites it, rather) in this tiny study of mine, it is like being compelled to listen to a pipe-organ in an hermetically sealed safe-deposit vault. Your ears ache, and so do your nerves. The "Kallyope" *is* a *YELL!* He leaves no doubt of it.

Yet the fresh humanity of the man—his beautiful exuberance—

fills you with delight. He is a real lover of mankind, with a humorous tenderness for its weaknesses. You forgive the celluloid collar and the long craning neck that seems to grow unspeakably when he lifts his voice in recitation.

You will like him. He has, quite literally, clean hands and a pure heart. He is coming back again in a week or so, and I'm looking forward to it. In his conversation there is the same racy fluency that there is in his prose, and here in St. Louis, where everybody is in New York (Irish bull) it is a joy to have him come.

It was Vachel's "beautiful exuberance" that captivated Sara. There was a second visit, and a third, and then the letters from Springfield came every day. Sometimes the letters were accompanied by gay griffins and prancing unicorns; sometimes they were a large single sheet of verse; sometimes they were fourteen pages of sheer high-spirited fancy. Sara protested that neither of them was in love—protested too much and too often—but never once did she reprove the letter-writer or discourage the man. Two months after she described her first vivid impression of him, she wrote me again:

Vachel had expected to spend the day with me today. But the hoped-for check didn't come that was to have brought him over the hundred prairie miles between Springfield and St. Louis. So he is languishing (he says) in loneliness.

His daily letters are a delight, though I realize I am only a peg to hang correspondence on. There never is and never could be anything but friendship between us. But he adores to pretend devotion, and since he does it with charm and humor, and since he doesn't expect any return, all is well.

The strange courtship went on. Vachel wooed his Gloriana with badinage and vehemence. She did not dissuade him, but he was too much for her. In his presence she was frailer than ever; after his visits she felt drained and spent. Nevertheless, the poetess of passion had a well-developed streak of caution and a touch of canniness. She thought something of her heart, but more of her future. She wanted desperately to get away from St. Louis—"I don't see how I'm going to stand it here. My parents are fairly well, but the atmosphere of antiquity seems to brood over this house, and I long to be off." But where and how? Her friends were married, abroad, or embarked on careers. She was eager to be loved, but she was still more anxious to be secure. What could Vachel offer? What did he have to give a sickly, protected woman of thirty, besides flowery adoration and inexhaustible (and exhausting) energy?

The strain was too fatiguing for her. "I have been living under the torrent that flows from Vachel's pen for six months daily, and now (under the vernal influence) sometimes twice-daily letters." She, who had always been half ready to fall in love with a poet, began to suspect that poets might not make the best companions for life, even for long. Her friend Orrick Johns had married "a painter-person" from Babylon; the town was Babylon on Long Island, but to Sara it might as well have been the original fountain-head of wickedness. She suddenly became obsessed with two fears: the fear of becoming an old maid and the fear of marrying a poet. Significantly she wrote, "What shall I do about Vachel? Would there be any excuse for my marrying him? I wish you would tell me some way definitely to say no—and yet I do not want wholly to lose him." And again: "Sterling, as you probably know, has been divorced and is remarrying a nineteen-year-old heiress. He intends building temples to Aphrodite in the Cyclades, and other delicate poetic affectations. . . . John O'Hara talks of returning to Ireland and living in his ancient baronial hall. He declares that he is a baron of something and that Asquith intends to reinstate him. . . . So do the bards build their houses of cards.'

Sara's house was to be no house of cards, no insubstantial poet's palace of art. She ceased to be charmed by the itinerant dreamer; she grew critical of Vachel's poetry. She appreciated his devotion and his dedications, but she mocked his fantastic structure of "whim and glittering dream"; she could not live in it. She learned to say no to Vachel in everything but words.

Her decision was made somewhat easier by the support of her friends, to whom she constantly turned, and by a person who had long admired her work but who was scarcely acquainted with her. This man was Ernst Filsinger, a shoe-merchant of St. Louis, later to become an authority on international trade. Ernst was tall, foreign-looking without being romantic, serious in a rather lugubrious way, sympathetic and vaguely literary. When he talked about Sara's poetry (which he did whenever he talked) his voice took on an almost hushed portentousness. I saw him constantly in New York and, though I was fond of him, I never felt the desire for close relations which Sara established so easily. He always seemed to me a little like a diplomat on a secret mission and a little like the head-usher in a funeral parlor. He was the perfect background for a poet; he was—or should have been—the perfect husband for Sara.

Sara's first reference to Ernst foreshadows the conclusion.

In April she wrote, "If it were not for a splendid new friend, a business-man who knows about everything (a very rare bird in St. Louis) named Ernst Filsinger, whom I want you to meet, I'd be terribly blue." A month later she was more despondent than ever. Her father was seventy-five and had suffered a stroke; her mother (who lived to be over eighty) was continually "failing." Sara was warned that there might be a fatality as the result of the least excitement. She dreaded to make a move or even an announcement; she became a paradox of responsibility and resentment. ("There seems to be no escape; it stretches ahead for years.") On the verge of a nervous breakdown, she ran away for a week in the country. There, with a combination of secrecy and shrewdness, she successively entertained her two suitors. She pitted the color and irresponsibility of the one against the dependable sobriety of the other. "We took long walks over the hills and found a lot of bright, cold springs hidden away in the rocks, and the nights were glorious with the moon—so, after all, it was better than writing down emotions in a notebook."

Frightened by the imminent death of her father, fearful of being alone, she could not decide what to do. But a decision was imperative. Sense and sensibility fought within her; there was no possibility of compromise. She came to New York for a respite and consultation. Here, too, the counsel of her friends was contradictory. She returned home feverish and cold at heart. Then, overwhelmed by Vachel, she acted. On August 24, 1914, she wrote from Charlevoix: "This very gay card brings happy news. I am deeply in love with Ernst Filsinger and am engaged to him. My family and his are both well pleased and everything looks joyous. I want you to be the first people to know it."

V

For a while after their marriage, Ernst and Sara lived with her parents; they established a New York residence only after her father died. Marriage should have cured Sara of most of her malaises. But it did not. She tried California for a season, but was bored by "the lovely and perpetually uninteresting climate." Ernst, who had left the shoe business, went abroad to investigate trade conditions in Central and Southern Europe; but, though she longed for the Mediterranean, Sara could not summon sufficient strength to accompany him. Even when Ernst was at home, "social evenings" were more than she could manage, and, though she loved music, she rarely went with him to concerts. Sara had no children; she never tried to increase the circle of her few friends. Ernst made almost no demands upon her, but she retreated further into a withdrawn privacy. She did not resent Ernst; she resented marriage.

Twelve years passed. The surface remained undisturbed. Her poetry grew warmer and wiser; her life grew steadily more spinsterlike. There were no scenes, no ruptures, no complaints. But one day, without a word to her most intimate friends, Sara went to Reno under an assumed name and divorced Ernst.

Now she was really alone. She came back to New York, moved into a small apartment, saw practically no one. For a while it was thought she had made a sad adjustment but found a new tranquillity. Her poems were not merely re-

signed, they attained a kind of somber radiance. Already in
Dark of the Moon, published toward the end of her marriage, there was a preoccupation with the autumnal beginnings of age, the omens of night, the unhappy mutability
of life. Now the note grew more stoical. Without parading
her hurt and boasting of her bravery—a combination beloved by the lyrical sisters of Niobe—she made courage tangible. She refused to indulge in querulous moods and cries of
frustration. The emotion was enriched and yet restrained,
compressed into the essential spirit, a last serenity. It is a
final irony that her readers grew less as her work grew
greater. The heart was too deeply moved to flutter light
pulses.

More and more she withdrew into herself. Premonitions
of loss and death began to appear in her lines. Even her
early verses were curiously prophetic:

> *I must have passed the crest a while ago*
> *And now I am going down—*

It is sounded in the exquisite:

> *Let it be forgotten, as a flower is forgotten,*
> *Forgotten as a fire that once was singing gold,*
> *Let it be forgotten for ever and ever.*
> *Time is a kind friend, he will make us old.*

And again, with a not altogether convincing note of pride,
the pride of the solitary:

> *My heart has grown rich that the passing of years,*
> *I have less need now than when I was young*

> *To share myself with every comer,*
> *Or shape my thoughts into words with my tongue.*

She tried to escape again, but this time it was even more futile, for she was trying to escape herself. After the divorce, she visited the Adirondack mountain-farm from which I write, and brought me a chart of the stars. Earth concerned her less now than the heavens; she had always been interested in astronomy—she had once written that my trip to Florida would be worth while if only for a sight of Canopus —but now she was centered in Arcturus. Arcturus, the bright bringer of spring, left toward the end of summer, and its decline reminded Sara too poignantly of her own autumn:

> *I saw you sink and vanish, pitiless Arcturus;*
> *You will not stay to share our lengthening night.*

It was a lengthening night indeed. Sara hoped to break it with a return to England; but her income had dwindled, and she, who never had to worry about economies, began to dread poverty. She started to work on a critical biography of Christina Rossetti, her earliest influence, but she lacked the power to complete it. Her life, like Vachel's, was darkening to its close. There was a brief respite from loneliness and melancholy. She found a late rapport with a young girl who was both her secretary and her solace. But the rift within her own nature was widening. Nothing could bridge the desire to be loved and the greater desire to be alone.

The death of Vachel Lindsay increased her sense of solitude. She wrote that her brief joy in the Adirondacks "seemed to be given as the prelude to what was so soon to be a tragedy—Vachel's death. To me it was a special tragedy, for he was one of the half dozen people who ever meant anything real to me."

How much further could she be isolated? Where could she retire? How much longer could she suffer estrangement from the world? She asked the heaven of stars; she asked the darkened sea. There were no answers. The last letter I received from her ended: "These days are rather like living in a prolonged hurricane. I think we look up in surprise to find that a roof is still over our heads."

Deliberately she began to put her affairs in the precise order characteristic of her. She thought again of Sappho—and remembered the Leucadian rock. She prepared to take the final plunge.

> *I have grown weary of the winds of heaven.*
> *I will not be a reed to hold the sound*
> *Of whatsoever breath the gods may blow. . . .*
> *The gods have given life; I gave them song.*
> *The debt is paid, and now I turn to go.*

The debt was paid. She turned to go. In January, 1933, a year and a month after Vachel's suicide, she swallowed an overdose of sleeping tablets. They found her body submerged in the bathtub.

THE BAD BOY OF BALTIMORE

THE QUALITY of friendship, unlike that of mercy, is continually being strained. But it is the essence of friendship that it can stand the strain. When I think of what my friends have had to put up with before I attained the venerable calm and rustic dignity which have now transformed my once unpleasant features . . . But I prefer not to think about it.

It was Cicero, I believe, who said that a friend is a second self. But that is not enough. The self is all too apt to turn upon one with distrust and self-consciousness; a second self would be critical beyond endurance. A friend offers that combination of intimacy and loyalty which can be expected only of one's family—and the friend has the advantage of not being a relative. I suppose I am trying to say that friendship is like love at its best: not blind but sympathetically all-seeing; a support which does not wait for understanding; an act of faith which does not need, but always has, reason.

Hundreds of acquaintances have entertained, amused, and instructed me; it is my friends who have saved me. "Nobody knows the trouble I've seen; nobody knows but—" And here I think of perhaps a dozen people dead and living who have really known me when I would not care to know myself. They can use me as they will. It is right, not shameful, that friendship may be valued in usefulness. For who but one's friends can use—and abuse—one so consistently with so little resentment.

No one has abused me more variously than Lee Simonson, and no one has held my affection for a greater length of time. Whatever I have been to anyone else, I have been Lee's whipping-boy. I have served him faithfully in that capacity ever since we first met at the Weingart Summer School in the Catskill Mountains. I was twelve years old then, two years Lee's senior and many times—I hope I am not boasting—his physical superior. But, even at ten, Lee was the school sophisticate; the first intellectual I ever knew, and I (then one of the lesser members of the second-string baseball team) let him tell me what to do. I have, except during a few revolting intervals, done it ever since.

When I was struggling out of my adolescence and into the jewelry business, Lee was sitting at the feet of (and probably prompting) Santayana. During the years when Lee was attending Harvard, I was selling lockets and link-buttons to Jordan Marsh and Company in Boston. I would take Lee to the Parker House for dinner, and, in return, Lee would read me a lecture on my bad taste and his own literary gods, who happened at that time to be Swinburne, Whistler, Shaw and Chesterton. When I began to write and Lee went to Paris to become a painter, his spirited animadversions (by mail) would make my verse sound prosy and frighten me out of writing prose entirely. He goaded me into a kind of comic rivalry. We tried to outdo each other in work, puns, children, homes in the country, lecture engagements, and perennial gardens. We still do. When I have been really distressed, Lee has suffered with me; but when I am temporarily discomfited, Lee is pleased. This, in turn, pleases me. Lee likes to triumph, and I like him to be happy.

Lee is perhaps happiest when he is disemboweling one of

my chapters. He can sniff a cliché six paragraphs away and spot a loose construction before it is put together. I will never forget the time I gave Lee the first section of my Heine biography. It was the quick rough typescript, and Lee took it over to our guest-house for an hour's casual reading. He met us at the swimming-pool late in the afternoon with a manuscript that I recognized only because of its size. There was more of Lee's writing than mine on the sheets; the original paragraphs were finely shredded; not a sentence was left unscratched, not an epithet unscathed. Never has there been such painstaking—and pains-giving—evaluation.

This is not to imply that Lee is ungenerous. During the summer Lee rarely comes to swim in our icy pool without bringing some of the glories of his garden: enormous sunset-colored snapdragons, rare hemerocallis hybrids, seven foot spikes of delphinium. I raise delphiniums myself—hedges of them—and Lee never fails to compliment me upon their mass and color. But he also never fails to show me how inferior my strain happens to be, how much smaller the individual florets are, and how impossible it seems for me to grow the true, deep bishop's purple. I could point out to him that my commoner varieties thrive, whereas his hand-fed aristocrats develop black-spot and refuse to come up the following season. But I do not. Lee has great borders of iris, and he dutifully admires the rich velvet Ambassadeurs, Butos, and Brunos which line my stream on both sides. Once he even went so far as to express regret when root-rot and borers devastated some fifty tall Asias, yet his condolence was a trifle forced, definitely tinged with *Schadenfreude*. But, though I am discomfited, I do not complain. The motto of a close friend might well be: chagrin—and bear it.

It is curious to observe how Lee's creative life has de-

scribed a complete cycle. He began as a writer, a prose
stylist. Then there was a change of allegiance; he made a
brilliant debut as a painter, and immediately thereafter
abandoned painting. Next he turned to the theatre; he put
on plays, invented lighting systems, created some of the
finest settings of the day. From the theatre he turned to furniture and industrial design—he made a piano and called it
"Death of a Simile" because it stood delicately on graceful
metal supports instead of the proverbially thick wooden
legs. Then the circle came full, and Lee was once more a
writer, a prose stylist. He incorporated his researches and
speculations in the brilliantly written *The Stage Is Set*.

Lee came back to himself with renewed vigor; he flourished in critical reappraisal and luxuriated in epigram. I
particularly cherish his "The news in our newspapers is
written by the garrulous for the gullible." And Rochefou-
cauld himself might have said, "Nothing is foreordained
except in retrospect." In fact I once thought it was a translation; but I am assured—by Lee himself—that I was wrong.

There are times I am tempted to criticize Lee's packed
paragraphs, his almost too constant use of balance and
aphorism. But I would no more think of assailing his style
than attacking his profile, which, differing from my own
undistinguished lineaments, has all the qualities of a good
(though slightly rubbed) Rhajput miniature. I do not want
to alter our rôles. There is no mirror like an old friend, and
I prefer to see myself the way Lee sees me.

II

I must have had playmates. Like Charles Lamb, I must
have had companions in the days of my childhood, in my

not too joyful schooldays. But, with the exception of Lee, "all, all are gone, the old familiar faces." Not until I was in my mid-twenties, married, a designer-salesman of jewelry, and the author of a book of saccharine lyrics did I form another friendship which lasted the rest of my life—or as much of it as I have lived up to this sentence. The friend was, and still is, Henry Louis Mencken, then a writer and occasionally a book reviewer for *The Baltimore Sun*. Mencken began by (quite properly) abusing my book of verse; I retaliated by abusing his book on Nietzsche. It was an auspicious start. Had I winced or cried aloud I never would have heard from him and we would never have been friends. The attack achieved more than any defense could have accomplished. I did not then know how much Mencken relished violence and invectives. I could not know that some day he would be reckoned among the masters of malediction, libel, and critical cursing; but his first letter to me, early in 1912, ended: "Why doesn't someone start a magazine for criticizing critics? They need it badly—and honest invective is always readable."

The adjective in the sentence just quoted is somewhat irrelevant and immaterial. Mencken never insisted on the honesty of invective as long as the diatribe was sufficiently thumping and calculated to "stir up the animals." He up-braided others and received a triple measure of vituperation in return. He enjoyed the hoots and castigations; he collected them. It was characteristic of him that he issued a *Schimpflexikon* about himself; an extraordinary collection of cat-calls, billingsgate, venom, lies, lampoons, larrupings, ugly names, uglier insinuations, and downright obscenity.

But this was to come later. It was on the basis of poetry

that we first established a contact. In his second letter he confessed it: "I used to be a poet myself—and not such a bad one either, by gar!" It was with a book of poetry that Mencken had made his debut. Its unblushing name was *Ventures into Verse,* and it contained an orthodox lot of ballads, ballades, rondeaux, triolets, roundels, to say nothing of sweetly assorted songs, quatrains, and even an ode or two. The book is now a collector's item of the rarest; it was said that the author spent years locating incriminating copies, snatching them from his friends' shelves, and even stealing them from public libraries. It was not until many years later that Henry became an anti-poet, a man who could never read a sonnet without comparing it (to its disadvantage) with Lizette Woodworth Reese's "Tears," and who admitted to me that the only kind of poem guaranteed to make him weep was a poem about a dog. In 1912, however, he was not only taking poets seriously, he was discovering them. He urged me to write an article on Mary C. Burke, whom he considered louder and funnier than James Byron Elmore or even J. Gordon Coogler. I had roared over Miss Burke's gorgeously bad verse in F.P.A.'s column, but Henry insisted that Adams got acquainted with her absurdities through a threat of a libel suit against him and his journal. He called my attention to another poet of a different order, a poet who was just beginning to submit shy songs to the metropolitan magazines. "Keep your eye on Sara Teasdale. I haven't the slightest notion who she is, but some of her lyrics come very near *It.* They show the influence of Lizette Woodworth Reese."

Then we met.

I had expected to see a sly, satanic fellow, dark-browed,

fierce, with a suggestion of brimstone, and I had looked forward to hearing lewd heresies and mutterings of the Black Mass. Instead I saw a chubby, moon-faced familiar, a cross between an English Puck and a German *Spitzbube*. His yellow hair was parted in the middle and neatly plastered down; his eyes were jolly and blue; his snub nose was impudent. His expression reminded me a little of the traditional Rabelaisian priest and a little of the boy who has just delivered the meat to the wrong address.

In speech Henry Mencken was equally incongruous. Chuckles punctuated every conversation. He would dislodge pretentious reputations with a toppling exaggeration, and deliver the foulest epithets with the sunniest innocence. Implacable enemies would find themselves capitulating within the first few minutes; the coldest hate would have to thaw before such easy warmth. He despised humanity, the great "booboisie," and loved persons.

Soon we were eating and drinking together. As a traveling salesman I sold jewelry to the leading Maryland installment houses, which, in turn, sold it to the more affluent members of the better brothels. But I visited Baltimore oftener than the trade warranted. The chance of combining Mencken and Maryland food was something not to be resisted. My headquarters were at the Hotel Rennert, but my misguided sense of taste made me eat in the stuffy dining room with stuffier prospects and buyers. It was Henry who rescued me from the heavy curtains and the matching table d'hôte. He took me down to the basement lunch-counter, then the best restaurant in America, with the exception of Antoine's in New Orleans, the original Mouquin's on New York's Sixth Avenue, and Krebs's in Skaneateles. There he

introduced me to imperial deviled crabs such as the world
has never seen before or since; to oyster potpie crammed
with a mysterious succulence instead of the heated rubber
found in most oyster stews; to broiled shad, which a few
hours before had been cavorting along the Eastern Shore; to
thick slices of young boiled turkey thoroughly immersed in
oyster sauce, a dish which has never been so cunningly prepared except in Henry's own home. No one in this world
of casualty can hope to choose his own death. But if I were
allowed such a boon, I would choose to die in the basement
lunch-counter of the old Hotel Rennert—not the renovated
chain-store hotel now in operation—eating shad-roe and listening to Mencken with one ear and *Die Meistersinger* with
the other.

It was after our first prandial orgy that the letters began.
Of all my friends, John Crowe Ransom is the world's worst
correspondent, Henry Mencken is the best. Certainly he is
the promptest as well as the most voluminous. He never
fails to reply to strangers as readily as to intimates; he answers appeals, inquiries, and controversies—usually on the
same day that the mail arrives. What with moving about the
world and establishing various habitations, I have failed to
keep most of my correspondence. Yet my incomplete files
have disgorged more than three hundred letters, cards, and
"items," many of them pure banter and not a few bawdy.
The "items" are perhaps the most characteristic. They include inscriptions in Mencken's volumes; e.g., "An early
edition for a late connoisseur, not for review," "To Louis
Untermeyer, in the hope of rescuing him from his Socialistic
debaucheries," "To Louis, on the day of the solemn refer-
endum" (obviously Election Day), "To my venerable brother

in God, Louis Untermeyer, this free copy, *not to be sold.*"
They also include a series of hoaxes, practical jokes, and
grotesqueries. For years Henry, who is the blondest of
Nordics, sent me an annual Jewish New Year's Card with
an appended translation in sentimental rhyme. Every February fourteenth I could expect a large comic valentine—
a cartoon horribly colored which cost ten cents a dozen;
Henry bought them by the hundred. His letters frequently
enclosed illiterate tracts, job-printed religious folders, mor-
tuary verses, articles on malicious animal magnetism and
tributes to somnopathology. I still have, in payment of a bet,
a beautifully engraved but worthless first mortgage bond of
the Maryland Brewing Company which Henry sent me, complete with unclipped coupons of $30 each from March, 1918,
to March, 1938. In 1917 I received a series of pamphlets in
plain envelopes (mailed from Baltimore) on the wonders of
the Emanuel Movement; this was followed by a series of
advertisements (in the same postmarked envelopes) recommending a course in sex hygiene. Once a week for several
months I received the same impressive handbill; it read
"Prepare to meet thy God TODAY!"At another time I was
the recipient of a long one-sided correspondence from
Llewellyn Jackson, who wanted me to help him write a
thesis on the lesser contributors to *The Yellow Book.* For
no good reason I assumed my correspondent was some relation to Holbrook Jackson, the authority on the literature
of the Eighteen Nineties. Finally I replied, evasively but
pleasantly. Whereupon I received an ornately inscribed
cabinet photograph from Mr. Jackson himself. The picture
was that of a colored gentleman in a badly fitting second-
hand suit, obviously a porter dressed for Sunday and the

photographer. There was no doubt about its origin; it came in a large envelope from *The American Mercury*.

III

In a long list of pleasantries, perhaps my favorite incident is one that has already become a legend. I was recovering from a touch of grippe when a letter arrived from Henry. It was one of his more medical documents—Henry used to be in and out of Johns Hopkins and was continually giving advice to doctors. He counseled me to get rid of my physician, drink three stiff glasses of *Glühwein,* and sleep on a stolen Bible. The last injunction, he assured me, was most important; "the poor whites among whom I live find this more effective than voodoo or wood alcohol. Besides, it brings good luck." This, I thought, is another of Henry's Menckenisms; I laughed, and forgot the matter. Two days later, a worn Bible arrived by parcel post. The cover was blazoned in gold: "Property of the Hotel Astor," and the flyleaf bore this inscription: "To Louis Untermeyer, with the compliments of the Author."

If I were to sum up Mencken in terms of alliteration— something that only a Swinburne would feel called upon to do—I would fix upon the letter "v": vehement, vivid, voluble, vituperative, vulgar (in the sense of *vulgus,* the common people, whom Mencken affected to despise), vital, various, and volatile. The only things unalterably set were his strange political aversions, his anti-social protestations, and his undisturbed skepticisms. Everything else about him was incalculable—even his manner of accepting manuscripts. Oftener than not there would be a brusque line accompanying the check: the larger the check, the shorter the note. Sometimes there would be a lengthy, pseudo-scholastic analysis of the piece, and, if it were in prose, recommendations toward condensation—always to its advantage. Once in a while, the acceptance would be written as though it were dictated by a Lithuanian pants-presser or couched in Potash and Perlmutter's best business style. For example, this, received sometime in 1917:

Louis, Untermeyer, and Company
Makers of Fine Verse
The Parnassus Store, Inc.

Gents:

I have went through your samples, and have decided to lay in two models. Our check will reach you by return mail, so to speak. These goods are stylish, and we expect a good spring trade with them, as it were. On one model we notice some bum trimming. The tag is "Betrayal." You have used one "stabbed" in the front and then hung on another. Please have your designer fix this. Otherwise the model greatly pleases our Mr. Blumblatt.

We would be glad to inspect more models March 1, May 2, July 3, Sept. 4, Nov. 5, u. s. w.

At that time Mencken and George Jean Nathan were editing *The Smart Set*. The co-partnership was an ideal arrangement, especially when either editor had to reject manuscripts by friends. Mencken would blame the rejection on the absurd prejudices of Nathan, and Nathan would soften the blow by saying that Mencken's low taste was responsible. I had been a contributor to *The Smart Set* during its many metamorphoses. I had appeared in its pages when it was a decorous semi-society sheet that tried to live up to its name, when it was struggling to work its way into literature against the opposing aims of the brilliant Percival Pollard and the puzzled Norman Boyer, and when it began experimenting boldly under Willard Huntington Wright, who, as a disciple of Mencken, was almost as audacious and disturbing as his master. But, during the duumvirate of Mencken and Nathan, I became Old Contributor himself. I was dubious about the social implications (if any) of the collaboration, but the editorial combination of the boisterous Mencken and the suave Nathan created a journal such as had never been seen in America. It was impertinent but probing, almost incredibly funny (as in the departments entitled "Americana" and "The American Credo") but prevailingly critical, a flabbergastering mixture of gusto, nonsense, politics, truculence, sociology, enthusiasm for new talent, and a genuine passion for honest criticism, fine literature, and good music.

During this period my letters from Mencken begin to reveal the man. For a while the comedian is uppermost, but, though he still wears the mask of the clown, there emerges the earnest anti-reformer, the Methodist-baiter, the erudite foe of academicians, the exposer of literary shams and national hypocrisies, the pioneer crusader against crusades, the patriot roused to indignation against the professional patrioteers. The mixture is often baffling. Here, at least, is a small but significant excerpt:

By this mail goes a copy of my debate with La Monte, *Men versus The Man*. [The title page lists the authors as Robert Rives La Monte, Socialist, and H. L. Mencken, Individualist.] The book has been the worst failure known in the publishing trade for 200 years. . . . Meanwhile, I look forward to a long joint debate when you arrive. Admire Marx all you please—but how can you defend his whiskers!

Another:

I must get Viereck's stuff and swallow it; he seems a genuine comique. One thing only I object to in your review: you went at him too seriously. The prescription here was ridicule. A few sharp cuts, and he would have lost his gas and collapsed.

Another:

Just home from the inauguration—the usual stench and debauch . . . I shall throttle my disgust and read your poem in the *Century*. But that way madness lies. You will sprout whiskers and end a Henry Van Dyke. You will be praised for your "magic" by Jessie B. Rittenhouse. You will lecture at Harvard. You will break the heart of
Thine (as yet)
von und zu Mencken

(All of Mencken's predictions, with the exception of the first and last, have come true. I have not yet worn, or ended, a Van Dyke, and I have not quite broken Mencken's heart. But the lecturing and the rest have happened to confirm his worst fears. He offered to send me a set of forged college degrees when he heard the regents had appointed me "professor in residence" at the University of Michigan in 1939, and he saluted me with a letter of mock reverence and repudiation when I delivered the Henry Ward Beecher lecture in the Johnson Chapel at Amherst.)

Another:

Is your "On the Birth of a Child" topical? I like it a lot. What is life, after all, but a tedious torture? The trouble with most of us is that we are not ever tragic, but feebly comic. Death itself, in all save a few splendid forms, has a touch of low comedy. Imagine dying of angina pectoris, blue-nosed and gasping! Or of chronic interstitial nephritis! Or gonorrheal endocarditis! . . . I am enthusiastic, in particular, over your "God's Youth"—it is the perfect marriage of a good idea and the right words. Think of the Creator as a low comedian, and at once the world becomes explicable. . . . Rabelais was far nearer God than Xt.

Serious documents were followed by bursts of extravaganza. Mencken was so afraid of appearing to be the pedagog, which his Teutonic forbears had fashioned him to be, that he often revolted against the pundit by playing the buffoon. He worshiped music, but that did not prevent him from writing (in "The Artist," a drama without words) one of the funniest burlesques of a concert-performance ever written. It was on the rock of music—music buttressed by malt liquor—that our friendship was riveted. Henry and I were both first-rank devotees of the three great German Bs. (We never admitted the Gallic Berlioz in the same concert hall with Bach, Beethoven, and Brahms.) We were confident second-rate pianists and ninth-rate composers. I shall never forget the night we pounded our way through four-handed arrangements of the Brahms symphonies, Mencken keeping his foot on the loud pedal, breathing heavily through all the lush passages, and sweating profusely. What we did to Beethoven was something between sabotage and sacrilege. We never got around to Henry's beloved Papa Haydn, but we managed to commit mayhem on Richard Strauss. A few days later, at the end of a frolicsome letter, I found this:

Thanks for the news about Schoenberg. Did you know that Richard Strauss, early in life, played alto in the band at the Hofbrauhaus in Munich and suffered severely from Bismarck-herring-eaters' colic? Also, wist you that Tschaikovsky carried on an intrigue with a charwoman and got her with foal? Or that Brahms owned only one collar, and that a thing of cellulose?

That such statements were scarcely fact did not spoil Henry's pleasure in communicating them. On the contrary, he maintained that the truth in a democracy was something which was believed by, say, fifty-one per cent of the people because it was discreditable to someone. He once defined the truth which survives as "the lie that is pleasant to believe."

I V

There was a period when Mencken's sportiveness turned bitter; the World War did not quite cure him of waggishness, but it confirmed his grim skepticism. He was opposed to America entering the cataclysm partly because of his devotion to German music and literature, partly because he felt that America would be both a cat's-paw and a milch cow for the British Empire. Many of his letters were headed *"Gott strafe England"*—sometimes varied by *"Gott strafe San Marino"*—and usually ended piously "Yours in Xt." While the Y.M.C.A. was uplifting the boys in France, he usually referred to Christmas as "the birthday of your late co-religionist, Dr. J. C. Josephsohn." He almost stopped baiting the "smut-hounds" and Chautauquans to belabor the confused liberals and challenge the assumption that an American was the noblest work of God because he lived in a democracy. "My objection to Americans is that they like to fight with the enemy strapped to the board. Hence the persecution of Germans during the war, the robbery of helpless alien business men, the American Legion, the attack on Spain, the wars with Nicaragua, Santo Domingo, etc. This poltroonery is not essentially American, it is simply democratic; the inferior man always shows it." He even condescended to praise *The Masses* to which he subscribed chiefly to please me. "I begin to think that Wilson may have to abandon his plan to make the United States an English colony. The last issue of your *Masses* was packed with good stuff. Almost you persuade me to become a velvet socialist."

With the first number of *The American Mercury,* which was founded at the beginning of 1921 by Mencken and Nathan, Henry had little time for high jinks and horseplay. After traveling about Europe, I was living in Vienna, and had heard nothing of the new venture. Yet even then it was impossible for him to announce the event without a flight of introductory fictions.

Dear Louis: You have perhaps heard all the news: that Dreiser has married an enormously rich Peruvian widow; that Sandburg is in jail in Oklahoma for train robbery; and that Knopf is about to set up as a periodical publisher.

The name of the new one is to be *The American Mercury,* and I have quit *The Smart Set* (selling all my stock) to go over to it. We hope to be out by January 1st. A high-toned, but *not* too solemn magazine. Object: to survey and picture the whole American scene—politics, the sciences, and belles lettres. No foreign stuff. No *Dial* complex. And *no damned liberalism! . . .*

How long are you staying in Vienna? You are missing a superb show at home, what with Teapot Dome, the Anderson trial, and half a dozen other such gaudy spectacles. Poor Cal is sweating blood. But I believe he will be renominated and re-elected. He is a fine Christian man.

Almost at once *The American Mercury* reached the heights of magazinedom; it remained there for several years. It became a vogue as well as an influence, a Jolly Roger for the young insurgents, a weapon for the anti-respectable, and a wealth of fresh trails for the exploring student. It gaily assaulted professorial petty-mindedness, and it was read by associate professors on every campus. It shocked, but it instructed; even its queer mixture of scorn and badinage scarcely concealed its essential earnestness.

Then Mencken and Nathan had their first quarrel and their final severance. For a while, Henry ran it alone. But dividing his time between Baltimore and New York was too difficult; and, besides, he was concerned with larger works of his own, such as the growing revision of *The American Language*. Then the magazine passed from one editor to another. Finally, under Paul Palmer, it shrunk in size and spirit; its audience changed; it became a pocket omnibus of unashamed pornography and apologetic fascism. Alas, it might have made a gallant if not more decent end.

Recently there has been another reaction; the assault has come on a new front. Formerly Mencken's adversaries attacked him for his literary and philological progressivism; latterly he has been under fire for his political conservatism. He, who inveighed against "rabble-rousers," has been accused of rousing the very rabble he detested by echoing the infamous Father Coughlin on Spain, joining the popular sport of "red"-baiting, and taking a definitely anti-democratic attitude. To the last charge he might well reply that he never has pretended to worship democracy. He need not even make the rejoinder. Years ago he wrote to Burton Rascoe: "To me democracy seems to be founded wholly upon the inferior man's envy of his superior—and of the man who is having a better time. . . . If the notions of the right-thinkers are correct, then such stuff as mine ought to be put down by law. I believe that, in the long run, it *will* be put down by law—that free speech is too dangerous to democracy to be permitted."

He has said all this consistently for years; he continues to say it. The premise is so wobbly a paradox as to be treacherous for anyone except an acrobatic dialectician, but Henry's hold is rigid. In 1917, when *The Masses* was denied the use of the mails, he wrote me letters ranging from rough jocularity to unconcealed indignation. Here is one of them:

The ferocity of *The Masses* business is almost beyond belief. But, after all, it is nothing new. In time of war, democracy always falls into such extravagances. . . . Its difficulty is this: that the very free speech it is based upon makes war impossible unless the desire for it is practically unanimous. When such unanimity is absent, as is usual, it has to abolish free speech by orgy. The spectacle is staggering, but not without its logic. To argue anything in such a time seems to me to be as impossible as to stop a stampede by playing on an E clarinet.

All appeals to any intrinsic love of free speech are futile. There is no such passion in the people. It is only an aristocracy that is ever tolerant. The masses are invariably cocksure, suspicious, furious, and tyrannical. This, in fact, is the central objection to democracy: that it hinders progress by penalizing innovation and nonconformity.

Again, at about the same time:

What I can't understand is why Eastman et al. go to the expense of a defense. Why not simply stand up, ask for sentence, and go to jail? Surely it is a damn sight better to be in jail these days than to be outside, entirely surrounded by detectives, snitchers, informers, and so on. . . .

What we need is an accurate and objective record of the present process. Why don't you do it yourself? I don't mean a passionate protest, but a calm and analytical record, as cold-blooded as possible. No such writing has ever been done in America. In the midst of endless clinical material, we haven't a single study of democratic psychology. Give this your prayerful thought.

And again:

The trial is indeed shocking, but it has its logical side. What can you expect? A libertarian attitude on the part of the liberty-hating mob?

Here he impales himself upon a dilemma of inconsistencies. Mencken is against the status quo, with all its repressions and (to use one of his favorite words) obscenities. But he is not for doing anything about it. There should be accurate records, clinical studies, powerful documents, but no protests. These are evil times, but he is against change; he is convinced that any change would only be for the worse. He is in favor of an intelligent aristocracy; yet he does not know where to look for it. He jeers at the willing slaves misled by every demagog, yet he detests their masters. Humanity to him is both a shabby spectacle and a gaudy show, something to tickle the risibles and provoke a belly-laugh; but he grows serious, even as a prophet of doom, when he recounts the errors of the Government. Seemingly a philosophic anarchist, he has never championed the underdog and espoused no cause; he has always railed against the *Sklavenmoral* and has refused to worry about badgered minorities. Yet, almost against his will, he interrupts his cynicism to speak up for "the free and honest administration of fair laws, the dealing of plain justice between man and man, the protection of the weak and helpless."

Thus I see Henry trying to reconcile the irreconcilables. And here I find the key to the inconsistencies in—of all places—a review of one of my books of poems, a review which he wrote many years ago. Henry is trying to reconcile the "insistent earnestness and genuine passion" (which he distrusted in poetry) with the sheer sensuousness ("the magical escape from the soddenness of metabolisms and the class war"), the "sough and sigh" in the verbal music which he adored. Toward the end of the review he wrote: "What Untermeyer gets into all his serious verse is a passionate exultation—a sort of esthetic drunkenness, odious to the right-thinking, but not specifically forbidden by the police. This is the explanation of all his bawling against orthodoxy, which he himself often mistakes for moral indignation. He is really no reformer, not even in poetry; he is merely one privy to the taste of Greek and Sinaian grapes, and hence gagged by the national buttermilk and coca-cola."

These sentences well might summarize Henry L. Mencken himself. Apart from such sober scholasticisms as *The American Language,* that colossal and pioneering task which purged his blood of inherited pedantry, Henry's work has been full of an "esthetic drunkenness, odious to the right-thinking, but not specifically forbidden by the police. This," and I say it with gleeful emphasis, "is the explanation of all *his*

bawling against orthodoxy. . . . He is merely one privy to
the taste of Greek and Sinaian grapes"—plus a fine taste in
malt liquor—"and hence gagged by the national buttermilk
and coca-cola." Henry a politician? A heavy thinker? A poet,
my masters, a poet!

V

This, at any rate, is the way I picture Henry. Future historians may disagree. I often wonder in what rôle he will
finally be appraised. Will he be considered chiefly as a
writer of aggravating polemics? A rowdy but reactionary
journalist? An immured philologist, a fanatic student of
the vernacular? A critic with a bludgeoning vocabulary? A
disgruntled moralist masquerading as the Nietzschean *Über-
mensch* beyond good and evil? A defeated poet who took
revenge in some of the most devastating and provocative
essays of his day? An editorial discoverer, a literary midwife,
stimulating new-born talent into the life of letters? A recorder and also a creator of the contradictory American
scene?

It is the contradictions that may trip the commentators.
They will have to be wary of conclusions; they will do well
to suspect all the legends, particularly those circulated by
Henry himself. It will be hard, for example, to reconcile the
cold and ruthless individual, which his enemies have depicted, with the devoted son, the affectionate brother, and
the warm companion which he actually is. There is the con-
scienceless seducer, the mythical rakehell; the author of the
vulpine and maliciously entitled *In Defense of Women;* the
shaper of such epigrams as: "Love is the delusion that one
woman differs from another" and "On one issue, at least,

men and women agree: they both distrust women." And
there is the solitary, hard-working bachelor who, at fifty,
married Sara Haardt (a writer, an intellectual, the very type
of woman Mencken pilloried) and remained a faithful and
extraordinarily tender husband until her premature death.
The appraiser who repeats (for the hundredth time) that
A Book of Prefaces and the series of *Prejudices* are a set of
perverse exaggerations and truisms turned upside down
should remember the formula of George Bernard Shaw as
summarized by Mencken: to put the obvious in terms of the
scandalous.

Early in 1939 an article in *The Nation* described Henry
as a "graying, bright-eyed little man, astonishingly Hoover-
ish-looking." I suppose he is now. He did not seem so as he
sat across the table from me at Shellhase's beer "kaif" during a long evening only a few months ago. Doubtless I was
seeing him through the astigmatic eyes of old friendship.
For all his gathering rotundity, he did not remind me of
any dispenser of Republican platitudes; nor, in spite of his
malty bitterness, did he seem the fabled local Schopenhauer.
I forgot that Henry had become a portent, an arbiter, an
editorial influence, "a kind of prime minister without port-
folio." I even forgot the peppery satirist, the virtuoso in
words, the fashioner of a flexible native idiom; a man who,
as Edmund Wilson wrote, "is the civilized consciousness of
modern America, its learning, its intelligence and its taste,
realizing the grossness of its manners and mind, and crying
out in horror and chagrin." It may have been an aberration,
a throwback in time. But, instead of the aging misanthrope,
I saw the young shamefaced poet—shamefaced because he
had deserted us when we needed him most.

THE NORTHEAST CORNER

THE FIRST time I saw the name of Robert Frost in print was in December, 1913, in the fourth issue of *Poetry and Drama,* a new quarterly edited by Harold Monro and published in London. The contents of the magazine were distinctly British, not to say Georgian—I was acting merely as American field-worker and occasional correspondent—and I took it for granted that Robert Frost, appearing in company with Rupert Brooke, W. W. Gibson, and Lascelles Abercrombie, was another and hitherto unknown member of that group. No volume of Frost's had yet appeared; his name had not been signed to any poems except a few published when he was a youth and I was a child, in *The Independent,* of whose existence I knew nothing. Yet, what Englishman, I thought, could have written these two poems? They were "The Fear" and "A Hundred Collars." True, the drama of the former might have happened anywhere, and the place-names in the latter might have been acquired by any English visitor with an ear for quaintness. Yet there was something beneath local color and far beyond background here; something which, in its very inflection, fixed identity. This was the solid yet extraordinarily subtle turn of ordinary language, the fresh conversational idiom unerringly exact and unequivocally American. It was the accent of common speech and, at the same time, the accent of uncommon poetry. What was more, this was blank verse; yet it was a blank verse so different from the traditional English medium that it had acquired a whole new tone and direction.

A month or two later the confusion was explained. I learned what has since been enshrined in every American textbook: that Frost's career had been founded on contradictions. The chief interpreter of New England, "the northeast corner," Frost was born in the Far West, in San Francisco; until he was ten, he did not know the towns and hills where his forefathers had lived for eight generations. The most American of poets, his first book was printed in London, brought out by a Frenchwoman, the widow of an obscure English publisher. Considered by many of his critics as a bucolic philosopher—a compromise between Wordsworth in New Hampshire and Virgil in Vermont—Frost's early life was spent in cities, in action rather than in meditation. He had twice run away from college (from two colleges, to be precise); he had shamed his grandfather by working as a bobbin boy in the mills of Lawrence, Massachusetts; he had earned his living as cobbler, farmer, editor of a weekly paper, and (he said this was at the end of a descending scale) a schoolteacher. Once he had tramped through the Carolinas—not, like Vachel Lindsay trading his rhymes for bread, but looking (unsuccessfully) for work. Seemingly a recluse, one who had lived more than a dozen years in poverty, unaware of, and certainly untouched by, the literary world, he suddenly sold his farm and took his growing family to England. There, gravitating to the countryside, he found himself in the very midst of literature. Gibson and Abercrombie were his neighbors; Ezra Pound, establishing himself in London, patronized him but introduced him to the Sargasso Sea of movements and studios. This last was something of a concession, for Frost was the friend of Abercrombie whom Pound had challenged to a duel, the weapons to be unsold copies of their books at thirty paces.

It was upon Frost's return to America early in 1915 that I met him. His first volume, *A Boy's Will,* with its characterizing title out of a poem by Longfellow, had been published second in the United States, preceded by *North of Boston,* a title even more characteristically suggested by the unpoetic time table. Alfred Harcourt (my friend, though my publisher) had persuaded Francis Hackett to print "The Death of the Hired Man" in the first issue of *The New Republic,* and the poet who never cultivated the poetic attitude came back to find himself a sensation. Critics fought over him—I boasted of having written one of the earliest reviews—movements claimed him. Pound had failed to make him an Imagist; later appraisers were no more successful in their efforts to classify him as a Classicist, a Humanist, a Traditionalist, a Realist, a Ruralist. In one of the first letters I received from him when we were lightly arguing about labels and the emphasis of understatement, he wrote the often-quoted characterization: "If I must be classified as a poet, I might be called a Synecdochist, for I prefer the synecdoche in poetry—that figure of speech in which we use a part for the whole."

As for being a realist, he did not wholly object to the connotation at a time when most American poets were swooning over the landscape, populating the local heavens with imported skylarks, and setting idealized workers to repeat grandiose clichés among the always alien corn. But Frost wanted to make it plain that his was a book of people, not merely a translation of backgrounds, and that the tone

—the sound a poem makes—was rooted in something besides realism. It was a free transcript, but, for all its freedom, held in form. It was not enough to render the vernacular accurately; still less was it desirable to twist the speech into the dialect with which Amy Lowell hoped to intensify her New England monodramas. With a genius for suggestion enriched by observation, Frost took the amorphous talk of everyday and gave it a shape. Prodded into admitting something of the sort, he wrote to me: "There are two types of realist—the one who offers a good deal of dirt with his potato to show that it is a real one, and the one who is satisfied with the potato brushed clean. I'm inclined to be the second kind. To me the thing that art does for life is to clean it, to strip it to form."

I I

I could quote endlessly from those letters. Some day I hope to publish a volume devoted to more than two hundred of them. They supplement Frost's life and work in the same way that Keats's letters round out the poetry. The letters came at irregular intervals ever since the first one arrived almost twenty-five years ago. Sometimes there would be an interval of months without a line; sometimes there would be a burst of several within a fortnight. Distance made no difference. On the contrary. The closer we became geographically and less in need of written communication, the greater grew the correspondence. Never have letters been so personal and yet so documentary, so frankly intimate and so intense a record of the times.

I could not realize this at the beginning of our friendship. I did realize, however, that I had met a man of immense stature the moment I saw him. I have known hundreds of brilliant, charming, profound, interesting, and even exciting people at home and abroad; I have known only three men whose greatness rested in what they were, rather than in what they said or did. The three men are Arthur Schnitzler, the Viennese novelist and playwright, now deceased; James Weldon Johnson, the Negro poet, teacher, and leader, who died so tragically little more than a year ago; and Robert Frost.

This was obvious at first sight. The breadth and quality of Frost's landscape were in the man's face. Carved out of native granite, the effect would have been cold had it not been for the pale blue but quizzical eyes, the quickly bantering smile, and the sensual bee-stung underlip. It was a stubborn scholar's face masking the irrepressible poet's. Years later, in a preface to his *Collected Poems,* he made the distinction: "Scholars and artists thrown together are often annoyed at the puzzle of where they differ. Both work from knowledge; but I suspect they differ most importantly in the way their knowledge is come by. Scholars get theirs with conscientious thoroughness along projected lines of logic; poets theirs cavalierly and as it happens in and out of books. They stick to nothing deliberately, but let what will stick to them like burrs where they walk in the fields."

Frost was continually walking in all sorts of fields—not to acquire anything, never on assignment, "not even self-assignment." I like to remember some of the ways I walked beside him; how often our paths crossed at home and in transit, from a hillside at Franconia to a campus in Florida, where we were surrounded and goaded on by an embattled faculty. One of the first letters from him, early in 1915, tells me he had been acquainted with my name long before I knew his, having heard it "so often mentioned under a certain thatch roof in Ryton, Dymock, Gloucestershire, England"—the home of Lascelles Abercrombie, a remarkable though underrated English poet and teacher with whom I had been corresponding. I began on the sidewalks of New York; Frost on the streets of San Francisco. Our orbits gradually approached each other; Robert, whose passion is acquiring farms and never selling them, now has me bounded on the north, south, and east. There was a time when we almost went to the South Seas together. It happened—or, rather it didn't happen—this way.

During the summer of 1920 Robert and I received almost identical letters from a Mr. Rhinehart of California. There, on the west coast, under the influence of the salubrious sun and the emanation of a hundred cults, Mr. Rhinehart planned a Utopia for some ten or twelve advanced spirits. He told us that he had divorced himself from the white race and had lived with primitives more than seven years—"O God, the years wasted living in Whiteland!"—and he hoped that we would not defer our bright communal future until too late. Mr. Rhinehart acknowledged that each of us had some good work, but there was no chance of our doing anything more in "a mode of life foreign to that possible for the human species. I can understand the endurance of the dumb, but not that of the intellectual." His plan was simple. Our home was to be in one of the purely Polynesian islands. Each man was to have his own hut for a trifling $300. We were to live, at a trivial cost, on a beneficently meatless diet of banana, orange, mango, guava, avocado, cocoanut, fei, custard-apple, melon, wild potato, and fish. If pocket-money were needed (if there were pockets) we would cultivate vanilla, "which is an orchid inoculated by hand, in the shade; tinted petals of white beauty, the world's one perfection. . . . I am an expert grower; know at sight first class vanilla land. Can tell it a mile away, like you can a page of good prose. The net profit isn't far from seventy per cent— and grant a wage rate above that current, and treat your natives like Christ would." Chiefly, however, we were not to labor or do any work. Godlike, we were to rest during a perpetual Sabbath, sitting on our verandas with a sleepy smile, "listening to the fronds of the nut-trees, letting the trade-winds fan and forget the hour, the day, forget all save a sooth-spirit."

The nucleus of the group which was to "leave the word 'speed' in its birth-home in the Land of Go," was to include Frank Harris, a novelist; Charles Edward Russell, a socialist; Bayard Boyesen, an anarchist; Clarence Darrow, an attorney, although a lawyer in a vanilla Paradise seemed an irrelevance; Luke North, unidentified; Robert Frost, a poet; and myself, although it was not stated whether I was to be the colony's jeweler or its anthologist. Each letter ended, "If you cannot go, please pass these papers on to some quality friend who might be interested." I have no record of my reply, but I have the long letter which Robert received and his "memorandum" written across it. The latter reads:

Dear Louis, My Quality Friend:

I have had to decline this invitation on the ground that I want to stay in the world a while longer to see what is going to happen. Hadn't seen any finality in the war; must hang around till I see some in politics. Also on the ground that I prefer to contract my skin diseases from white people as being more likely to be white diseases. My latest information from the South Seas is that this man's island is to be open island for pearls next year; in which case it will be full of divers and entertainment dives such as movies, con games, and shoot-the-chutes. It would be literary (almost) to run away from such things here only to run into them there. . . . I told him *you* would probably go, as you were retiring from the jewelry business, and if he couldn't get you he could try Edith Thomas, who seems about to retire from poetry and even life itself from sheer satisfaction with the good work she has been doing the last ten years. If you accept and go, make it a condition that President Wheeler (of the Poetry Society) shan't go and spill the vanilla beans.

Gee, I wish I were done with life so I could go where I please. But if I *could* go I shouldn't light out for anybody's cast-off islands in the Pacific. Rockwell Kent knew a trick worth two of that for press stuff. I should bar Charles Edward Russell if it were my funeral. And who is this Luke North that, so untrue to his name, Looked South? . . . Neither do *I* understand how the intellectual keeps going unless it is by panning intellectuality like *The Liberator*. Catch on to the New Radicalism and vote for Harding. Anyway, welcome to the Beach.

Sinceriously
Robbered Frossed

Such a letter is one of many to discomfit those who appraised the poet as a grim realist. Even when he was most purposeful, he teased and twisted new values out of old commonplaces. He never ceased to play, not even when he was most "sincerious." Apart from his poems, where the play and profundity are most powerfully intermingled, his lectures, his casual conversations, were full of it. Those who saw Frost confined to the province of pastoral poetry, a sort of inspired rustic, never really knew him.

His was a kind of talk that was as extraordinary as it was exciting. It might (and usually did) begin with baseball or yesterday's headline, but it soon soared into the immensities. It was impossible to tell where small talk ended and where the large ideas began. It was talk that never sagged, that remained "on high," and that usually outlasted all but the hardiest. Twelve years of semi-isolation had made Robert shy of gatherings until he was almost fifty. Even then he would let conversation drift his way. Everyone talked aimlessly for a while, and Robert would contribute little more than a sidelong comment or an occasional puncturing phrase. Then, usually toward midnight, something would be said which roused him—and it was a rare night that the company broke up before three in the morning. The rest of us staggered upstairs or out into the dawn. But not Robert. Hitting a new stride, he was going stronger than ever.

Robert, like Mencken, always denied he was for making anything over. Yet I have never listened to such reconstructions of politics, poetry, social philosophy, and (a concern which he resented but which never let him alone) the use of education. It was not talk which skimmed and dipped, or flashed with surface brilliance. It plunged and explored, disturbed preconceived notions, exposed prejudices, and clarified motives. I am afraid this sounds as though the talk were heavy in texture and portentous in tone. The opposite is true. Everything said was said in a progress of fancy, in terms of something else, in the rich color of comparisons.

I remember one of the most unexpected and yet most logical of these conversational comparisons. Someone, I think a professor of English, had been trying to account for the quick rise and even more rapid fall of young poets. He used the expected metaphors: "meteor-like," "up like a rocket, down like a burnt stick," and turned to Robert for agreement.

"No," said Robert, "I see him as something more natural. Natural and undramatic. Something that drinks its substance from whatever it strikes—earth or water. A bean-sprout or a waterspout."

Most of the figures of speech are lost; the conversations have not been recorded. Robert cannot be persuaded to put his lectures into print. But this metaphor, at least, has been enlarged. In an introduction to a tiny anthology of Dartmouth undergraduate verse he wrote what well may be a final word on the matter:

No one given to looking underground in spring can have failed to notice how a bean starts its growth from the seed. Now the manner of a poet's germination is less like that of a bean in the ground than of a waterspout at sea. He has to begin as a cloud of all the other poets he ever read. That can't be helped. And first the cloud reaches down toward the water from above, and then the water reaches up toward the cloud from below, and finally cloud and water join together to roll as one pillar between heaven and earth. The base of water the poet picks up from below is, of course, all the life he ever lived outside of books.

These, then, are the three figures of the waterspout; and the first is about as far as the poet doomed to die young in every one of us usually gets. He brings something down from Dowson, Yeats, Morris, Masefield, or the Imagists (often a long way down), but lifts little or nothing up. If he were absolutely certain to do as doomed and die young, he would hardly be worth getting excited over. But you can't be too careful about whom you will ignore in this world. Cases have been known of his refusing at the last minute to abdicate the breast in favor of the practical and living on to write lyrics like Landor till ninety.

III

The young poet in Frost did not die, although the family elders did their best to kill the stubborn maker of metaphors. Those writers who complain that they are not sufficiently published, recognized, and rewarded as soon as they have begun might remember that Frost's first volume was not published until he was thirty-eight. When he sailed for England at the age of thirty-seven he was not beaten, but he was resigned to obscurity. "At thirty-seven, I had pretty well despaired of a reputation of any make. I went to England to write and be poor without further scandal in the family."

Free to be a poet, free to buy farms, free to leave the farm and meet people, he triumphed over the sense of isolation. ("I can't help thinking it is good for us after those years of detachment and disinterestedness.") He talked up his friends and talked down his enemies; he bewildered his opponents with a straightforwardness that had unexpected double meanings, and a kind of nonsense that suddenly made sense. He luxuriated in philosophic banter and flourished in the play of ambiguities. In the midst of a letter full of personalities he wrote revealingly:

Forgive me my nonsense as I also forgive the nonsense of those who think they talk sense. All I insist on is that nothing is quite honest that is not also commercial. You must take that as said in character. Of course I don't mean by that that it isn't true. Nothing is true except as a man or men adhere to it—to live for it, to spend themselves on it, to die for it. Not to argue for it! There's no greater mistake than to look on fighting as a form of argument. To fight is to leave words and to act as if you believed—to *act* as if you believed.

Sometimes I have my doubts of words altogether, and I ask myself what is the place of them. They are worse than nothing unless they do something, unless they amount to deeds as in ultimatums and war-cries. They must be flat and final like the showdown in poker from which there is no appeal. My definition of literature would be just this: words that have become deeds.

Remember all I say is said in character. I urge nothing.

The ivory tower cracks and a new kind of poet emerges; not the weaver of rainbow fragments and moon-wrought fancies, but the practical craftsman, the poet in action. "To *act* as if you believed." To put words into actions—"words that have become deeds" echoed, years later, in Archibald MacLeish's "A poem should not mean, but be."

At the beginning of the preceding chapter, I ventured (with a little help from Cicero) to define friendship. Looking over some old letters, I find a few sentences that act as a happy corollary; they emphasize the blend of earnestness and playfulness which is Frost's outstanding characteristic:

I shan't be at ease till we are on terms where there is no more controversy, neither is there any danger of crediting one the other with more or less than we mean. Thus we shall know when we are fooling, because we shall be always fooling like a pair gay with love. We shan't mean anything too profoundly much except perhaps, that we are friends and that nothing else matters between friends. That is the only sincerity: all else is an approximation. It sounds like the loss of something, and it is—of competition, of the sharpening of wits, and of the criticism that makes us look to ourselves. But friendship is like that. It may not be as strengthening as enmity. And then again it may. At any rate, it is different. The beauty of enmity is in insecurity; the beauty of friendship is in security.

Friendship and poetry, thought and emotion, instinct and intellect—the letters play about the interrelated themes. The approach is always tangential, but there is no uncertainty of the target's place; with a seeming aimlessness the arrow soars, wavers, dips—and the mark is hit in the dead center. For example, Robert begins a rambling letter with a little local gossip. This leads him from the town to the children and to a book which the children have found. It is a collection of current magazine verse, "lady-like, well-made, and empty," and it communicates nothing, he says, for it begins with thought rather than with feeling, and "feeling is first." Then this follows—an unforgettable summary:

Why go into details? Granted that there are a few good poems in the book—I read yours and liked it because it *says* something, first felt and then unfolded in thought as the poem wrote itself. That's what makes a poem. A poem is never a put-up job, so to speak. It begins as a lump in the throat, a sense of wrong, a homesickness, a lovesickness. It is never a thought to begin with. It is at its best when it is a tantalizing vagueness. It finds its thought and succeeds, or doesn't find it and comes to nothing. It finds its thought or *makes* its thought. I suppose it finds it lying around with others not so much to its purpose in a more or less full mind. (That's why it oftener comes to nothing in youth before experience has filled the mind with thoughts. It may be a big emotion then, and yet find nothing it can embody in.) It finds the thought and the thought finds the words.

Always the poetry—and always the poetry transcended itself in play. In his later work, understatement becomes a kind of persiflage and intensity is clothed in raillery. Even the early poems declare it; they could not conceal their spirit from anyone but the critics. Of the fifteen monologs in *North of Boston,* rated by the reviewers as the "grimmest" of the volumes, seven are indisputably humorous, and four are almost jokes. In the letters the humor is broader, more explicit. There are times when the Socratic dialog-roller is not above clowning, and at such times the results are both remonstrative and uproarious.

IV

In 1916 forums broke out in a rash of contemporary culture. Versifiers whose names had never been mentioned in any household were quoted as oracles; chairmen fought for the current best-selling poets; agents cajoled them with national tours and glittering percentages; the self-descriptive circulars grew suddenly and ever more superlative. Robert, who had resisted the platform when he ceased to be a teacher, found that lecturing was a personal torture but a fair way of supporting the farm. The most spontaneous of talkers, he could not get himself to prepare a "descriptive list" of lectures, let alone a circular. But one of his letters contained a magnificent burlesque of what was being done and what he could not do. I copy a good part of it:

ANYBODY WANT TO HEAR R. FROST ON ANYTHING?

Partial List of Subjects in Stock:

BOOTY. Derivation of the word from beauty. Two words interchangeable in age of bride-snatching. Poetry, the bride of elemental nature. Richard Le Gallienne. Kale Young Rice. Edith Thomas. Etc.

THE UNATTAINABLE. How much ought a poet get for showing (Hamlet, Act III, Scene 2) in public? How much is fifty dollars? Are the English overpaid? Masefield. Yeats. Noyes. Base suggestion that poetry is as often gloating over what you have as hankering after what you haven't. Strabismus and Idealismus.

POETRY AND SCIENCE. Is the conflict irreconcilable? How long will the war last? Piece of Utrecht and other memorable pieces. Aphasia. Pompadour. Nell Gwyn. Resolved that evolution is like walking on a rolling barrel. The walker isn't so much interested in where the barrel is going as he is in keeping on top of it. The Labyrinthodont. The Sozodont. The Cotoledon. The Dodecahedron. The Plesiosaurus. The Thesaurus (and Rhyming Dictionary). The Megatheorem. The Pterodactyl. The Spondee. And the Concordance.

THE INEVITABLE: AND HOW TO POSTPONE OR AVOID IT. How to keep from attaining what you don't want. Query: if what Shelley meant by Prometheus wasn't the philosophizing poet, Shelley himself. The world's gain could he have stood fate off for one year. Two years. Five years. Ten years. Futility of speculation.

THE HARRISON LAW. Some dull opiate to the drains. Swinburne's famous adjuration to his sister: "Swallow, my sister; oh, sister, swallow!" Picture: We were the first that ever burst; or the danger of mixing drinks. Jamaica Ginger. A plain talk to druggists. Given in England under the title: A plain talk to chymists.

MOANISM AND SWOUNDING. On larruping an emotion. Men's tears tragic, women's nuisance. Heightening. In this I make it clear—by repeated assertions—that I can use any adjective that anyone else can.

NEW HAMPSHIRE GOLD. Adventure with an examining doctor for an insurance company who, after looking me over and taking samples of me, decided I was just the romantic kind he could

unload a small wild farm on because it was blessed with a gold
mine that had been worked to the extent of producing three
wedding and engagement rings. The moral being that I am not
romantic.

TRUE STORY OF MY LIFE. Stealing pigs from the stockyards in
San Francisco. Learned to whistle at five. At ten abandoned sena-
torial ambitions in order to come to New York, but settled in
New Hampshire by mistake on account of the high rents in both
places. Invention of cotton gin. Supersedes potato whisky. A
bobbin boy in the mills of Lawrence. Nailing shanks. Rose
Marie. La Gioconda. Astrolabe. Novum Organum. David Harum.
Visit General Electric Company, Synecdoche, N. Y. Advance
theory of matter (what's the matter?) that becomes an obsession.
Try to stop thinking by immersing myself in White Wyandottes.
"North of Boston." Address Poetry Society at Great Poetry Meal.
Decline. Later works. Don't seem to die. Attempt to write "Crossing the Bar." (International copyright.) Time: three hours. Very
intimate and baffling.

(*NOTE:*) Some of these lectures are more intelligible if taken
in combination with all the rest together the same afternoon or
evening.

Dollar a minute or sixty minutes for fifty dollars. I have to ask
a little more where I introduce my adjectives immediately after,
instead of before, my nouns—as in The House Disorderly. Lists
of nouns and adjectives I am accustomed to use furnished in
advance to guard against surprise.

The fooling reference to the White Wyandottes disguises
a grief of ungratified chicken-farming. Too restless to remain in one place and raise them himself, Robert has
plagued me for years to start and market a fancy breed of
fowl, he to act as partner *in absentia*. The fact that I am
already surrounded with a complexity of animals, domesti-

cated and wild, and that I particularly loathe chickens (except with noodles) does not discourage him. He still dreams of persuading me to raise some long-feathered thoroughbred, one which is particularly susceptible to obscure and incurable diseases. Thoroughbreds, not the common manifestations of matter, are an obsession with him. He refused to allow his grandson to accept one of a litter of Eskimo dogs which we had bred because huskies were mongrels. Finally, he relented. But only after he had matched one of the puppies with a photograph of a full-blooded Norwegian Elkhound, which he had discovered in—of all authorities— *Vogue*. He has never ceased teasing me by deriding the classes; but he has never belittled class.

V

It was class that he admired in his senior New England fellow-poet, Edwin Arlington Robinson. Ill-wishers implied that the two had so much besides locale in common that a jealousy grew up between them. This is not true. Each poet had a few reservations about the other, but their relations were always cordial, not critical. When Robinson brought me his contribution to the *American Miscellany,* he regretted that he had not more to offer, especially, since he wanted to "stand shoulder to shoulder and back to back" with Frost. Robert was no less responsive; his introduction to Robinson's posthumous *King Jasper* is a discerning acknowledgment as well as a personal tribute.

Robert records one of their meetings concisely but vividly. The place was Boston, a bar near the Commons, and they referred to it as the Place of Bitters, "because it was with bitters, though not with bitterness" that they sat there and "looked out on the welter of dissatisfaction and experiment around us." Robert delighted in many of Robinson's acid-bitten etchings ("every one the closest delineation of something that *is* something") and he delighted to read the gently alcoholic "Mr. Flood's Party," reading it far better than Robinson did. Long before Robinson won acclaim or public awards, Robert wrote me, apropos of a review, "I'm glad that you found it in you to give Robinson his due. He gave you yours, you devil, the night of the Great Poetry Meal. The way he snickered over you was the next best thing to you there, confirming me in what I had made up my mind was the best quality in his books." That quality was wit, the play of sympathy, the style "with outer seriousness and inner humor," a characterization that describes Frost himself with even greater truth.

But it was another meeting that implicated me, the only meeting at which Robinson hazarded an opinion of his confrères. James Oppenheim described it in his reminiscences of *The Seven Arts:*

One day Robinson, Frost, Jean Starr Untermeyer, Louis, and myself had a poets' lunch at the Untermeyer apartment. Four of us were mute. Socially at that time Robinson was a clam with haunted eyes. (I see the defect of that statement but can't seem to change it.) Frost, though warmer than his name implied, was as silent as the snow on a New Hampshire hill. Jean was heavily morose. I was sunk.

I can imagine the frightful attempts we would have made if Louis had not been present. We would have attempted first to talk, failing that to eat, and failing that, even more dreadful, to go away. But Louis . . . So soon all of us were comparing our methods of composing poetry.

It is a telling picture, and it is too bad that most of it is wrong. For one thing I remember that Jimmie, instead of being "sunk," spoke volubly from the beginning and Robert had difficulty interrupting him. For another thing Robinson, for all his reticence, scarcely looked like a "clam with haunted eyes," although the figure is fetching. E. A. never resembled the picture of the proverbial poet with a moon-struck air, the rapt upturned gaze, the bardic profile. Once, when we were discussing "The Man with the Hoe," E. A. complained in mock-lugubrious accents, "It's easy enough to write like a poet, but it's much harder to look like one—and that's what Markham does."

Robinson was tall, and his thin frame made him seem taller. He was primly bespectacled, with curiously puckered lips, and a gravely owlish expression. He looked neither like a clam nor a poet, but like an expert accountant—which, in the literal sense of the term, is what he was. No poet in America has rendered more expert accounts of the lost strugglers, the incompetents, the dream-ridden mediocrities. Robinson identified himself with the Miniver Cheevys, the Richard Corys, the Bewick Finzers, and all those who, like their creator, had been frustrated and beaten by the current standards of commercial success. Even his portrait of Lincoln in "The Master" is that of a glorified failure. "Laconic and Olympian" (recalling John Hay's characterization of Lincoln as "a backwoods Jupiter"), he failed to live up to "our shopman's test of age and worth." But here I am in danger of confusing the man with his creations.

Yet, at the meeting reported by Oppenheim, Robinson emerged from his bivalvular shell, if only for a moment. The rest of us were variously praising certain contemporary English poets: Hodgson, Masefield, De la Mare, and Edward Thomas, Frost's favorite. Robinson smiled, but he did not commit himself.

"Well?" we challenged him.

"Well," he answered between sips, "every time you mention another poem by another Georgian, I think of another poem by Kipling—and a better one. He'll outlive them all." Then he added the only pun I ever heard him make. "He's a better man than they are for all their din."

We groaned appropriately while Robinson, unusually pleased with himself, continued to chuckle.

One thing Robinson definitely did not do at the meeting described. He did not discuss his method of composing poetry. He could not. He discussed little of anything; he was no more than barely articulate except when alone with a good friend and a better bottle. His talk, like his expression, was colorless; all the color was in his verse. Dissecting his work was, for him, an impossibility. Creation was a simple act with Robinson. He wrote continuously, almost unconsciously; he wrote industriously—toward the end far too industriously—but he uttered no theories. His poetry was sometimes impassioned, he himself never burned; when the conversation grew excited, he let the others coruscate. You learned to know him by watching for the little twinkles.

Sometimes the twinkles were audible. After supper at the MacDowell Colony, that artists' retreat in New Hampshire where Robinson was the acknowledged deity, most of the authors and composers would coagulate in thickly controversial groups. Robinson, however, preferred to play billiards, and even the loquacious Maxwell Bodenheim had to confine himself to clipped monosyllables when he handled the opposing cue. But, on rare occasions, E. A. would talk. I remember one discussion that had been going on for a long time. It was about birds, particularly about which birds and which poets seemed to belong together. We agreed that Keats's bird was obviously the nightingale, Shelley's the skylark, Swinburne's the swallow, Heine's the seagull, Whitman's the hermit-thrush, Poe's the raven, Frost's the ovenbird that knows "what to make of a diminished thing."

"But who," said one of us, "will write the perfect poem about the whippoorwill?" They had been particularly persistent that summer.

"I tried such a poem," said Robinson to everyone's surprise. "It began:

Thou iron-lunged incessant bird of Hell!

Then I had to stop. I found I had written the whole poem. That line said it all."

I did not agree with him. But there are nights in summer when the reiterations of what must be a damned spirit grow increasingly ominous and sleep refuses to come. Then I think he was right.

It was apropos of such a night—or rather an early morning after we had emptied an illicit quart of Scotch—that Robinson again turned to poetry. This communication, written on a postcard, was almost as brief as the one line apostrophe to the whippoorwill. It was delivered to my studio with the sandwiches left on the doorstep—at the Colony we were supposed to spend the day in uninterrupted creation—and, as far as I know, it has never appeared in any of Robinson's volumes. Yet the twist of the epigrammatic line stamps it immediately as his:

TOO MUCH COFFEE

Together in infinite shade
They defy the invincible dawn:
The Measure that never was made,
The Line that never was drawn.

A painstaking biography of Robinson has been published. But there is more to the man than is held between the covers. The facts are there; the quiet but contradictory spirit escapes. Some day a more intuitive biographer will explore the depths beneath Robinson's smoothly deceptive surfaces: the devotion under the detachment; the fear that underlay his celibacy; his curiously cramped and almost undecipherable letters; his fits of alcoholism; and the anxiety manifest in the over-concern with his own work. Such a book will explain the reasons back of his distrust of most men and his fear of almost all women. It will disclose the causes of his limitations, and the desperate lifelong sublimation of the tight-lipped, lonely man, a man obsessed by failure and in love with death. Before actual death overtook him in a New York hospital, Robinson was living a posthumous existence, an existence too withdrawn, too private and involved for any but the most devious biographer.

Robert Frost will escape his biographers even more nimbly. There are, to my knowledge, five or six works under way, but I am dubious of their success. His life, like his poetry, is a maze of disguised simplicities and delicate double meanings. I think I have the right to say this. Our friendship has grown over a quarter of a century. He is one of my oldest friends in time, one of the nearest in space—our mountain-farms are on opposite sides of Lake Champlain—and firmest in breadth, length, and thickness of endurance. Yet I do not feel qualified to be his biographer. Knowing him so long and well may be a handicap for me as a writer. I await the projects already begun with eagerness and (I may as well confess it) distrust. I am waiting (suspiciously, of course) for them to reconcile the calculating and incalculable artist; the teacher who resented teaching but could never let education alone; the far-spread influence and the stubborn individualist; the puritan, the man of the world, and the man who, in his intensity and probity, was always somewhat beyond the world.

BILL AND NEFERTITI

ELINOR WYLIE was one of the most beautiful women I have ever known, and the vainest. She was not vain about her work, which she regarded with the true craftsman's detachment, modesty, and critical appreciation. She was vain about the merit for which she was least responsible, her physical beauty. She studied her delicate grace in every posture; she translated the firm suppleness into the heroes and heroines of her novels; she mirrored herself in her verse. Sometimes, half mockingly, as in the autobiographical "Portrait in Black Paint, With a Very Sparing Use of Whitewash," she admitted:

> . . . *she might reform the world*
> *In those lost hours while her hair is curled.*

More often her stanzas reflected her intense and loving self-scrutiny. The portrait is serious and almost complete in "Preference": the mournful mouth, small and solemn,

> *Having, to confound the mourner,*
> *Irony in either corner;*
> *The limbs fine, narrow and strong,*
> *Like the wind they walk along,*
> *Like the whirlwind, bad to follow;*
> *The cheekbones high, the cheeks hollow—*

It is all here, all the external beauty, the eyes "large and wide apart," the ever-young skin, even the "small bones in

wrists and ankles." She was right. There was an exquisite-
ness about her that was as precise and as precious as a work
of art; a blemish here was, to her, as maladroit as a flaw in
a poem. When she was past forty a partial paralysis affected
a small spot on one cheek. It did not make her less attractive; the skin was a little smoother and the mouth a little
tighter. But she drew away from most of her friends; she
felt marred; she wrote, according to her sister, that "her
vanity, her precious vanity, was irretrievably wounded."

Elinor's sister, Nancy Hoyt, wrote a biography subtitled
"The Portrait of an Unknown Lady" which gives most of
the facts, though a more candid and more nearly complete
account would have been a greater service to the poet. "Personally," says Miss Hoyt, "I should think that they [people]
would have seen in her vanity, if it were that, a striving
toward the same perfection she reached in writing." Possibly.
Yet I could not help remembering the night that I intended
a compliment and effected a wound. Elinor had just come
out of the hospital after a particularly trying time. Nevertheless, she looked radiant if a little tense. I said something
about her recovery and added, "You look particularly lovely
tonight."

"Louis," she returned, with what sounded like asperity,
"have you ever seen me looking any other way?"

I laughed at what I assumed was a quick sally. Elinor did
not smile.

This was sometime in 1924 or 1925. Long before that,
long before I knew Elinor, I had known Bill. Bill was William Rose Benét, and we became acquainted in 1912 when
he was assisting the assistant editor of *The Century* and I

was beginning to contribute to that venerable magazine. We had much besides our mid-twenties in common: the writing of verse to challenge the world; a preoccupation with the lesser Pre-Raphaelites and the larger Browning; an amateur's fondness for drawing; and a passion for reciting in public the magnificently absurd strophes of James Byron Elmore and J. Gordon Coogler. There was even a military background in both our lives: Bill's father was an army man, later to be in charge of a huge camp; my father had been a member of the Ninth Regiment and, later, an honorary colonel in the Old Guard.

(My earliest memory of father is the sight of a little red-faced man in an enormous beaver precariously balanced, and a chestful of brass buttons about to pop off. He marched me up and down the room to snatches from Gilbert and Sullivan, but his set-piece was "The Mulligan Guards Parade." He sang it *con brio* and with undiminished energy. The childish rhythms of the movement, the music and the march, have so persisted that I suspect half my poems have been written to those measures.)

At the very beginning of our friendship we discovered another mutual bond: a devotion to the art of parody. Beginning to write burlesques of a limited sort, I had just discovered the travesties of J. C. Squire, and I passed on the information (along with a review of some minor poets) to Bill. Having come upon them myself only a week before, I rallied him on his ignorance. Bill, in one of the first letters I had from him, acknowledged this in a prose which barely attempted to conceal the rhyme. Written when Bill was twenty-six it proves that Bill, besides being a poet of distinction, could have been a master of light verse. There are couplets here which might have been fathered by Gilbert collaborating with Browning—but I promised, years ago, not to make the latter comparison. Browning was a source from which Bill fed, by which he was bound, from which he escaped, and to which he was always returning. This is the letter:

I'm not devoted to the masses nor to the cultured upper classes, but I was glad to get your screed, hurling abuse at me indeed; yet instinct with a merry spirit which I acclaim, though others fear it. As one who twangs and seems a liar, I want that book by Mr. Squire, mentioned by Mr. Untermeyer. That I not knew it irks me sadly. I want it now; I want it badly! Tell me in brief—or half a colyum—where I can get the little volume. At last a parodist appears whom I have waited for for years.

As for the others, though some hark her, I'm rather pained by Elsa Barker. And your remarks appear profound (because they echo mine) on Pound. Browning could pour it forth at spate, but Ezra sweats to imitate, with groans, and Celtic sighs, and curses, one line from out a billion verses. Oh, come, let's go into the diner. They're all so "minor," "minor," "minor"! And so am I, and so are you. But God's good grin may see us through.

Come then to lunch whenever suits. We'll hash a score of good reputes. I'm glad to hear remarks so rational about the hyper-international. As peace resolves a happy fugue-end, my mind is now made calm by *Jugend,* after chaotic illustrations. I only hope you have the patience to work toward drawings so supernal in your new socialistic journal. After such flings of "Ars Hysterica," say, can we do it in America? The beauty of a *Jugend* page is an oasis in this age!

This is the sort of running comment by which we know what David's psalm meant, when, for his rightful singing permit, he said "Lord, I know mine own infirmity!" So for the present God be wi' you, and pretty soon I hope to see you.

Bill's letters were embellished with grotesque colophons, rococo borders, and apt caricatures. The paragraphs themselves had a way of leaping from business-like prose to fantastic rhapsodies, to turns of farce and miracles of unmeaning. Inconsequence and farrago would be introduced without preamble; instead of the conventional ending there would be a concluding burst of nonsense. Some of these madcap rhymes are among the best of their genre. The following, for example, is almost classical—if there can be such a thing as an unprinted classic:

> *O God, that I were roaming*
>   *Where usen't I to go;*
> *Where vales were bright with gloaming,*
>   *And skies were black with snow.*
> *But if the luck should change, dear,*
>   *And love should turn to hate,*
> *I think I'd have the mange, dear,*
>   *And die outside the gate.*

> *Oh, purple are the Plymouth Rocks*
>   *That gobble grains of seed;*
> *And radiant are the flowers' frocks*
>   *(With here and there a weed).*
> *But rabbits roam the old ways,*
>   *Through showers of sleet I see*
> *The bold ways, cold ways—g . . o . . l . . d ways—*
>   *There usen't I to be!*

I I

In 1914 Bill began to talk of two people. One was Stephen, "my younger brother, aetat 16. I enclose some of his poems, which mother copied. You will see how violently Gallic they are—his hero is Napoleon. But also I think you'll see he has an unusual command of rhythm and rhetoric for one of his age. Really singing lines." And again, a few months later: "By the way, you'll find young Stephen heading a herd of poets on page 20 of *The New Republic* for August 7th. I'm prejudiced, but I think 'Winged Man' has more guts than all the rest put together.

Black 'gainst the crimson sunset, golden o'er cloudy snows—

That's *damned* good!"

Bill's enthusiasm was not founded on purely fraternal prejudice. At seventeen Stephen Vincent Benét made his debut with a vigorous set of Roman portraits, *Five Men and Pompey;* twelve years after the appearance of this first small collection, unknown to all except an intimate few, he won the Pulitzer Prize with the varied quasi-epic *John Brown's Body.*

Bill's other enthusiasm was for a young painter, one of his oldest friends; he predicted a great future for the young fellow. The friend had a private income, but Bill insisted that he wanted to get away from the traditions of his craft and his class, even though he was neither a socialist nor a post-impressionist. "It occurred to me that as long as he voluntarily stated his liking for *The Masses* pictures, perhaps you could get him interested in doing some sketches

or illustrations for the sheet on the side. Like all 'real'
painters he does not care about illustrating as a method of
pot-boiling, but *The Masses* is a different proposition. . . .
He is very fond of Forain, the Frenchman from whom Sloan
and Glackens and Shinn seem to have descended."

Alas for Bill's hopes. Although his friend, Henry Martin
Hoyt, Junior, was gifted, happily married, and fairly affluent,
he died prematurely, tragically. Bill had already met his
sisters. One of them was Elinor.

Bill's own work was growing in scope and strength. We
had quarreled often and amicably about his love of medieval-
ism, exotic language, and a general preference for "period
pieces." Now he began to explore the contemporary scene
and expand his interest in American legend and landscape.
He was getting ready to present "The Horse Thief" and
"Jesse James," two of the period's most vigorous and best-
known ballads. Meanwhile, he wrote:

If you say my new poems hold a trace of R. Browning, why,
I—I—why, I'll—by gravy, I'll hit you with the inside of a dough-
nut. . . . At any rate, you consarned modernist, it may amuse
you to know that two of my last three poems bear the titles
"The Push-Cart" and "The Quick-Lunch Counter," though I'll
admit they try to put the splendors of ancientry into the grim of
modernity. The third, "The Horse Thief," is this in plot: Posse
is out after a horse thief. His stolen horse breaks a leg, and he
sights a wonderful mustang up "on the purple canyon's lip." So
he crawls with his lariat, ropes the wonderful hoss, wrastles him,
manages by sheer luck to get a leg up—hoss stampedes with him—
sprouts wings—turns out to be Pegasus. They are soaring hilari-
ous on the Milky Way when old Sagittarius (rhyme, see!) comes
at 'em with his bow'narrer.

Pegasus shied and swerved aside and fled from the Splendor-
   Shod.
Through that flashing welter of worlds we charged. I knew why
   my horse was frightened.
He had two faces—a dog's and a man's—that Babylonian God!

So hoss thief is buck-jumped back to earth. Wakes up. Posse
catches him. Tells them of Pegasus. Then: "String me up now,
boys! I die happy." . . . Passed by the Benét Board of Censorship.

At thirty Bill assumed his full characteristics, physically
and poetically. Later, seeing him and E. A. Robinson together (and they were together often at the MacDowell
Colony), I was struck by the similarity of their build and
manner. Both were tall and lean; they walked with a curiously hesitant step; they spoke in a low and almost deprecat-
ing tone. But their facial expressions were altogether different. Robinson's was stiff, cool, and faintly acrid; Bill's
was continually wrinkling with warmth and pleasure. Remembering James Oppenheim's description of Robinson as
"a clam with a haunted look," I hesitate to describe Bill's
face as a winter apple. But that, even at thirty, is precisely
what he looked like—the roundness was criss-crossed with
fine lines, and the wrinkles were drawn with humor and a
great sense of kindness.

Kindness was, perhaps, Bill's chief characteristic. He may
have had enemies (although, knowing Bill, this seems highly
improbable), but he never spoke ill of them. He never spoke
ill of anyone. He was not saintly—saintliness is something
which attended his first wife Teresa—but no one even
casually acquainted with him could fail to perceive that here

was a man of generosity and ungrudging good will. Many
an established poet regarded the emergence of young singers
and new voices with distrust. But Bill was never jealous;
he welcomed poets not only for their own sake but for the
sake of poetry. When we discovered James Elroy Flecker's
"Old Ships" and "Gates of Damascus" simultaneously just
after the poet's death, Bill boiled over with excitement and
self-reproach.

I have bitter things to say to myself anent poor Flecker. I liked
something of his I had seen back in the old days, and wrote him.
He wrote me from Egypt or somewhere, sending me some poems
for *The Century*. The Underbrush [Bill's way of referring to the
bearded editor, Robert Underwood Johnson] was then so heavy
that, of course, his poems were howled out of court. But what I
have to curse myself for is that I wrote Flecker saying one of his
poems had a chance *if* he would do this or that to it, and inflict-
ing my criticism upon him. He very naturally wrote back and
told me, politely, to go to hell. . . . I often remember how in-
fernally clumsy I was with him—because, by God, and before the
Throne, he was a great poet.

I I I

Every prospect pleased, every new project aroused him.
Bill was one of Vachel Lindsay's earliest supporters, and
Vachel in turn hailed Bill's "Merchants from Cathay" as
one of the best of modern chants. When the colored broadsheets of Ralph Hodgson's poems reached America, Bill was
so drunk with the union of rich-hued words and brightly
tinted drawings that he thought of learning to make woodcuts. "Every poet should have a printing press, a color kit,

and maybe a draughtsman kept in a gold cage. He should produce all his poems on single broadsheets, and go through the city every week tossing them in doors, like circus or furniture-sale announcements."

Not that Bill refused to be critical. But, instead of laying about him with a cudgel (which seems to have been my method), he used a blade of so fine an edge that the victim scarcely realized that he had been decapitated. I treasure one of his few and, I believe, unprinted parodies for its double keenness. I had written a long monolog, "Eve Speaks," in which the first woman reproaches the Creator, and which Bill facetiously called "the greatest feminist poem of the age." Amy Lowell was writing her New England melodramas at about this time, and one day I received an anonymous poem which took my subject and treated it in her later manner. At first I thought this was another of Amy's mystifications; the postmark, the feminine handwriting on the envelope and the envelope itself, were unfamiliar. Finally, I recalled where I had seen the blue paper and the not-too-well-disguised script. It was at the Benéts', and I remembered that Teresa was not only an ardent suffragist, but a modest writer and translator. Teresa and Bill had evidently collaborated to place Paradise somewhere in Massachusetts; they had given my Eve a new speech, the dialect of Back Bay and Brookline. The parody was so neatly turned that even Amy Lowell enjoyed it. I quote it in full.

EVE KEEPS ON SPEAKING

Jest a moment, Lord God A'mighty!
Air you plumb sure you got th' hull rights of it?

Adam's no hand at explainin'. Lord! The number of times
  I've hed to do that man's thinkin' fer 'm!
'Twarn't that we wanted no ard'nary ahcherd apple,
What with peaches purt' nigh ez handsome ez if they wuz
  made in wax,
An' pineapples thet ye cud hev put under glass in the parlor,
Besides a hull passel o' fruit that we never even tasted!
Course, they told us thet it warn't poison.
But th' most of it looked too handsome to be hullsome;
Till the time come when 'twould hev been sort of a relief
  to be poisoned!
I don't say Adam wouldn't a stuck it out a while longer.
He lay under a laylock bush whittlin' out checkers;
Said they'd come in handy for winter evenin's.
Lord! How often I'd tell him there warn't goin' to be no
  winter evenin's—
No red sun settin' in a bank uh solemn cloud;
No snow so's ye didn't know ef ye cud make the cow-barn;
No cuppa coffee makin' it wuth yer while ter git up
  mornin's! . . .
Then there was the boys, Lord.
I don't know now what more we cud hev done for Cain
  than we did do;
Always hangin' on and sayin', "When air we goin' fer ad-
  ventures, Ma?" . . .
Seemed sif I cudda got th' boy on a ship I'd a knowed whar
  he was nights!
And Abel was most too good to live.
Couldn't put your finger on nothin',
But he was dreadful aggravatin'!

So I sez to Adam, "This is a matter fer prayer."—
An' we et it!

Then the war came, and Bill became a second lieutenant
in the Air Service, non-flying and, as he wrote from Texas,
practically non-combatant. Then, in 1919, a month after he
was honorably discharged, Teresa died. Bill went to Washington, where he tried to adjust himself to reconstruction
work, attempted to learn the jargon of advertising, and, poet
though he was, became assistant editor of *The Nation's
Business.*

I V

It was at this time that he first mentioned Elinor Wylie.
The name was unknown to me, as it was to most, in early
1920, and I was uncertain in what lines Bill was serious
when he ended a half-humorous reply to my request for
data:

. . . Thus *Who's Who*—brought up to date by me: My favorite
flower is the young spring onion. Favorite poem, Casey Jones.
Favorite hatred, solemn asses in political office. Favorite sport,
tennis. Favorite children, mine. Favorite American poet, male,
Stephen Vincent Benét; female, Elinor Wylie. . . .

Bill, it seems, had renewed his acquaintance with Henry
Hoyt's sister in Washington.

A few months later Elinor came to New York, Bill squired
her everywhere, and rumor thickened. I had already heard
some of the darker gossip: that Elinor, frustrated in an early
romance, had married Admiral Hichborn's son before she
was twenty-one; that she had left him and a child of two to

elope with Horace Wylie, a married man twice her age; that Elinor and Wylie had lived for years under an assumed name in various little English villages until the war sent them back and Mrs. Wylie finally consented to a divorce; that now Elinor was planning to leave Washington and her second husband, lead a literary life, and marry Bill. Because of this lurid tale most of Bill's friends were prepared for the worst; I think I expected to see the typical adventuress, dark, passionate and poisonous. Instead I saw a person made of cold silver whose bearing was puritan-patrician and whose being emanated chastity.

Where, I wondered as we all sat together, had I seen those features before? I recognized that combination of fragility and firmness, of delicacy and determination. But to whom did they belong? Then I remembered the face, the proud face that had always seemed the most exquisite in the world, a face more than three thousand years old. It belonged to Queen Nefertiti, wife of the idol-breaking "heretic" Pharaoh Akhnaten. The resemblance was more than a poet's fancy; the drawing which Peter Arno made for *The New Yorker* a few years later confirmed and emphasized the likeness. Here were the same imperious brows; the high cheekbones and the scooped-out cheeks; the proud and narrow nose; the small taut mouth; the carved and resolute chin; the long smooth column of the throat. Even the slight squint could not hide the quickly appraising glance. The eyes were bright and a hypnotic hazel—witch hazel, it seemed to me. To offset the stare and the general effect of stiffness, her hair was loose and lively.

"Is it chestnut?" I once asked her, recalling my failure to

define a certain tone of brown for Amy Lowell. "Or burnt gold? Or would you call it tawny?"

"I like to think of it as lion-colored," she said. And I thought of the happy exactness of the word, and of her description of autumn trees "that shake a burning spray against autumnal cool"—especially in the last lines which had not yet appeared in print:

> *They rise in silence, fall in quietude,*
> *Lie still as looking-glass to every sense*
> *Save where their lion-color in the wood*
> *Roars to miraculous heat and turbulence.*

Bill was the first literary person to see Elinor's manuscripts after her return from England. It was a great discovery, for he immediately recognized the difference between the facile outpourings of the gifted amateur and the clipped utterance, the nervous intensity, the unflagging brilliance, of this verse. Soon Elinor's sharp-cut, intellectually restrained lines were appearing in *The New Republic* and elsewhere. Her star ascended rapidly; it found a prominent place in the new poetic constellations. In 1921 my publisher brought out her first collection entitled, with implied deference to the metaphysicians, *Nets to Catch the Wind*. It was a dazzling performance, and the reviewers were quick to appreciate its pointed lucidity. The one reservation I made was that it was a little *too* brilliant, that it coruscated but did not burn, that the light it sometimes shed was the flash and sparkle of ice rather than the glow of earthly heat. Writers are so constituted that they overlook a column of praise and seize upon the one sharpened clause to inflict upon themselves a long-rankling wound. Elinor was no exception. It was a year or more before she forgave me; it was two years later, after marrying Bill, that she conceded I had not tried to belittle her. Four years later she healed the breach with a gift.

It was an unusual gift; it proved, among other things, that all of us were wrong in referring to *Nets to Catch the Wind* as Elinor's first book. Nine years before this volume had appeared, when Elinor was happily exiled in England, a book of early verses had been privately printed. Her mother had paid for it; there were sixty-five copies. It was called *Incidental Numbers*. There was no name, not even an initial, to suggest authorship; the title-page bore nothing more than the title, the designation of the London printer, and the date, 1912. Most of the poems are obviously immature and derivative. There are pretty tunes written in her teens; the little volume ends with translations from the French, a ballade, a roundel, and a rondeau. But there are a few poems which presage her later work in tone and even in treatment. "The Knight Fallen on Evil Days" anticipates the finely knit sonnets which were to follow ten years later, and her characteristic turn is apparent in "Pegasus Lost" and on other pages. Yet she referred to the book only to ridicule it; she pretended that the small section of juvenilia was superior to the rest. Her way of disowning the book was almost comic. The copy she sent me was inscribed:

> To my dear and honored friend
> Louis Untermeyer
> Who retains that title of Respect and
> Affection only so long as he faithfully
> preserves the Strict Anonymity of
> The Author

At that time Elinor was still pretending to be a "new-born author." So desirous was Elinor of preserving the "strict anonymity" that she did not write the inscription herself; she dictated it to her German cook in Connecticut. Appropriately enough the date signed at the bottom of the page was April First.

The same day and in the same mail Elinor wrote me on pink-edged blue stationery—but under separate cover:

This is Frieda's paper, dear Louis. *Just allemand*—very much so!

The verses are *so* incredibly bad, it takes my breath. Yet there is here and there a *never* or a *forever* possessing a certain tragic irony. Therein they share the fate of their betters. The same may be said of Milton and Shelley. But these are words better not to be written. . . .

It was Shelley, not Milton, that Elinor idolized. He was not merely a poet to her; he was her pillar of fire, her attendant spirit, and her mystical bridegroom all in one. He was her lodestar and her obsession. She departed occasionally from the destined course, but her poetry and her prose were dedicate to him. "A Red Carpet for Shelley" is a group of sonnets laid at his feet—"the legendary patchwork of a year flung into muddiness, like Raleigh's cloak, to ask the honor of your step." *The Orphan Angel* is a fantastic novel which, in an exaggeration of Shelley's rhetoric, rescues the poet from his actual drowning in Leghorn harbor, brings him to America, and sends him to the frontier West of the Eighteen Twenties. *Mr. Hodge and Mr. Hazard* is a poet's allegory in which Mr. Hodge represents the petty ledger-worshiping middle class and Mr. Hazard is the uprooted

romantic spirit which returns to England only to be defeated. The Shelley pre-occupation was not a pose; it was, as
Stephen Vincent Benét contended, entirely sincere, although
it may not have been, as he maintained it was, entirely mature. But there is no doubt that Elinor wrote her finest work
under the guiding principle of Shelley's subtle spirit. She
believed she was companioned by a cloud, a pardlike phan-
tom among men, an eternal pilgrim, "a woman by an arch-
angel befriended."

When I first knew Elinor it was hard for me to reconcile
her devotion to the burning Shelley with her dependence on
properties that suggested his very opposite: crystal, silver,
filigrees of frost, cool waters, frail glass, and pearly mono-
tones. But Elinor, somehow, fused the disparate elements;
she relished the contradiction and enjoyed the fusion. In
reply to a note on data, she wrote, "I like to think about
ice and snow and Blake and Shelley." And then, with bland
mendaciousness, she concluded, "I am sorry that there is
nothing interesting about my life or habits."

This was at the outset of her career; later the communications were less evasive. I particularly treasure a letter Elinor
wrote just after she began publishing, and an article of mine
had appeared in *The Nation* which played variations on the
theme of a Certain Condescension in Foreigners. Here is the
frank side of the writer who had known both sides of the
Atlantic.

May I for one tell you how much I like your article in *The
Nation?* The mere fact that it is brilliantly funny makes it none
the less profoundly true.

Being myself given to rather useless indignations, and loving to make the rafters of Irish oak ring again, but to little effect, in the cause you have taken up, your words are especially pleasing to me. During the five years I spent in England, I used to throw the *Spectator* and *Blackwoods Magazine* on the floor and stamp on them as regularly as they appeared. But the effect on these publications was nil. And since returning to my native land I have met with few to share my sentiments. I had begun to feel that we were a race of simple-hearted bootlickers with a taste for kicks. Now you give me hope; so permit me to transcribe myself

With admiration

E. W.

This was in 1922, after Elinor had decided to forgive me for my few critical dubieties. Although I did not praise her subsequent work unreservedly, there were no further ruptures. We grew to be good, though not close, friends. At my request, over Amy Lowell's murmur of dissent, as recorded on page 121, she became one of the contributors to the biennial *American Miscellany*. I was assembling the material for the 1925 edition in Europe, and she wrote to me at Vienna:

At last I rise from the complete oblivion of the last few months, and before beginning a novel or even finishing a poem, I want to tell you how glad I am to be one of your Miscellaneous, and to thank you for your kindness and sympathy in a less happy matter. . . .

I am particularly glad that "Peter and John" pleased you, as that poem is a favorite of mine. Bunny Wilson roared with laughter when he read it, and said, "You are Peter, and Bill is John" as if he had made a stupendous discovery. "Of course," I said. "Who could doubt it?"

"Peter and John" was a short dramatic ballad that turned upon an unexpected ending. The sharpened point of Elinor's rejoinder was that, in the poem, John ("whose brow was smooth" as Bill's) dreamed he was Jesus, while Peter ("whose hair was red and whose eyes were gold" as Elinor's) dreamed he was Iscariot.

Before I returned to America in 1925, Elinor had published another volume of poems and had written two extraordinary novels, one a "sedate extravaganza," and the other a fine-spun piece of diablerie. I was amused and a little touched to find myself in the first of her novels, *Jennifer Lorn*. In that almost perfect piece of artifice the young Prince Abbas is praising his father's poetry by quoting another's praise. "A goldsmith of Jerusalem, himself a poet of no mean attainment, said openly in the bazaars and market places of Shiraz that my father made songs to ring with a rare and spicy music evoked from seemingly casual words."

I was flattered, but I was not too sure that the "goldsmith of Jerusalem" was a tribute to my old trade and older race; even the phrase "himself a poet of no mean attainment" was not a certain identification. But I knew that the "bazaars and market places of Shiraz" were the contemporary journals of opinion, for the rest of her sentence was composed of the very words I had first used in a review of one of Bill's books and which I had incorporated in my *Modern American Poetry*.

V

The year after my return I saw Bill and Elinor more and more often. There were gatherings with Edmund ("Bunny") Wilson, Sara Teasdale, Alfred Kreymborg, the Herbert Gormans, and Mary Colum, whose accounts of Elinor are a fine combination of personal sympathy and impersonal appreciation. There were a few Prohibition parties, but Elinor drank little, and then chiefly in defiance of the law and her high blood pressure. There were a few theatres, but Elinor's eyes were giving her trouble. She was too vain to wear glasses, and would whip out a surreptitious pair of spectacles after the lights went out. I remember the night that four of us went to Edwin Justus Mayer's *The Firebrand;* Bill and Elinor particularly wanted to see it because of the richly medieval setting and its pastiche of the heroic style. But Bill, who feared I might not know it, wrote me at the last moment about Elinor's infirmity.

Though I know it is not in Doubleday's *Book of Etiquette,* could I whisper in your ear that my talented helpmeet (she always helps the meat) is really so blind, despite her orient gaze, that unless she is almost down among the saxophones she can't see the actors on the stage. Once I took her to *The Beggar's Opera* and didn't get seats far enough forward, and when I began to dilate on the beauty of the spectacle she tactfully changed the subject to a discussion of the actors' intonations. Like the good child, she had heard but not seen.

A summer at the MacDowell Colony, that nest of incubating studios in which we were supposed to be hatching golden eggs, brought us all together again. I think I was beginning to resent Elinor about this time. I had admired her as a person during her struggle between domesticity and literature, and no one could blame her when she found it impossible to divide herself fairly. But now she seemed petulant, full of childish whims, unreasoning demands. She sent Bill on silly errands, gave way to groundless fears, even to phobias of persecution. Because Bill showed no displeasure, his friends resented it all the more. She seemed not only to dominate him, but to absorb him. She, who had been his discovery, glittered and outshone him; she almost put out his light. He continued to write poetry, but the echoes of his rollicking staves and riotous whimsicalities were all too infrequent.

There was one occasion when I resented Elinor on my own account. Early one morning a few of us went for a before-breakfast swim in a New Hampshire lake near Peterboro. There was the "quick plunge into the cool, green dark," the rough badinage, and the spurt to the raft. The others returned leisurely, while Elinor told me about a nightmare poem she had begun, outlined the plot, and quoted the first chill stanzas. Then we, too, swam back. The distance seemed longer, and Elinor asked to rest one hand on my shoulder. I was proud to be a sort of temporary Christopher, or at least the vicarious delegate of poetry. Then I felt burdened; frail though she seemed on land, I was conscious of her weight in water. The shore seemed as distant as ever. I was making no headway; I was growing tired. I thought again of poetry, but that did not help, for now I thought of Shelley. I thought of him in the harbor of Leghorn—drowned. And, for a moment, I wished that Elinor was with her beloved idol. Then, as a happy anticlimax, Elinor swam the rest of the distance alone.

Elinor lived in her work with a vehement exclusiveness; she was a fever of creation. Her writing life covered only eight years, and in this short time she composed four novels, a dozen short pieces of prose, and more than two hundred poems. It is little wonder that she overtaxed herself physically and mentally, that her amazing fecundity was shot through with fits of doubt, spasms of arrogance and outbursts of irritation which could not help irritating others. Sara Teasdale, who admired her greatly, once said, "She seemed heroic if you liked her, hysterical if you didn't." She was always at concert-pitch; an overstrung instrument, a set of tense wires, ready to snap. She became a legend during her lifetime. She was idealized and caricatured; distortions of her are in several contemporary works; she is the central figure in Anne Parish's biting roman a clef *All Kneeling* and, by implication, Kathleen Coyle's *Immortal Ease*.

Her son was growing up with his father's family; Bill's three children by his first wife were with Teresa's sister, Kathleen Norris. Elinor tried simple housekeeping, but the self-division was too great. There was always the double pressure of temperament and the fear of time. If she made demands upon others, she made twice as many on herself. Literature possessed her; she claimed herself for her work as fiercely as though she knew how soon there would be an end of writing.

In 1926 she went to England alone. Except for short visits from Bill and her family, she remained alone. Gossip was busy again. There was a wild story that Elinor had been persuaded she was the reincarnation of a Druid priestess, that she had danced on Stonehenge and had recited poetry among the prehistoric monoliths. There was a wilder tale that she had wept for hours over an obscure grave because someone had told her that a lock of Shelley's hair had been buried there. There was, it transpired, some truth in both stories.

Then Elinor returned to America for a short stay. Within a few months she was back in England. She seemed unable to settle in either place. Her friends heard that she had had an almost fatal accident, that her back had been broken, and that she would never walk again. Fortunately, the reports were exaggerated; a vertebra had been dislocated and the coccyx had been fractured. She recovered sufficiently to plan a new home in the Wiltshire downs and to return to America for the Christmas holidays in 1928. She brought with her the manuscript of *Angels and Earthly Creatures,* the height of her expression, and the sublimation of all her gifts.

She was still suffering from the results of her fall and the first shock of paralysis, but she could not know that she was about to be struck again. On December 15th, 1928, she made the final arrangement of her book, affixed the motto from another of her favorite metaphysical poets—this time it was John Donne—and corrected the last comma, ready for the printer. The following day she was dead.

V I

In his introduction to her *Collected Poems,* published some three years after Elinor's death, Bill emphasized her deftness and wit, recording her lighter side. The book arrived while Sara Teasdale was visiting here, and we stayed up half the night reading the hitherto uncollected poems, which Bill had justly praised, and the last high utterances, which were Elinor's pinnacle. Sara recalled hearing her recite "The Persian Kitten" on the last occasion they were together—"almost the whole book comes to me in her voice,"

she wrote later—and I remembered the moments when
Elinor relaxed in play. But we both agreed that the best
of Elinor found its expression in those half-proud, half-
pessimistic and strangely premonitory verses which she
wrote shortly before her death.

Elinor had begun with a trim and dangerous cleverness.
Poems of the purest sensation were followed by experiments
in sheer technique. For a while it seemed that the elegant
technician would triumph. As late as her third book she
was still being the virtuoso; she delighted to build baroque
structures upon Gothic ideas and erect elaborate scaffoldings
around an essentially simple form. "Malediction Upon Myself" was an example of the verbal architect at her showiest;
some forty lines were packed with overloaded precisions and
false intensity merely to reproach herself for disliking the
city in summer.

No contemporary poet grew so quickly; none marched
forward to so rapid and radiant a climax. She was progressively schooled by her craft, by her mind, and by her spirit.
After the displays of exquisite artifice, an intelligence, fastidious and even finicking, commanded the utterance. The
reader began to recognize the poet herself, free of her mechanics, especially in the self-portraits she drew from time to
time: metaphysically in "Nebuchadnezzar," curiously altered
in "A Red Carpet for Shelley," barely disguised in "Pere-
grine." But she was revealed most richly in her last magnificent poems, traditional in language, individual in symbol:
in the eloquent sonnet-sequence "One Person"; in "O Vir-
tuous Light," with its unhappy wisdom; in "This Cor-
ruptible," in which dialectic is lifted into drama; and in

the organ-music of "Hymn to Earth," one of the most moving valedictories ever written.

The spirit of Shelley persisted, even at the last. In the concluding stanza of the noble "Hymn to Earth" Elinor wrote, bidding farewell to the elements:

The air flings downward from its four-quartered tower
Him whom the flames devour;
At the full tide, at the flood,
The sea is mingled with his salty blood.

The lines tell us (unconsciously, perhaps) thus, before his time, was Shelley doomed and drowned. And we remember that she, too, was flung down at her height, "at the full tide," she whom the flame of living poetry had devoured.

Amy Lowell's force and influence outlived her own work; Elinor Wylie's frail self was consumed in the uncorruptible passion of her craft. It is good that the art should survive the person. It is the prayer of every worker.

THE FANTASTIC TOE

NATURE never (alas) intended me for a dancer. Yet there was a time in my confused life when I thought my body might somehow express the complexity of rhythms which poetry had never mastered and which music could only suggest. It was a great interpretive dancer who provoked the illusion; it was a terpsichorean mystic (a sort of non-dancing dervish) who fostered it; and it was a creative mime who finally destroyed it.

I saw Isadora Duncan for the first time in Philadelphia. I sat in the gallery of the old Chestnut Street Opera House—or was it the Walnut Street Theatre?—with George Wolfe Plank, whose impressive English address became Little Twits, Five Ashes, Sussex, but who was then only a boy from Bethlehem, Pa. George was printing and publishing a magazine called *The Butterfly,* making all the woodcuts himself, assembling the material and preparing the pages with the help of a few art students who followed him somewhat in the manner of the limp languorous ladies in the wake of Bunthorne. There were less than twenty of them, but they were as rapturous as a Gilbert and Sullivan chorus when Isadora pierced the sleepy stage quietly and dramatically, like a sudden shaft of light. This was the revolution of the body, a revolution that was also a revelation. Brought up on music and rhythm, I had always instinctively responded to the dance. I had relished its dexterous formalism and its prescribed patterns. But no body had ever moved like this;

no legs, arms, and torso had ever dared to say these things.
This was a sacrament and a summons; it was a living flame
of protest; a challenge and wordless cry of freedom.

When I met her later she told me (possibly because she
heard I was a poet) that she first wanted to dance when, a
schoolgirl in San Francisco, she read Keats's "Ode on a Gre-
cian Urn" and, in her imagination, the figures came alive.
It was this union of form and freedom that drove her beyond her time and place, that took the whole Duncan family
to England in a cattle-boat with little more than one hundred dollars, that made her haunt the galleries half-starved
for hours, while she studied the painted vases in the British
Museum and the Greek sculptures at the Louvre.

It was in the Greek dances that I saw her first. The stage
was completely bare; Gordon Craig's bellying gray curtains
were dimly lit to suggest the columns of a Temple on some
vague height; Isadora appeared in the peplum and tunic
worn by the Greek girls. Yet she contradicted costume and
setting in a swiftly established paradox. The designs she
wove in movement were from so antique a source that they
were fantastically fresh to the modern world. She accomplished the common miracle of the creative interpreter: she
made the strange seem familiar, and the old seem new. But
the paradox was deeper than this: here was the Greek way
expressed in what was the essential American spirit. In these
free steps and barelegged leaps, so different from the strict
measures of the conventional dance, tradition was revived
and, at the same time, rejected. It was both an adaptation
of ancient form and a repudiation of formalism. These limbs
moving in light destroyed the rigidity foreign to the American sense.

The American sense, however, was not above being shocked. Several cities refused to let Isadora appear on their chaste platforms because she refused to draw stockings over her rebellious toes. Symphony Hall in Boston was outraged because, in the *Marche Militaire*, Isadora flaunted a red scarf, fearful symbol of revolution; but they were even more indignant at her naked knees. (It is no more than poetic justice—or is it nature's revenge?—that the children of those who hissed Isadora's frankly uncovered, and unglamorous, legs exhibit their almost complete nudity on every beach and in every ballroom of these benighted states.) Finally the rebel triumphed. She influenced her country in spite of itself. She broke down the barriers between music and motion. Whether she translated a folk-song or a symphony into liberating gestures, she turned sound into sight and made the invisible palpable.

I did not realize how far her influence was to spread, how it would affect and change even so highly stylized an organization as the Russian ballet. It was many years before I appreciated Isadora's contribution to the new frontiers in native culture. When I met her I wanted to talk about dancing and she wanted to talk about poetry. We compromised by listening to music. Even this was interrupted by Isadora who could not bear being anywhere but in the very center of interest. She talked of her work by thanking me for some semi-descriptive, semi-fantastic poems about her which I had published in *The Butterfly*. She began to pace up and down the room; she lifted her arms in heavy, futile gestures, as though she were carrying them against their will.

"I want to do a dance that says everything with my hands.

I want the hands to find words. It is dark now and I cannot find them. Some day I will."

The day came. Isadora had been absent from America for several years. She had mixed personal vanity and impersonal magnificence. She had tasted cheap sensations and great ecstasies. She had gone from one lover to another, living on scandal and champagne. She had married Serge Yessenin, a young futurist Russian poet ten years younger than herself. She was no longer fresh and lovely. Her hair was dyed a bad red; her belly was large, her legs were thickening; she looked coarse and bloated. Yet her day had come again. The Russian Revolution had come. She expressed it with her hands.

She came out on the darkened stage of Carnegie Hall, walking slowly, her arms held as though by heavy weights. The hands were locked behind her. Gradually the bonds seemed to be loosening; the hands freed each other; the fingers moved. The arms swung loosely now; they began to lift. She looked at her hands in simple wonder, looked as though she were seeing them for the first time. She smiled at her hands; they laughed back. She reached them forward. Then up, up. . . . She waved them exultingly, victoriously, deliriously. Never have I seen a more vivid symbol; never had I felt liberation so wordlessly yet so powerfully expressed.

A few years later she was dead. She had lived by an excess of motion, and she had died of it. A motor had caused the death of her two children; the engine balked, a brake had slipped, and the car they were sitting in had plunged into the Seine. The automobile, monster of motion, and the red scarf, symbol of freedom, had killed her, too. A trailing end

of the scarf had caught in the whirling spokes of a racing
car, choking her in her own noose. That was in 1927. Had
she lived a few months longer she would have been fifty,
a pagan who had become priestess and prophetess.

I talked with her sister Elizabeth at the school she and
Isadora had established near Tarrytown on the Hudson.
Elizabeth was trying to explain the ideas which Isadora had
communicated without a text. But no one could teach what
Isadora had done, for Isadora never taught; she infected.
The young group, composed mostly of her adopted children, attempted to continue the innovation which had become a tradition. But, though Anna and the other Isa-
dorables were charming, they were not exciting. They
moved gracefully, but they moved no one profoundly. They
had the youth, the lightness, and the bodily beauty which
the older woman had lost; but they lacked the errant and
revealing loveliness which can neither be taught nor transmitted.

I I

Isadora's imitators increased in number and declined in
appeal. They succeeded only in making interpretive dancing
pretentious and somewhat ridiculous. The programs became
more and more purposefully cosmic, the performances unin-
tentionally comic. I mocked their empty posturings—but I
wrote an appropriately vague introduction to a compilation
of misty photographs and mistier verses entitled *Poems of
the Dance*. I laughed at them—but the ghost of Isadora saved
them from complete foolishness. And it was her ghost that,
absurdly enough, brought me into camp—a camp of dancers.

It was a health-camp situated on the shores of a lake near

the Canadian border. Its presiding genius was another eman-
cipator. She, however, planned not only to liberate the body
but to save the soul. This was to be accomplished by simple
living, a little yoga, a great deal of vegetarianism, and the
understanding of the elemental laws of "organic rhythm."
Organic rhythm was the camp's spiritual slogan; with this
talisman we abjured meat, drank quarts of Wesson oil,
munched raisins while we misquoted Indian epics, and slept
with our toes pointing to the East so we might catch the
creative instead of the destructive radiations of earth. Music
was the compelling source, but we did not leap boldly into
an allegro without proper mystical preparation. We had to
initiate ourselves into certain rhythmic rites.

Miss Bea had read the Books of the East after teaching
music in the schools of the west, and her mind was a fasci-
nating maze of cross purposes, of spiritualism and science,
of supernal detachment and earthly shrewdness. Her camp-
followers listened to the word of God as revealed by Gluck
and Ouspensky, Darwin and Dalcroze, Mozart and Montes-
sori. Privately, we were a disorganized and skeptical lot; as
a group, we were credulous and co-operative. We flexed our
muscles and limbered up our minds.

Before our bodies could translate the intricate rhythms of
the great composers and poets, we were conducted to the
source of rhythm, even to its pre-organic origins. This necessitated a journey of a few million years while we progressed
retroactively through the heaving of continents, the ebb and
flow of metronomic tides, the rise of the moon and its corresponding lunar rhythms, the march of the seasons, the re-
flexes of night and day, the minute pulsations of light, the
huge swing of the solar system, and so back to the nebular

hypothesis. Then, slowly, we were allowed to go forward in time: to trace the rise óf animal motion as it worked its way through the amoeba, and to follow the first footed creature as it hesitantly lifted itself above the primordial slime.

We were trained to embody this progress. In tune with the infinite, the girls lounged in diaphanous "rhythm gowns" and the few men sprawled consciously in bathing-trunks while the aeons danced through our veins. Even the setting-up exercises were designed to reflect the relation of man to all mobile life. Before Schubert was permitted to speak through us, we squatted upon the ground and kicked our hind legs vigorously in the manner of bull-frogs or wabbled about with dangling arms like a bear prematurely roused from hibernation. Some of the more advanced zoologists went on to become kittens and colts; one or two, with their eyes on professionalism, loped in the morning and leaped through the afternoon as expressively as any Nijinsky faun.

Mine was neither a light nor fantastic toe, yet I did my best to imitate the simpler rhythms. I resolved to be a terpsichorean song of joy and innocence; at the very least a tripping couplet out of "L'Allegro." I may have been somewhat inhibited, but I was not ashamed of my cavortings. I remembered (and wrote about) the Greek warriors who did not disdain to dance in public, but, on the contrary, were so skilled in the art that tributes to their dancing were carved on their tombstones and immortalized in epigrams. But nature and an untamable lust for sweets conspired to defeat me. The swimming was superlative; the landscape was lovely; the girls were lovelier; the conversations were as surprising as the lives of the narrators. But I was gaining weight and losing patience. I never (alas) returned to that health-camp on the lake. My career as a dancer was over.

III

My next preoccupation with dancing was as remote from Miss Bea's conceptions as it was from Isadora's. I had seen Ruth St. Denis and her husband, Ted Shawn, attempt to express the instant's local communication by way of the Orient. But neither her adaptations of Hindu ritual nor their combined Denishawn school of impressionists seemed to contribute anything new to the cultural landscape. When Irene and Vernon Castle stepped out of a Julia Sanderson musical comedy (in which my uncle Samuel had an interest) I could not foresee that another liberation had taken place. But I followed their progress with growing awareness while the European importations were discarded and the two suave pioneers established new and distinctively American rhythms in the ballrooms of the four hundred and the dance-floors of the forty million. I watched the countless imitators of Isadora grow more and more arbitrary, abstract, and generally absurd. But it was not until I saw Angna Enters—first in New York, then in London, later all over the States—that the dance once more emancipated the audience and itself.

My friendship with Angna Enters has been a long and intimate one, but it has had a strangely itinerant nature. We have had tea together in darkest Soho and in her apartment which nestles, oddly enough, among the most expensive dress shops of Fifty-seventh Street; she has introduced me to old sherries in a refugee Spanish restaurant; our latest

reunion was across a Statlerized luncheon in Detroit. It was
by accident we first met, and our meetings continue to have
an accidental quality.

It was in an incongruous dance-and-musical-review that I
first saw Angna Enters. She was still in her teens; she had
the double desire to be a painter and to do something in the
theatre, possibly scenic design. She had never thought of
dancing, but someone had seen her sketches for costumes
and persuaded her to appear in them. Partly to satisfy her
well-wisher, partly because she was desperately in need of
cash, she consented.

Her debut in a hodge-podge of traditional comedy and
strained modernism was quiet but extraordinary—a dancer
who did not dance, a diseuse who did not speak, a panto-
mimist whose every gesture suggested another painting. She
was not, according to prevailing standards, overwhelmingly
beautiful, nor did she set out to win her audience by being
coy or calculating. She stood in semi-darkness, as in a shadowed niche, a Byzantine figure heavily draped, never moving out of the spot of light which emphasized the black hair
and intense eyes. It was impossible to recognize race or
nativity; she belonged to no age or place. By the posture,
the stylized economical gestures, the cupped hands and
pointed elbows, the long line of her arms and the sculptured folds of her gown, she was a composite of a hundred
medieval paintings, centuries of stone.

A few years later I was living in London, and I saw her
again. She had, in the interim, planned a series of wordless
scenes and dramas. She had hired a theatre on nerve and
twenty-five borrowed dollars; she had sent out her own
simple announcements, picking names at random from the

New York telephone book until her stamps ran out, uncertain whether or not the curtain would rise until the box-office had the required amount in the till. London had never heard of her, but after the first performance her name was everywhere. Among those who went backstage were Rebecca West and Arnold Bennett as fellow-artists, and Charles Morgan and J. B. Priestley as critics. They did not attempt to pigeon-hole the young American; they made no remarks about her departure from the conventional ballet or her failure to fit the new modernistic conventions. They spoke only of her rightful place: the place of the creator in the theatre. Later Aldous Huxley said that one of Angna Enters' programs contained enough ideas for a volume of short stories and half a dozen novels.

"You Americans!" said Bennett as we were leaving—the only sentences he addressed directly to me. "You people have every talent except the ability to recognize your own genius. You lost Whistler and Henry James to us—and I hope you lose this girl who is a little like both those expatriates. She, too, is a painter of portraits."

It was her portraits, in a new genre, sketches comic and critical, grave and exalting, which established her. Soon she became a legend. When I returned to America the legend was still growing. I was told that she had changed her name from Anita to Angna because names which were the same spelled backwards or forwards had a peculiar mystical power. She was, I was informed, an escaped nun, hiding an ancient family name under a *nom de danse;* I was also assured that she was of origins so mixed that her blood was a reservoir of all races. She was born, if all the reports could be trusted, in Bucharest, Vilna, Memphis, and Morocco. No one bothered to suggest that Enters was an eminently respectable German name and that the bearer of it actually was a child of Manhattan. She never stopped to dispute the wildest tales; she went on experimenting and extending her gamut. She traveled in both hemispheres, and brought back new ideas in form and feeling. She exhibited her work in crayon and oils throughout the country in arresting "one man shows." She published a valuable if strangely evasive autobiography, *First Person Plural,* enriched with fluent drawings, describing the costumes which were not only designed but executed by herself. She wrote a tragedy about "the mad Joanna," and when she could not find appropriate music for certain numbers she calmly turned to composition.

Not primarily a talker, her conversation developed the color and graphic quality of her mingled arts. I particularly remember her expression of disappointment in Germany, a *kultur* of which she had expected so much. She could not stop excoriating the ruthlessness of the rich, of the bullet-headed, fat-creased Junkers who out-caricatured the caricatures of Georg Grosz. She said that, time and again, she saw heavy-jowled Prussians, repulsively buttoned in short leather knickers, come into train compartments followed by a small servant-girl who carried enormous suit-cases and who lifted them up to the baggage-rack without any offer of assistance. She was, I gathered, more shocked by the people rushing out to gobble frankfurters between the acts of *Siegfried* than the crude farce of the health movements which culminated in the Nudist camps—epitomized by Sally Rand in her "Nude Ranches"—and sublimated in the Nazi slogan *Kraft durch Freude,* which a psychoanalytic wit contends should be *Kraft durch Freud.* I remember her swiftly drawn pictures of the

Grand Tour, the half-humorous account of her failure to find the ashes of Isadora Duncan in Père Lachaise, and the gatekeeper's complete ignorance of the dead dancer's place in the world of the living or the dead. I remember telling her that Heine had refused to be buried in Père Lachaise because he feared that the ghosts of the famous would spend the nights wrangling throughout eternity, and so Heine chose the cemetery of Montmartre as a quieter place to sleep.

But chiefly I remember the multiplicity of her effects, the protean shifts of mood, the seemingly endless portrait gallery to which she nonchalantly summoned archaic Greece and medieval Spain, an odalisque of the Bosphorus and a high-school girl of the Bronx, Mozart at breakfast and the not-so-Gay Nineties at the card table. Her immediate medium was the stage, yet her performance overflowed the theatre and carried far beyond the concert hall.

IV

I remember a typical recital. It began with something called "American Ballet: 1914-1916." The audience tittered, gasped, broke into chuckles of amusement and incredulity. Here, with broadly humorous strokes, with exaggerated glides and a false grace, Angna Enters was recording the forgotten steps of a gauche decade—the Bunny Hug, the Castle Walk, the Texas Trot, the Grizzly Bear—and recording them with a faint but unmistakable touch of burlesque. With just the right accent of wit, she made you realize that nothing dates so quickly as the innovation of yesterday. A satirist, you concluded, a comedian with a wicked glint in

her eye and a definitely ironic leg. She can, you told yourself, please the eye and provoke the mind but she cannot
stir the heart.

And then, with her very next number, you witnessed the
beginning of an enigma. "Ikon—Byzantine" revealed the
same empty stage—she used no more scenery than an occasional chair or table. But, instead of the flashy pre-war
flapper, here stood a carved figure, spare and austere. The
humorous commentator had vanished and someone serene,
almost sacred, had taken her place. The grave suggestion of
countless cathedrals filled the auditorium; one sensed the
great nave and the dim arches, one could almost smell the
incense. Something deeper than the intellect was stirred.
A triumph of gesture and arrangement, you conceded. She
is, you said, remembering her background, essentially a
painter. A painter, but not a dancer. "Compositions in
Dance Form," announced the program; a further proof that
Angna Enters was preoccupied with the painter's problems
of line, composition, and color.

And then she surprised you again. The next number
was entitled "Delsarte: With a Not Too Classical Nod to the
Greeks." Here was no elaborate costume, no effort to capture a period by contrast or comparison. In simple flowing
chiffon, following the astonishing routine which once was
regarded as a "Key to Esthetics," the performer registered
Joy and Grief, Hope and Despair, Doubt, Delight, Fear,
Abhorrence, and all the other capital-letter emotions so dear
to our grandparents. And then she danced, gracefully—a
little too gracefully, perhaps, a little too self-consciously—
danced and drooped and posed and pirouetted and scattered
flowers, all to the tune of Nevin's "Narcissus." The sly,

almost submerged travesty was reinforced by the next number, "Oh, the Pain of It!" which was very modern-abstract,
a left-handed tribute to the heavily emotional interpretive
moderns, and which said, by inference, that the dances which
"expressed" the soul of the machine, party tactics, and the
latter-day psyche are as strained and artificial as the anti-
quated rhetoric of the Delsarte ritual.

With nothing more than the projection of her multiple
personality, that "first person plural," she crowded the stage
with vivid people, and in each person she evoked an epoch.
Singly but with uncanny certainty she populated the theatre
of the imagination.

For example, in "Vienna Provincial: 1910" a chair, a table,
and a sewing box created the illusion of a room in one of
those suburbs which surround Vienna: Grinzing, Mödling,
Pötzleinsdorf. The young girl who entered crystallized the
effect. A prim little *Bachfisch,* neat to the last button, proper
to the pressed fold of the stiffly arranged frock, she was the
very pattern of what, some day, would be the model *Haus-
frau.* She had evidently just come back from church, and,
drawing off her black Sunday gloves, it was plain that one
of them needed mending. Carefully she inspected the offend-
ing hole, carefully she put on an apron—no well-reared
Viennese would think of sewing anything, no matter how
small, without first putting on her sewing-apron—carefully
she repaired the damage, and carefully she laid the dark pair
away. From the bottom of the drawer she drew out a pair
of white gloves, a handkerchief, a scarf, all of them folded
with housewifely precision. Donning these, she left the room
and moved, through imaginary doors, to another place. This,
it became apparent, was a gayer and more crowded room. A

party was in progress; there were bright lights and brighter quips, laughter, music, a waltz. At first a listener, the girl soon became a participant. She, too, sparkled; she entered into the badinage; she danced. But the best of parties must end; the guests began to withdraw; reluctantly she left. You saw her once more, back in her room, now tinier than ever, folding up her precious scarf, blowing out the fingers of her party gloves, putting away the company handkerchief. And in that combination of gaiety and gravity, of mild pleasure and severe discipline, you saw an entire period—the *vorstadt* Vienna gone forever—the end of a cycle, the mingling of suburb and metropolis so memorably depicted by Arthur Schnitzler. Here was a "slice of life" which the imagination could easily have expanded into a full-length novel.

Or there was the memorable "Boy Cardinal: 16th Century." Here, re-creating that fusion of beauty and brutality which characterized the Renaissance, she again revivified an age by concentrating upon an episode. Here, bold in his scarlet regalia, was one of those medieval boy prelates—possibly a Borgia's "nephew"—little more than a child, yet already cynical, touched with decadence, but still retaining the exuberance of boyhood. This was made clear by the mincing steps, the disillusioned eyes and the curled lips, as the already tainted youth went his way, blessing parishioners, listening abstractedly to questions, kissing the hand of some fair communicant. Whenever he thinks he is unobserved, he slyly produces a pair of castanets hidden in his sleeves and, while he practices new rhythms, his feet, not yet trained to ecclesiastical solemnity, instinctively break into the steps of a lusty folk-dance. Again, proving that she is not less at home in one century than in another, there is the American series called "Piano Music," which is partly played, partly mimed, and partly communicated by states of mind. Here is the adolescent girl in the throes of her first love affair, dutifully and dully practicing her Chopin assignment, leaving the piano to look out of the window, dreamily plaiting her hair, gazing across the way where He lives, and returning to the piano to sob her heart out over a sentimental music-hall tune. And there is her sister—or maybe it is she, herself—at Commencement, nervously fingering her diploma and sheet-music, waiting her turn to play, a performance which is a triumph of application, pathos, and comedy.

Or there is "Aphrodisiac: Green Hour," a study of a Parisian *fille de joie* (a denial in terms, for she is no longer a girl and she is certainly without joy) waiting, patiently but not too hopefully, for her prey; watching the sky for the rain which will ruin her evening's work; down to her last cigarette—a study from the crayon of Daumier and the pen of Maupassant. As a complete contrast, there is the reverent and lovely "Queen of Heaven," possibly the most commended of her compositions, a perfect embodiment of all the Gothic madonnas, and which, by using the sacred rose as a symbol, tells in parable the greatest of Christian legends.

The range is from antiquity to tomorrow's headlines, from sheer pattern-making to savagely critical cartoons. Intuition joins with observation; in 1937, a year before the Munich betrayal, Angna Enters created "London Bridge Is Falling Down," which ends as the once-proud Britannia falls to her knees waving a small swastika flag. In "A Modern Totalitarian Hero" the combined brutality and homosexuality of the Nazi regime are symbolized by a gas-mask and a powder-puff; the goose-step is pitted against a rose which happens to prick the hero and is consequently torn and trampled under foot. The mime as satirist often gives way to the clown as critic. A burlesque of the Monte Carlo Ballet develops into a devastating skit which she calls, with a grimace to a popular song, "Riviera, Stay 'Way from My Door," and which has roused the ire of fanatic balletomaniacs. There is "Field Day" which is childishly outspoken, and there is "Odalisque" which is frankly unspeakable.

Here, in its own way, is another native exploration, a new cultural frontier. The function of the mime may have been older than Greece, but the contradictory spirit born under a dancing star, the spirit of play and purpose, has become as indigenous as corn and skyscrapers, as American as the music of George Gershwin, the water-colors of John Marin, the architecture of Frank Lloyd Wright, the flashing repercussions of Walter Winchell, the tap-dancing of Bill Robinson and Fred Astaire, the prose of Ernest Hemingway, the plays of Clifford Odets, the poetry of Robert Frost. Isadora Duncan and Angna Enters—they, too, have declared a native independence.

And yet . . . And yet . . .

With the sigh that accompanies the surrender of a great career, I can at last regard my failure as a dancer with resignation and not too much regret. Look, I say to myself, at Ted Shawn and his male coryphees. Look at Nijinsky immured in an insane asylum. It is a woman's world, the world of the dance. I comfort myself that, glorious though it may be, I am no longer in it. It is, I conclude with a final alas, not for me.

GOD IN GREENLAND

MY FRIEND James N. Rosenberg has made a specialty of helping his intimates through their malaises and maladjustments. He is ideally suited for the self-imposed task, for James has understanding, patience, and two beautiful houses in the country. His town apartment is a combination of studio—James is a painter as well as an authority on reorganizing private corporations—clinic and hospice; his Mamaroneck home is a refuge for expatriates and wild swans. But it is in his Adirondack camp that he seems most at home, and it was there' that I discovered the acres which mean home to me.

I had watched James change a wilderness of pines and birches into the domain too modestly called "Shanty Brook." I had observed his passion for water grow into something like hydromania. James was always diverting, especially when he was diverting rivulets, misguiding trout-streams past his bedroom window, forcing brooks where they never wanted to go, and attempting to make a pool of a leaching mud-basin which now contains nothing more than an indestructible diving-platform to commemorate his mad optimism. His friends chaffed him that he was bent on transforming his houses into house-boats, that his favorite character in history was Noah, and that in the basement of his law office he was secretly drilling for wells to flood the city with canals. I had envied him as he built and rebuilt, patched and enlarged, employing the prodigal economies possible only to the rich—until his wife made the classic remark about his penchant: "Jim has such a good time doing it this way, and it doesn't cost him *much* more than if he did it right in the first place."

There came a time when I needed an abrupt change of environment, and it was Jim who found it for me. Jim was really seeking a place for Rockwell Kent who had a similar need, but Rockwell wanted something richer, vaster, more Kentian than was offered by the country near Elizabethtown. Rockwell scorned the Bartlett farm which had only one hundred and fifty-seven acres, two small trout-streams, a pheasant hedge, and only half a mountain of sugar maples. I bought the farm.

I needed a change not only in scene but in tempo. I was tired of the mechanized noises, the futile speed, the carbon monoxide gas which suffused my native city. I planned to escape the routine gatherings, the cocktail parties to which one never wanted to go and to which one always went, the public way of the arts, the publicized method of the artist, and the hothouse atmosphere of art colonies.

The village of Elizabethtown folded in the mountains promised such a retreat; a farm two miles from the rural courthouse seemed a safe and almost hermetically sealed haven. I was wrong. I had reckoned without my friends. A few years after I had discovered the difference between a hemlock and a tamarack, and had learned to name all the birds without a gun, my friends surrounded me. They still do. Lee Simonson lives near Port Henry, eighteen miles south of our cow-shed. Rockwell Kent is at Ausable Forks, twenty-eight miles north of the tool-house. Six miles closer, at Upper Jay, Donald Ogden Stewart has built something in the grand manner. Raymond Knight, the playwright, is at Westport-on-Champlain, ten miles away. Gino Mangravite, the muralist, is bringing up his family at Wadhams, seven miles distant. During the summer Wayman Adams, the portrait painter, conducts a busy school of more than fifty at the edge of town, in what was Elizabethtown's old mill. Pauline Lord, the actress, lives in lavish simplicity on the very dirt road which I had come to consider my exclusive right of way!

There are times when I think of moving back to the city for quiet and privacy. But I love the country and my friends with a fixed and almost unreckoning attachment. The plowed fields fill me with possessive pride; the new-budded potato patch is fair as any garden in Hesperides: the warm ammoniac smells of the barnyard are more satisfying than the roses of Sharon. It may be coarse, but to me it is always compelling, rotten-rich, instinct with life. I seem to be to the manure born.

II

In a way, so does Rockwell Kent. But he was born to be and do so many things. From the first he was traveler, a lover of distance, the further and more barren the better. Cold and difficult places had a special fascination for him; rigorous ice and snow did for him what the romantic tropics did for Gauguin. His fullest expression has been reached in the extremities of frost and loneliness, in the wilderness of Alaska, in the bleak hardships of Tierra del Fuego, in the wild treeless leagues of Newfoundland, in the harsh islands off the north of Maine, in the frozen wastes of Greenland.

Terror has been a stimulus and a challenge to him. No one has ever so loved and so recorded such extremes of vigor, such beauty in barrenness.

It was expected that Rockwell would be an architect; he was trained for the career. But the prospect of spending his life in an office, forever applying the seat of a chair to the seat of his pants, was too much for him. Anything else was preferable. He did everything else. He became a lobster-fisherman, a peripatetic carpenter, a day laborer. In Maine he became a grave-digger. One of his specialties was well-drilling; from drilling he graduated to dynamiting; and, since the ground in Maine is frozen half the year, digging and dynamiting graves in frozen ground became his forte. An episode in which the dynamite was thawed out in an oven while doughnuts were frying is nonchalantly told in *N by E*. One of his occupations when he was living on Monhegan Island was cleaning privies. The pay was fairly high: five dollars a privy. He says it was worth it.

All men are inconsistent, but Rockwell is the most self-contradictory person I know. He luxuriates in the domestic life; but he dreads domestication. He is all for artistic form and social discipline; yet he distrusts laws and is an order unto himself. He delights to play the patriarch, commanding his wife and five adult children, four of whom are married; but his own thoughts and acts are free beyond question. He was born under a restless star; at fifty-six, six times a grand-father, he is still restless and reckless.

Tossed upon thunderous seas below the Straits of Magellan, he dreams of a farm on fixed earth; calm and coddled in New York, he writes of Patagonia. He appreciates the paradox only too well; he realizes how impulsively, how

unreasonably, he is willing, even eager, to be off somewhere—
anywhere. Again and again he embarks for the little-known,
the desperate seas, the hazardous passage and the glacial
shore. In the midst of happiness the footloose spirit makes
its fierce demand and the heart "cries out its own despair,
speaks its own doom and banishment."

Rockwell has always been hounded by a demon-angel who
promises him that the vision is attainable, even though it is
always beyond. Always beyond the vision flies; it tricks and
eludes him; yet he follows happily if blindly. Often the
vision is a social vision; often it is an apparition of sheer
line and color. But, whether it is a passion for pure justice
or for pure wonder, he is always ready to take ship and
plunge into fresh pursuit. He is William Blake one moment,
Captain Ahab the next. "I want! I want!" he cries, erecting
his ladder against the moon. "Yield! Yield!" he prays, strain-
ing after the white whale of beauty, the never-captured
Moby Dick of the unconscious.

He has recognized this himself with only occasional mis-
givings. At the very beginning of *Voyaging* Rockwell writes:
"How unobserved and silently is the deep measure of the
soul's endurance filled; it mounts the rim, troubles a moment there; then like a torrent overflows—the vast relief of
action. This hour you are bound by the whole habit of your
life and thought; the next, by unerring impulse of the soul,
you are free. How strong and swift is pride to clear itself
from misery or joy, from crowds, from ease, from failure,
from success, from the recurrent brim-full, the too-much!
Forever shall man seek the solitudes and the most utter
desolation of the wilderness to achieve through hardship the
rebirth of his pride."

Yet Rockwell is no isolationist. Although he has worked alone at a hundred homely tasks—building a house, making woodcuts, setting the beans to soak, writing an illustrated diary—he loves to work among men. It is not only in the solitudes but in society that he has achieved the "rebirth of his pride." Ten years ago his latest odyssey brought him to this corner of the world. He has gone a long way around to come home. Home it is, and never has man found a more appropriate one. Wilde (or was it Whistler?) claimed that Nature was always imitating Art; Rockwell's "Asgaard Farm" proves the contention. The dramatic contour of the land, the far-reaching vista, the powerfully ascending climax of hills are those of his visionary drawings. "My God!" exclaimed one of his friends as he drove up the first time, "Rockwell *would* live in a landscape that looked exactly like him!"

Rockwell is one of the painters who have discovered themselves in their backgrounds, who have found their own soul in their own soil. He, too, echoes Whitman in believing that the running blackberry adorns the parlors of heaven, that a mouse is miracle enough to stagger sextillions of infidels, and that the cow crunching with depressed head surpasses any statue. Grant Wood, of Iowa, definitely declares that the common cow is a greater source of inspiration than the most beautiful model in Montparnasse. Thomas Benton, of Missouri, goes further and exalts the ass; the despised mule, says he, "is a damned dramatic animal." Rockwell takes and leaves his animals where he finds them; he animates mountains. Mountains take on a new meaning in his work; sometimes they are attended by symbolic figures, sometimes they have a humanity of their own. Here again Rock-

well establishes an intuitive wisdom, a kinship with Blake
who wrote:

Great things are done when men and mountains meet;
This is not done by jostling in the street.

III

It is Rockwell's vigor, even more than his versatility,
which is the wonder of his friends and the stumbling-block
to his critics. He lives on high, whether he is arranging fes-
tivities, planning a book, or driving a car. When he is doing
the last, he is a *deus ex machina* of the most dynamic, even
demonic, sort. His best friends hold their breath and cower
in the back seat while Rockwell takes all curves on one whis-
tling wheel. As Donald Ogden Stewart once said, "To drive
in an automobile with Rockwell Kent at the wheel is to
know God—or want to know God."

A party at Rockwell's is even more breathless. His daughters have been married *al fresco*, on the side of a hill, between Rockwell's living room and an oversize swimming
pool. The weddings have been something between a community affair, a marriage feast out of Breughel, and a robust ritual in which only the fittest can hope to survive.
The ceremony begins long before Supreme Court Justice
Brewster puts on his officiating robe. Many toasts are sol-
emnly proposed in what is the most comically intimate bar
ever built by an artist who is not afraid to satirize himself. After the legal stamp has been put upon the proceedings, the varied guests—among whom are eminent publishers, hired men, Broadway actresses, members of the

Vermont Symphony orchestra, local contractors, assorted
artists, and near-by roadhouse keepers—entertain each other
with acrobatics on the lawn, high diving, ground and lofty
tumbling, quartet playing, and kayak stunting. I remember
seeing Tony (of "Tony's") practice his yoga, standing on
his head and singing the entire prolog to *Pagliacci* without missing a note or disturbing a grass-blade.

Dinner follows, in the Kentian tradition, gay and gargantuan. There are tables of more *smörgåsbord* than were ever
set in Sweden. There are whole roast piglings, haunches of
"mountain lamb" (the native euphuism for venison), a variation of Shepherd's Pie invented by Frances Kent, vast communal bowls of salad, great cakes and lordly cheeses—baronial to the last mouthful. All this is interlarded with fresh
toasts during which the ceremonial *aquavit* (a caraway-
flavored gin) is washed down with goblets of beer.

Dinner over, the party distributes itself to gossip in front
of the appropriately huge fireplace, to play The Game, or
merely to relax. But Rockwell has other ideas. He hates
nothing so much as inaction, and he is not going to allow
his guests to sink into a lethargy humiliating to his repute.

"Up!" he shouts. "There is still plenty of light left. It
won't be dark for hours, and you can sleep tomorrow.
Up!"

Not too resentfully we are up—and doing—with a heart for
any fête. Some of us are dragged to the tennis court, while
Rockwell demolishes his opponents with berserk smashes and
viking war-whoops. Some of us are hoisted upon horses, and
ten minutes later Rockwell is spurring us on as though he
were leading the charge of the Light Brigade. Some of us
are thrown into the swimming-pool, while Rockwell dives

between the startled strugglers, disappears over the dam only to emerge as a seal, a spouting walrus, an irrepressible white whale.

Afterwards there may be music or reading (usually Coleridge and Laura Jean Libbey) or weak matching of wits or violent debate or a little unorganized sparring. But never silence, never pause or boredom. At midnight the least hardy of the participants begin to crawl upstairs; an hour later a few more find their way to one room or another; at three in the morning the toughest of them have surrendered.

This is Rockwell's great moment. It is quiet—quiet enough to play a flute. Which is precisely what Rockwell does. It is the closing ceremony. I go to the piano, and we two play over the songs of Schubert, Schumann, and Brahms. This brings us to the simpler German folk-tunes and, with a little shortening of breath, we attack these. "Ich weiss nicht was soll es bedeuten." "O du fröhliche, o du selige." "Sah ein Knab' ein Röslein stehn." "Der Maie bringt uns der Blümlein viel." "Muss i' denn, muss i' denn. . . ." It is now about four. Reluctantly, Rockwell says good night.

I am up at eight, not because I am an early riser, but because of a bad dream and the third helping of herring salad. I creep down to the kitchen by the back stairs, not wishing to rouse the household. "When Mr. Kent wakes," I tell Nellie, "let him know that I am down at the pool."

"Mr. Kent?" Nellie asks by way of answer. "He's been up hours ago. He's always at his studio by seven."

Shamefacedly I remember that, no matter when Rockwell goes to sleep, he is up shortly after dawn. Ordinarily I admire such alert industry. Today I hate him for it. Feeling like the weakest scion of a decadent race, I totter toward my cup of coffee, reflecting that this is only the first day of a Kentian week end.

A few minutes later Rockwell joins me, brighter and more damnably energetic than ever.

"As long as you're not doing anything, Louis, Gordon would like to play a couple of duets with you," he says briskly. Gordon is Rockwell's youngest son. "Would you oblige the boy?"

"Why not?" I answer wanly. "I didn't know Gordon had become a musician. Tell him to come in."

Gordon comes in, and I go to the piano again. I move over for him, saying, "I'll play the left-hand part. You take the melody. Is that all right?"

Gordon nods, but he does not move.

"Aren't you going to sit down?"

"No," he replies. "I'd rather play standing up."

"Suit yourself, but it's harder that way. You *are* going to play the piano, aren't you?"

"No."

I become a little alarmed. "What are you going to play?"

"The trumpet."

And so we blare and pound out Sousa marches while the guests, in various tones of green, slink, horror-stricken, down the stairs. This, however, is a refinement of Rockwell's usual method. Ordinarily Rockwell's guests are summoned to breakfast with the call of the Valkyries, the *Hoyo-to-ho* being repeated fortissimo on the Victrola until the last recalcitrant is shocked back into life.

It is Rockwell's bounding health and his boundless energy which are responsible not only for his creativeness but for his controversial temperament. He takes to controversy the way other men take to drink—and he drinks, too, "as large in liquor as in love." He has been engaged in dubious battles ever since I have known him; I particularly recall three of the most recent. There was the single-handed fight with the Delaware and Hudson Railroad, in which Rockwell, slashing his way through a maze of red tape and a labyrinth of lawyers, came off victorious. He forced the company to send a passenger train over the abandoned spur of track from Plattsburg to Ausable Forks. But it was an empty victory, for the railroad scheduled a single coach at an impossible hour and, when it was not used, discontinued it altogether.

There was his struggle with the Republican "ring" of Essex County, New York, during which Rockwell took the stump with all the passion of Savonarola and the outraged resonance of William Jennings Bryan. He championed the common man, exposed the leeches who fattened on him, quoted the Bill of Rights, and predicted a Better Day. Alas for moral rectitude; Rockwell's common men cheered his harangues, drank his health at Monaco's Tavern, and unhesitatingly betrayed him at the polls.

There was the prolonged wrangle with the government because of an almost invisible detail in a mural which Rockwell had been commissioned to paint for the new Post Office in Washington. After the murals were completed and placed, it was discovered that one of the characters in the design held a letter, presumably sent by airmail from Alaska—Rockwell contrasted the dog-sled with the plane as a method of communication. The letter was seen to be covered with script. This, in turn, was deciphered but not understood, since it was in an obscure Eskimo dialect. Angry but undaunted, the government researchers finally had the message

translated by "authorities" and, to the horror of the patrioteers, the epistle spoke of the benefits of liberty and the
rights of free men. It took many months and many head-
aches before the seditious sentiments were finally allowed to
stand. This contretemps led to an attack on (and from) the
ruling powers in Porto Rico, which led to Rockwell's going
to Brazil to investigate the threat of fascism, which brought
him in conflict with the entrenched right as well as the
embittered left, which forced him . . . But here I descend
to party politics and internal factionalism. This is unfair to
the man, for the issues which compel Rockwell into action
may be doubtful, they may be impulsive, but they are not
petty. He does nothing by inches; his faults and follies, his
very foolhardinesses, are on a large scale.

I V

It was foolhardiness, perhaps, that first sent Rockwell to
Greenland in a small sailing vessel through storms which
would have sickened the average man and privations which
would have killed him. Rockwell landed on the very inch
of Greenland at which he had been aiming. He fell in love
with the forbidding country, the new experience, the unromantic, undemanding primitive men and women. He returned to them all, not because they were material for the
artist—Rockwell always considered art not an end but a
means, a by-product of life—but because they were rich in
the very simplicities which Rockwell regarded as the best
of existence.

To the natives of Ubekjendt (literally, the Unknown) and
Igdlorssuit Rockwell must have seemed the mythical deity

offering himself and his bounties to his favorite tribe. (His friends joked him about playing God to his Frozen People.) He brought them the world in a wooden chest and music that spoke by itself out of a magic box. He distributed hundreds of records and thousands of cigarettes. He had drink for the men and bolts of calico for the women. But he did not only give things, he did them. He made paintings for the people, erected his own house, showed them carpenter's tricks, built a dance-hall for them, and became the craftsman *in excelsis*. He invented games for them to play, sang for them, taught them new dances, arranged their parties, and never attended a Kaffemik without bringing presents. Since at Igdlorssuit alone there were one hundred and eighty kaffemiks, or birthdays, in one year, Rockwell had to be something of a miracle-worker. No wonder he became the overlord, the hero-king of the community. Women fought to become his housekeepers; men offered their wives as *kifaks* for a few gifts and the honor of serving the dispenser of good things; children were named after him.

The situation was serious, but Rockwell did not take it too seriously. He has told it all simply in *Salamina,* sometimes slyly, even with self-satire. Concluding his introduction, he writes that the book is about "Adventure, Romance, brave men, and beautiful unmoral women. (Good Lord, this is the twentieth century and I must lure on the gentle reader!) In short, great stuff. And since it does add glamor to *Pilgrim's Progress* and *Fanny Hill* to know that they were written in prison, I am pleased to say that *Salamina* was written in a 10 x 12 x 5⅓ foot turf house which I hastily constructed, fled to, and barricaded, that by escaping the

ardent solicitude of my heroine I might in peace pay her
the tribute of a book."

The book was completed in Greenland and, at his request,
Carl Zigrosser and I helped prepare it for the printer. We
were zealous proofreaders, and Rockwell thanked us profusely on his return. The thanks, with Rockwell's own twist,
appeared this way in the second edition:

> In this book all the mistakes in grammar and punctuation are
> to be attributed to the perverseness of the author who, unex-
> pectedly returning from Greenland, put back some of those
> errors that his friends Louis Untermeyer and Carl Zigrosser had
> so carefully eliminated from the proofs.

To assuage the feelings of an outraged editor Rockwell
sent me the new edition on my wedding anniversary with a
characteristic dedication: "To Esther and Louis—upon their
having, by God, and to the amazement and delight of the
good people (their friends) and the chagrin of their enemies,
weathered out another year of matrimony. And so, God having thus blessed, may he (we do!) continue blessing and
blessing them forever."

In such passages—and Rockwell's books are full of them—
one glimpses the man's damnable charm. There are times
when it must be difficult to live with one who has been
God—even the mythological ladies found Jupiter trying
when he was not terrible. But it would be far more difficult
to live without him. As host to a community, or public
figure, or private friend, he leaves behind him a long trail
of affection and generosity. A few years ago he redesigned
my home (without pay) down to the last drain-pipe, which
was cannily concealed in an imposing but false beam. The

living-room, completely paneled in knotty pine, is the scene of most of our gatherings. But Rockwell was not altogether pleased with it.

"It looks like the inside of an elegant casket," he complained. And, before the furniture lent gaiety and the books added color and intimacy to the shelves, the room probably did have a slightly funereal aspect. It was the large expanse over the fireplace that particularly troubled Rockwell.

"I don't know just what I'm going to do about it," he said. "But I'll have it fixed by the time you get back from your lectures."

He did. Making a frame of thin pieces of the same pine, he enclosed one of his most vivid paintings, "Valley of the Var," a faint impression of which is given in the black and white of *Rockwellkentiana*.

"I hope you like it," he said, "for it's nailed to the wall, and it would be a lot of trouble to take off."

This is a slight indication, not a measure, of the man as friend.

There is nothing that the man has not tried. At one time he was a draftsman-humorist and masqueraded as "Hogarth Jr." At another time he tried a combination of photo-engraving and hand-engraving, a process which he claimed was a great labor saver. He has worked in every medium from the delicate line drawings which embellish *Candide* to the more than two hundred superb illustrations for *Moby Dick,* his masterpiece, in which he finally freed himself from the overweighted symbolism of his Blake-and-white period. Perhaps it is as illustrator that Rockwell has won most praise. But, rather than accomplishment in any one manner or medium, it is the gamut of his work which expresses the man, a scope which ranges from muscular lithographs to whimsical bookplates, from huge murals to a Greenland air-mail stamp. He has illustrated, decorated, designed, and originated more than twenty volumes, from his own pseudonymous *The Tales of Tom Thumbtack* to *Beowulf*, from the neo-pagan *Venus and Adonis* to the neo-barbarian *Leaves of Grass.*

But there is one rôle in which he has been inadequately praised—even insufficiently appraised—and that is as a writer. I know no one who succeeds in expressing himself so richly, so simply, and so personally as Rockwell. His books have that completely unaffected, richly delineative, wholly revealing quality which great art is supposed to possess. They are extended letters to the reader; they are what correspondence between intelligent, and sometimes inspired, people should be and so seldom is. Correspondence—that is what they are: a corresponding flash, a sudden reaching out, a vibrant hail, a fulfillment of communication. All his volumes are letters, graphic and detailed and beautifully illustrated epistles, documents to his contemporaries. They never have the studied air, the false nonchalance and finicky style, of letters aimed at posterity, although posterity (that contrarious division of the human race) will undoubtedly read them. They are fresh and provocative; immediate in their conception, immediate in their compulsion.

Multiple though Rockwell's essays, articles, and accumulating volumes may be, I think of them as a series of extended notes, notes in a gathering autobiography. The writings mount steadily in interest and intensity. Some day the unpublished (and unpublishable) gaps in the narrative will be filled in, and then there will be the connected saga of author and artist, wanderer and home-builder, lover and fighter—the complete man. Some day a chronologically arranged *Collected Works* will show how full and yet how simple, how unpretentious and yet how profound, autobiography can be. I hope Rockwell lives long enough to complete the thoroughly Kentian task. And I hope I am there to see him do it.

PRODIGIES AND FUGITIVES

NATHALIA CRANE, the most remarkable literary prodigy since Marjorie Fleming, was eleven years old when I met her. She was already famous. She had published her first volume, *The Janitor's Boy,* when she was little more than ten. Kings County had proudly hailed her as "the baby Browning of Brooklyn" and the English Society of Authors and Playwrights, a society of which Thomas Hardy was president, had invited her to become a member.

I had already made her acquaintance in print and by correspondence. I had read her first astonishing lines and I had heard the story of their publication. In 1922 Edmund Leamy, then poetry editor of the *New York Sun,* accepted some verses signed by an unknown name, accepted them wholly on their merits, delighted with the curious twists of phrase. After two of the poems had appeared, Leamy wrote his contributor suggesting an interview. A few days later there appeared in the editor's office a young woman in her gay twenties accompanied by a child of nine.

Leamy naturally addressed his questions to the vivacious woman until the child, hearing a reference to the publication of future verses, interrupted: "But I'm the poet. I'm Nathalia Crane. That's only my mother."

The mother, I learned after I came to know the Cranes, was an Abarbanell, a descendant of the famous family of Spanish Jews who had been poets, musicians, artisans, and ministers of state. Nathalia's father, who was some thirty years his wife's senior, was a distant relation of both Frank and Stephen Crane, and claimed descent from John and Priscilla Alden. It was an amazing ménage.

The Crane family lived in a small flat on Brooklyn Heights. There were, until Nathalia was out of her teens, two rooms (besides an invisible kitchen) which were always overcrowded and overheated. As far as I remember, the windows were never opened and the phonograph was never off. This did not interfere with conversation. On the contrary. The Cranes were at their best when things were most feverish; they luxuriated in a welter of happy noises. Nanny, whose full name was Nathalia Clara Ruth Crane, frequently did her school-work with the phonograph fortissimo, the telephone ringing, the parrot Sinbad screaming vituperatively, Nelda Crane calling from the kitchen, and Clarence Crane arguing with me that war was not only a normal but a noble way of life. In the midst of this, Nathalia remained an unspoiled child. Reporters kept calling for facts and opinions, editors asked for new work, researchers pried into her home-life to test the validity of her gift; but Nathalia did not even suspect that she was a *Wunderkind*. She adored her father, who had had a melodramatic career and lived on conversation and coffee; she fluttered around her mother; she was concerned with nothing more abstruse than her immediate world. Early in our friendship I offered her a visit to the theatre—I think I suggested the Hippodrome—or anything else she preferred to do.

"Anything?" she asked.

"Anything," I assured her. "What would you like to do most?"

"Go to the Five and Ten. The big one on Fifth Avenue.

You can see much more there than you can in the theatre, and it lasts longer."

I remember particularly one of our afternoons in the red and gold emporium on Fifth Avenue. It was literally an afternoon we spent there; Nathalia never allowed herself to be dragged away from Mr. Woolworth's gleaming counters in less than three hours. She had forty cents to spend and she spent them gravely, with the deliberation, ardor, and energy of the experienced shopper. She had exhausted her budget when she saw an old-fashioned hour-glass. Immediately she wanted to exchange all her other gifts for it.

"I'll give you another ten cents if you'll tell me why you want it," I said. "Is it to help you cook four-minute eggs?"

"Oh, no," she replied. "I want to see how time goes by."

It was the first thing she had said to make me remember I was shopping with a poet.

As a poet she puzzled me. There was a strangeness about her writing; an almost too pronounced childishness coupled with a most unchildlike vocabulary, a (was it cultivated?) quaintness which made her seem not so much a creature from another world as a visitor from another century. The work was alternately juvenile and mature, frivolous and profound, absurd and mystical; it was a mixture but not a fusion. There were the captivating jingles which began:

> *Oh, I'm in love with the janitor's boy,*
> *And the janitor's boy loves me;*
> *He's going to hunt for a desert isle*
> *In our geography.*

And:

I linger on the flathouse roof, the moonlight is divine,
But my heart is all a-flutter like the washing on the line.

And then, without warning, one came upon poetry that
was as indubitable as it was grave, epigrams that startled with
their accuracy and daring, images that stabbed the naked
soul. There were poems which began:

> *I sing a song of greatness—*
> *Of grandeur in a grain;*
> *Of seas that rim the minim,*
> *Of dust that breeds a plain.*

And:

> *Crumpling a pyramid, humbling a rose,*
> *The dust has its reasons wherever it goes.*

And:

> *I shall escape all the scholars,*
> *Giants who chant of belief;*
> *Pebbles will open their caverns,*
> *Pastures will call from a leaf.*

It was as if, in the midst of quiet play, a child had begun
speaking like Emily Dickinson or (as in "I sing a song of
greatness") had recited "Little drops of water, Little grains
of sand" the way William Blake might have rewritten it.

Here, and in the succeeding volumes, the lightly tossed
rhymes and rope-skipping rhythms suddenly announced concepts and phrases as breath-taking as "The aeons ran like
rain," "The fountains jetted slowly in the faith that they
would last," "A summer incantation tied the shimmer to the

trees," "A planet held the plumb-line," "Your towers turned to torrents, your walls waved like a fan" (this referred to Babel), the graves in Gobi were "the tombs Time left un-latched." She wrote a poem about homesick angels who long for the games and knickknacks they have left, even for "the hurdy-gurdies in the Candle Maker's Row"—

They listen for the laughter from the attics of the earth;
They lower pails from heaven's wall to catch the milkmaid's
     mirth.

Every poet has attempted to describe the combination of suspense and suddenness which marks the hummingbird. Emily Dickinson spoke of "a resonance of emerald" and "a route of evanescence with a revolving wheel." To Robert Frost the hummingbird was a feathered comet:

> *The meteor that thrusts in with needled bill*
> *And off a blossom in mid-air stands still.*

To Nathalia's keen eye the living spark was not only a route of evanescence suspended in mid-air; her imaginative observation found the hummingbird "pivoting on empti-ness." The rose, her favorite symbol, was "infected by the tomb," yet, indifferent to death:

> *Great is the rose*
> *That challenges the crypt,*
> *And quotes millenniums*
> *Against the grave.*

II

What obscure source was responsible for the casual wisdom, the precocious implications, the metaphysical boldness? What unguessed afflatus could cause such divinations to be uttered by a child not yet in her teens? Some said that Nathalia was not a real person, that she was a conspiracy, a composite of several older poets—which greatly amused those who knew the child. Others declared the whole thing was a hoax, and several critics supported this theory. This was ridiculous for at least two reasons. For one thing, a hoax perpetrated upon a child—a hoax which required the co-operation of the two parents and the daughter as victim —was unthinkable. For another, it was pointless. Nathalia's father certainly influenced her, and he was, more or less consciously, responsible for many of her "plots"; but the poetry was written by one who was simply a poet and only a poet. It was obvious who the poet was, and I saw no more reason to question the genuineness of Nathalia's gift than to doubt Pamela Bianco's or Yehudi Menuhin's.

Others contended that Nathalia was an unconscious mystic, an automatic medium unaware of what she was transmitting. In a sense I agreed. Definitely she was a medium of truths beyond her experience. But, even at eleven, her intuitions were more highly developed or, rather, more keenly sensitized than most people's. What is more, she believed in her intuitive powers. She spoke of them without pretentiousness, but also without naïveté. She was told, "You must learn arithmetic"—which she hated.

"Why?" she asked defensively.

"Because it will help you to learn astronomy"—which she loved—"and you will get to know more about the stars."

To which Nathalia calmly replied, "I know all about the stars."

"But, Nathalia," her mentor persisted, "how can you know all about the stars? The greatest scientists, with all their figures and instruments, can only guess about them."

"That's just it," flashed back the intuitive poet. "With all their books and telescopes they can only guess. But I know!"

Nor was she wholly unaware of what she was saying in her verse. Usually she knew. What is more, she could explain. She could, but she rarely did; she was so naturally a child she took it for granted that anything she knew must be common knowledge to her elders. I remember making a list of the more unusual terms in her poetry; in the second book, *Lava Lane,* published when she was twelve, I found "sindon," "perris," "sistrum," "barracoon," "parasang," "sarcenet," "nullah," "cincture," "cicatrix," "blastoderm."

"What's a blastoderm?" I asked Nathalia one day while we were at the Central Park Zoo. "It sounds like a huge animal, a kind of pachyderm. Is it?"

"You know," she reproved me. "You're just teasing me. You know as well as I do."

"Honestly I don't," I said. "It's a word I've never seen, and I forgot to look it up."

"Well," she said without a trace of embarrassment, "it's the thing which makes the eggs form; the thing which makes life."

And then I realized that what her mother told me was true, that Nathalia read the dictionary for pleasure. She was as fond of archaic terms as Francis Thompson. She collected unusual words, from the Greek to the Hindu, the way other children collect postage stamps, and she knew where to place the queer-sounding syllables just as the young philatelist knows where to put the queer-looking bits of colored paper. At twelve she had read *Ivanhoe,* the *Jungle Books,* and *The Arabian Nights,* but her favorite reading was in the Encyclopaedia, and I saw no less than half a dozen mammoth dictionaries, torn and thumb-marked, which she had gone through "for fun."

Words were her delight. Their shapes and colors were as tangible to her as pieces in a jigsaw puzzle, as serviceable as parts in a mechanical building set. Even the commonest conjunctions fascinated her. Only a genuine poet—a poet irrespective of age and sex—could have realized the firm solidity accomplished by the connecting monosyllables, the little welders of language. Nathalia said it in eight whimsical lines:

> *The little* ands, *the tiny* ifs,
>   *The ardent* ahs *and* ohs,
> *They haunt the lanes of poesy,*
>   *The boulevards of prose.*
>
> *Small primpers of the passages*
>   *With very slender limbs—*
> *And yet they make alliances*
>   *With lordly paradigms.*

This was at twelve. Then came *The Singing Crow,* published when Nathalia was thirteen, and *Venus Invisible,* which came out when she was teetering on sixteen. I watched her, with some misgiving, compose a novel on an odd theme ruined by a dry and stilted diction; it was called *An Alien from Heaven,* and it appeared when she was not quite seventeen. By this time she was the author of some seven volumes of prose and verse, including the extraordinary *Pocahontas.* *Pocahontas* was a phantasmagoria written in 1930 and placed in 1941. It described, among other things, two lovers, a misguided prince of Samarkand and the Empress of America, who live happily ever after on the lawn of the White House; a Red uprising in which the neglected Indians are persuaded to oppose the rebels—thus, by an act of more than poetic justice, fighting the Reds with Reds; and a gratifying rescue by my intimate friends:

> *Thus while the horror stalked a daunted land,*
> *Eight patriotic poets formed a band—*

The eight poets were disguised, but not too much to prevent readers from recognizing Hubert Crost as Robert Frost, Ira Arlington as Edwin Arlington Robinson, the two Monets as William Rose and Stephen Vincent Benét, Jarl Randberg as Carl Sandburg, Dean Parkham as the veteran Edwin Markham, brave Kinsey as Vachel Lindsay, and Lovis Vanderspire as—well, Nathalia's adjectives brought a blush to my hardened cheeks.

Since my favorite confrères figured prominently in the wild allegory, I was promptly charged with fathering a hoax. Some of the reviewers went further. They intimated that I was not only the author of Nathalia's poetry, but the creator of Nathalia herself, that Nathalia was my feminine *alter ego* just as the mysterious Fiona MacLeod was William Sharp's. Once more Nathalia became a national literary problem; once more Nathalia (and, to some extent, I) became involved with feature-writers, self-appointed investigators, psychoanalytical sleuths, and an army of amateur snoopers. Then, as other matters grew more pressing, I lost sight of Nathalia. She went to college, and I went abroad.

I I I

Several years later I learned that interested persons, to whom Nathalia mysteriously referred as "unknown powers," had offered to send her through college on one condition: that she publish nothing until after graduation. In Nathalia's letters these anonymous sponsors seemed alternately to be Olympian deities and eighteenth century patrons in the nobility. At any rate they kept their promise, and Nathalia kept hers. She waited (impatiently I imagine) until her twenty-second birthday, and then she published *Swear by the Night*.

The critics did not know what to make of the new work. They pecked at it gingerly. Unable to resolve her contradictions, they concluded that Nathalia had failed to mature and that, contrariwise, the maturing of a child prodigy was not an enviable occasion. In a way they were right on both counts. Manifestly there were few signs of growth, but this was not surprising; Nathalia was poetically mature at eleven. If the sensibility, even the calm sententiousness, no longer had the charm of novelty, it still was capable of such flashes as: "Forego the crutches of the moon and sun," "The chorals of the crow," "The thunder scolds the cricket for a noisy afternoon," and "The Dead Bee," which is a flash of whimsical insight that might have been mothered by the recluse of Amherst. Even had the book been trivial, even had Nathalia never written another line, she was a poet—and it is by his best that a poet persists, whether, like Keats, his life work is over at twenty-five or, like Whitman, barely begun at thirty.

Nathalia now teaches poetry to other children. Her native Brooklyn has found a gratifying place for her at Pratt Institute. She still writes poems which are, by turns, unusually graceful and unexpectedly awkward. The language shifts from simplicity to elaborate obscurity, as though a child had turned pedant. Her talents have not integrated: they still refuse to unite in a reasonable solution. I said that when Nathalia was eleven years old she puzzled me. She still does.

I V

They called themselves, mocking their own escapism, The Fugitives, although they never indicated from what they fled. They issued a magazine and signed their contributions to the first number with fancy pseudonyms: "Roger Prim," "Dendric," "Robin Gallivant," "Henry Feathertop." Vanderbilt University, in nostalgic Nashville, Tennessee, was scarcely the spot one might select for a cultural hatching ground; certainly it was an unpromising place for a group of prodigies, and experimental prodigies at that. Yet there they were, an odd dozen of them; young students, and teachers not much older than the undergraduates they taught. They became full professors, polemists, psychiatrists, biographers, historians, agrarians, dialecticians. But they all began as poets, and poets most of them remained.

There were seven of them to begin with in 1922, but before publication was discontinued in late 1925 there were double that many. Some of the contributors, all of whom originally met to discuss poetry and philosophy, forsook learning and literature; the two businessmen went back to their shops; the organizing philosopher retired to his private metaphysics. But the majority soon established themselves as the most interesting group in the country. Starting as local insurrectionists in the "Sahara of the Bozart" (the phrase is Mencken's) they seemed less exciting than the Imagists, that group of innovators which had just ceased to hold popular attention, but they were far more penetrating. Their influence was slower but deeper; they were less interested in visual effects and surface sensations than in states of sensibility. Whereas the Imagists issued credos and continually stressed the startling detail and the exact word, the Fugitives never formulated a program but emphasized the neglected commonplaces and the *allusive* word. Theirs was not always a poetry which could be enjoyed at first reading; their use of new connotations and intricate phraseology often retarded recognition. But the reader was rewarded with a pleasure no less lively and intense because it was postponed.

After the group had been scattered by time and geography an anthology of eleven of the members appeared. Interesting in their differences as well as in their similarities, six of the poets were particularly effective in their native originality, the serious accent and the undertone of irony, the tight grace and the richly imaginative vocabulary. These six were:

John Crowe Ransom. Born in Pulaski, Tennessee. Rhodes scholar at Oxford. On the faculty of Vanderbilt University and, more recently, of Kenyon College, Gambier, Ohio, where he organized and edited *The Kenyon Review*. Author of four volumes of poems, three of prose, and contributor to the group-book, *I'll Take My Stand,* which championed a curiously patrician agrarianism. Ransom, more than any of the others, was responsible for the new awakening of poetry in the South. As teacher and practicing poet he profoundly influenced all with whom he came in contact by his grave wit and unaffected gallantry.

Donald Davidson. Born in Campbellsville, Tennessee. Son of a schoolteacher, he taught at Vanderbilt University, issued three volumes of poems, and wrote essays protesting against those who favored an industrialized South dominated by the North. His work was first praised for its "mysticism," but its outstanding characteristic was its fiery localism.

Allen Tate. Born in Clarke County, Kentucky. He and his wife (Caroline Gordon, the novelist) were twice awarded fellowships by the Guggenheim Foundation. Author of three volumes of poems, three biographies of Southern soldier-heroes, and a novel. Taught at universities in Tennessee, North Carolina, and Princeton, New Jersey. Although the impulse prompting his work is frankly sectional, Tate's is a personally pronounced and intricate style. His circumambient method is perhaps the most intensely allusive of all the Fugitives; his critical attitude is revealed in the collection of papers grimly entitled *Reactionary Essays*.

Laura Riding (Gottschalk). Born in New York City. Studied at Cornell and the University of Illinois. She came to Tennessee by way of Kentucky, from the University of Louisville, where Louis Gottschalk taught history. Later with Robert Graves she founded the Seizin Press and published quantities of poetry disastrously influenced by Gertrude Stein and introduced by almost ludicrously pretentious prefaces. Her career as a Fugitive was brief, but—though she never forgave me for saying it—nothing in her later work surpasses the simple early "Afternoon" and the sub-acid "The Quids."

Robert Penn Warren. Born in Kentucky. He attended Vanderbilt, the University of California, the Yale Graduate School, and New College, Oxford. Upon his return to America he taught first at Vanderbilt, later at Louisiana State University. With Cleanth Brooks, Jr., he became one of the editors of *The Southern Review* and collaborated with Brooks on a college textbook. After publishing a volume of biography and one of poetry he turned to fiction. A Houghton Mifflin Literary Fellowship resulted in the *Night Rider,* a novel packed with social drama and almost inexhaustible vigor. Warren's poetry, like his prose, is tense, knotted in its passion, "strung with the bitter tendons of the stone." Departing from the Carolinian suavity of his colleagues, Warren's is a stripped Saxon utterance.

Merrill Moore. Born in Columbia, Tennessee. Son of John Trotwood Moore, the historian. He received his B.A. at Vanderbilt in 1924; his M.D. in 1928. Except for Warren, Moore is the youngest of the Fugitives. At first . . . But this prodigy is too prodigious to be confined in a paragraph. Besides, although I have had many friendly sessions with the other Fugitives, Merrill Moore is my constant fidus Achates. He has become our medical consultant; his boys and mine are growing up good comrades; our family lives have grown increasingly interrelated. He is so multiple a personality that I can scarcely consider him as just one person. Nevertheless, I remember . . .

V

I remember attending two of the early meetings of the
Fugitives. They were earnest but lively sessions. Each member submitted a poem or two, sometimes anonymously, sometimes signed. The poems were read and freely criticized. At
the next meeting other (and presumably better) versions were
brought in. All the members followed this procedure—all
except Merrill. Merrill never brought the same poem back.
He offered, instead, no less than twenty or thirty new sets
of verses because it was easier for him to write a new poem
than to revise an old one. His was such an alert and sug-
gestible mind that every comment prompted ideas, images,
and concepts for additional verses. His work grew not by
accretion but by proliferation; every tendril of thought bore
buds a hundredfold, burst into amazing bloom.

When Merrill turned to the sonnet, that strict and hal-
lowed form, he was no less unorthodox and profuse. Someone said that Merrill did not write sonnets, he shed them.
Even as an undergraduate his facility was a legend. I doubted
the rumors that he had a fabulous amount of sonnets in hiding; when, during a consultation about the arrangement of
his first book, he told me that he had written five or six
hundred I thought he was exaggerating. It was not an exaggeration; it was an understatement. Merrill's first volume
contained one hundred informal and highly individualized
sonnets; his second volume contained one hundred and fifty;
the third contained an even thousand.

I took some pride in the phenomenon, not only because of
my growing fondness for the man, but because his communal,

collaborative attitude reminded me of Vachel Lindsay's. Everything he heard, everyone he touched, every item he read, suggested a poem. Never has there been such a spontaneous creativeness. He learned shorthand so that he could get his fourteen-liners down the more quickly; I have heard him dictate a sonnet in his car during the change of traffic lights. He is now so strongly conditioned to the form that I suspect his conversations fall unconsciously into units of fourteen lines.

As a psychiatrist Merrill is brilliantly analytical; as a poet he has no gift for selection or self-criticism. Whenever he contemplates publishing a volume, which is practically all the time, he depends upon two or three friends. Out of a mixed fifteen hundred I had selected the one thousand sonnets which went into the appropriately entitled *M;* but before that Dudley Fitts had threshed some three thousand. When Merrill presented me with the material for his second book he permitted me to arrange the contents and give them a more or less unifying title. I called it *Six Sides to a Man,* dividing the sonnets into Seeing, Hearing, Touching, Tasting, Smelling, and, for good measure, Knowing—the intuitive or sixth sense. It was then that Merrill rewarded and horrified me. He made me his literary executor.

My horror increased when I took stock of my trust. Merrill has two houses, one near the Boston City Hospital, one at Squantum, Massachusetts. Both are crammed with manuscripts. A rough inventory of the bound sheets in the house by the sea and the contents of the filing cabinets in Springfield Street gave me the approximate total of forty thousand sonnets. Merrill says there are probably fifty thousand. If he is right, he has written more sonnets than all the sonneteers who ever wrote in English. He accepts the fact without boasting and without surprise. He says that, since his eighteenth year, he has written an average of five sonnets a day. Of course there have been scoreless days; but, to compensate for such inactivity, he has on occasion written as many as one hundred in four hours. He says he timed himself. An ultra-conservative estimate would make him the author of thirty thousand sonnets, to say nothing of uncounted lyrics, fragments, quatrains, experiments in free verse and free association. And Merrill, at the moment, is only thirty-six.

One might suppose that such industry would keep Merrill hermetically sealed in a completely isolated ivory tower. The contrary is true. Being a poet is, if not the least of Merrill's activities, merely one of his busy concerns. He spends most of the day at his office engaged in successful psychiatric practice. He instructs in the Harvard Medical School and pursues his researches at the Boston City and Boston Psychopathic Hospitals. His studies in cases of attempted suicide and in the problem of alcoholism were given wide publicity by the Associated Press. His published medical papers already number more than twenty and include such examinations as "Tumours of the Brain Associated with Marked Pleocytosis in the Cerebrospinal Fluid," "The Iron Reaction in Paretic Neurosyphilis," "Subdural Hemorrhage in Psychotic Patients," and the idyllic "Syphilis and Sassafras." He is an enthusiastic walker and a semi-professional swimmer; he competes annually in the twelve-mile race from Charlestown to Boston Light. Father of three sons and a daughter, he looks forward to a steadily increasing family. Far from seeking quiet, he loves a noisy household. During one summer visit there were, besides his own four youngsters, two of my sons and my wife's two nephews. Eight children under one roof are several more children than I can live with unprotestingly. My wife and I ran away to the beaches at Maine; but Merrill, backed up by Ann Leslie, his wife, insisted on keeping the children. He says he never had a more creative week end.

The duties of doctor, author, and paterfamilias do not, it seems, take up enough of Merrill's time. Since the European crisis he has devoted many hours to the refugee problem; he has found laboratories and sponsors for doctors from Germany and Austria. He has his fingers on an intricate network of wires; there seems to be no one whom he cannot reach. Without being boastful, he is frankly proud of this. His very setting confesses it. His bedroom is a spacious affair facing the Atlantic Ocean; he likes to feel he has the elements at his door. On each side of his bed is a large marble bust. "Your two selves," I said. "Caesar Augustus, the dominating self, and Apollo Belvedere, the self that wants to be the vatic poet."

"You're right, Louis," he smiled. "I didn't know it when I got the pair, but I'm sure that's why I bought them."

There was one more detail in the room which symbolized the machine-driven poet of modernity. Around the base of the Apollo and halfway up the column were newspapers— hundreds of newspapers that Merrill had not yet read, probably would never read, but that no one was allowed to throw away.

V I

What of the sonnets themselves? Although on varying levels of accomplishment, even the most casual have char-

acter; they are individual, as definitely Merrill's as Wordsworth's or Sidney's are their own. This is not to imply that
they are equally good. At the best Merrill's is not a work of
perfection; in such quantity it could not hope to be. But
at his height the poetry is fresh in spirit, startling in range,
and exciting in effect. His contemporaries have recognized
this. John Crowe Ransom hailed Merrill as the most spontaneous of poets, "free and easy in his way of generating
poems beyond anybody I know." William Carlos Williams
wrote that Merrill's sonnets were nothing short of magnificent: "What Moore has done is more or less what we have
all been striving to do in America since Whitman; he has
broken through the blinding formality of the thing and gone
after the core of it; not of the sonnet, which is nothing, but
the sonnet *form* which is the gist of the whole matter."

Here the experts differ. The purists have been outraged at
Merrill's riotous assaults upon the classic structure; the ex-
perimentalists believe that he has conceived and constructed
a form of his own, an American sonnet, a new method as
recognizably native as Petrarch's was Italian and Shakespeare's English. I agree with the latter opinion. The tone
is so seemingly careless, the manner so impromptu that some
readers have been deceived into thinking that the lines are
slipshod and the results trivial. But it is only the rigidity
which has gone; the old form of the sonnet has not been
destroyed, it has been reanimated. Most of all, it is the mass
and mixture which is imposing: the incalculable scope, the
abrupt shifts of interest, the fevered energy, the quick succession of plodding fact and headlong fantasy. Everything
is here in a rich disorder. There is never time for hesitation
or editorial improvement, never a pause or letup. "Hurry!

Hurry!" his frantic daemon urges him. "It is later than you think! It is always later than you think!"

Meanwhile the sonnets grow alarmingly in number. By the time Merrill is forty, there will be another five or six thousand. By the time he is fifty he will, if nothing stops him, be the author of more sonnets than have been printed since Wyatt brought the pattern to London in the sixteenth century. Even if Merrill publishes occasional volumes of one thousand sonnets each he will never catch up with himself. He is his own psychiatric problem. Can he apply an inner check, a drastic inhibition? Can he forego creation entirely? Can he declare a self-imposed moratorium?

The problem is also mine. I remember again that I am Merrill's literary executor. It is a career in itself. I sometimes suffer from nightmares when I contemplate the situation: I see myself pursued by an army of determined octaves and sestets, gaining upon me with every rhyme; I find myself slipping down an ever-growing mountain of verse or drowning in a sea of sonnets. There is just one consolation. I am seventeen years older than Merrill and, by the law of expectancy, he should outlive me. I hope he takes good care of himself.

GRAUSTARK TO MAIN STREET
AND BEYOND

THERE was a period in my youth when I lived happily in Graustark. I was not alone there by any means. Most of my generation were living in countries off the map; they left Graustark only for such equally remote and romantic havens as Zenda and Ruritania. Romance, of course, took place wherever you did not happen to be in actual life, and the most popular books were those which offered the speediest (as well as the surest) methods of escape. I remember some of the more alluring titles: *When Knighthood Was in Flower, The Prisoner of Zenda, Rupert of Hentzau, Under the Red Robe, Saracinesca, The Deemster, King Solomon's Mines.* . . . The very names stole the heart away.

We were still, culturally speaking, in the nursery; we could not give up our beloved fairy tales. We identified ourselves with the glamorous figures in the exciting never-never land because the real world (so we thought) lacked glamor and excitement. Worse, we suffered from a mass inferiority complex, ashamed of our backgrounds, distrusting the present, fearing the future. The fairy tales of Grimm and Andersen brought up to date continued to justify us. As boys we had watched the ugly duckling grow into beautiful Horatio Alger swans by way of *Ragged Dick, Fame and Fortune,* and *Mark the Matchboy;* they were translated and glorified in the somewhat older Rudolph Rasendyll. The disinherited youngest son triumphed all through G. A.

Henty, and Cinderella kept on growing through *The Little Princess* and *Janice Meredith*. Such books took us out of ourselves and the world which was too much with us. We did not care where they took us as long as they took us out of America.

We did not like being brought back to vulgar reality. We resisted the plodding purpose and heavily accumulating honesty of Theodore Dreiser in favor of the slick legerdemain (the old fairy tale formula) of O. Henry. We pretended to admire the delicate realism of Sarah Orne Jewett, but we preferred the gaudy romanticism of Robert W. Chambers. It was a long time before we tired of running away, running in several directions at once. We demanded nothing of our literature but speed and amusement. Suddenly we were weary, and we were no longer amused.

For years Sinclair Lewis had been writing short romances with tricky endings, success stories, polite and profitable fictions. Something happened, and Lewis felt he could not invent another variation of another fairy tale.

"I want to write something that will get the truth out of my system. I want a change. I want to write a novel about real people in a really representative middle-size, middle-class American city. It will be unpleasant and, of course, unprofitable. Maybe nobody will read it. But I've got to do it."

"What are you going to call this bid for unpopularity?" I asked Lewis.

"Main Street," he said.

This was a new kind of liberation. It was not an escape from the world but a deeper penetration into it, not a release but a re-examination. We began to demand recreation which was also a re-creation; we came of age in fiction not by evasion but by possession. Even when we broke through reality we insisted on a liberal measure of truth. We hailed *Jurgen* and *The Silver Stallion* not because of their glittering manicured prose but because of their penetrative irony; Cabell's rhetorical heroes may have been more fustian than Faustian, but we relished their thinly disguised declamations because they represented more truth than poetry.

Lewis, Cabell, Mencken—they were strangely dissimilar, yet they spread a common contagion. In their very distortions ordinary life was intensified, experience became more meaningful. The reactionaries, yearning for fabulous morals, complained that we learned nothing from the realists. We replied in the same terms that Goethe replied when questioned about Winckelmann's purpose: *Man lernt nichts wenn man ihn liest, aber man wird etwas*—"You don't learn anything when you read them, but you become something."

We *became* something when we encountered the Kennicotts, Babbitt, Arrowsmith, Dodsworth; these people lived as contrariously, as roughly and richly, as American life. And we lived with them: even at home they extended our horizons, pushed back the borders of our mind. Theirs was a national contagion. We were infected by their irreverent questioning; writers as well as readers caught not only an unworshipful audacity but a fundamental habit of interrogation which was, in itself, an integrity.

This native blend of boldness and enthusiasm, of skepticism and affirmation, has been characteristic of Sinclair Lewis from the beginning. I have known "Red" on the heights and in the depths, but he has never lost the fortunate combination. He takes pride in the very characters he pillories; his private burlesques of the smoking-car Lotharios and the blatant Rotarians have grown naturally into his most famous dramatis personae. Compare, for example, Lewis's actual understanding of common people with most of the determinedly class-conscious novels. Lewis repudiates easy solutions and political cant as he suspects the cultural snobbery which systematically praises the illiterate and exalts only the ignoble, a kind of third-class consciousness.

It may be this distrust of shibboleths which accounts for Lewis's failure to write the long labor novel expected of him. Ever since I have known him he has been contemplating the work, making exhaustive researches, filling his notebooks with encyclopaedic data. Possibly he may yet write it. He is usually engaged on three novels at one time; he may temporarily discard two of the three, but he never wholly abandons them. His critics, misled by his uncertain fertility, have a habit of predicting his creative death. After the Nobel Prize had been awarded to him, and he had celebrated the event in his lusty manner and at somewhat more than the usual length, his antagonists again predicted his end.

"Lewis is through," they announced cheerfully. "This time he's finished for good."

Whereupon, after delivering himself of a preliminary novel or two, he wrote *It Can't Happen Here.* It was unforeseen, but it was to be expected. "Red" has a way of rising, like a gangling phoenix, from a nest of empty bottles and the ashes of criticism.

I remember a recent visit to the Lewis-Thompson household in Vermont. Dorothy, with the aid of a servant she had brought from Vienna, had given us a dinner which could no longer be obtained anywhere on the Ringstrasse, not even at Sacher's. We talked long past midnight, Dorothy and "Red" achieving a perfect balance of history and legend. Dorothy was just being acclaimed for her unprecedented column, and no less than five unwritten novels seemed to be brewing in the vat of "Red's" imagination.

My wife and I had expected a short and early breakfast since we were driving north to Montreal. But "Red" came to the table with the outline of still one more novel. This was another typically Lewisian combination of current problems and quickening personality. It would be unfair to detail the plot—"Red" may be at work on it even now—but it concerned the Jewish problem. What surprised me most was the extraordinary perceptiveness displayed in the rapid sketch. It was not just the knowledge of broad issues which astonished me—for "Red's" factual powers were proverbial—but the analytical wisdom, the almost too-sensitive sensitivity, which only a Jew among Jews could express. We stayed on past lunch.

I I

The contagion spread; the new novelists infected themselves as well as their readers with the virus of discovery. They began to investigate the far-spreading vistas and further-reaching implications of the present scene, to explore the robust dignity of their own regions, to relate the individual to the mass. Graustark had given way to the hinterland; the lines of communication ran far beyond Main Street; the frontier was everywhere. No longer parochial or escapist, literature became nationally inclusive. Instead of the impossible composite, "the great American novel," there grew up a rapid series of novels outlining a new literary map, novels that were both sectional and symbolic.

New England was recorded through the fine-edged austerities of Sarah Orne Jewett and the blunt ironies of John P. Marquand. New York's changing social scene was illuminated by Edith Wharton. The politer phases of the South were delineated by the suavities of James Branch Cabell (whose mythical Poictesme was only a few miles away from Albemarle County, Virginia) and the more delicate but no less destructive malice of Ellen Glasgow. The pioneering backgrounds as well as the antebellum remnants of the less affluent South were unforgettably heightened by Elizabeth Madox Roberts. The impolite and once inarticulate stretches of Georgia, Alabama, and Mississippi were given racy tongue by Erskine Caldwell, who mixed a fantastic humor with frightening realism, and William Faulkner, whose people seem to exist on the levels of subconsciousness and whose furious settings form a neo-Gothic though native Chamber of Horrors. Florida, hitherto exploited for its sweetness, light, sunkist oranges and old folks' Eden, finally achieved its laureate in Marjorie Kinnan Rawlings, who wrote not from the fashionable beaches but out of the uncultivated scrub. The Northwest learned to speak through the careful accents of Willa Cather and Ole Rölvaag, who summed up the credo of his colleagues by saying, "The unforgiveable sin is to write about life untruthfully."

Regions which never had been explored and people who never had been expressed found their interpreters in every district. John Steinbeck progressed with gusty energy from picaresque tales of the western coast to *The Grapes of Wrath,* which his contemporaries hailed almost without a reservation; they compared it to such panoramic works as *Moby Dick* and *Leaves of Grass,* while Clifton Fadiman asserted that this Homeric chronicle of the great migration from the dust-bowl was an *Uncle Tom's Cabin* for our decade. Sherwood Anderson pioneered in a celebration of people whom his predecessors had considered "unliterary" if not illiterate; before he became ensnared in his own technique he revealed the vitality in plain speech and simple scenes. Ring Lardner used the American vernacular with surgical precision and devastating mockery. An entire literature, antiromantic yet persuasive, was founded on the "hard-boiled" tenderness and taciturnity of Ernest Hemingway. James T. Farrell searched for the least detail of daily experience and occasionally made the trivial seem tremendous. Katherine Anne Porter perfected a prose that reverberated as though it were written in counterpoint. John Dos Passos employed every device—the newspaper headline, the camera eye, the newsreel, the popular song, the condensed biography, interrelated narrative—to emphasize the decay of a system. Thomas Wolfe surpassed them all in energy and breathlessness; he wrote out of a rapid inner burning, a pulsating and tumultuous fire which consumed itself and its author.

Such writing touched a new awareness. It plumbed hitherto unsuspected depths in America; it pierced the layers of intelligence and reached levels beyond consciousness. It was solid and yet suggestive. Beyond all, it kept on growing.

III

What the novelists achieved in prose the poets accomplished in every type of verse. Whether traditional or experimental in form, the liberated spirit ranged across the states. New England spoke authoritatively and variously through Robert Frost, Edwin Arlington Robinson, and Amy Lowell. The theatrical coast of California loosed its thunderous tides across the country in the nightmare melodramas and fiercely surging lyrics of Robinson Jeffers. The patrician South found itself again in the elaborate idiom of The Fugitives. The mechanized cities of the Atlantic seaboard were heard in the messages—half secret code, half sky-writing—of Kenneth Fearing and Muriel Rukeyser. The vast industrial Middle West, pitting its prairie silences against the roaring mills, was sketched by Edgar Lee Masters, sounded by Vachel Lindsay, and spread out by Carl Sandburg.

Of the three Midwestern poets, Sandburg was the most powerful as well as the most panoramic. He employed curious and contrary devices: slang and mysticism, bizarre imagery and barber-shop gossip, private allegory and familiar folkstuff. His were a set of colossal memoranda, as brusque and as garrulous as the land that bred them. Following Whitman, they "expand the air." The notes are in everything Sandburg recorded: the monumental biography of Lincoln, the omnibus collection of folk-tunes, *The American Songbag,* and the rambling poetry of *The People, Yes.*

(I hear Carl's rumbling drawl as I write. I hear it lifted in song, accompanied by his guitar, to delight an assembly of young students. I hear it in public speech, championing the waning rights of the individual. I hear it—and enjoy it most—in private.

There was the time when we met in an Indianapolis bar, when we were arguing about the Hoosier frontier, and the bartender came over to the table to add his contentions to Carl's.

There was the time when Carl lectured in Toledo, Ohio, then my wife's home, when we brought him to the house for a hurried meal. Carl was to take the next train west. It was, we gathered, a train leaving "somewhere about eight in the evening." At eight we suggested calling the station for information, but Carl would not let us stir. "I'll take the next train," he said. At nine we thought of it again, but Carl was talking so expansively, so happily unconscious of time, that nobody moved. At ten we began to worry, but Carl settled himself down to a new anecdote. At one in the morning we took him to the station in the midst of another tall tale, Carl protesting that we were trying to get rid of him.

There was the time I was sleeping in a Chicago hotel. It was a deep sleep, for a long lecture had been followed by several friendly nightcaps. But I was roused peremptorily by the insistence of an angry bell. The telephone was at the other side of the room, and I stumbled to it, trying to recall where I was. Everything was wrong; the hour was wrong; the windows were in the wrong place; there was a sense of wrong in the bewilderment that hung over me. But the voice that came over the wire was right. It was Carl's voice.

"Hello, visitor." He dragged the syllables in his low baritone. "It's nothing to worry you. Nothing at all. I just thought it was an idea. It's a good thing for a man to be wakened in the middle of the night in a strange place once in a while. Once in a while he ought to feel how alone he can be—alone and a little frightened. That's all. It's three thirty. Now go back to bed. And forget it."

I think I mumbled, "I'll try to."

But it was impossible to forget. At the time it was even hard to forgive.)

IV

Playwrights and poets came into their own through venture and ridicule, daring and change. The poetic drama, after having been almost asphyxiated by the stale rhetoric of Stephen Phillips, was revived by the living language that came clean through the plays of Maxwell Anderson and vibrated over the air waves in the radio dramas of Archibald MacLeish. Words themselves were being transformed, distorted for emphasis, grafted with astonishing new growths. E. E. Cummings twisted words methodically in a mad typography. MacLeish fitted them into new cadences or put them to work on a sound track—witness *Air Raid* and *Land of the Free*. Hart Crane redistributed and joined them in seemingly impossible relationships, yet his apparently irrational associations affected and influenced writers as logical and divergent as Horace Gregory and Allen Tate.

("I want to do something with words," Hart Crane said the first time I visited him in Cleveland. "I want to make them strange and rich—rich in every way; in sound and sense and, most of all, in suggestion. I'd like to make them over, to make them jump—even jump two ways at the same time. Old words with new associations—startlingly new—queer but, somehow, exact. Of course, I can't do it—not yet, anyway. But that's what I'm trying for: the abrupt transition, the unexpected swoop, the long leap."

Alas for Crane. The leap was too much for him. Poisoned by drink and emotional disorders, returning to the America he loved and feared to face, he jumped out of a nightmare into the Bay of Mexico. He had liberated himself at last, but not before he had freed his words.)

From Graustark to Main Street and far beyond the new impulse carried. It established itself in discovery and flourished in reappraisal. Here it persists, possibly in the only place where gusto can survive, and the artist is still allowed to question and probe, experiment and play. This America, so casual-careless, so unafraid, may be the last outpost of uninhibited creation. In a world of censored whispers and dictated lies, this may be the one sanctuary of the freely printed word, the final safeguard of civilization.

LAWRENCE AND
ULTIMA THULE

THE FIRST time I saw Lawrence in Italy, in a suburb of Florence, we had little to say to each other. The second time I met him in London I talked too much. "H. D." had brought me to Dorothy Richardson's, and the two women had brought Lawrence to the flat in which I was living. Frieda, Lawrence's wife, was also there, an almost theatrical contrast to her husband. Solid, simple, assured, she was health itself: the earth-mother Lawrence was always seeking and escaping, but to which he always returned. She was proud of her rôle and of her past, even of her lineage. She made you know she was a von Richthofen and that Lawrence was a commoner. She refused to be pitied for the hardships she and Lawrence endured during the war when they lived, servantless and unfriended, in a flimsy shack on the coast of England.

"But you mustn't sympathize with me. I didn't do any of the menial work. Lawrence did that. Lawrence scrubbed the floor. He loved it."

Lawrence smiled and went on discussing the scenic designer Robert Edmond Jones and the psychoanalyst C. G. Jung and Mabel Dodge Luhan. He crossed and uncrossed his legs continually while he spoke; his voice, curiously high-pitched, jerked from sentence to sentence; his silky beard was a hank of what, in the artificial light, seemed a bright pink; he had an almost falsetto giggle. Perhaps he was ill at ease.

Perhaps I only thought he was. At any rate, I did the wrong thing. I tried to outrace him in conversation.

It was a literature-crammed evening, but I had learned nothing of Lawrence that his books had not continually revealed again and again. What he thought of me was not apparent until Mabel Dodge Luhan published *Lorenzo in Taos* six years later. In a letter dated September 23, 1926, Lawrence wrote to Mrs. Luhan: ". . . I have seen a few of the old people: and yesterday the Louis Untermeyers: extraordinary, the ewige Jude, by virtue of not having a real core to him, he is eternal. Plus ça change, plus c'est la même chose: that is the whole history of the Jew, from Moses to Untermeyer: and all by virtue of having a little pebble at the middle of him, instead of an alive core."

I was, I suppose, a little flattered at the association with Moses, for I had told Lawrence that I was planning to write a semi-historical novel, a free fantasia on the Biblical theme of liberty and exile, law and leadership. In the book I drew a new portrait of Moses. I pictured him as part-Jew, part-Egyptian prince, a rebel deeply influenced by Akhnaten's One God—a characterization followed and analyzed by Freud eleven years later in his *Moses and Monotheism*. But what did Lawrence know of me? Or Moses? Or the Jews?

Lawrence would have been the last to see a relation between himself, the eternal artist, and the eternal Jew. But the relation was there.

I I

The artist starts with a wish to make something. Close upon this desire comes the wish to make something new. The Jew, as artist, usually starts with the second impulse instead of with the first. Too often for his purpose (and his own good) he tries to make something over before he has decided what to make.

So it was with Lawrence. Doggedly, and often belligerently, Lawrence pursued his confused loves and hatreds, revolting against fixity yet trying to domesticate the absolute. None of the Chosen People ever followed their own tragic heritage more tenaciously, more desperately, than Lawrence followed the dark dictates of the unconscious, trying to make something over—over and over again—without knowing precisely what. Again and again, like the blindest cabalist, he went off into mystic orgies, rhapsodized against reason; he announced that his one religion was a belief in the blood. Had Lawrence lived he might well have bridged the racial gap between Hebraic mysticism and Hitlerism.

Lawrence suffered from an angry, inverted puritanism and from an impulsive perceptiveness at war with experience. Here the likeness, which Lawrence would not have relished, is still closer. The Jew, bound to his own negative commandments yet fascinated by opulence, is a sensual moralist: an Oriental and a prig. Asceticism and estheticism fight it out in the same breast. This accounts for the Jew's proverbial contradictions: his excessive humility and his spiritual arrogance, his longing to lose himself through the flesh and his determination to save the world, his underlying melancholy and his ability to turn all grief into material for a joke.

Lawrence's self-contradictions were equally obvious, precariously balanced. He hated colonies, yet he was always starting a colony of his own. A much-mothered child, he was continually dependent on friends, and he continually repudiated them. He fought violently to preserve his "secret and sacred individuality"; yet he denied individuality to others and wrote, in the very accents of mad nationalism: "The mass of men are fragments of the collective consciousness; it is a mistake to say that the State is made up of individuals. It is made up of a collection of fragmentary beings; the State cannot be Christian." Lawrence pretended to ignore both the aristocrats and the intelligentsia; but as Hugh Kingsmill, one of his biographers, wrote, "though not a conscious charlatan, he had an instinct for exploiting the large areas of imbecility in the English upper classes." Lawrence was precise about the small affairs of the household, undisciplined about life. He filled *Lady Chatterley's Lover* with painstaking pornography, but he was shocked when Katherine Mansfield sang a somewhat suggestive French song at a Christmas party.

Lawrence's difficulties with his readers, as well as with his critics, rose from his itch to reform and dictate, his stubborn resolution to let nothing and no one alone. He challenged standards, questioned liberties; he was in complete opposition to his surroundings, most of all when he was in America. "I don't believe either in liberty or democracy. I believe in the divine right of natural aristocracy, the right, the sacred duty to wield undisputed authority."

Here was the real split between Lawrence and myself. As a Jew I could not accept dictatorially inspired authority; freedom was not a "detestable negative creed," but something for which one never ceased fighting. The Jew suffered because he constantly denied divine authority in mortal man; he was hounded, put to the rack, beaten and broken because he refused to take power for granted. The Jew doubted perfection, and agonized himself to make something, anything, better. He was hurt (literally) not because he could not adapt himself to strange people, but because he dared to believe he could help them, even when they did not want to be helped. It was not merely the itch to reform; it was a constant *weltschmerz*, a sad but stubborn moral yearning. He pitted himself foolhardily against inertia. Doomed by his very nature to resist complacency, which he identified with rigidity and death, the Jew offended those who did not wish to be roused. The objections to him were logical. He was, in the strictest sense, an agitator; he excited and irritated those who wanted no change. From the point of view of those who prayed never to be disturbed, the Jew was truly a disturbing element. The Jew might well have expected the reaction. He should have remembered that the pioneer is ridiculed by the stay-at-home, the disturber is cast out, and the prophet is stoned.

It has been said that, if the Jews are actually the Chosen People, they have been chosen to suffer. (The precedent was set even before Jesus.) At least they have been chosen to differ. They have never been able completely to accept the status quo politically or culturally. They are congenitally non-conformers, uncomfortable and critical. Bent on obtaining the unattainable they remain, even in their skepticism, determined if disillusioned idealists, God-forsaken but God-seeking.

III

God-seeking, the Jews have sought their temporary home all over the earth. The victims of national aspirations and antagonisms, hunted across borders, driven abroad by cold pogroms, betrayed by their allies and protectors, they have

found only insecure havens. Without a common home, with
nothing in common but a dream, they established themselves
in refuges which they hoped might be "the brave, new
world."

Lawrence, scorning the Jew for attempting to live in exile,
was constantly running away. Never did a man try more
furiously to escape from himself. "I wish I were going to
Thibet—or Kamschatka—or Tahiti—to the ultima, ultima,
ultima Thule," Lawrence wrote Lady Ottiline Morrell as
early as 1915. "I feel sometimes I shall go mad, because there
is nowhere to go, no 'new world.' One of these days I shall
be departing in some rash fashion to some foolish place."

All his life Lawrence was "departing in some rash fashion
to some foolish place." It was not a new world he was seeking, but the poet's old security, the ivory tower, Axel's castle.
He sought it around the world—Florence, Sicily, Ceylon,
New South Wales, Taos, Mexico, back to Florence—around
the world and back again. The wandering went on forever.
Wherever he was, Lawrence wanted to be somewhere else,
and soon after he arrived at the new goal he would write,
"This place is no good." Then off again to the bright illusion and the dark dream—ultima, ultima, ultima Thule . . .

Frieda, the high-spirited and indefatigable, could scarcely
keep up with the pace. The quest for the ultimate which
was also the primal drove Lawrence headlong from old
haunts to ever-new goals. His letters were broadcast from the
Rhine, from Cornwall, from Lago di Garda, from Taormina,
from Australia, from Guadalajara, from Scandicci, from
the Valley of the Var—from a hundred temporary stops on
the never-ending pilgrimage.

No wonder Lawrence could look with neither humor nor pity at the ewige Jude, the eternal Wandering Jew.

I V

Six years after Lawrence's death I saw Frieda Lawrence again. It was during the Christmas holidays in Boston at one of Merrill Moore's cosmopolitan week ends. Frieda was round and exuberant, handsome, lustier than ever. We spoke of Lawrence's happy days, when he baked the bread and Frieda served it; of the many women who tried to mother him and the quarrelsome biographers who claimed him—Frieda's own *Not I, but the Wind* still seems to me the most unaffected and revealing of the portraits—of the intense and comic rivalry between Frieda and Mabel Dodge Luhan; of our meeting in London and Frieda's subsequent experiences in Taos' "Mabeltown."

Then Frieda told us an incredible story. Someone who wanted Lawrence—and Frieda named the possessive admirer—wanted him in death as well as in life. Frieda's house was invaded and Lawrence's ashes were stolen.

"You can believe," said Frieda, "I had a hard time getting them back. But I recovered them. And I made up my mind that nothing of this sort should happen again. So I fixed it."

"How?" we asked. "What did you do?"

"I had the ashes mixed with a lot of sand and concrete. Now they are in a huge concrete slab. It weighs over a ton." She laughed heartily. "A dozen men could not lift it."

It may not have been ultima Thule, but at last Lawrence was safe. His long wanderings were over. Peace to his ashes.

ANTHOLOGIST'S HOLIDAY

ACTUALLY I was President Alexander Ruthven's responsibility, but the entire University of Michigan was my host. I never learned what my official status was—I think it was something like "Poet in Residence" or "Professor in Idleness"—but I was allowed to conduct seminars, to meet classes in the lounge of the Union instead of in the classroom, and to follow my lectures with round-table discussions, free-for-all, catch-as-catch-can, no holds barred. It was the most stimulating month I had ever spent on any campus, and my center of activity was not the literary college but the college of engineering.

This did not seem to me at all incongruous. I had always maintained that the creative arts were not primarily academic pursuits but forms in which men worked naturally, as functional as ships and skyscrapers. The Japanese landscape gardeners sometimes built bridges for purely esthetic line, not for use. But most bridges were meant to work, to span a river, to convey men and machines. A small percentage of literature existed for the sake of abstract line and pure composition. But most works of art were made to be used, to convey intellectual freight, to carry an idea or emotion across space. The young engineers, presumably anesthetic to culture, showed unexpected but gratifying powers of appreciation; one of my best audiences consisted of several hundred miniature bridge-builders, the student body of the dental college.

It was here that I studied the disparity in contemporaneousness between the teaching of the arts and the sciences. The latest findings in medicine, the most recent experiments in the tension and flexibility of steel, the latest speculation about the atom were examined by the young scientists. It was only in literature that contemporaneousness was scorned and experiment rejected. The young internists at the medical college were fascinated by the new uses of nicotinic acid in cases of vitamin deficiency. But the student of literature was made to feel that experimental writers were merely freakish, that historical perspective was more important than immediate participation, and that the product of our own times was scarcely worthy of study. It was significant (and, I thought, logical) that the only place at Michigan where a course in modern poetry was given was at the engineering college.

Long ago my friend and publisher, Alfred Harcourt, had warned me about this time-lag. He said that there were at least twenty years between the acceptance of an idea and its adoption in the academic schools. First the experiment; a decade later its prevailing use; a score of years had to ensue before it was incorporated in the textbooks. It was Alfred who urged me to shorten the gap. He had already published a volume of mine entitled *The New Era in American Poetry,* a set of essays on new figures and current tendencies. He encouraged me to experiment further: to make a textbook of strictly modern verse. It was to be an American collection and, if it was not too universally damned, would be followed by a companion volume devoted to modern British poetry. We planned a condensed little volume; it was to consist chiefly of lyrics; it was to begin with Emily Dickinson and end with Stephen Vincent Benét, then twenty years old. This was in 1919.

I have the tentative little volume before me now. It has almost every defect that an anthology can have. It is arbitrary in its choice of poets; it attempts to cover too many types and kinds of verse, movements and individuals; it purports to record an entire period in a too limited space, a panorama in an Easter egg; it is limited by the taste and temperament of its compiler. But (to be fair to one's backward child) it also attempted to suggest certain interesting phenomena and fresh material, to present a new alignment and indicate a new approach. Also it included, among the more than one hundred selections, some thirty little-known poems which have since become famous.

Alfred Harcourt was not wrong about the first reactions. The examination copies evoked a mixture of puzzled criticism, pedantic condescension, and downright contempt. One outraged teacher, the head of the department in an Eastern preparatory school, lost her temper completely. She returned the book to my publisher with angry comments scribbled across the pages. Alfred smiled and passed it on to me.

The marked copy is one of my dearest possessions, a memento of a person and a reminder of a period. These are some of the penciled notations: "She wrote too much" is placed at the end of the selection from Emily Dickinson. After a piece of rollicking light verse by Charles E. Carryl, I find "This is not poetry in any sense of the term, and it shows poor judgment to put it anywhere *near* 'Little Boy Blue'" which she marks "Perfect!" She barely concedes that Lizette Woodworth Reese's best sonnet ("Tears") is "Not bad," but the few pages devoted to Edgar Lee Masters inspire her to pure invective. "This is *not* poetry—it is poor prose." "Rot!" "Horrible, hopeless stuff." *"Spoon River Anthology* is not poetry. It is *filth!"* (These conclusions are hurled across the printed page in large black script.) She is a little kinder to Edwin Arlington Robinson, obviously sorry for him because he cannot be as good a poet as Eugene Field; "Richard Cory" is "not worthwhile as poetry," but "The Master," Robinson's memorable Lincoln poem, is "worthwhile because it has some fine stanzas." Ridgely Torrence's graphic and eloquent "The Bird and the Tree" merits only her contemptuous: "How stupid to put this into second-rate verse." Robert Frost is dismissed with a wave of the hand. An ironic question mark is put along the side of "The Road Not Taken"; "Birches" is definitely *"not* poetry"; "The Tuft of Flowers" is merely "poor"; "Mending Wall," which became one of the most quoted poems of the period, is "remarkably stupid." She ridicules Amy Lowell—"What poor prose!" "Rot!" "Poor paper! To be so abused!" "Wow!!!" —but Carl Sandburg brings out her ripest invectives. She sputters, in bigger and blacker pencilings: "This is mere prose with capitals in the wrong places." "Might have been made into a poem but is certainly not one." "This"—the poem happens to be Sandburg's tender "Cool Tombs"—"is vulgar and degrading as well as degenerate." The defacements in the rest of the volume showed a consistent and typical hate of experiment, a hate that is also fear.

But—other times, other rhymes. Here, again, Alfred Harcourt showed foresight as well as faith in new ventures. He emboldened me to continue; he tempted me to prepare a series of textbooks for high schools and colleges. He gave me the freedom to depart from the customary form, to revise and amplify, until in seventeen years the original collection of one hundred and thirty poems had grown to a fifth edition of seven hundred and ninety. Thanks to him, we had succeeded in occasionally shortening the time-lag in poetry.

I I

How does an anthologist determine which poems to omit and which to include? By what standards does he judge his contemporaries? How can he tell whether or not a poem will last?

These are simple questions which have been continually asked, but they cannot be answered with simple finalities. You read and you forget—or you read and you remember. When it is impossible to forget, you are ready to assume that there is a vitality which will not let this piece, this poem, die. But there is the next consideration, which asks: Besides vitality, has it "value"? Here a complexity of determinants and uncertainties comes into play: memory and association, familiarity and novelty, time and training and natural taste. There is the pleasure of recognition, and there is the pleasure of surprise. There is the delight in being charmed and soothed, and there is the other fascination in being piqued and excited. Somehow the selective mind strikes a balance. Somehow it appreciates how common words have made the familiar seem strange or the strange seem familiar, how they have assumed a fresh personality, even a fresh potency.

With an intelligent awareness, an open though discriminating mind, the quality of a poem can be apprehended. But—here enters the inhibiting fear, the fear of being wrong —will it last? We must assure ourselves not only with something that temporarily pleases, but with something that persists beyond us. Time is, of course, the final anthologist. But what reader can wait for time to confirm him? Here Robert Frost has given memorable comfort. He wrote, "It is absurd to think that the only way to tell if a poem is lasting is to wait and see if it lasts. The right reader of a good poem can tell the moment it strikes him that he has taken an immortal wound—that he will never get over it. That is to say, permanence in poetry as in love is perceived instantly. It hasn't to await the test of time."

This quick permanence, this "immortal wound," cannot be mistaken. It is not only a conviction but a compulsion. It tells us, as Edwin Arlington Robinson declared poetry should tell, "something that cannot be said," something, at least, that cannot be said in any other way. Definitions are hazardous, and definitions of poetry are notoriously unsatisfying. We can no more account for the essence of a poem than we can explain a color or translate a perfume. Hot for certainties, we are thrown back upon A. E. Housman's "I can no more define poetry than a terrier can define a rat, but I think we both recognize the object by the symptoms which it provides in us" or John Squire's halting but unquestionable "Poetry is the thing which is written by poets." But the reader (and especially the reader who may be an anthologist) accepts recognition without definition. He recognizes it, first of all, in the tone of voice which issues from the printed page, in the nice measure of sound and sense, the balance of meaning and music, in the bright image, the caught breath, the ring of truth and ecstasy.

The anthologist, however, is not so much in danger of being arbitrary as of being overcautious. Bewildered by contemporary differences, afraid to trust himself in a rapidly rising welter of creation, he usually turns to the collections of his predecessors. There were many instances where it seemed that anthologists read only anthologies. As an anthologist myself, I pitied my competing colleagues; as a poet I despised them. Five or six of my poems were continually being quoted to the exclusion of all my other and (I thought) better verses. Fellow-poets made the same complaint. Conrad Aiken, whose early "Bread and Music" had been repeated ad nauseam, told me that the anthologists published only "anthology poems"—poems that had been printed and reprinted in other anthologies—that they rarely bothered to open the poets' own books. This seemed fantastic, and I determined to test Aiken's skepticism. I invented a poet. I wrote several verses (mostly technical exercises) and signed them with my grandfather's name turned backward: Michael Lewis. (My grandfather was safely dead; besides, he never read poetry even when he was alive.) I scattered these verses in various anthologies and in *The Forms of Poetry*, an elementary handbook and dictionary of verse. Within a few years I found some of the manufactured stanzas appearing in imposing-looking volumes; an eminent compiler included two of them (without my knowledge) in a now-standard collection with this biographical note: "Michael Lewis. Data unavailable."

More years passed. Dorothy Thompson and Sinclair Lewis had a son. They named him Michael, unaware of my own brain-child. I did not tell them of my pseudonym. I thought it better to wait. It is possible that the real Michael Lewis may not grow up to appreciate poetry; it is even possible that he may not be too pleased with the body of verse written in his name before he had a name to begin with.

III

When the busman takes his proverbial holiday he takes a bus; when a sailor gets a holiday he hires a rowboat; when an anthologist has a holiday he thinks of another anthology. After it seemed likely that a few schools would adopt my American collection as textbooks, I planned to make an enlarged companion assemblage of contemporary English and Irish verse. Unable to continue to burn my candle at both ends—the manager of a jewelry factory during the day and literary person at night—I burned my bridges. I resigned; my partners were not only resigned but rejoiced. I turned over my stock and the vice-presidency to my brother Martin, whose offenses against art have been retailed in the first chapter and who had shamed me not only by entering college but by staying in it. I had been too long a part-time worker in literature. Besides, I wanted to examine the local scene from a new perspective. Early in 1923 I sailed for London.

At the time of my first visit to England the literary world was sharply divided into two opposing camps. The more powerful faction was controlled by John Collings Squire, editor of *The London Mercury,* and his group was often referred to as the Squirearchy. It included most of the contributors to *Georgian Poetry,* the biennial collections which had introduced Ralph Hodgson, Walter de la Mare, W. H. Davies, W. J. Turner, Harold Monro, and other exponents of the new romanticism to America. Its character was gen-

erally naïve, wistful, vaguely rustic, and somewhat too dependent on words as magic. The opposition was headed by
the three Sitwells (Osbert, Edith, and Sacheverell) and their
smaller clique of poets, painters, and musicians. The Sitwell
group scorned the elaborate simplicity of the Georgians, and
dedicated themselves to deflation. Mocking what they considered the false ingenuousness of the Georgians, the Sit-
wellians struck out with sophisticated unreality, with rococo
grotesqueries and purposely over-colored burlesque, combining the mood of the Russian Ballet with that of the music-
hall. They advertised themselves impudently; they even
capitalized their own queerness and unpopularity. I remember an occasion when Edith Sitwell, accompanied by the
acrid music of William Walton, intoned her poetry behind
a fiercely painted screen through which a megaphone had
been thrust. The Sitwells, anticipating the surrealists, idealized posture as an art; they distorted sense-effects, luxuriated
in fantasies, and mirrored a nightmare world which was the
nightmare of a child.

Both groups fought continually, each in their own ways,
and emphasized their differences. They filled columns of
dignified and impudent controversy; they hand-picked the
reviewers of their volumes. I had been warned about the
prevalence of log-rolling in England. I was unprepared for
anything so systematized and so small in detail. With the
exception of a few figures who were above the conflict, the
literary foreground seemed to consist not only of log-rollers
but of log-rollers who were using saplings.

I noticed the change beginning after my second visit to
England. During the third and longest stay the difference
was obvious. A new taste and tone were being manifest not

only by the younger writers but by those who had established their manners. The lesser Georgians had ceased to populate the landscape with lambs and curlews and clock-work nightingales; readers were no longer soothed by pastoral reassurances. They preferred the frank ironies, the prim but bitter hymn-tunes of A. E. Housman; they discovered the genuine pathos and terror in Wilfred Owen and Siegfried Sassoon; they turned to "the hot blood's blindfold art" of D. H. Lawrence and the "intense levity" of T. S. Eliot; they began to echo the sprung rhythms and onrushing fervor of Gerard Manley Hopkins; there was talk of a new social poetry, half vulgar, half visionary. I watched the gradual shift from an obsolete romanticism through a literature of nerves toward a firmer set of convictions.

My sojourns in England ranged from two weeks to a year. Memory tends to become kaleidoscopic, but there are places and people that never lose the first vivid color.

There was the day at Thame to which Minna Curtis (then Minna Kirstein) sent me, where I lunched at some length, and where I met the amazing John Fothergill. Fothergill was a local innkeeper who was also a great cosmopolite; he seemed to be the intimate of every living author. What is more, he made his friends collaborate upon one of the most curious works of the period. Fothergill had been harboring an idea for a story for many years. The plot was this: By accident a man gets into correspondence with a woman whom he doesn't know. He finds romance in it, though the two never meet. Then he sees a girl, falls in love with her in the ordinary way, marries her, and drops the academic correspondence. Happiness and distress. Then friction. In an effort to find consolation he writes again to the unknown woman, till by another accident it is discovered that the married couple are writing to one another.

At first Fothergill tried to write the story. Then he would, on occasion, ask one of his favorite authors to develop it. Finally he hit upon the scheme of having *all* his friends engage upon the work, each one writing his own version around the one plot. The point of the plot lay, as R. G. Collingwood pointed out, in the contrast between two kinds of intimacy: the intellectual intimacy that comes by writing letters, and the very different kind that comes through sharing bed and board. But the subtler point was the changing treatment, the application of method and style, the conflict between what the reader knew and what he could not surmise. The theme was less important than the dazzling set of unexpected variations. Eighteen authors set to work to tell a story in eighteen different ways; among them were G. K. Chesterton, Frank Swinnerton, A. E. Coppard, E. M. Delafield, Storm Jameson, Margaret Kennedy, Sheila Kaye-Smith, Elizabeth Bowen, Helen Simpson, J. C. Squire, and Rebecca West. The eighteen variations were extraordinary in the way they developed and managed to fill the known theme with suspense, even with surprise. They were gathered together and printed in a volume appropriately entitled *The Fothergill Omnibus,* and they caused something of a sensation when they appeared. Yet as far as I know, the volume has never been published in America.

There were the late afternoons in The Poetry Bookshop on Great Russell Street near the British Museum. After my day's work in the Museum's chill Reading Room, I would relish the hearth-fire of the room above the shop and the warm welcome of its owners, Harold Monro and his beautiful wife, Alida Klemantaski. Harold, a poet and fighter, debated furiously, and Alida read poetry more movingly than anyone I have ever heard. There were continual skirmishes between us regarding the American and English points of view, but, in spite of stubborn clashes, we remained friends. I think Harold made allowances for me as an American; he forgave my persistence and my local pride—everything except my puns. He had discovered my favorite weakness and, in common with the rest of humanity, he let it be known that a pun is something at which you groan unless you make it yourself. I reminded him that the erudite James Joyce was engaged upon a book that seemed to be one stupendous if incomprehensible set of puns, but Harold was not impressed.

I will never forget his most telling rebuke. Alida had brought out a particularly lavish tea which included an almond-encrusted Dundee cake and, to please her Scotch husband, a plate of hot scones.

"No bread?" I asked, knowing there was none. Then, preparing the absurdity, I complained, pointing to the plate, "I asked for bread and you gave me a scone."

There was a fine Scotch silence.

"All right," I said. "You don't have to laugh. But I think it's fairly appropriate. Poetic, too. You know—like the epitaph on Butler's monument in Westminster Abbey:

> *The poet's fate is here in emblem shown:*
> *He asked for bread, and he received a stone.*

In the New Testament, too," I went on repeating desperately. "And you gave me a scone."

Harold looked at me sadly. "We pronunce it 'skun,'" he said.

IV

There was Dorothy Richardson, seemingly the central character in her monumental *Pilgrimage,* a work on which she labored for about a quarter of a century, twelve volumes finally collected in four crowded books. She was as plain and subtle as her own style and, like her style, she gave you an intense awareness, a heightened consciousness of common activities. Quiet but dominating, recalling her own Miriam Henderson, she communicated a new kind of comedy, unobtrusive, even unimportant, but richly human. Her touch was in everything; it persisted by virtue of a rich sensibility; it grew in comedy that was realistic and, at the same time, classical.

There were the other teas which I remembered with more than the usually mixed emotions, the teas at which I kept silent. The best of these took place at Ridgeway's near Piccadilly Circus. Perhaps "took place" is the wrong term; the meetings merely happened. Four of us—Ralph Hodgson, James Stephens, W. J. Turner, and I—would happen in at about three on a Friday, and the following Friday we happened to be there again. We four would always say good-by to each other, as though we were leaving for the four corners of the earth, never again to meet. And every Friday we would be appropriately surprised to see each other at Ridgeway's.

We would begin our sessions with anything but shop; the three Englishmen almost pretended not to be poets at all. Turner spoke as a music-critic and biographer. Stephens talked as a novelist and collector of folk-lore. Hodgson dis-

cussed pugilism and the breeding of bulldogs. Only another
poet could have seen through the disguise. Anna Wickham
wrote a sly piece of light verse which rallied Hodgson, but
was really a teasing tribute:

> This gentleman will only talk to us of dogs
> Because he wishes to disguise that he's a poet.
> If he should mention lions, dolphins, frogs,
> He thinks, by misadventure, we should know it!
>
> I cite a dog I once set eyes upon
> Which, lacking doggy lore, I say looked like a swan;
> He takes me, says, "That hound was bred in Russia,
> Three such are owned by Henry, Prince of Prussia."
>
> O, modest violet! Cowering in your green,
> Your scent betrays you though you are not seen!
> Only unveterinary wights, like you and me,
> Would see in dogs a swanny quality.

It would not be long, however, before one of us would
quote a line or mention a poet. Then the talk would begin
in rapid earnest. The conversations at the Mermaid Tavern
were, perhaps, more sonorous, but I am sure they were not
more animated. Guests three tables away let their tea grow
cold, or did without it altogether, while the waitresses
neglected their clients to listen to Hodgson's tales of a London that had passed, or to Turner's apostrophes to Mozart.
Perhaps the most memorable occasion was when, prompted
by one of my remarks about recent American poetry, James
Stephens declaimed most of "The Congo." Nothing like it
was ever heard in that setting: a drum-banging poem by an
American poet on a Negro theme chanted in an English

restaurant by an Irish mystic with an accumulating brogue.

There was Anna Wickham herself, a magnificent gypsy of a woman, who always entered a room as if she had just stamped across the moors. Almost unrecognized by her compatriots, much of her work unpublished, she had more color and character than many of the poets who were so quickly acclaimed. Wayward, ironic, spontaneous, she was the very opposite of another poet known only to the few: Charlotte Mew, whose work, like herself, had a deceptive fragility, a cameo cut in steel. Anna Wickham's work was fierce, not fine; rough and disturbed, gnarled in her own nervous protests. The protests were not only against the age but against her sex; they were doubly tense because she put her arguments into epigrams. Tormented, bound "first to passion, then to sentiment," she alternately praised and despised feminity. She began a half-angry, half-pitying poem:

> *I have to thank God I'm a woman,*
> *For in these ordered days a woman only*
> *Is free to be very hungry, very lonely.*

In turn I quoted to her part of Elinor Wylie's "Let No Charitable Hope":

> *I was, being human, born alone;*
> *I am, being woman, hard beset;*
> *I live by squeezing from a stone*
> *The little nourishment I get.*

But Anna Wickham had not heard it, nor did she seem to want to hear it. Her favorite American woman poet was Ella Wheeler Wilcox. "What passion!" she cried in exaggerated admiration. "What power! What pleasure!"

"And what a woman!" I added. But Anna Wickham was not interested in Wilcox the woman; she was concerned only with Wilcox the singer and seer. I tried to interest her in that other great American bard, Edgar Guest, the uncrowned laureate of Michigan, born in Birmingham, England. She waved him aside. It had to be all-woman, all-American, or nothing.

A few days later she sent me a long and unpublished poem. It was headed "To Men" and subtitled "Variation on Ella Wheeler Wilcox, after a poem of the same name." It began characteristically and ironically:

> *Sirs—though we fail you—let us live;*
> *Be just, have pity, and forgive.*
> *Think how poor Mother Eve was brought*
> *To being as God's afterthought.*
>
> *How can you wonder, if we stray*
> *Through coward night and sloven day*
> *When power in us can but reflect*
> *God's wifelessness and man's defect!*

Before I left England Anna Wickham excited me about her latest and most serious discovery. He was a young English boy, seventeen years old, who supported himself by printing chemists' labels on his own hand-press. He gave me a little, paper-bound booklet, "Nine Experiments," which he himself had printed and which he had signed with his initials S. H. S. His name was Stephen Spender.

When I returned to America in 1928 he sent me two or more groups of his "later" manuscripts. Spender was then eighteen, about to enter Oxford and begin his career as the most powerfully impassioned of the post-war poets. His first volume was issued in America in 1934. I congratulate myself that seven of Spender's poems appeared in the 1930 edition of my *Modern British Poetry* before Spender had been published even in England. Here, at least, the anthologist's holiday had justified itself.

THE DONKEY OF GOD

IT WAS a donkey who started it. Or, to be precise, it was two donkeys. They belonged to Signor Daneu and I first saw them in the Corso Umberto in Taormina. They were attached to those gaily colored miniature wagons which, in spite of their absurd littleness, manage somehow to carry the usual Italian family of seven with a grandfather or two thrown in, several liters of wine, a hogshead of olive oil, and most of the family bedding. The tiny two-wheeled carts were everywhere in Sicily, and the poorest of them were flamboyantly painted; the shafts sparkled, even the spokes were freaked with color. The vehicles, symbolic of the Sicilians, denoted the rank of their owners. The humbler ones carried crude scenes from the life of the local hero-brigand, while the rich farmers outdid themselves with ancient myths and biblical legends spread over every crowded inch—history, so to speak, à la cart.

Though the esthetic appeal of the dwarf donkeys was instantaneous, I suspect they charmed me still more because of their associations in art and literature. I remembered Sintenis' little bronze donkey at the Detroit Art Institute, a creature so beloved by the children of Michigan that his back and muzzle were worn smooth. I thought of the rôles donkeys had played in life and legend all the way back to the Bible. There was Samson's potent use of an ass's jawbone. There was the weather-eaten ass of Balaam who spoke in pure Hebrew. There was the magic ass's skin in Balzac's

343

Peau de Chagrin. And there was the donkey who was beloved by a queen, even though she was only the queen of
the fairies and it happened on a midsummer night.

These two, however, were the mildest-mannered donkeys
I had ever seen. And they were without doubt the most
beautiful animals ever created. Feet of a young faun, eyes
of a new-born Jersey, a muzzle of silk, a dove-gray body and
a black cross laid dramatically upon the back. I fell unreservedly in love with them, and I think my passion was
reciprocated. I was not too affluent, but I determined to
have them. I wanted them not only as pets, enhancing the
Adirondack scene, but as potential sources of profit. The
pair I coveted were more than decorative; they were more
dog-like than dogged; they were the only docile donkeys in
the world. I would breed them; Westchester gentlemen-
farmers and Long Island millionaires would beat a path to
my stable. If people paid disproportionately large sums for
small dogs, they would, I figured, disgorge handsomely for
the littlest and loveliest of donkeys, not much larger than a
somewhat overgrown Great Dane. I was determined, and
Signor Daneu was not difficult. After an exchange of compliments and a little cash, the matter was arranged. There
were, of course, fees for the immigration authorities, for the
collector of the port at Messina, for the owner of the donkey's grandfather who had loaned the original male at
Palermo, for food and drink during the journey—when the
bill of lading was presented I was convinced that the animals had lived on caviar and Lacrimae Christi—and a special
fee for a distant relative who was going to meet the boat in
New York.

When the ship-news reporters accosted me upon my return—this was in pre-depression 1929—I told them about my scheme. They were delighted. So were the editors. The papers, lacking more epochal events, devoted columns to my enterprise. "Poet Turns Donkey-Breeder," "Smaller and Better Donkeys," "From Muse to Mule" were some of the inspired headlines; and few of the stories failed to mention that, whereas the winged horse had always been the symbol of the poet of the past, the donkey might well represent the poet of the present.

The publicity did not offend me. I read the articles, filed the inquiring letters which followed, rubbed my hands, and counted my future donkeys. I began naming them. The male donkey, due to arrive in a month, had a proud Castilian look; I named him Donkey Hote. His wife-to-be was pretty in a rather German way; I called her Donkey Schön. If the first child happened to be a boy I determined to call him Maxwellton. If it were a girl I would, brazenly enough, name her Isadora Donkey. I was, in the full meaning of the phrase, all set.

Then two things occurred which destroyed the dream. Long Island millionaires suddenly went out of fashion; and the female donkey, having had only one look at the Statue of Liberty, sickened of the fare at Ellis Island and turned her face to the wall. There was quite a correspondence with the port authorities. They wanted to know whether I intended to exceed the quota on donkeys, whether the remaining animal had been examined for cholera or moral turpitude, and whether I was planning to attend the female's funeral. Regretfully I informed the government that I had come to raise the creatures, not to bury them; that I could not afford further importations; that I was down to my last donkey, and would they please ship him to me instanter.

Donkey Hote arrived alone and lonely. He remained that way for a year. There was no brilliantly bedecked cart for him to pull, no familiar Sicilian to kick and curse him, no one to feed him *risotto alla Bolognese*. I, too, was sad. It was manifestly impossible to have a progeny with only one disconsolate male. Worse, Donkey Hote's docility vanished and his protests increased; he took to making fun of my guests and nipping my small sons in tender places. I determined to advertise for a more consistent donkey-lover than I turned out to be.

Fortunately, I found the very man. Seeing my heartrending "Personal" which started the Agony Column in the *Saturday Review of Literature,* Angelo Patri, the country's outstanding authority on problem children, sent for the beast. I was now about two hundred dollars out of pocket, and no Untermeyer has ever taken his losses complacently. Something, I said to myself, must be done, and done quickly. That donkey, somehow, must pay for himself. It was a literary association that arrested me; I resolved he should return to literature. Thereupon I put him into a story.

Remembering the dark cross upon his back, I traced his lineage. Back I tracked him through history and fable, relating him to his illustrious predecessors until I reached the Bible. Then from the Creation I followed him out of the Garden of Eden, accounted for his ridiculous ears and his horror-striking voice, and so to the New Testament. The great-great-great-etc.-grandfather of my donkey, I concluded, was the very one who carried the mother of Jesus on her wanderings, who played with the carpenter's son when he was a child in Bethlehem and suffered thorns for his sake, and who finally bore his master in triumph into Jerusalem. Because of these services, Jesus allowed him to wear his symbol as a mark of honor, and thus the little animal could shoulder burdens which larger animals could never carry. After he had been blessed, the donkey, who had been forced to eat nettles, fed on thorns and thistles for now they tasted like sweet salads. And then he, too, was allowed to wear the cross upon his back throughout eternity.

The story brought me many letters when it was published, especially from young people; I followed it with another which had a similar setting. It takes little enough urging on the part of a person to persuade an author to write a book, and when that person happens to be your publisher—! So the book was written. It was called *The Donkey of God*. It was handsomely embellished, aimed at a youthful but not too juvenile audience, placed on sale, and—a pox on modesty—enthusiastically reviewed. Parts of the volume were reprinted; the royalties continued, though in somewhat decreasing amounts; librarians spoke to me respectfully. A year more and, being engaged on another work, I forgot all about the book.

II

A year later my publishers informed me that, at no expense to me and with little hope for them, they were entering *The Donkey of God,* along with several other volumes, in a contest for cash and kudos. The contest was open to the world; it was to determine the best recent book on Italy written by a non-Italian. The results were to be announced in Rome; the judges were to include journalists, professors of literature, and Mussolini himself. I smiled, not too broadly, and, remembering the character and title of my book, forgot about it again.

A few months after this, I learned that, although some three hundred entries had been submitted, I had split first prize with a French author who had offered three volumes glorifying Il Duce's life, his works, and his high place in history. I could not believe the award; I doubted that the judges had read my book. I still doubt it.

But the announcement was official, the stationery was gold-encrusted, and the check was indubitable. It was then that I did one of the few wise things of my career; I acted on an impulse which was both poetic and practical. I wrote to Signor Pantaleone, the New York correspondent, that I was not a publicist, but a poet; as a poet I was, true to the tradition, uninterested in money. Therefore I must return his check. But I added, in a canny postscript, I had recently remarried. My wife was a busy attorney and an ex-Judge who had never had a honeymoon; if the Donkey of God's country wanted to do something for culture, to say nothing of connubiality, it would arrange for our passage on one of its less conspicuous vessels. I intimated that a modest stall in a not too crowded cattle-boat would do. I even promised to find enough money to pay my own transportation through Italy, for the newspapers were beginning to mention threats against Ethiopia, and I wished to be neither a burden nor a muzzled guest.

My earlier excursions had been spent in the spiritual company of Giotto, Dante, Michelangelo, St. Francis, Verdi, Boccaccio; this visit (so the judges warned me) was to bring me in contact with Mussolini! I told myself that, though the idea of fascism was abhorrent to me, Il Duce was not an ogre who ate poets; Mussolini himself had been a teacher and a socialist. Neither a fanatic nor a bigoted reactionary like Hitler, he was probably an opportunist; the rumors of a possible war were part of his political strategy, a dangerous but obvious bluff. Italy, I reassured myself, could never change; the people were careless and pacific, the art was imperishable. Meanwhile, there was the never-failing excitement of the journey.

Signor Pantaleone discovered that we had mutual friends and, after a little high-handed wire-pulling, forwarded two tickets for the *Saturnia*. It was a comic crossing. My wife and I were prepared to spend our belated honeymoon cabined, cribbed, confined between a modest port-hole and the darkest corner of the dining-room. Instead, we found ourselves occupying a balcony suite—so that, I was told, I could have my inspirations in private—saluted by the ship's officers, and seated at the Captain's table. At first we were impressed. Captain Iviani was a portly gentleman of the Old Italian School; he was charming to my wife, deferential to me. But conversations with a Captain of a large ocean-liner are definitely limited. The prevailing winds, the excellence of the food, the prospect of a continuing calm sea brought us through the first five minutes of every meal. Then conversation grew limp and died without one pregnant pause. Gossip about fellow passengers was, of course, taboo; Captain Iviani was a diplomat as well as a navigator; he would not say anything which might reflect on anything, not even on the weather. After the first three days we would have been glad to exchange our seats for less coveted but livelier places.

Fortunately, it was not long before we were enlivened.

Fellow-Americans presented themselves; Captain Iviani ceased to struggle with his bad English and my worse Italian; parties grew less official and more convivial. The Mark Lenkes, a young couple married the night before sailing, became our partners in crime. Mark had been a lawyer before he married into the world's largest dried egg industry; he painted semi-abstract landscapes under a pseudonym and still fancied himself as a violinist. No matter how late the hour, he refused to let us go to bed before playing his *Nachtstück.* This nocturnal—or early matutinal—horror was always "Love in Bloom" decorated with unintentional falsetto flourishes, and it was always rendered in his bridal suite. Other memories of that journey have faded, but I can still see (and hear!) Mark seated on a pile of steamer-presents, scratching away *amoroso e furioso,* while his next-door neighbor pounds on the walls, curses the virtuoso, and rings for all the stewards.

This next-door neighbor was Dr. Logan Clendening, author of *The Human Body* and innumerable syndicated articles in which readers were advised to regard the facts of life with resolute calm. Perhaps the strain of travel was too much for him; perhaps Mark's assaults on the slipping A string warranted homicidal impulses. In any case, Dr. Clendening forgot his public essays and his private resolutions whenever Mark tortured the cat's gut with his stick of frayed horse hair. There was talk of the ship's brig; and it was only Mark's youth and my intercession which saved Rea, the new bride, from being a fiddler's widow. . . . Four years later, when Mark and Rea were paying us their annual visit—paying it literally with a carload of dry groceries—we were all delighted to learn that Dr. Logan Clendening had lost his temper again. It seems that, while writing calmly about controlling the nerves, Dr. Clendening imagined he was listening to a congregation of giant woodpeckers trying to put holes in his brick building. He realized that this was an absurd fancy; at the same time he also realized that the distracting drumming had been going on for what seemed incalculable eternities. According to the reports, Dr. Clendening did not grin and bear it. On the contrary; he left the calm of his sanctum, put down stethoscope and fountain pen, and, though he was not a surgeon, found an ax. Armed with this instrument of quiet he went out and (calmly) smashed the safety valve of the air drill beneath his window. We were more than ever impressed by this action. It showed that our fellow passenger was not only human but consistent.

Besides the Lenkes and Dr. Clendening, we were entertained with the usual coterie of royal pretenders, second-class cousins of the Mdivanis, and fur-buyers who let it be known that they were once Romanoffs. There was also a German countess who suddenly appeared on the third day out and disappeared on the fourth. I was flattered that she had consented to dance with me, a commoner and a Jew, until Captain Iviani ostentatiously took me to his table and kept me there until the evening was over. It was only after the German espionage system had been exposed in America that I understood Captain Iviani's cautionary gesture. Nevertheless, I still think that the lady gave a poor imitation of an international spy; she should have known that a poet has no secrets except the secrets of his craft, and these he is glad to divulge to anyone who will listen.

I thought I had found my readiest listener on board ship.

He was a boy of ten or eleven; delicate of feature and poetically dreamy-eyed. He followed me about and (so I thought) hung upon every syllable. He was a silent boy—overawed, I concluded. Thus encouraged, I embroidered old tales and new legends for him. It was when we were passing the island of Sardinia that I invented a new fantasy for his pleasure.

"Once upon a time," I began, while my wife, the Lenkes, and Captain Iviani formed a properly respectful background, "there were mermaids in these waters. Their home was in the deepest, bluest corner of the Mediterranean. But they always sunned themselves on the rocks of that island because their lovers beached their boats there. These lads, fishermen of the island, brought gifts which maidens, and particularly sea-maidens, have always desired: rings, ribbons, hand-mirrors, hair-combs, and other trinkets which are hard for mermaids to find except after a shipwreck. The mermaids were grateful, and in return for these favors they would sit on the rocks and sing their magical songs. These songs had a particular effect on the small fish which were so swift that no one could catch them. Lured by the voices, they would lash their little tails and swim shorewards by the million, wave after wave of them. This was the moment for which the fishermen had been waiting. Running down to the shore, the men would scoop up the tiny fish, pack them tightly in flat tin cans, and sell them all over the world. And that," I concluded, with a gesture toward the great silhouette on the horizon, "that is why they call it the island of Sardinia."

My audience was silent—appreciatively, I thought.

Finally my dreamy-eyed youngster spoke. "I don't get it."

"Sardinia," I repeated. "Sardinia—isle of sardines."

"Oh," said the lad with the delicate air. "Smart guy!"

It was the last I saw of him; our circle shrank back to the Lenkes and Captain Iviani. As a special concession, the Captain arranged unexpected shore excursions since, he said with casual prophecy, the *Saturnia* might be a transport ship on her next journey. The *Saturnia* never made the return voyage to America. Within a few weeks she was carrying soldiers to Abyssinia, and those who had booked passage on her were transferred to the *Rex*.

III

It was at Lisbon, our first stop, that I realized how fast and thoroughly the world had shrunk. We were lunching in a restaurant which had been recommended by Captain Iviani, when Mark Lenke, with his customary mixture of impudence and serenity, began a conversation with a delegation of journalists at a near-by table. One of the men, a Brazilian author, recognized me, or said he did; at least he mentioned the titles of some of my books. More interesting, however, were his references to *The Seven Arts*. He told me he had translated several of the articles, and that the short-lived monthly had made South America more conscious of the culture of the United States than any other magazine of the period. His literary heroes were Randolph Bourne and Waldo Frank—and once more I was impressed by the annihilation of time and the indelibility of the written word.

There was Gibraltar, where we crossed from the English city—a combination of fortified molehills and a sleepy village in Sussex—across the neutral ground into the seething color of Spain. There was Algiers, the world's greatest self-con-tradition of a city: a disorganized silhouette of architectural modernism built on seemingly organized filth; enameled Citroën autos scraping the flanks of unwashed oxen; the austere hills, the stretch of flawless sand, and the Kasbah which housed more varieties of prostitutes than could be found in Maine and Minnesota, with Mississippi thrown in for good measure. Finally there was Naples again, with Vesuvius unconcernedly smoking away, and the people at its base gathering grapes, cutting cameos, inlaying wooden boxes as their fathers had always done, impervious to a world of eruption.

The Amalfi-Pompeii-Sorrento peninsula was a familiar wonder, but Capri was new to me—a confusion of grandeur and gaudily painted backdrops, a genuine and ancient mountainside peopled by a milling crowd of extras in technicolor. Besides the fantastic crescendos of rock, there were sufficient unreal realities. There was the aggressively modern house which had been built for a second wife who was a futurist, but which was haunted by the ghost of the first wife who insisted upon singing the florid arias of Rossini to the great discomfiture of the guests and the defeat of the bride. There was the unoccupied tower which had been completely rebuilt because all its owners had flung themselves from the turret into the waiting sea, and from whose stones the latest owner, laughing at the legend, had slipped before the scaffolding was removed. There was Edwin Cerio, the polylingual wit who gave us tea in a setting one would expect of an author whose best volume was entitled *Aria da Capri*. And there was Duke Dusmet, the mayor of Capri, with whom my wife danced until morning, while the rest of us yawned into the coffee cups and dreamed of featherbeds, not daring to leave until the *Podesta,* mayor and dictator in one, decided that we might go home.

The little Sicilian donkey had brought us far. Thanks to him we spent eight kaleidoscopic weeks in and out of galleries, ghettos and gardens, markets and museums, playhouses and palaces. We were housed among notables in the most pretentious hotels and left alone in a villa on Lake Garda. The days, each one brilliant in itself, blurred past. I remember my renewed acquaintance with Naples not on account of its dull society and its motley waterfront, but because of a lecture at the University that I was supposed to give and which, through a series of misadventures, was never given. (For one thing, no one in my prospective audience had studied English, and my Italian was the kind that is understood only by advanced linguists and waiters in restaurants.) I remember my return to the hill towns not because of the zebra-striped cathedral in Siena or the amazing square towers of San Gimignano, but because of the unequal division of "public conveniences" for men and women. My wife, a one-time feminist, complained that whereas all the males of Italy were ostentatiously either buttoning or unbuttoning themselves, no refuge seemed to be provided for her sex. She was told that a woman might demand entrance into anyone's home simply by going to the door and asking to use the toilet. In fact, she was seriously assured, this was a way in which women often became acquainted and struck up friendships which lasted a lifetime—a touching phenomenon when one considers that a long-standing intimacy may be founded on nothing more powerful than a weak bladder.

I remember my third visit to Florence not because of the

twin treasuries of the Pitti and Uffizi galleries, but because we arrived on a labor holiday (since abolished), the climax of which was a gorgeous anachronism. After a speech proclaiming the prowess of modern mechanized Italy, there was a chariot race. But the charioteers were butchers and bakers, and the traditional plunging steeds were work-horses that were not only laboring but belabored; they shied desperately at the disguised Roman senators, gladiators, and local vestal virgins whose faces they may have recognized, but whose strange and badly fitting garments struck panic to their workaday hearts.

I remember Milan not because of the ever-fading, over-exploited mural of Leonardo and the lace-work cathedral with its two thousand statues in appliqué, but because it was in Milan that our unofficial host became our sudden confidant. A prominent industrialist, he motored us across the border to Lugano so that he could talk freely.

"Italy is a country reborn," he announced, as we purred along the new motor highway. "But whenever possible the men visit Switzerland to read uncensored papers and the women go there to have their abortions."

"Yet," I hazarded, "the government is popular."

"The government?" He shrugged. "You mean Mussolini. The young people believe in him. We older men do not know what to believe. We have seen him take too many opposing attitudes. We remember his socialistic attacks on the monarchy and his murder of socialists. Now he's saying we must bring civilization to Ethiopia—with bombs. But I am talking treason. Besides, you will see him in Rome—and you will know less than you know now."

I V

He was right. We were in Rome during Easter week while the Pope blessed us and two hundred thousand others, blessed Rome and (with the aid of loud speakers) the rest of the world. Never was there such a publicized peace. Mussolini had just returned from the conference at Stresa which heralded a new diplomacy, and we went about our sight-seeing, confident that the Head of Government was too occupied to be interviewed by any poet. We were wrong. The day before we left for Perugia I was summoned. Although it was contrary to the established rule, my wife was permitted to accompany me—probably because Mussolini had never met a poet's wife who had been a Judge in the Municipal Court of Toledo, Ohio.

It was when we were approaching the Palazzo Venezia that I gasped. "Your handbag!" I pointed in horror.

"What's wrong with it?" my wife asked. "It's a brand-new handbag, and I thought you liked it."

"What's wrong with it!" I repeated. "Everything! For one thing it's the wrong color—red; a bright, brazen, bolshevik red. For another thing, it's too big. You could carry a sawed-off shot-gun in that baby suitcase. Now you will have to submit to being searched and possibly stripped, and it will end by you and your handbag being thrown out together. And serve you right."

I was wrong again. We were admitted with due ceremony but without delay; my only credentials were a letter of invitation and the prize-winning volume. (I also carried a copy of my *Food and Drink* by way of largesse.) The dangerous handbag was never even examined. Pairs of guards handed us from one elaborate room to another. I had been prepared for this. I had been told that the visitor was taken through a veritable Chinese puzzle, room after intricate room, until the final doors opened and, trembling, one crossed the threshold on shaken hands and knees. There was time enough, I told myself. I refused to let hearsay and the palatial setting intimidate me. Besides, unless Horace had misinformed us all, the man who has led a pure life need fear nothing, especially if his wife is also his attorney.

The fateful doors opened. It was a skillfully planned contrast. This, after the art-crowded rooms, was austerity itself: the huge, blank space at one end of which Caesar himself was sitting. It was a modern desk from which he rose and the coat was cut in the twentieth century, but it was still Caesar, even to the Roman jaw, the bulging forehead, and the lampooned baldness.

V

We fumbled for a common language. It was a jerky conversation, conducted in broken English, in ungrammatical Italian, in French (which my wife bandied about), and in dumb-show.

There were the usual amenities. I presented my volume, complimented His Excellency on the good roads, the punctuality of the trains, and the new quiet which he had imposed on Rome, hitherto the noisiest city on the Continent. He complimented me on my book.

"But," I said, "the book is pure fantasy. There is not a

word of praise for the new state; nothing about the aims of
fascism. Your Excellency is not even mentioned."

"Ah," he smiled, "that is a very subtle kind of propaganda."

Mussolini then went on to talk about America, of whose
culture he knew nothing except the works of Edgar Allan
Poe, but whose political battles he followed in detail. He
asked particularly about Hoover's present status and the
possible future of Huey Long. I tried to say that Long was
a minor Mussolini, a homespun dictator with a streak of
genius—if dictatorial genius could be defined as the infinite
capacity for taking gains. But I distrusted the pun; moreover, I knew no way of bringing it over into Italian. Instead
I said something about democracy being an experiment in
which most Americans still believed.

"Why not?" he replied. "For you Americans it is fine. But
we Italians are poor. We cannot afford democracy; it is too
wasteful. You elect a president for four years, and he must
spend the last half of the term making plans to get re-elected.
A great waste of time. Then there are the costs of the election, the funds that have to be gathered, the interests that
have to be bought to put one man out and another man in.
A great waste of money. We do away with all that. The
time lost in campaigning is put in planning for the people
as a whole, not for one party. The money spent on delegates
and big conventions goes into clearing the slums, reclaiming
the land, and draining the marshes. You have seen the new
cities like Littoria? The new sections of Rome? The speed
highway to Pompeii?"

I told him I had heard of his projects against malaria and

superstition, but I had not yet seen the cities which once were the much-feared marshlands.

"You shall see them." He made a notation. "You have been to Verona before, yes?" I nodded. "But you have not seen the new motor road through the mountainsides on Lago di Garda. More than fifty tunnels. You will see new frontiers."

"I have lived in Austria," I said. "The feeling there has changed considerably."

"Why not?" he continued. "The Austrians know that we guarantee their existence. We are not a democracy, but there is a wish for the democratic spirit. That is why I went to Stresa."

(These may not have been the exact words. It was in early 1935, long before the axis was conceived, when Italy was seeking a rapprochement with France and England, rather than with Germany. But this was the substance.)

"Your Excellency," I said, "I am not a politician. I am not always a poet. But I am undeniably a Jew. As a self-appointed spokesman for my people, let me say that the Jews of America appreciate your sense of fair dealing and sympathy with Jews in Italy—especially in these times."

"Oh, I see," he smiled broadly. "You are speaking of that man up there." He pointed to what I supposed was the location of Germany. Then slowly and seriously he went on, "But we in Italy do not know the difference. We do not have races; we have citizens. If a Jew is a bad citizen, he is a bad Italian. And there are plenty of bad Italians. Jew—Gentile—who can tell the difference? Who wants to, here in Italy?"

(Now in the name of all the gods of chance, upon what

meat did this same Caesar feed that he is grown so great a hypocrite? Hitler, at least, has been true to himself and his consistent lies. But Mussolini has betrayed every dream he followed, every ideal for which he spoke. Age, thou art shamed.)

At the end of the interview Mussolini presented a signed photograph of himself to my wife. It was Mussolini as leader of the Black Shirts, the head thrown back, the arm upraised, the hypnotic eyes shouting from their sockets.

"But your husband," he smiled again, "I am afraid he does not like soldiers. I shall not give him a picture like this. For you," he turned to me, "this is more apropos. One artist to another."

The photograph displayed the Other Self. Here Mussolini was in ordinary clothes, the simple soul, the lover of art and culture. The brow was not belligerent; the public eyes were lost in reverie; the famous chin was thrust out only to hold a musical instrument. The Head of Government, august Imperator, was playing a violin!

I wanted to say something about another Caesar who had played the fiddle. I did not say it. I wish I had.

ANOTHER EUROPE

FOR THE second time the telephone interrupted President Roosevelt's speech. I cursed it and kicked myself for having installed the instrument after having resisted it happily for nine years. This time it was long distance: New York calling. "Did I know Ernst Toller had just killed himself in the Hotel Mayflower? When had I last seen him? What did we talk about? Would I say something?"

I put down the phone and returned to the other room. But I did not hear the end of the challenging address. I did not care if the budget was ever balanced. I forgot about the plight of the reactionary Republican party and my over-taxed, non-existent grandchildren. I even forgot about this America. I thought about another time and another continent; about Europe—the other Europe—and the friends who were no longer there.

Toller and I met for the first time in a prison outside of Frankfort, in the Germany of 1924. A few months before this, the Theatre Guild had produced Toller's *Masse Mensch* ("Man and the Masses") which I had translated in Toller's elliptical "telegraph" style, and which had been designed and directed by Lee Simonson. Lee had used groups of actors as instrumental choirs and, discarding scenery, he had employed lighting effects as leitmotifs. We talked in German—Toller could read and understand English, but he did not speak it—talked about the problems of translation and the greater problems of putting revolutionary ideas into the

tight, dark box of the theatre. He outlined a new play
(*Hinkemann*) in which a war-cripple symbolized the impotence of the sensitive individual faced with the savagery of
a world that exalted only physical strength. Himself an
experimenter, he spoke of Reinhardt and the more experimental producer Jürgen Fehling with an enthusiasm that
was almost a passion.

Passion voiced itself in whatever he communicated, in the
short sentences and brusque gestures. Toller was just thirty.
Born at the close of 1893 in County Bromberg, then a part
of German Poland, he ran away from a Prussian high school
and studied at the French University of Grenoble. He was
in a fair way to become a wandering cosmopolite when the
war broke out. He returned to Munich and reported as a
volunteer, convinced that it was his duty to defend his
"attacked fatherland." Like his colleagues on both sides of
the trenches he soon found he could not distinguish muti-
lated "French" from "German" corpses. Like Siegfried Sassoon, he entered the struggle with patriotic ardor; and, like
the English poet, it was not long before he began to voice
protests against the humanity which fouled itself and the
madness which gloated in "the *danse macabre* of blinded nations." He was invalided and discharged. He grew to be a
rebel; he wrote manifestoes, held meetings, and searched for
comrades. He organized groups that were dispersed, reas-
sembled, and dispersed again. He headed a news bureau to
circulate the truth that was seeping behind the lines. In
1918 he helped plan the strike of the munitions workers
which led to the November Revolution. A price of ten thousand marks was set on his head. In 1919 he was arrested,

tried, and condemned to imprisonment for five years in the fortress of Niederschönenfeld.

He did not complain. He did not voice a personal outrage, but he spoke with smoldering intensity. The eyes burned with a black fire; even his hair seemed to be burningly alive as he talked of abstract justice. Although young, he looked ageless; his broad brow and deeply etched face suggested a half-Jewish, half-Slavic Beethoven.

Masse Mensch had symbolized the re-echoing conflict, but the struggle in this drama was between passions in man rather than between nations. Here man battled with himself: the individual against the member of the community. The chief opposing figures in the drama, the Man and the Woman, expressed the two impulses in modern life which were beginning to dominate the scene when Toller, in his mid-twenties, conceived the play and which, shortly afterwards, came to a climax in the grapple between the totalitarian and democratic ideologies. The Man represented the completely disciplined State, the unquestionable belief in government as God. The Woman was the radical humanitarian; she refuted the mechanical and merciless State; she championed a civilization where people would be free for creative labor. To the emerging new force (the Nameless One) this was pretty romanticism, futile sentimentality. The Nameless One stood for Revolution, as ruthless as the soulless State; he, too, was willing to send millions to their death for a principle of power. Between the equally terrible and uncompromising forces the Woman was sacrificed.

"It seems to me," I said, "that there is nothing subversive here. Yet, once again, you have offended the sacred prejudices. The old cry has been raised about propaganda versus art."

"Yes," said Toller with a twisted smile, "some of the journalists said that I was trying to make a drama out of an editorial. In a way they were right. I don't see why the theatre cannot sometimes act as critic and commentator, a sort of living newspaper. This is a time of upheaval, of disturbances that cannot be localized. These disturbances, 'news items,' will come to have increasing significance not only for us Germans, but for people everywhere."

"And that," I went on, "is what I suppose will limit the production of your work still further. Next they will accuse you of being a proletarian writer."

"They have already done that," said Toller. "I can understand it. Those who live a life free of worry find all references to labor 'propaganda' and mere 'phrase-making.' But those who live close to the working world know that the terms we use are the expressions of vital consequence, of life—even of life and death."

"Then you wouldn't distinguish between a proletarian art and any other kind of art, would you?"

"No," Toller replied slowly. "All art must rise from the one great source, the submerged, sometimes choked, but always human depths. There cannot be a proletarian art per se—not a single part. That is, it can only speak for a representative body of mankind if it speaks for all humanity."

We went on to discuss the writers who were planning to circulate their work in secret or, if necessary, leave the country.

"But it will not come to that," he said. "After all, this is Germany—oppressive and clumsy and authoritative as it always has been—but it is not barbaric. You can depend on that."

The prophet in Toller was less intuitive than the playwright. Twelve years after our first meeting I saw him again. It was in New York, at one of the meetings in a commercialized Greenwich Village still struggling to preserve the neighborhood's tradition. He looked twenty years older, a defeated worker, a harassed exile. I started to speak to him in German. He stopped me.

"I don't want to talk German. I can't even write in it any more. I'm writing in English—or trying to."

I misread the cue. I was overeager. I spoke about Thomas Mann's new work and Heinrich Mann's anthology, *Deutsches Lesebuch*—records of the homelessness of German literature. I mentioned Berthold Brecht's mordant lyrics. I asked for details about Erich Mühsam, who had recently been murdered in the concentration camp at Oranienburg. But Toller was reluctant to respond. He was tired, I thought, not despondent. We were both relieved when the refreshments made close conversation impossible.

Later he told a friend who was pessimistic about world affairs, "No one can take the short view. One must study history and think in terms of a century—not five years. Otherwise," he shrugged, "otherwise one might commit suicide."

Now—this is May, 1939—he is dead by his own hand, another Hitler victim. There is one less champion to defy barbarism and evil, one less honest worker in the world. Perhaps Toller felt he had fought and worked enough. But he knew that there could be no end of work and that the fight is never over. He was needed. I wish he had waited.

II

Although my own work for the theatre had been limited
to one or two adaptations, I seemed to be more or less backstage much of the time in Central Europe. I met and talked
with the playwrights Arthur Schnitzler, Richard Beer-
Hofmann, Sil-Vara, the actors Max Pallenberg and Alexander Moissi, the translator Siegfried Trebitsch, and the
director Max Reinhardt.

When I first met Reinhardt, he was living in a setting
more theatrical than most of his lavish productions. Schloss
Leopoldskron, outside of Salzburg, was a baroque castle
equipped with balustrades, columned halls, terraces, sculptured nymphs, and a practicable lake; it was also a producer's heaven. It could be turned into a series of realistic
wings and back-drops without the confining limits of a
proscenium. It was a temptation, and Reinhardt yielded to
it. He had already remodeled an old circus, and his actors
had rushed through the audience, making the spectators
participants in the action. He had discarded this "Theatre
of the Five Thousand" for still more co-operative experiments. He had transplanted and filled a cathedral to bring
The Miracle to life. He had staged *Everyman* in an open
square at Salzburg in a further attempt to break down the
barrier between actor and audience. Now he wanted to
achieve a still closer intimacy. To show that he was a master
of miniature effects as well as a manipulator of grandiose
pageants, Reinhardt was putting on a social comedy in one
of the reception rooms at Schloss Leopoldskron. About a
hundred of us were invited to watch Max Pallenberg create

a new *Stimmung* in a German adaptation of Molière's *Le Bourgeois Gentilhomme*. It was an unqualified success. The mood of the play and the manners of the period were evoked by the last piece of furniture, the least gesture. There was no stage, no footlights to confine the actors; Pallenberg's "asides" were addressed to our ears as if he were one of us; half the time he seemed to be playing in our laps.

Having proved what he could do with satire, a crystal chandelier, and a few chairs, Reinhardt planned a fresh departure. He wanted to come to America and follow his production of *The Miracle* with its complete opposite—a musical comedy. It had to be a musical comedy which was also a classic, but a classic which could be modernized to suit the times and the American tempo. Reinhardt turned to his favorite Offenbach, the French composer whose parents had been German Jews, and decided (prompted by his aide-de-camp Rudolf Kommer) that I was the man to transform *Orphée aux enfers* into "Orpheus Goes to Hell" or "Love in the Underworld" or something equally appealing. I warned him that the music would need adaptation even more than the plot; that it would be easy enough to broaden the never too refined libretto of Halévy, but that it would be far more difficult to transport the light volatile wine of this *opéra bouffe* to a climate that preferred fortified spirits. But Reinhardt (together with Morris Gest, his American partner) persuaded me, and Pallenberg convinced me. Pallenberg was to play Jupiter in the production—he swore he could learn English in ten easy lessons—and we planned the rôle. Pallenberg was to be anything but the awe-inspiring Father of the Gods. He was to be a grotesque deity, badgered, bewildered, semi-senile; a henpecked Olympian and a frustrated lover.

We saw him as a fattish man with uncertain legs, a few wisps of hair carefully plastered over his bald head, usually stuttering and forever adjusting a pair of badly fitting, gold-rimmed glasses. (If it ever is produced I hope Victor Moore can be induced to play the affecting part.) We planned to divide the action into three acts: Earth, Heaven, Hell. We predicted new careers for everybody. I was easily convinced that I was just what the American theatre needed.

Then, on the first day of 1925, I returned to America and began work on the text and lyrics. By March I had completed the first act. By April I had sketched the second act and completed a scenario for the third. Then began the unhappy conferences, compromises, delays, doubts, arguments, apathy, particular quibbles and general uncertainties. Kommer made approving noises over the manuscript, but approbation was not enough. Pallenberg could not learn English; Reinhardt postponed sailing; Gest was always elsewhere. Otto Kahn was said to be interested, but the interest of Mr. Kahn, true to a banker's principles, was expressed only in a golden silence. By the end of June I acknowledged defeat. I discovered I was temperamentally unfitted for the theatre. My own training had been along lines which called for directness, punctuality, decisive yeas and even more enthusiastic noes. In the theatre, I realized sadly, the real work begins after the labor of creation is over. It was good to return to my publisher who accepted my manuscripts, had them set in beautiful and imperishable type, squandered his substance and perjured his soul by furnishing the books with effusive jackets—without procrastination or attempting to collaborate, even to my advantage. I was glad to be taken to his (figurative) bosom.

III

Toller, Pallenberg, Reinhardt . . . One dead; another in exile; another in Hollywood, his experiments at an end—only three of the hunted thousands who have no place in a Europe where art is a word pronounced with a sneer. ("When I hear some sigh for 'Culture,' " said Goebbels, "I reach for my revolver.") I think of other members of the persecuted minority I met in Germany and Austria—Schnitzler, Beer-Hofmann, Stefan Zweig, Franz Werfel, Felix Salten, Lion Feuchtwanger—and I think that death was the easiest escape for some of them.

Schnitzler had been the center of gossip when I first came to Vienna. His wife had left him; a daughter was in the midst of an unhappy affair; his son, an actor, was rarely home. But, though alone and grown old, Schnitzler was never dull or morbid. He remained the alert Viennese; his mind was quick to expose shams; the eye blazed under the lock of hair which fell across his forehead. He looked vaguely Wagnerian—like a shrunken Wotan—especially when a rumble of anger thundered in his voice. We exchanged books and visits. I would go out to the cottage district where he lived in diminished splendor; he would come in to join me in The Neuer Markt and dine at *Meissl und Schadn,* where he was at home among the old waiters and echoes of his past.

Two meetings with Schnitzler remain vividly in my memory. The first persists because it was then he taught me how to prepare *Liptauer garniert*. To the average gourmandizer *Liptauer garniert* was a cheese; to Schnitzler it was a ritual. He gave the order for the ingredients with solemn exactitude: two small cream cheeses, four pats of butter, a teaspoon of capers, four boned anchovies, one finely chopped shallot, paprika, mustard, salt and caraway seeds. When the waiter had placed all these before him, Schnitzler dropped all persiflage and became as serious as a high priest; I could almost hear him intone as he mixed the cheese and butter into a smooth paste. "Never use a spoon," he said with the craftsman's precision. "It packs too hard. Always work it with a fork—and slowly—slowly." Then he chopped the anchovies, added them, and, always in the same order, put in a scant teaspoon of salt, a heaping ditto of paprika, ditto capers, ditto the chopped shallot, a good smear of mustard, finally a liberal sprinkling of caraway seeds. When the perfect blend was achieved, he presented it to us as though he were offering his latest drama to a select audience. The audience always applauded—and with good reason.

The other meeting with Schnitzler persists in memory because of a proud and trenchant remark. We were talking about another Jew. Two Jews cannot foregather more than twice without discussing the Jewish problem—discussing it the more obstinately because it is insoluble. Faced with the Jew's contradictory characteristics, we had tried to agree on what the Jew actually was, whether he could be defined at all except as he may be defined by exclusion. What unity could he possess without a common home, without a common type, without even a common language? How far could he be "assimilated"? Without a homeland, how could he repatriate himself in exile? Granting a measure of wholeness, could he maintain his integrity in a disintegrating world?

"Vienna is no longer your sentimental *Alt Wien*," I said. "It is a socialist city. Yet even here, where the professional circles make no racial distinction, I hear murmurs of political anti-Semitism. Is it due to the war?"

"I am afraid it is older than that," said Schnitzler ruefully. "Even in Vienna. Even in professional circles."

"Of course," I said. "I should have remembered. It is good of you not to remind me that you wrote *Professor Bernhardi* over twelve years ago."

From a discussion of this play, in which a Jewish doctor is caught between the demands of his calling and creed politics, we went on to talk about an American author whom Schnitzler knew only in translation, not in person. Schnitzler was puzzled.

"I don't know what there is about his work that I don't like," he muttered in his Wagnerian growl. "He seems to boast and ask for pity in the same breath."

"Perhaps that's the worst of his Jewishness," I suggested. "He wants all the distinctions—when they improve his status or inflate his ego—but he complains about every difficulty."

"What!" exclaimed Schnitzler. "Does he expect to be a Jew for nothing!"

I V

Looking back at it now, I cannot imagine what persuaded me that I might become a dramatist. But, during the two years I lived in Europe, I had one eye cocked on the stage. Even when I was adapting the Swiss tales of Gottfried Keller, I spent half my time alternating between the popular *Volkstheater* and Reinhardt's rather precious little theatre in the Josefstadt. I wrote a long article about Alexander

Moissi, comparing his unforced method with the exaggerated theatrics of our own actors, chiefly so I could say that the quality of Moissi was not strained.

I interviewed Sil-Vara and Siegfried Trebitsch on successive days. Sil-Vara looked and wrote like a fashion plate; his plots were as neatly tied as his cravats, and his style was almost as well creased as his trousers. Siegfried Trebitsch was designed by art and nature to be Sil-Vara's opposite. Trebitsch was the cartoonist's idea of middle-class complacency; a thick-set little man, well-to-do but untidy. A playwright in a lumbering way, he was spoken of merely as the German translator of Bernard Shaw. Like Shaw, Trebitsch was a shrewd businessman, and he looked it—a stock-broker suffering from indigestion rather than a dramatist afflicted with imagination. Locally he was best known as the brother of the notorious Jew who had given himself the resounding name of Ignace Trebitsch-Lincoln and had successively become an eminent Anglican priest, an Arabian sheikh, a Chinese spy, and a Buddhist abbot.

But, next to Schnitzler, I most admired Richard Beer-Hofmann. Each new visit made me esteem him more. He lacked the quick thrust of Schnitzler, but his penetration was even deeper. Beer-Hofmann was a poet and dramatist; his work had been produced in Vienna's show-place, the *Burgtheater;* he had been acclaimed as a verbal composer, an author, whose orchestral words needed no music. For years he had been writing and rewriting a cycle of plays, *The History of King David,* but only the prelude had been published. This prelude, *Jacob's Dream,* was a most extraordinary fusion. The language was simple yet intense; there was little physical action, but every scene was moving; the subject was remote, yet the reader was caught up in a sense of immediacy. What might have been an allegory, a literary cantata, became an exciting event. Two translators had failed to adapt it to the American stage. I resolved to atone for their failure. I translated the first two scenes with increasing difficulty but with continuing enthusiasm.

Then I bogged down. I read over what I had written. It was completely without force or conviction; it was not only dull but dead. It was hopeless as theatre, helpless as poetry. It was some time before I realized that Beer-Hofmann was completely untranslatable. His words, even more than Heine's, were deceptive in their simplicity; the spirit of the characters was expressed in the unalterable character of the words. The slightest change of value distorted them; the very differences of color reduced them to a lifeless rhetoric. . . . The truncated fragment of the play is in a drawer with other uncompleted schemes; I doubt that I will ever finish it. But I will be glad to lend the manuscript to anyone who is more persevering and confident.

V

It was another Europe indeed—the Europe of faith in art and hope in man. It was real comradeship I remembered, a spontaneous friendliness which united men of good will; it was not a hotbed of manufactured suspicions which kept them apart. It was a natural loyalty that freed the Germans of the Republic, not a fanatic ritual which chained them. The Germans I met as I journeyed down the Rhine, and tramped (with the customary rucksack) through the Black Forest from Heidelberg to the Swiss border, were not only tolerant and kindly but eagerly co-operative. It would have been fantastic to assume that they would ever accept hate as a daily diet and brutality as a way of life.

Now the idyllic Freiburg in Breisgau is a breeding place for spies; the soothing villages around Karlsruhe seethe with frightfulness; Munich, home of the classic Pinakothek, is a synonym for betrayal. It is a small but significant phenomenon that the square in which I lived in Vienna, the Freiheitsplatz (literally the Place of Freedom) has been Nazified into the Hermann Goering Platz. The most innocent letters are intercepted; your friends are agents provocateurs. Force has become the one regulator of social discipline.

I recall Fritz Haber, whose discoveries in the fixation of nitrogen had brought him to the head of Kaiser Wilhelm Institute for Physical Chemistry and the University of Berlin, and who, as scholar and soldier, was revered by his colleagues. He resigned when his two chief assistants were made to "retire" by the zealously pure-blooded State, went to Switzerland, and died there in 1934, a suicide. A year later Professor Philipp Lenard "officially" refuted the heresies of free investigation and unprejudiced research. In his introduction to *Deutsche Physik* Lenard wrote: " 'German Physics' ? Some may question the term. I might have called it 'Aryan Physics' or 'Physics of the Nordic Genus'—the physics of those who have fully sounded the depths of reality. . . . I shall be told that science is international. It is false. Science, like every other human activity, is racial and is conditioned by blood!"

It is unbelievable. But it is only a small variation on an incredible but continuing theme. They tell me conflicting stories. Some of my friends say that the Germans are their own victims, that they have suffered with the Jews, that they are limp and resigned. Others assure me that resentment is growing against the power-hungry leaders, that "nests" of objectors are meeting underground, that the German soul will save itself. They say, repeating Leopold Godowsky's sinister epigram, that most of Europe has divided itself into two kinds of people: "non-aryans" and "barbarians." No one knows. I only know that Europe once represented to me a high cultural level and the peaks to which the human spirit yearned. I wonder if my sons will ever know it.

HOME IS THE PLACE

MORE than ever, the world is too much with us. The morning newspaper shrieks itself off the presses to thrust the latest terror across the breakfast table. The midnight radio anticipates tomorrow's headlines and sends us to bed to dream of unprecedented perils surpassing any nightmare. The neighborhood movies hurry us through the innocent humors of Mickey Mouse to plunge us into the horrors of organized insanity. Every hour our privacy is assailed and our liberties are threatened; every day we must decide how much the world is to be with us and how much we are to be against the world. In no case is there any chance of escape. We retreat, but there is no refuge; we are faced by a series of systematic offensives. "We are no longer able to act as if tyranny did not exist," Jules Romains said at the New York World's Fair. "Therefore, we must act in order that it shall not exist." The ivory tower is down forever. There is no home for the frightened fugitive.

And what is home? The definitions contradict each other. Robert Frost gives two of them. The disillusioned man mocks gently:

> *Home is the place where, when you have to go there,*
> *They have to take you in.*

The kinder spirit reproves him quietly by adding:

> *I should have called it*
> *Something you somehow haven't to deserve.*

Home, then, is not merely the place of temporary peace, but the sense of permanent serenity—a child's faith, a dream of security. Yet how oddly, how almost incongruously, the words sound today: "peace," "serenity," "faith," "security." They are like concepts we no longer understand and terms we fear to use. Must we leave the home, desert the world of love and art, and pit ourselves against the world of action? Children of light, can we live in darkness? Live—and perhaps die—in conflict?

In one way or another, we make the compromise. Rest and rouse, play and fight, sleep and arm—they are the balanced and commanding measures; we alternate between them wherever we are. In the warm circle of friends, on a cold lecture platform in a strange city, across a blank sheet of white paper, writers struggle somehow to revive an old world or create a new one. So is it with me here. The old and new mingle where I live; they interpenetrate each other. Scarcely aware of it, never deserving it, I am enriched.

The home I have found, through no merit of my own, is a constantly surprising compromise. Except for the times when I am "in residence" at some university, or traveling to spread the gospel (not too thickly) through civic forums, I live on a freehold which is also a mountain-farm. I divide my time between writing and transplanting, attempting to make six iris grow where only one burdock grew before. My wife's day is less diverting; when she is released from secretarial duties the farm claims her. Here she becomes experimenter and manager in one. For several years she broke her heart because she could not breed fancy birds for expensive palates. In the end she profited by the mistake of Archibald MacLeish, poet-agrarian and, like my wife, once a practic-

ing lawyer. MacLeish had tried to raise a fine strain of pure
white turkeys only to discover that they succumbed without
warning to thunder, the first threat of rain, overeating, un-
dereating, or a severe frown. My wife thereupon eschewed
the culture of neurotic fowl and other temperamental game.
Her present bucolic program is simpler and sterner. With
the assistance of the Farm Bureau she has taught our idle
acres how to bear alfalfa, timothy, rape, field-corn, and soy
beans in sufficient quantity to feed our two Clyde-Percheron
mares, half a dozen Jersey cows, multiple litters of Red
Duroc pigs, and (since the meat problem is an ever-vexatious
one) a steer or two. I regard the greening fields with pleasure. She studies them for profit, analyzes the soil, inoculates
the seed, and counts (in advance) the bushels of potatoes, the
hills of corn, the rows of carrots, the mysterious vegetable
confitures planned for the local market and (if she is lucky)
the metropolitan trade. In the past the proceeds of my lecturing went to support the farm; part of the time my hired
man worked for me, but most of the year I worked for him.
Now it is pleasant to feel that my wife *and* my hired man
are collaborating to safeguard my comfort. Unless the soil
deceives me and the account books lie, victory is only a
decade away: within ten years the farm should almost support itself. Each year the losses are a little less than the year
before. And that, it seems, is the ultimate in successful
farming.

Friends of mine, it is true, have rallied me on my change
from the city skeptic to the expansive countryman. They
have affected to see a certain comic, even a comic opera,
quality in my change of scene and costume; my entry into
the barnyard, said one of them, seems less like the occupa-

tion of a farmer than a cue for music and the irruption of a bevy of slim-legged milkmaids. Alfred Harcourt has never ceased to remind me of my first month on the place when I boasted that I had transformed an ancient henhouse into a playhouse for my children and, unconscious of the value of phosphate and fertilizers, had congratulated myself that I had got a farmer to cart away the droppings of twenty generations of hens for only four dollars a load. Now, with the collaboration of a wife who is a student of legumes and nitrogen-producing nodules, I can afford to smile at my own ignorance. In a world of instability and unpredictable change, I can feel safe with a few acres of ground and a cellar full of potatoes.

After all, we farm as a way of life. Over the entrance to the upper pasture we have (figuratively) engraved the old upstate adage: the farmer who farms for a living sometimes makes money; the farmer who farms to make money goes broke.

If the farm does not guarantee a continuing profit, it ensures a variety of guests who have little more in common than an indiscriminate love of nature and a taste for freshly churned butter. Our national and domestic holidays bring us, besides our neighbors, perennial visitors who are continual novelties. F. P. A. drops in for tea, remains three days, indulges himself richly if not riotously, and leaves with a handsome tribute, "Well, when you're roughing it, you mustn't complain!" Challenged as rival raconteurs, Abram Chasins rises from his latest piano concerto and Sydney Kaye puts aside his accumulated briefs to become dialectical folklorists, to interrupt each other and argue about the medieval origins of this week's popular double entendre. David Mc-

Cord, poet and essayist, comes here to confront the Adirondack hills with a box of water colors and to teach the boys how to cast for trout. My harassed but still faithful attorneys, Alexander Lindey and Ralph Colin, earn their keep by repainting our signs and making camera records of the landscape with their Zeiss Super Ikomats. Helen Grace Carlisle brings her manuscripts and waits (always successfully) for the telegram which informs her that the *Ladies' Home Journal* and Hollywood have capitulated again.

The faraway world is with us, even though we sometimes cry:

O who would trust this world, or prize what's in it,
That gives and takes, and chops and changes every minute?

Thus the poet Quarles, in the seventeenth century, anticipating our fears. But Quarles, too, heartened himself by adding:

The road to resolution lies through doubt—
The next way home's the farthest way about.

I I

Home is where the truth is, but one goes a long way to fetch the truth home. It was a long search in Europe; it was a longer time before I found it in America. After I learned its changing form and color, I discovered it in the strangest places. It wore rough homespun in the midwestern town of Galesburg, Illinois, where Knox College came to renewed life for its hundredth anniversary. It disguised itself smoothly in cap and gown but was outspoken in the Teachers Colleges clustered about proverbially effete Boston. It rose with pioneering accents in the agricultural campuses of Utah and the unacademic forums in Arizona. It made itself heard in the Kentucky mountain classrooms as clearly as in the industrial universities of Missouri. Without union, seemingly without strength, students, teachers, and writers rallied to defend their last right—the right of the spoken word.

In the beginning was the word—the word that made men free—and, as Dorothy Thompson announced, today in most lands the word itself has been made captive. "It walks in chains. Those who would free it do so at the risk of their lives. . . . Our tools appear very weak. They go unarmed. They fall into the wastebasket; they crumble into dust; they are forgotten upon dusty shelves. But time and again they have opened prison doors; they have shamed the powerful; they have mobilized nations; they have held together the discouraged and oppressed. . . . Great nations have been built on words and, above all, this nation."

I applauded these sentences, I am afraid, a trifle self-consciously and with some self-gratification. Years before I heard them, I had written:

> *This is man's noblest edifice. All else*
> *Crumbles and rots; his loftiest stone is thrust*
> *Into the patient and ironic dust.*
> *His iron ships, his scornful citadels*
> *Are blown apart by gas and fiery shells.*
> *They mingle in forgotten pools of rust.*
> *But words, mere words, invulnerable, august,*
> *Become his statesmen and his sentinels.*

How can there be freedom when the word is enslaved? How can we hope for sentinel law or reanimating literature when the letter is broken and the individual spirit is outlawed?

III

Within the last few months I read three comments on literature by the heads of three major governments. They were all the more startling because they were seemingly non-political.

Benito Mussolini, speaking through Dr. Gherardo Casini, Minister of Popular Culture, said: "Our aim is ᴛo raise children in the firm imperialist spirit of Fascism. We have to look after the spiritual formation of youth. We have decided to revive in a totalitarian manner the principle underlying juvenile literature. We must follow Il Duce's orders to sleep with our heads on a soldier's knapsack."

Adolf Hitler declared by proxy in a widely circulated document: "There must no longer be artists who create willfully, haphazardly, or in any other but a national way and with a national purpose. Every artist who refuses to do this must be opposed, branded as an enemy, and hunted by the nation until he gives up resistance."

Prime Minister Chamberlain, in an interview, complained that world affairs too frequently interfered with his retreat into a literature "that takes me out of my daily life and away into a world as remote from reality as possible. Often I cannot read for twenty minutes without a visitor coming in and saying, 'He [Hitler] has done it again.' "

The brutality of the first two utterances is surpassed only by the inanity of the last. It is pathetic that Mr. Chamberlain is not permitted to immolate himself in a remote and hermetically sealed bower of roses, that he cannot fly for another conference to Ruritania, not even with Mary Poppins and her umbrella. It is regrettable that he cannot escape the world, and even more regrettable that the world cannot escape him.

But the statements of the totalitarian powers freeze the blood. The artist is to be regimented out of "haphazard" thought; if he refuses he is to be hunted down. He is to be trained to serve as automatic mouthpiece and machine-gun; the young idea is to be taught to shoot—straight. It is one thing for the classical schoolmen to "rear the tender thought and pour the fresh instruction o'er the mind"; but not even the most dogmatic drill-master of the past could have advocated the elimination of all fun and fantasy from the child's world. Only a régime gone mad with armaments could have "decided to revive in a totalitarian manner the principle underlying juvenile literature"; only a government of military sadists could have ordered children in the nursery to sleep with their heads on a soldier's knapsack.

With science reshaped into a lying instrument, with creation twisted to fit the supreme State, with aimless play suppressed and inquiry branded as treason, there is little hope for the free mind abroad. Europe faces new nihilisms, new slogans for progressive revolutions, further decay of art and distortion of culture. Torn by proscriptions, mesmerized by false messiahs, riddled by phobias, Europe plunges through a wasteland of increasing sterility. It is only in America that the questioning soul can hope for answers and the redeemed intelligence can remain independent. Here, if nowhere else, the creative urge re-establishes itself, turns

away from a rendezvous with death to an appointment with
life.

Almost three quarters of a century ago Walt Whitman
predicted that America would liberate itself and the arts
simultaneously. He declared that the poets, the painters, the
musicians, builders in sound and substance, would rip off
the European strait-jacket, stretch their limbs, and bring
forth a new race, strong and melodious. He invited the
Muse to respond to his summons and become an illustrious
émigré:

Come, Muse, migrate from Greece and Ionia;
Cross out please those immensely overpaid accounts,
That matter of Troy and Achilles' wrath, and Aeneas',
*   Odysseus' wanderings;*
Placard "Removed" and "To Let" on the rocks of your
*   snowy Parnassus.*
The same on the walls of your German, French, and Spanish
*   castles, and Italian collections.*
For know a better, fresher, busier sphere, a wide, untried
*   domain awaits, demand you.*

Here, in this "better, fresher, busier sphere," workers and
dreamers would find their material and their salvation.
Again Whitman abjured them:

Turn from lands retrospective, recording proofs of the past,
From the chants of the feudal world, the triumphs of kings,
*   slavery, caste;*
Turn to this world, the triumphs reserved and to come—
*   give up that backward world.*

*Then turn, and be not alarmed, O Libertad—turn your
    undying face
To where the future, greater than all the past,
Is swiftly, surely, preparing for you.*

The ancient accounts have indeed been immensely overpaid. Time now to strike a balance, turn the page, move
forward. We in America can well look toward wide democratic vistas; we have finally turned from that backward
feudal world, "the triumphs of kings, slavery, caste" to a
world "greater than all the past." We can go forward with
insatiable curiosity to where impulse has a fresh energy,
where liberation rises from the rich soil, the uncanny techniques, the limitless resources of the confident mind. Here
the free range, the spirit of affirmation, continues untired
and unconquerable. Here stimulus never flags, and truth,
dispossessed abroad, is at home. Home is the place.

INDEX

INDEX

389

BOOKS BY MR. UNTERMEYER

POETRY

FIRST LOVE ROAST LEVIATHAN
CHALLENGE BURNING BUSH
THESE TIMES ADIRONDACK CYCLE
THE NEW ADAM FOOD AND DRINK
SELECTED POEMS AND PARODIES

PARODIES

THE YOUNGER QUIRE INCLUDING HORACE
—AND OTHER POETS HEAVENS
COLLECTED PARODIES

TALES AND TRAVEL

MOSES CHIP: MY LIFE AND TIMES
THE DONKEY OF GOD BLUE RHINE—BLACK FOREST

TRANSLATIONS AND ADAPTATIONS

THE POEMS OF HEINRICH HEINE
THE FAT OF THE CAT (*after Gottfried Keller*)
MAN AND THE MASSES (*Toller's Masse Mensch*)
THE LAST PIRATE (*after W. S. Gilbert*)

ESSAYS

AMERICAN POETRY SINCE 1900
PLAY IN POETRY

CRITICAL COLLECTIONS

AMERICAN POETRY: FROM THE BEGINNING TO WHITMAN
MODERN AMERICAN POETRY MODERN BRITISH POETRY
THE FORMS OF POETRY: A POCKET DICTIONARY
DOORWAYS TO POETRY

ANTHOLOGIES

THE BOOK OF LIVING VERSE YESTERDAY AND TODAY
THIS SINGING WORLD RAINBOW IN THE SKY

COLLABORATIONS

POETRY: ITS APPRECIATION AND ENJOYMENT
(*with Carter Davidson*)
NEW SONGS FOR NEW VOICES (*with Clara and David Mannes*)

BIOGRAPHY

HEINRICH HEINE: PARADOX AND POET
FROM ANOTHER WORLD

LOST
ICONS

Reflections on Cultural Bereavement

ROWAN WILLIAMS

T & T CLARK
A Continuum imprint
LONDON • NEW YORK

T&T CLARK LTD

A Continuum imprint

The Tower Building,
11 York Road,
London SE1 7NX

370 Lexington Avenue
New York 10017–6503
USA

www.continuumbooks.com

First published 2000
Reprinted 2000, 2001, 2002 (three times), 2003

ISBN 0–8264–6799–7

British Library Cataloguing-in-Publication Data
A catalogue record for this book is available from the British Library

Typeset by Fakenham Photosetting Ltd, Fakenham, Norfolk
Printed and bound in Great Britain by MPG, Bodmin, Cornwall

In memory of Murray Cox
and Gillian Rose

Contents

Preface

There have been times when I thought this book might more honestly have been presented as a sort of journal of the 1990s. It has been several years in the making, and has been constantly reshaped as the decade unfolded (including a change of government in Britain and a war or two elsewhere). But the reflections here set down still seemed to circle around a few fundamental themes, and to make something a little like a connected argument; so it remains in the shape of an essay. I hope, though, that its readers will try to discern behind the surface a continuing story of reaction to the strange decade that has closed the twentieth century, a decade that has given us plenty to worry about, economically, internationally and culturally; most worrying, perhaps, because of our awkwardness in confronting the fact that certain styles of human self-understanding, styles that might conduce to a sense of irony or humility or trustfulness or solidarity, are fast becoming unavailable. This book attempts to identify some of these and to interpret and even defend them before they are quite forgotten. It does so from the point of view of a Christian priest; but I hope that most of what is written here will be accessible to those who do not share the theological position from which I begin.

The conversations that have helped to form this book have been with many people over many more years than it has taken (even) to write it. I must express my debt to my wife Jane; to Val Martin and my colleagues in the Church in Wales Division for Social Responsibility; to Tim Jenkins, Sara Maitland, John and Alison Milbank, Catherine Pickstock, Paul Rahe and Graham Ward. The dedication of the book inadequately marks two especially deep influences, personal, spiritual and intellectual. I miss them grievously and give thanks for them.

ROWAN WILLIAMS
Newport, July 1999

Introduction

The word 'icon' has come down in the world. It is probably more familiar as a term of art in the world of communication technology than as the designation of a sacred image; perhaps for most people its commonest use is to designate a particular kind of public figure. 'Icons' appear on computer screens or on television screens. They classify instructions for managing a machine or they mark the fashionable significance of a singer, model, actor or sporting hero. The late Princess Diana was regularly described as an 'icon'; Madonna and the Spice Girls likewise (interestingly, it seems to be a word applied more easily to women than to men in our culture, even in fashionable talk about 'gay icons'). An icon is apparently in this context something like a classic statement of a particular kind of life, a particular kind of *style*. This may not necessarily be a life or a style simply presented as something to *aspire* to, an ideal; 'iconic' status means something more like becoming part of the code of a community,

1

becoming in some way an image that binds people together, provides a common point of reference and a common touchstone of acceptability. A mediaeval commentator might have said that it was a shared source of 'delight' ... Its meaning belongs in the complex realm of public presentation, the marketing of personalities. It defines possibilities for a cultural group; it doesn't need a reference in some represented or evoked reality beyond itself, because its power and substance lie in its capacity to focus the desires of a public or a constituency. It 'refers' to these desires, it represents imagined futures; in itself, it needs no relation to a hinterland of meaning. It aims at an authoritative, self-contained presence – an *obviousness* in its structure and conventions.

But there are other meanings to be retrieved or suggested. The traditional icon of the Eastern Christian world is never meant to be a reproduction of the realities you see around you; it is not even meant to show what these realities will ever look like. It shows some part of this world – a scene from history, from the Bible, a particular person or group of persons – within a structure that puts them in a distinctive light. What is shown is their significance against the background of a source of illumination independent of them. This is, incidentally, illustrated graphically by the convention in iconography of building up the colours on a gold base: from this the rest of the representation 'emerges'. The point of the icon is to give us a window into an alien frame of reference that is at the same time the structure that will make definitive sense of the world we inhabit. It is sometimes described as a channel for the 'energies' of that other frame of reference to be transmitted to the viewer.

Something of this is what I want to explore here. Human cultures, up to the dawn of modernity, have generally worked with verbal and moral 'icons' – patterns of reading and understanding human behaviour and relationship that don't simply arise from what any particular group happens to find helpful or interesting, but that are supposed to represent some of the basic constraints on what human beings can reasonably do and say together if they are going to remain within a recognisably human conversation. It is a cliché and an unhelpful one to observe that these structures have not been universally the same. The point is that they have been there at all. The sort of thing I mean would include, for example: language about kinship; ritual marking of death and a set of conventions about what to do with human corpses; the ritualisation of eating; the regulation of sexual activity; the assumption that there are appropriately different expectations of human beings at different stages in their lives, and various ways of codifying these; the making of promises; the recitations of a common history. All have in common the presupposition that we cannot choose just any course of action in respect of our human and non-human environment and still

3

expect to 'make sense' – that is, to be part of a serious human conversation in which our actions can be evaluated and thought through and drawn into some sort of rough coherence, by ourselves and by other speakers. These are not moral ideals or demands, in the sense of being things required by authority for the sake of a granting of approval; they are a bit more basic, to do with the conditions of common life and language. They are, in what is now a well-known phrase, the points or levels in human talking 'where our spade is turned'. Where such things obtain, people do not know how to *belong* with each other and with their environment in the absence of these – what should we call them? Not conventions, as that implies a certain contingency or arbitrariness in them, nor ideals, as they are not goals to be pursued; hence my choice of 'icons', structures for seeing and connecting in the light of something other than our decisions, individual or corporate.

Modernity has been suspicious of all this, assuming that the reasoning mind can sort out a sensible common agenda for human beings, a process in which these 'iconic' structures will either prove their rational usefulness or turn out to be, indeed, arbitrary and therefore deserve to be discarded. The result – a banal enough observation, this – has been a prolonged and highly complicated story in which 'modern' society, mostly North European and North Atlantic, has tried to disentangle structures that have served limited and oppressive interests, yet have been defended and justified as 'natural', from those that have some claim to be intrinsic to human welfare and sense. The very recognition of the former has made it harder to identify the latter: suspicion becomes endemic. Current confusion over the family or gender roles or 'sexual preference', over religion and secularity, over race, sovereignty, language and economics and many other things suggests that no consensus is going to appear in a hurry, whatever pressures there are to identify 'values' we hold in common.

So this short essay does not set out to offer any theories about the precise content of a plausible list of iconic structures. More modestly, it looks at a limited number of areas in which some kinds of discourse seem to be getting more and more laboured, more and more inaccessible to our culture; and it asks whether the consequences of the loss of these icons might not imperil so deeply the possibilities of corporate sense-making (and so of just social order) as to suggest that here we might find a few pointers to where spades are turned. It will be clear that the practical concerns behind this book have a lot to do with the education of our children. The first chapter presses the question of whether we now have any confidence about what we mean by 'childhood' in our culture; because if we haven't, there is no chance at all of our having a coherent idea of what education might be. But there is a further suggestion, that we won't make sense of childhood unless we have an idea of what we under-stand by *choice*; and the background question is, What happens to our sense of the human when it is divorced from a grasp of the self as something realised *in time*? The 'iconic' issue here is how far a picture of the human as constructing identities in would-be independence of the temporal flow can serve as a structure for human sense.

In fact, this issue, in one way or another, will be around throughout these pages. The second chapter looks at the erosion of those mechanisms in society that control or limit rivalry – particularly those that have little to do with conscious choice or policy. To recognise that the choices of the individual will cannot demand instant and unconditional fulfilment in the material and inhabited world we in fact live in is to acknowledge the necessity of spending time in the management of conflicts of interest or desire. But the readiness to spend time in this way already presupposes certain bonds, certain convergences of interest. Paradoxically, to be able to 'negotiate' differences (rather than trying to resolve them by the contest of violence) entails an assumption that differences can be *thought*, not just thrown against each other; that the present conversation takes for granted a common world and that the interests of its inhabitants can never be intelligibly considered except by thinking of relations and interde-pendence, even if only at a very formal level. But to arrive at this understanding involves the recognition that the self itself is learned or evolved, not a given, fixed system of needs and desires. And this leads on in turn to a reflection in the third chapter on the phenomenon of *remorse*, in which we come to terms with the unwelcome fact of our presence in other people's histories, a presence we can't control. There is that of us, it seems, which lives outside what we think of as ourselves.

Following through the implication of this leads to the further acknowledgement that my loss and the loss of other subjects (that is, other feeling and thinking entities) are not two distinct matters: my life-in-the-other, theirs in me, means that it is possible to discover a kind of 'mourning' that does justice not simply to any individual's privation or pain but to the shared nature of human grief. Again paradoxically, comedy as well as tragedy carries that recognition; both are potentially painful to the extent that they constantly undermine self-contained and controlled models of the self. And in the final section of these reflections, the conclusion is drawn out that what is common to all the imaginative crises and deprivations discussed is the loss of the language of the *soul*.

The last chapter attempts the ambitious and indeed thankless task of defining what this might mean. Something other than arguing about the presence or absence of a supposedly non-material 'element' in the human constitution is involved, and this discussion takes it for granted that the post-Freudian insistence that the self is not a *given* form of inner unity has to be given due weight. One recent writer has spoken of the self as what emerges in the process of 'defining conflicts' – that is, conflicts that provoke sufficient interrogation to generate a new way of speaking, of articulating a position. In a culture that tries hard to minimise certain sorts of conflict or contradiction – either by a mythology of the goodness and givenness of an inner self or by the (equally mythological) picture of the agent as simply enacting a chaos of timeless desires – a vital language of selfhood wastes away. But in using the word 'soul' as well as 'self', in treating the latter as very nearly a synonym for the former, I have deliberately trailed a coat. 'Soul' is – at least – a religious style of talking about selfhood; and the issue finally raised here is whether a wholly secular language for the self can resist the trivialisations and reductions outlined in the book as a whole. This is dangerous territory. It is religious language that has borne most of the responsibility for keeping alive the story of a substantial soul that can live apart from the body and its history, and it may seem an odd ally to turn to in order to challenge just that model. But, if for the moment we keep our distance from what might be properly called religious doctrine, and ask about the nature of the religious self as articulated in some styles of religious culture, mainly but not exclusively Christian, I hope that the relevance of these styles to our present cultural bereavement may emerge as worth discussing. It is certainly interesting that psychoanalytic theory continues to engage in a cautious and complicated pavane with the language of the Christian tradition in seeking to make sense of how the self is formed in response not simply to the contingent other, but to an Other which may be necessarily fictive and empty – or necessarily not, depending on a good many variable and involved factors.

So this is an essay about the erosions of selfhood in North Atlantic modernity; and also, therefore, about the accompanying erosion of certain ways of imagining *time*. It will emerge, I think, how these issues are bound up together. Wilfully standing back from the different kinds of questions about how meaning relates to a history of *production*,[1] the common feature in many of the areas discussed here, leaves us with one or another form of the given and absolute self, the self that stands outside language and interchange. Now to use a term like 'production' invites the suspicion of Marxist influence; but in fact one of the really substantive *philosophical* insights of Marxism was to focus attention on the ways in which meaning is bound up with the processes by which we engage and transform a material environment. It also

[1] The significance of production as an issue affecting what we say of ourselves is given prominence in Nicholas Boyle's brilliant collection of essays on our current crises, *Who Are We Now? Christian Humanism and the Global Market from Hegel to Heaney* (Edinburgh, 1998).

alerts us to the fact that cultural questions can't be separated ultimately from questions about power – about who has the freedom for what kinds of transformation of an environment. Chatter of a certain kind about freedom of choice needs chastening by reflection on who is being served by particular models of freedom, since there is no possibility of talking usefully about freedom without looking at the way power is distributed in actual societies.

These will be issues in the background rather than the foreground of what follows; but it is important to note in advance that these broader questions of political discernment press in very insistently when we speak seriously about cultural change and cultural deprivation. Part of the frustration of our contemporary position is that political language becomes increasingly dominated by the marketing of slogans, sound bites, and the calculation of short-term advantage, in a way that effectively removes politics from considerations about the transformation of human culture; while a fair amount of what passes for cultural studies relies on fundamentally anti-political accounts of desire and imagination. This book will not bridge that gap, but it is at least an attempt to read the gap as a wound, which neither conventional right nor conventional left are currently doing much to recognise or repair. Indeed, the job is *not* to 'mend' this or other breaches so much as to suggest how the raw edges can awaken us to questions about our humanity which even the most mature kinds of political and cultural discourse handle only with difficulty.

And the last introductory word, which may already have been hinted at, is that this is a book attempting to articulate *anger* – not anger only, and not necessarily an anger that requires more and more insistent and explicit statement, but anger nonetheless, at a recent history of public corruption and barbarity compounded by apathy and narcissism in our imaginative world. Fiona MacCarthy's 1994 biography of William Morris, one of the most solid and resourceful books of the decade to deal with the politics of culture and the culture of politics, concludes its introduction by evoking Morris's likely reaction to the prevailing ethos of the 1980s and 1990s.

> Electronic addiction? Drug culture? Inner city planning? Bottom line banking? Political correctness? Post-Modernist architecture? ... Sound bites? Opinion polls? Chat shows? Designer clothes? Executive phones? Pulp literature? Video porn? Corporate sponsorship? Market-orientated society?
>
> 'Damn'd pigs! Damn'd fools!' You can hear Morris expostulate, robust, fidgety, tremendous ... [2]

We seem to have no contemporary Morris; but it may still be possible to wake an echo of that imagined expostulation.

[2] Fiona MacCarthy, *William Morris. A Life for Our Times* (London, 1994), p. xix.

1

❧

Childhood and Choice

A few years ago, the excellent education supplement of the *Guardian* carried a series of articles under the general heading of 'Education 2000'. The writers were fairly representative of educational and political orthodoxies; much emphasis was laid upon training, skills, socialisation, from contributors of the left and the right alike. The week after the series ended, there was a letter from someone who had long been engaged in some less orthodox experiments in private education; it pointed out rather acidly that not a single article in the series appeared to have contained the words 'childhood' or 'play'.

This is a heavy indictment; an accurate one, unfortunately, as far as this (in many ways admirable) series was concerned, and so a pretty accurate measure of the orthodoxies represented. What it speaks of is a profound *impatience*. Childhood, after all, is a period we've come to think of as 'latency', the time before certain determinations and decisions have to be made. But to manage such a period requires a certain confidence that the society we inhabit has the resources to carry passengers, a confidence that we know how to live alongside people whose participation in our social forms is not like ours. It is not that the child doesn't have a share in society; but, on the whole, developed and not-so-developed cultures alike have granted that the child does not have the same kind of negotiating role in society as the adult. Hence, of course, the prevalence of rituals of transition – putting on the *toga virilis*, adolescent circumcision, bar-mitzvah ... The child is brought out of a latent or free-floating state to become a social agent like you and me. But this implies that we as adult social agents are obliged to bear with what goes before, with the indeterminacies of childhood. A society with clearly marked transitional rituals is committed to *guaranteeing* the integrity of such a period; and a society for which the education of children is essentially about pressing the child into adult or pseudo-adult roles as fast as possible, is one that has lost patience with that kind of commitment.

A lot could be said about the prolonged 'latency' of the human young. It is not only a function of the sheer biological vulnerability of human infants, so much more protracted than in other species; it also has to do with the fact (connected with, but not simply reducible to, biology) that humans perceive

14

themselves, form their attitudes to their bodies and to other bodies, as users of *language*. The acquiring and refining of language is a long and complex process, never moving at precisely the same rate in different subjects. And part of that process, as every parent and teacher is (at some level) aware, is play; because to learn language is to discover, by trial and error, what I can seriously be committed to when I open my mouth, what I'm ready to answer for. This is something I cannot begin to do with intelligence or confidence unless I am allowed to make utterances that I *don't* have to answer for. We do not treat children as adult speakers whom we expect to take straightforward responsibility for what they say according to recognisable conventions: we accept that there is a sphere of legitimately irresponsible talking, of fantasy and uninhibited role-playing, language without commitments beyond the particular game being played. Without such an acceptance, the learning of language is paralysed by the fear of making mistakes – not just mistakes in grammar or diction or whatever, but the disastrous fate of having game taken as reality, being *bound* by things thoughtlessly or ignorantly said. We are familiar, from fiction and autobiography, with the trauma that can be suffered by a child whose fantasy is taken for distorted or intended fact, whose imagination is interpreted as lying, by a hostile, stupid or tyrannous adult. And there is a sharp little tale ('The Looking-Glass Boy') by that surprising Edwardian

15

children's writer, E. M. Nesbit, which turns on the fate of a boy who himself does not appreciate the difference between fantasy and lying; as a result of the kind of morally robust magical intervention Nesbit enjoyed providing, he has to experience as reality the fantasies he concocts – that is, he has to take responsibility for what he says. He thus learns, if in a somewhat drastic way, a lesson about adult discourse and indeed about the *social* or at least interpersonal dimension of speech. The morality of this story is crude, but it illustrates neatly the point being made – the difference between talking we can be expected to be answerable for and other kinds of talking.

Children growing into mature speakers will naturally want to try out projects and identities. Adults overhearing children fantasising (the stories a child tells herself in bed, a game in the corner of a room or a schoolyard) may be shocked at times as well as amused: the uncensored tribal mythologies of schoolchildren as collected by the Opies in their wonderful books, are shot through with fantasies of terror and violence and half-understood sexual threats. Alison Lurie observes of playground rhymes that 'everything we might want to protect boys and girls from is already in these verses'; and in her novel, *Foreign Affairs*, the central character, Vinnie Miner (a scholar of children's literature), is dismayed and disillusioned when her field research on children's rhymes and games uncovers what are to

her obscene, cheap and disgusting imaginings.[1] But –
without wanting to deny that children's language
and imagination can genuinely be corrupted and
cheapened – we have to remember the multitude of
roles and vocabularies that every child uses. If we
allow that there is a proper and protected space for
children to be 'irresponsible' speakers, we must
budget for the fact that their uncommitted speech
will not be uniformly nice, docile or harmonious –
understanding that the freedom to try out roles and
images and words that are not 'nice' is a rather
significant part of learning speech. In other words,
latency should not be muddled up with *adult*
fantasies of innocence.

If children's fantasies can be anarchic and amoral,
or, at least, at an angle to our constructions of plausibility and rightness, it should not surprise us if the
children's literature that seems to have staying
power includes texts that sit light to realism or moral
tidiness or both. It will seem strange, perhaps, to
bracket together two such wildly different children's
writers as Enid Blyton and Roald Dahl; but they
have this at least in common, that they are both
abidingly popular, to a degree that can be baffling to
sensitive adult observers, and this despite the weight

[1] Alison Lurie, *Foreign Affairs* (London, 1985), pp. 113–16; on
playground rhymes in general, *Not in Front of the Grown-Ups:
Subversive Children's Literature* (London, 1990), chapter 16
('Everything we might want ...', p. 215).

17

of adult disapproval, from parents, teachers and librarians. Blyton is castigated for her flatness of style, for class prejudice, stereotypical characters and speech forms, and lazy plotting; Dahl for his vulgarity, collusion with violence, sexual stereotyping, racism and cynicism. To the adult reader – in practice, the long-suffering adult reader-aloud – these charges are beyond dispute; and they are capable of uniting the orthodox of left and right in a most striking way. But what both writers do (with, I suspect, rather different levels of self-awareness) is precisely to indulge 'irresponsible talking', to inhabit the child's indeterminate world with hardly a hint of apology. Fantasy is given free rein, in a world from which 'ordinary' adult agents are largely absent. Dahl presents us with monstrous or subhuman adults, tyrants and fools, varied with rather ineffectual, if benign, elders. Blyton's still phenomenally popular 'Famous Five' books are to the adult no more than interminable and wellnigh indistinguishable variations on a single plot. The children, separated completely from their parents, engage in and solve some kind of 'mystery', usually in a mildly exotic setting (island, castle, moorland, circus). To the young reader, they are very much about the freedom to try out a sort of adult identity: to be in control of an environment where adult power and presence is not visible, *and* where the prosaic externals of the 'normal' environment in which adult power operates are also forgotten or suspended.

It is because this is a non-standard environment, a holiday in unreal surroundings, with the children living unsupervised (and eating the 1950s equivalent of junk food a lot of the time) that it is possible to imagine new and unconstrained identities. This is not a world in which the ordinary sequence of acts and consequences operates at all strongly, and so it becomes possible to 'speak without commitment', to test possible courses of action without anxiety, to try on clothes.

A recent and highly provocative study of children's fantasy by John Goldthwaite argues with passion that: 'To pretend that children's books are the playground of the imagination, with no intrinsic pedagogic content and no accountability to reality, is to deny the very nature of the reading experience in childhood';[2] on this basis, a number of classics in the canon (including *Alice* and the Narnia books of C. S. Lewis) are severely castigated for erroneous teaching about the world. Either, like *Alice*, they lack – or even subvert – coherent moral purpose,[3] or, like Narnia, they inculcate false and (surprisingly) blasphemous views of the world. In the latter case, fantasy becomes a malign substitute for the real world, a place to work

[2] John Goldthwaite, *The Natural History of Make-Believe. A Guide to the Principal Works of Britain, Europe and America* (Oxford/New York, 1996), p. 195.

[3] Ibid. chapter 3; pp. 164ff. on 'the absence of *agape*' ['love' as in Paul's first Epistle to the Corinthians].

out grievances against the world God has actually made, rather than a space for learning how the real world may properly and faithfully be negotiated.[4] There is some point to this thesis, though I find its characterisation of a good many writers, not only Carroll and Lewis, eccentric and overdrawn. What matters is indeed where we end up, what moral suppleness and insight have been won in the course of the story; and in such a light it is hard to rule wholly out of court the 'parallel world' style of fantasy, as exemplified in Lewis and his precursors and imitators. (It is equally hard, I'd say, to rule out the kind of anarchic and parodic fantasy found at its darkest in *Alice* and at what Goldthwaite terms its most 'frivolous' in Jim Henson's triumphantly surreal adaptations of children's classics for his Muppets; Goldthwaite, sadly, doesn't at all approve of these resourceful and ironic transformations.[5]) The salient question is whether and how we are returned to our own setting, and how, in the interim, we have learned to 'read' it. Lewis sails very near the wind, admittedly, in including a final Narnian episode dealing, a little ambitiously, with the end of the space-time universe: the sequence does indeed seem to end in a decisive

[4] Ibid. pp. 220–44, esp. 242 ('This is what you do when your God asks things of you that are unthinkable; you create another world where you can sneak in your complaints under the guise of make-believe').

[5] Ibid. p. 195: 'it teaches frivolity' is his judgement on the Muppet Workshop.

escape from the choices and tensions of the temporal order. And the way in which 'Narnian' lessons are put into practice in our world can indeed look lame at best and at worst just as silly and offensive as Goldthwaite argues. Yet the lessons themselves can often stand; the problem is less, I think, with Lewis's method than with his unmistakeable clumsiness in handling a good many aspects of the contemporary world in plausible fictional terms.[6]

The 'alternative world' vein has been mined almost to exhaustion in the past few decades, though new publications continually recycle its themes. Like Blyton's books, these fantasies are often flawed by stereotypes of class, race and sex, and present, to adult eyes, anything but a morally rounded universe. But the basic premise, that children may find themselves transported to a magical or mythological level within the familiar world, now grown strange, or to a parallel and normally hidden world, is a powerful intensification of the licence to 'irresponsible talk'. The sheer distance of this imagined environment makes possible an even greater range

[6] Lewis's best effort, *That Hideous Strength*, must be set against this negative assessment; but, despite its considerable achievement in savage satire of a realistic kind, it is strongest when dealing with the invasion of the contemporary by the mythical. Goldthwaite's annihilating hostility to Lewis overall ignores Lewis's extraordinary ability, at his very best, both to relativise his own prejudices and to uncover moral self-deception at every level.

of styles and identities. But perhaps the most liberating thing about such literature is the sense conveyed that the 'normal' world, the habitual ways in which life is structured and control exercised, is not so self-evident that we can't think ourselves around its edges. The child learns to look with a curious, even sceptical, eye at the everyday, ready to ask what are its non-negotiable bits, what are matters of convention or even distortion. What aspects of persons, objects, feelings, relations (landscapes, for that matter) look the same even when some of the ordinary ground rules are shifted? And, in imagining other sorts of beings, other sorts of agents, where, if at all, do we recognise a gap opening up between *that* kind of life and ours? At what point does a peculiarity of behaviour *there* enable us to see for the first time that some aspect of human behaviour *here* is strange and questionable?

Alan Garner is a notable exponent of the parallel world style, his fictions becoming steadily darker and more troubling up to the mid-1970s. Even in the earliest books, though, there is an undertow of disturbing re-visioning. *The Moon of Gomrath* was his second children's fantasy, involving the familiar pattern of children precipitated from the ordinary world into a realm of mythical conflict between strange creatures. Throughout the book, we're made aware of a tantalising oddity, a sort of detachment and chill, in the behaviour of the 'light-elves'; and, fairly well on in the narrative, an explanation is

offered by another of the 'fairy' species. The elves
fight with bows and arrows, not hand-to-hand, with
swords: they can kill at a distance, without seeing
the eyes of their victims. ' "You will find in the bows
of the lios-alfar much to explain their nature, which
was not always as now." '[7] But human beings use
bows and arrows, don't they? And guns? So the child
reader might ask. Well indeed: now look at human
beings again, a bit more carefully. What might the
difference be between knowing you're killing a
specific person and indiscriminate slaughter? And
does the latter make you another kind of person?
Were *we* not always as now?

  This kind of moral exploration, by way of the play
between the familiar and the often outrageously
strange, is properly a function of all imaginative
writing; and the fictional space as an opportunity for
testing styles and identities – even at the level of the
suburban soap – goes on being important for anyone
trying actively to relate to the world. Even the kind
of book popular at 'first reader' level, a vigorous
narrating in word and picture of familiar settings and
experiences, with some comic dimension or comic
distortion (animals doing human things, for instance
Spot goes to School), is a space for seeing the self and
its world afresh. So *that's* what I'm like (or am I?).
Being an object to myself, a story for myself – I'm
like that, I'm not like that – is the beginning of

[7] Alan Garner, *The Moon of Gomrath* (London, 1963), p. 142.

reflective and imaginative talk, or the irresponsibility that finally shapes us – in ways I'll go on to
consider – into choosing agents, answering for
ourselves.

This irresponsible talking of children, at whatever
level, is set free by the unspoken presence of the
habitual, adult-controlled world. You can dispense
with the adult in the story precisely because there
are adults around to guarantee that the play or the
fiction stay within bounds. I shan't suddenly be left
stranded, bound to a 'playing' role that I was only
testing. The background world allows me to drop out
of a fantasy that's become too dangerous or
compulsive; I know that, just as I'm discovering the
'normal' world isn't the only possible one, I can also
be sure the alternative frame of fantasy isn't the only
truth either. Sophisticated older children's or
teenagers' fiction can explore the dangers here, to
memorable and haunting effect. Some of the abiding
power of *Treasure Island* derives from the agonising
prolongation of a 'game' of pirates and treasure into
painful, sordid and ambiguous reality, with lots of
loose ends. The later Alan Garner (*The Owl Service*
and the really chilling *Red Shift*) works at the same
dangerous edge, as does William Mayne, whose
extra-ordinary novel *A Game of Dark* is one of the
most searching essays in this genre: in both Mayne
and Garner, an emotionally disoriented child, for
whom the 'normal' has fractured (parental death,
sickness, divorce, traumatic puberty) can become

trapped in worlds of mythical force, violent compulsion, that are profoundly frightening and damaging. And fantasy of this kind tells us that fantasy itself relies upon unspoken contracts, on the symbiosis of irresponsible talk with the secure background in which acts *do* have 'ordinary' consequences and fictional identities can be abandoned without emotional shipwreck. At the simplest level, all parents will know the experience of explaining that an over-vivid story (book, video, play, film) is taking place *there* not here, that it has boundaries fixed and controlled by the 'ordinary' world, boundaries for which the adult in some way assumes responsibility: it can be banished without disaster and the familiar world resumed.

The responsibility of the adult in all this is crucial. We are understandably repelled these days at the deliberate cultivating of fiction designed to frighten and subdue children (more worried than some of our ancestors seem to have been); this sort of thing abandons the nurturing responsibility. Perhaps too (with Dickens's Gradgrind in mind, demanding facts and nothing else) we're repelled by an approach that sidelines fantasy and what I've been calling irresponsible talk. More seriously, we are, or should be, shocked and sickened by the picture of thirteen-year-olds conscripted into an army (as in the Iran–Iraq war, and in some of the rebel militias of Africa); by parentless, homeless, criminalised children in the urban streets of Brazil or Guatemala, regularly butchered by police and security forces; by child prostitution – *not* a phenomenon confined to Thailand or Latin America – and sexual abuse. There is a peculiar horror and pathos in children not – as we say – *allowed* to be children. And this was a significant aspect of the wave of nausea that swept Britain in the aftermath of the murder of James Bulger at the hands of two ten-year-olds, and that is echoed every time a child is convicted of killing; these are events that prompt an unusual level of heart-searching by the mass media.

I've used 'we' in the last paragraph, as people do, to mean the sort of people I expect to be reading these words: those who understand the importance of exercising a responsibility that allows the child room to explore in safety, not to be prematurely committed. But 'we' is always in danger of being a complacent word. There are enough currents around us to suggest that this is in fact a responsibility only dimly understood in its fuller implications, and that the 'we' who believe we are aware of what's involved in the nurture of childhood need to think harder and more systematically about the subject. If in fact we live in an environment in which the definition of the child as a choosing and consuming subject undermines the whole enterprise of nurture, we ought to be asking sharp questions of ourselves and what we take for granted or collude in; so I shall be turning next to look at what kind of 'subject' our culture seems to think a child is.

II

The perception of the child as *consumer* is clearly more dominant than it was a few decades ago. The child is the (usually vicarious) purchaser of any number of graded and variegated packages – that is, of goods designed to stimulate further consumer desires. A relatively innocuous example is the familiar 'tie-in', the association of comics, sweets, toys and so on with a major new film or television serial; the Disney empire has developed this to an unprecedented pitch of professionalism. Rather less innocuous (more obsessive, more expensive) is the computer game designed to lead on to ever more challenging and sophisticated levels. Anything but innocuous is the conscription of children into the fetishistic hysteria of style wars: it is still mercifully rare to murder for a pair of trainers, or to commit suicide because of an inability to keep up with peer group fashion; but what can we say about a marketing culture that so openly feeds and colludes with obsession? What picture of the acting or choosing self is being promoted?

If the child is a consumer, the child is an *economic* subject – even if someone else actually provides the cash, the demand is the child's. And what economic subjects do is commit their capital, limit their options by so doing, take risks for profit or gratification. They make property or assets take on meanings, values, in a pattern of exchange: things become a kind of language. Which is why, as a few metaphysicians have observed, economics is indeed an inescapable part of human business, one of the things we 'just do' as human beings, as makers of meanings. Good: but the rhetoric of consumerism (the arts of advertising) necessarily softens the elements of commitment and risk. It is important to suggest that gain may be had with the minimum of loss. All advertising tends to treat its public as children – tends, that is, to suggest that decisions can be made without cost or risk. This is in the nature of the enterprise (people are seldom attracted by being told about cost or risk): adults can be expected to know something of how this works. But the child targeted by advertising is not likely to be aware of this. He or she becomes an economic subject without the opportunity to recognise those painfully-learned truths about how economic activity commits and limits you. The child as consumer is always a *pseudo*-adult – which may explain something of the confusion and frustration of the child or teenager ('young adult', if you insist) pressured into the obsessive patterns that arise when economic activity is divorced in imagination from the problems of adult commitment. The most merciless example of this is, of course, the marketing of addictive drugs to children; merciless not only to the children, but in reflecting back to the marketing world the logic of so much of its 'mainstream' strategy.

The language we use about being an economic subject is not unlike what we say about being a *sexual* subject. Here too what we might want to talk about is commitment and its risks: the whole body becomes, intimately and dangerously, a giver and receiver of meanings or messages, with all that this implies about limit and potential loss. Advertising, once again, loves to suggest that being a sexual subject is fairly unproblematic: the right exercise of economic choice equips you for a better and fuller range of sexual opportunity – which is really rather like economic opportunity. Both kinds of 'market' are presented as relatively risk-free. Now it is notoriously hard to say just how far the advertising of children's or even young adults' goods *deliberately* plays with consciously sexual images; let's assume, generously, that it does not to any great degree. The difficulty comes in, more subtly, with a whole vocabulary of choice and gratification, in the unspoken complexities of rivalry and desire that are not addressed head-on; the business of learning what it is to be desired, to be enviable; in the codes that the body is being habituated to, the messages it learns to give. And in any case, the world of adult advertising is always visibly at hand to reinforce the message with its own (often imaginatively and beautifully) erotic idioms. Things are desirable to make *you* desirable; even before you quite know the nature of the desire in question, the language is learned. At its most crass, this can be seen in the postures and gestures of children, girls particularly, in children's talent competitions, beauty contests and so on: the stereotypes of predatory male and seductive female are happily exploited and thought to be rather touching in children of six to eight years old. But the problem is not restricted to this crude setting; as I've hinted, it is everywhere where the display of 'desirability' is fostered in the child, in the very idea of fashion as a proper category for thinking of the child's appearance.

So pressure on the child to be a sexual subject is not simply about the age at which children become sexually active in the usual sense. Cultures, even within our own country, differ and have long differed over this: teenage motherhood (and attendant teenage mortality, often forgotten in this context) has been common enough in many times and places, from mediaeval (especially aristocratic) Europe to parts of modern Asia. When it has suited dynastic or economic ends, the early initiation of sexual activity has seldom been a problem for moralists (whose difficulties have come more with the matter of *controlling* the initiating of sexual activity). The problem is more one of *how* sexual choices are learned and made: how consciously, in what context. Much of our continuing abhorrence of incest seems to rest on the assumption that sustainable adult sexual choices are made more or less impossible if there are *no* areas of our lives and relationships uncoloured by erotic potential. In a weaker form, this is why we establish

professional codes for clergy, physicians and others; there needs to be a territory where this question can be put on one side. And incest taboos are like taboos on sexual activity involving children – with which, of course, they frequently coincide. The abusing parent offends us doubly (offends us enough for Freud, famously, to deny the clinical reality of parental incest in the histories of his female patients; still a painfully controversial issue in Freud interpretation – and in modern analytic practice). Both prohibitions effectively claim that there must be regions where the pressure of being object or subject of sexual desire is held off. And, where children are concerned, this has much to do, once again, with the safeguarding of a space where identities can be learned and tested in imagination before commitments have to be made.

The child drawn into sexual activity by the adult has no chance of managing or controlling the meanings his or her body is made to bear. And while loss of some kinds of control is itself *part* of the experience of sexual encounter, we assume that its danger is contained by mutual consent, by the *sharing* of risk. We don't and can't assume that such containment is possible in a radically unequal situation (we know the damage to self-perception that is caused by rape). As for sexual activity *between* children, a similar point holds as for the incest taboo. We are not necessarily faced here with the exploitative inequalities of adult–child sex; but there

31

is the same erosion of a 'space' not dominated by the pressures of erotic desire and choice – and by the vulnerability and uncertainty thus introduced when my body becomes something that may or may *not* be desirable to another. Exactly *when* sexual latency ends may be a less important matter to settle than recognising that there is such a thing as sexual latency, and that it needs serious attention and protection if sexual maturation is in any way to keep step with the whole process of imaginative maturation. If there is no such recognition, or if we have no sense at all of the rationale of according such a recognition, we are culturally guilty of the equivalent of conscripting the teenage guerrilla; not to mention the child prostitute.

The point could be expressed most simply by saying that children need to be free of the pressure to make adult choices if they are ever to *learn* how to make adult choices. For them to be free for irresponsibility and fantasy, free from the commitments of purchasing and consuming, is for them to have time to absorb what is involved in adult choice. Failure to understand this is losing the very *concept* of childhood. But it is just this failure to understand that is evident in the slippage in our public images and practices towards treating the child as a consumer, an economic and erotic subject, in ways that obscure the whole business of *learning to choose*. And the loss in question here is sharpened by wider economic pressures. We (the liberal-minded) may and do complain about the pervasively middle-class atmosphere of much 'classic' children's literature (including all the examples so far cited here). But this feature of the literature has a lot to do with the bald fact that poverty is a poor environment for protected spaces of freedom, or for having time to learn through unpressured play. It may well be that some of what goes into our concept of childhood derives from a very specific Western 'moment' after the Industrial Revolution, when significant numbers of children among the new middle classes were relieved from the direct pressure of contributing to an agrarian or cottage-industry economy, and, quite simply, had time on their hands. And while every culture has the notion of protecting the young in some important aspects, Western bourgeois families undoubtedly prolonged this period, creating new markets for education and entertainment. Be that as it may, the *decline* of industrial society, the steady growth of a sector of the population excluded from the processes of production and wealth creation, brings new problems for childhood. In areas of major economic depression, especially urban deprivation, the environment is commonly one in which material poverty and the pervasive images of consumerism sit side by side; there is little to soften the pressures of those images, while at the same time there are few straightforward or legitimate ways to gratify the desires nurtured by them. Thus the drug economy flourishes and small-scale crime is almost too common to notice. Furthermore, this is an environment in which adult stress and depression – often intensified in, though not exclusive to, the lone parent household – limits the ability and willingness of parents to secure pressure-free space for children, or to provide models of adult choice – if only because the range of real options available, economic, political, even sexual, is narrow. It is an environment in which heroic efforts are made by many adults, parents and teachers alike, to sustain the possibility of experiencing childhood in the ways already discussed; but the dice are heavily loaded against them.

In this context – but also in many that are supposedly more 'privileged' – the effect of blurring the boundaries of childhood and limiting the choices of adults is a situation in which adults revert to childlike behaviour, uncommitted and fantasy-driven, and children and adults can come to see themselves as *rivals* in a single arena of competition. Sexually, socially, economically, the child may seem to be bidding for the same goods, and the difference between a child's and an adult's desires is not grasped. In another much-publicised scandal of 1993, a mother who left her eleven-year-old daughter alone in the house while she disappeared for a holiday, spoke of this almost in terms of punishment for the child's pert or flirtatious manner ('a right little madam'). More than one commentator remarked on the implication that the child was being presented as a competitor in

34

'desirability'. Regressive adult and precocious child meet in a situation where the child's actual vulnerability can be overlooked until too late, a situation which is thus fraught with possibilities of violence.

The 'safest' adult to have around is one who is aware of having *grown* – one, that is, who knows in his or her own experience how transitions are made from one sort of choosing to another (which also means one who hasn't forgotten what it is *like* to be a child). A society that is generally disabled in its choice-making will produce childish adults, bad at the nurture of children because they are not secure in their adult freedoms. There are some paradoxes here, of course. It is not unknown for totalitarian societies to channel quite high levels of creative energy into child-rearing and education; there were aspects of the educational system of the old Soviet Union, at some moments in its history, that were not completely contemptible. But in the long run, unintelligent political education will produce either conformism or cynicism – or a debilitating mixture of the two – and will undo any good that emerges elsewhere in the system (as in the Soviet Union again). If people are not developing into real political subjects, there is a major area of adult freedom that remains uncultivated.

There is also a rather different problem, accentuated in the past couple of decades. Learning to *assert* ones claims, needs and dignities as an adult has become a matter of immense cultural importance;

and it can be an aspect of learning how to foster the needs and dignities of children effectively and without resentment. The Neanderthal Right quite regularly blames feminism for the collapse of the family and the menaces to childhood in our culture. But the woman who is left unfree to negotiate economic and other choices in a society where choice overall is more varied and more pressured is, if my earlier argument was right, more at risk of regression and of rivalry with a child. There are so often chains of violence and abuse transmitted from the powerless, childish male adult in a situation of deprivation to the still more powerless woman and on to the child; and these are chains unlikely to be broken without a clear feminist analysis of cycles of violence and powerlessness – as well as the broader economic transformations needed. To say this is also to recognise the need for critical work on male self-perception, especially the ways in which economic powerlessness reinforces the regressive aspects of 'standard' male behaviour and male bonding – machismo as a response to poverty or status uncertainty. The problem arises – and it is a problem we shall be returning to more than once in these pages – of the point at which the assertion of right becomes a less-than-adult claim to nothing more than access to an open market, an assertion of the right to compete. When that happens, we are back to the destructive situation of adult and child in potential competition for limited goods, losing the *distance* between adult and non-adult desire that preserves the dignity of both.

The implication of all this is that if children are to be allowed to be children, we have to ask about what prevents adults being adults. Not only parents, but adults in general, adults in their social organisation and their political choices, have to grasp what is involved in becoming responsible for the nurture and induction into human society of new human subjects in process of formation. A recent book by a Roman Catholic writer meditating on Rembrandt's great painting of the return of the Prodigal Son concludes with reflections on the difficulty of taking up the role of the parent in the group depicted, compared with the relative ease of identifying with the older or the younger son: 'Do I want to be not just the one who is being forgiven, but also the one who forgives; not just the one who is being welcomed home, but also the one who welcomes home?'[8] A society that pushes us towards dependent and frustrated patterns of behaviour will not enable adults to be 'at home' with their limits and their choices in a way that makes it possible to welcome or nurture those who are bound to be dependent, who are still learning their own freedom. How then

---

[8] Henri Nouwen, *The Return of the Prodigal Son. A Story of Homecoming* (London, 1992), p. 115 (p. 122 in the 1994 edition).

do we, how are we encouraged to, understand the nature of adult choice in our environment?

III

We are told often enough that our society is set more and more to maximise choice. Is it, then, one in which adult choices are better grasped and more easily possible? The signs are not encouraging, if we take the signs to include the marks of alienation – juvenile crime and adult abuse, the growth of a non-working population with no stake in society, the chaos in personal and familial relations in areas of deprivation (and elsewhere), and the general confusion and bitterness over methods and goals in state education. If we think of adult choice as the choice of 'somewhere to live', settling on options that allow us to act more freely and intelligently by giving us definition, giving us graspable material to work on, we have to reckon with the fact that such choice closes off avenues by giving my life definition, a definition it can only have by refusing certain openings. I am changed by my choices, and I can't simply revert to the position I had before – which is itself a position already defined and limited by choices. Real choice both expresses and curtails freedom – or rather it should lead us further and further away from a picture of choice that presupposes a blank will looking out at a bundle of options like goods on a supermarket shelf.

And here originates a good deal of our trouble. Is this in fact how choice is presented to us? If we think back to what's been said about the culture of advertising, it is more or less in the nature of the beast that the 'choices' here put before us are presented to an *abstract* will or personality, to nobody-in-particular; they address, of course, bundles of instincts, fears and desires, sometimes the instinct or prejudice of a group or class, but never a person with a history or a specific kind of vulnerability. Advertising could not work otherwise, and the best we can hope for is an education that lets us notice what is going on, how advertising 'constructs' its abstract consumers, its impersonal but impassioned audience. But what about other areas where the rhetoric of 'choice' is powerful at the moment? I want to look briefly at two such areas, asking how far our current practice really looks to or equips *adult* choosing: the parent's 'right to choose' in respect of children's education, and the woman's 'right to choose' as presented in contemporary debates about abortion. I am aware that this is a contentious juxtaposition.

For a decade and a half, we have been consistently told by government that the protection of 'parental choice' in educational matters is one of the most fundamental imperatives in a proper education policy. The appeal of this is genuinely powerful, because it has a ring of altruism – wanting what's best for a growing generation – at the same time as having a comforting ring of tribalism – wanting what's best for our own. The harder you look at these two sorts of appeal, however, the more difficult it is to hold them together in terms of *choice*. I want to be able to choose a 'better' education for my child, and so I must require educational institutions to furnish me with information about their relative success or failure; without this, there is not much sense in speaking at all about the right to choose, and it is quite logical that a policy stressing such a right should involve pressure on schools to provide a copious flow of information about their performance (test results, league tables and so on). But who in such circumstances *chooses* a school identified as 'failing' (to use the current jargon)? Just possibly, a parent with a strong commitment to – say – education in a multi-ethnic setting might say that it's more important to equip a child to live acceptingly in a diverse society than to secure a particular cluster of qualifications, and might accordingly opt for a school with higher diversity and lower average examination results. But that is a consciously risky business, and it is a bold parent who is sure enough about this to jeopardise a child's possible vocational/professional future. Those doing so are obviously *choosing*, though on the basis of different criteria of excellence: they are not choosing what they see as failure. But more generally it should be self-evident that the notion of failure here already begins to limit the supposed availability of choice. To attract custom, a school must 'succeed'; and this almost invariably means selection by academic promise. Some will be rejected, and will end up in schools by definition less 'successful'; and who wants to choose them? Yet they will be the only possibilities for some parents. The language of choice is beginning to look far from innocent.

If the parent (on the child's behalf) is a consumer and the school a provider or producer, the school competes in a finite market, a market where one producer's gain is another's loss (there is not a lot that a rival producer can do in this context to 'diversify' to avoid failure). A school's excellence, measured in the apparently straightforward ways specified in present policy, is bound up with its capacity to attract customers away from competitors. Within a finite geographical area, this becomes a means of attracting not only 'custom' but resources – local enthusiasm, the support of parents with managerial and fundraising skills; and so a model such as this necessarily involves a spiral of failure for the less successful competitors, and the consequence diminution of *real* choice for some parents. And a parallel spiral is set up among consumers: the 'successful' school can, to some extent, negotiate conditions, intensify its selectivity, setting terms that only a certain percentage of applicants can satisfy – a necessary move, since the school itself is a finite system whose resources have to be economically deployed. Parents can become caught in anxiety about their ability to negotiate with the school to establish the viability of their choice. The end result is a situation in which certain schools and parents are effectively *without* choice, because resources are slanted in one direction by the imposition of uniform standards of excellence, and the experience of choice for the more fortunate is shadowed by anxieties about how to meet increasingly stringent conditions for the exercise of that choice.

In short, the language of choice applied to the educational system is deceptive. By concentrating our attention on parental freedom to choose the 'best' available provision, it distorts both our moral and our more narrowly educational perceptions. It encourages us to ignore the context and effects of such choice, nudging us insistently away from the awkward question of how everyone's supposed right to choose could be honoured in a framework like this. It also encourages us to assume that there is a single and fairly easily measurable standard of success in education. In both respects, the language of choice helps us to postpone or set aside questions about education as something that has to do with expressing and fostering a *corporate* responsibility – the shared responsibility of inducting children into a social environment with at least some common values, and the providing of what is needed to understand and question that environment in terms of its success in embodying values. Since we currently don't seem to know, as a society, what we want to 'induct' children into or what we consider to be the foundation of our society's moral legitimacy (that is, what makes this society worth belonging to or defending), it isn't surprising that we take refuge in treating education as the process of purchasing blocks of training material. When our consciences are particularly tender on all this, we consider adding a block called 'moral education'. This will inevitably have a somewhat abstract feel to it – as does the valiant but rather elusive document on 'Values and Education in the Community' produced in 1996 for the School Curriculum and Assessment Authority. And it is a gloomy fact that left and right often mouth the same clichés here. By accepting the polarisation of 'academic' and 'vocational', by applying simplistic tests of relevance or accessibility, educationalists on both sides of the political divide can successfully bracket out the most fundamental issue: how are people to acquire a language in which they can *think* about the character of their society? For that requires both a fluency in the traditions, even the mythology, of the society you're in, *and* a confidence sufficient to test and challenge its inconsistencies or deceptions. There was once a powerful socialist vision of education as learning tradition so as to make it a critical tool; but voices like those of Raymond Williams, Richard Hoggart or E. P. Thompson are none too audible on the left these days.

'Choice' in education is a term that must be stripped of its false innocence. The prevailing use of the word conceals a deep scepticism about the whole idea of education as serving a common interest, providing a language for public debate and moral wrangling. Choice in this context looks remarkably like the successful assertion of *will* when you analyse it; and the supposed goodness of free choice in education is not very different from the desirability of my being able to defend and sustain my interest – albeit through another party, the child, whose interests are seen as an extension of mine. Now where the assertion of my will is simply about matters of relative indifference to other agents and their interests, if it is indeed like selecting a brand from the shelf, it does not seem too problematic – though campaigns about South African produce or Nestlé have opened our eyes to the fact that even supermarket choices may have moral and political connotations. The truth is that very few indeed of our human options are like that. I said earlier that 'real' choices both express and limit freedom; if we are encouraged to ignore the elements of limit, the limiting of myself and, just as importantly, the limiting and determining of someone else's horizon, we end up in fantasy or confusion or both. We will not be making adult choices and we will not be taking responsibility – in the educational context – for inducting children into a properly *social* world: we will be deploying them, conscripting them, into thinly concealed conflicts over whose interest will be allowed to

44

prevail. To bolt on components of 'moral education' to a system whose *methods* already communicate a particular moral message (conflict and rivalry) is not likely to help. Furthermore, part of the strategy of this conflict of interest is the refusal to articulate what's going on, the truth that choice for one group is preserved or defended at the cost of the freedom of others to choose what they want or need. An educational strategy that conceals this is not going to induct children into any lively sense of goods and goals that are not sectional, interests that are not local or in some way tribal.

The rhetoric of choice as a controlling good in education is one of the factors that makes for a society profoundly inept in handling adult self-determination and responsibility. We don't particularly want to know how our choices make a difference – to the possibilities open to others, and thus to our relations with those others, and thus to our own longer-term possibilities. The involvement of our own good or interest with that of others is a theme that will recur frequently in this book. If we lose the edge to our thinking about choice, lose the awareness that choice means loss, and that the morally taxing questions are about how that loss is 'distributed', it is natural enough that we lose the awareness of the distinction between how adults choose and how children choose. We end up with the child as consumer, economic and erotic, and thus as potential rival. We end up assuming that human beings do not have to *learn* to choose; will triumphs over the messy and time-consuming business of reflection, the thinking through of our relationships and dependencies. And one consequence is the loss of an integral understanding of what childhood is, with the corrupting and violent results which are becoming familiar.

Education is one example among many of the debasement of choice that has become current, the now almost universal reduction of agent to consumer. Similar points could be made about the encouragement given to cable television, let alone the 'consumerising' of primary health care. But these are quite familiar themes; instead of exploring the fairly obvious parallels with education, I want to look at a far more complex and contentious example – the use of 'pro-choice' as a designation for the position of those in favour of liberalised abortion laws. One or two preliminary points had better be cleared away before further discussion. I accept that in anything other than strict modern theological terms, there is a widespread uncertainty as to when one can begin to speak of an identifiable *individual* in the first few weeks of a pregnancy, and that this uncertainty colours the emotional responses of many who would be unhappy with unrestricted access to abortion for women at any stage of pregnancy. I accept also that the termination of a pregnancy is not necessarily in all circumstances the worst possible moral option, even though I consider this to be the termination of a human life. And, like many others, I am sickened by the rhetoric and practice of anti-abortion activists whose respect for human life turns out to be curiously selective, activists who are prepared to threaten or kill surgeons involved in abortion, or simply those who see no contradiction between their views on abortion and their endorsement of militarism. I am genuinely puzzled by political parties, governments or churches that appear to find a greater moral problem in abortion than in the manufacture, marketing and use of indiscriminate weaponry, from cluster bombs and poison gas to nuclear warheads. Confusion, dishonesty and misplaced dogmatism in this area have lowered the moral credibility of any critical questioning of liberal orthodoxies on abortion in the eyes of many, if not most, articulate citizens of the North Atlantic world.

But this does not alter the ambiguity of 'pro-choice' as the designation of a moral position. 'Not the Church, not the State, Women must decide their fate' is a well-known slogan; and what it appeals to is in fact a deeply moral perception, that any system programmatically denying to someone the liberty to become 'subjects of their own history', authors in some degree of their destiny, is indefensible in moral terms, *precisely* because it rules out certain groups or persons as possible candidates for making what I've been calling adult choices. However, what the slogan silences or encourages us to ignore is that the moral world is not very

47

satisfactorily defined in terms of individuals 'deciding their fates' in a vacuum. No one at all 'decides their fate' in the sense that their choices shape only their own lives and possibilities, or that *only* their choices shape their lives and possibilities. The question that arises, as with the rhetoric of educational choice, is whether the word 'choice' itself translates simply as the freedom to protect your own interests at the inevitable expense of other makers of choices.

This is where the complications begin in earnest. We don't treat the foetus as a real subject, a maker of choices, it is argued. It would be absurd to speak of its 'freedom' being violated. Can we therefore speak of its 'interests' in the same breath as those of an independent human agent? We call it 'it', because its human identity is still unformed as far as our adult perspective is concerned: we haven't until recently been in a position to know its sex before birth. We don't treat the issue of a miscarriage as a human corpse – though we feel differently about a stillbirth or a very late miscarriage, a point well made by Mary Gordon in a careful and nuanced 'pro-choice' essay.[9] Surely here if anywhere the language of free choice as a good for the adult subject can be used without too deep a shadow?

This would be an easier argument to sustain if we did not at the same time treat the foetus as having

[9] Mary Gordon, *Good Boys and Dead Girls and Other Essays* (New York, 1991), pp. 140–1.

48

'claims' of its own – for which purpose, the textbook will begin to write about the *child* rather than the *foetus*. When we discourage the pregnant woman from smoking or alcohol consumption, when we make recommendations about exercise or lifestyle, we treat her as someone morally constrained by interests not completely defined by her. She may, outside pregnancy, 'innocently' choose to indulge in practices that may undermine health: only when these affect others – smoking in a non-smoking railway carriage, alcohol abuse causing violence or criminal neglect – does the moral temperature go up. A choice we may not applaud but are content to tolerate becomes a more public matter. And it seems as if the relation of mother to foetus is morally nearer to this public territory than to the liberty of an individual to treat her body as she chooses; her choices have become recognised as setting limits on some other subject's possibilities. We may not regard the issue of miscarriage as if it were the body of a named individual; yet we do regard it as having a place within a network of human interests, as a notional partner in possible conversations, as carrying the particular charge of being an object of love.

Possible conversations: but surely this is different from the relationships we have to *independent* others? The foetus exists, for at least the greater part of the gestation period, in a state of absolute physical dependence upon the mother: it can have no life outside the womb. What does it mean to treat it as a real 'other'? It means, at the very least, to recognise a coherent life-system which, however closely dependent upon a 'host' system, possesses a relationship to its entire environment that is not the same as that of the 'host' system. Indeed, the dependence itself is a mark of that difference; we cannot avoid speaking of *relation* here, in a way we do not and cannot speak of my relation to my finger or my kidneys. Is this enough for real *moral* otherness? As one or two recent commentators, notably Fergus Kerr,[10] have observed, we should be careful about the possible implications of saying 'No' to this. If we want to say that there are pieces of evidence that can help us decide whether or not we give this or that biological phenomenon the status of person, we run severe risks. If 'moral otherness' depends on the right accumulation of properties on the part of a putatively human system, we shall always risk enumerating or categorising those properties in a way that rules out some controversial claimants. People regularly, when they try to specify in this area, refer to qualities such as rationality, capacity to take responsibility for actions or respond coherently to stimuli, to participate in communicative or meaningful action in some way; and such suggestions leave us with a nest of difficulties about the status of the newborn, the senile, the severely

[10] Fergus Kerr, *Theology after Wittgenstein* (Oxford, 1986), pp. 176–7.

handicapped in mind or even body (where communication skills are impaired). Just why are we licensed to consider them as moral others, endowed with interests comparable to ours, claiming access to a good like ours? The question is hard to answer; but, despite the robust conclusions of one or two recent philosophers, like Peter Singer, the plain denial of the granting of such a status to, for example, a newborn infant, seems to be counter-intuitive.

But, it could be replied, in any theoretically doubtful cases like these we – concretely and physically – recognise an organism existing in its own right, sufficiently like our own independent organic existence to be a plausible sharer of our interests; not so with the foetus, or at least not before a certain point in pregnancy. Again, though, is this so clear? Pro-choice activists are quite right to say that technology has in some ways made their position emotionally harder, because of the ready availability of photographic images, variously enhanced, of the foetus. When abortion legislation was last debated in the British parliament, a 'pro-life' group sent MPs lifesize models of twenty-week foetuses, and much outrage was expressed by campaigners on the other side. Similarly, when the *New Statesman* a couple of years earlier carried on its cover the photograph of a well-developed foetus, there was a good deal of angry correspondence: this, it was said, could only play into the hands of the 'pro-life' agitation. The anger is revealing, and rather disturbing. It acknowledges the significance of sheer instinctive recognition, 'animal' recognition we could almost say, in responding to something as a moral other; and it implies the desirability of learning to suppress, ignore or minimise such an element in the forming of a rational moral response, the desirability of – in some circumstances – arguing people out of these reactions. But once that has been granted, houseroom has been given to a very ambiguous principle – that we should be taught to question what I have called 'animal' recognition. This in effect raises the question once again of the possibility of criteria for 'counting' as a human being, and whether there is a plausible way of articulating or listing these. But if there is, we are clearly into the territory where the claims of some putatively human organisms is to be decided by others unilaterally: the question has become one of power, the profound power of definition. The power to decide the human claims of others is, of course, precisely what feminism rightly rebels against – the long and shameful history of educating people to ignore, distort or minimise certain kinds of biological community and the recognitions that are or should be bound up with them. The history of patriarchy – not to mention racism – shows that such a project is by no means impossible.

Yes, but perhaps this is only a back-projection of the form of the second-trimester foetus on to the barely determinate 'streak' of genetic material that exists at the beginning of a pregnancy. So the objector might respond, and with some justification. The 'pro-life' use of images from later in gestation might reasonably be challenged as giving the impression that the embryo of the first weeks of pregnancy is already *visibly* a 'small person'. Yet the structure of the embryo is what it is in virtue of what it will develop into: it is not a different *kind* of organism from the second-trimester foetus, and what happens to it determines what becomes of foetus, child and adult in all kinds of ways. As the 'pro-choice' advocate insists, there is a long and complex process going on even between conception and the formation of what we can call an identifiable nervous system; we can easily be hurried to a conclusion when the obvious is pointed out – that the qualities we instinctively associated with 'being a person' seem to be present in the pregnant woman and absent in the contents of her womb during the first weeks of gestation. But if the real issue is not 'counting as a person', qualifying to join the company of fully-fledged possessors of personal rights, but simply being a moral other, the possessor of interests not reducible to mine, the case is not so clear. As Fergus Kerr notes, almost in passing,[11] the

[11] Ibid. p. 177: 'Paradoxically enough, the more animal we remember ourselves to be [that is, the more we move away from defining ourselves as autonomous reasoners first and foremost], the weightier the theological objections to abortion and embryo experimentation might become.'

recognition of this rests on a recognition of our own fundamentally animal condition, as material systems involved in varying kinds of material relationship to an environment, relationships of dependence and interdependence. The pro-choice argument may say, 'Granted there is an area of uncertainty, there is surely some clarity about the ends of the spectrum – genetic streak and quasi-infant (third trimester, say)'; but the point has to be pondered that this is a spectrum extending between different *levels* of dependence and biological organisation: at no point can we mark a transition from one *kind* of life to another.

These considerations are not meant to settle the fiercely debated question of the law's role in all this; my concern is more with the kind of moral discourse within this debate that exhibits disturbing features, a simplifying of the notion of free choice into the terms of a purely individual good. Reversion to a pre-1967 situation would only be attractive, even morally defensible, in the context of a massive reconstruction of attitudes to childcare and nurture, to the professional lives of childbearing women, the availability of other forms of fertility control to women, and many other things besides. The entire question is also badly in need of informing from the standpoint of those who have examined the psychologies of pregnancy and childbearing: a recent book on this makes great play of the fact that, like it or not, the *relation* between mother and conceptus is from the first precisely that, a relation, with all that that involves of projection and the need to free the other from projection, negative and positive. But this seems an issue worth spending time on, if only because we have now reached a situation where most of the onus appears to lie with those arguing the moral otherness, the distinct and irreducible interest of the unborn – a situation reinforced by current trends and practice in genetics involving the 'breeding' of human embryos for research. It is now far easier and more fashionable to defend the moral otherness of animals, or even of the inanimate environment, than to persuade people of the appropriateness of defending unborn humans in this way, although there is intense *clinical* pressure to identify the foetus as a quasi-child whose welfare the mother is obliged to foster. The *reductio ad absurdum* of would-be legal definitions of foetal rights only serves to pinpoint the bizarre confusion British and American society tolerates in this area, where the defenders of the moral status of veal calves and rainforests seem to find no problem with the moral invisibility of certain categories of embryonic humans.

But there may be a point capable of being owned by both sides of the abortion debate, a point bringing us back towards the main argument of this chapter. 'Pro-choice' is a slogan that can very easily be a recommendation to *ignore* something, just as it is in the educational world. By treating the availability of 'choice' in a situation as *the* moral issue of decisive importance, it can again collude in the reduction of

ethics to the question of who is able more successfully to defend their interest against others: ethics as
a conflict about power. Feminist ethics has had a
vastly important role in unmasking the ways in
which supposedly 'disinterested' talk about ethics,
sexual, economic or familial, has an unacknowl-
edged agenda that is to do with the control of some
human beings by others. It is a bit of a paradox that
the discussion of abortion, quick to suspect a patriarchal anxiety to control women's power in relation
to their own fertility, so easily sidesteps the problems
of power that lie in the shadow of 'pro-choice'
rhetoric – if you are prepared to grant some level of
genuine moral otherness to the unborn. The very
rhetoric itself does less than justice to the acute
sense of the tragic experienced at some stage by
many women opting for abortion, who may be
haunted by an otherness denied, even if they stand
by their decision.

IV

If we are able to demythologise the goodness of
choice as the affirmation of the consumer's will, we
may have learned something of value in understanding the relation of child and adult, the main
burden of this opening essay. Protecting the human
young from some of the pressures of adult choice
implies a recognition that such choice is weighty,
potentially tragic, bound up with unseen futures for

the agent and other agents. To learn about this, I have argued, requires a space for fantasy, a licence for imagination, where gradually the consequences, the self-defining knots, of adult choice can be figured, fingered, experimented with. To look at the child as economic and sexual consumer is to flatten the landscape of our own adulthood, to make universal a model of choice that is at best partial and trivial; and also to treat the child as a market rival, confirming that ambivalent strain of rivalry that both energises and skews culture. It is, of course, possible to say that 'protecting' the child is again about power or control; but if it is true that the child doesn't come into the world fully equipped for moral self-definition, if the very language of selfhood has to be *learned* as we grow, we are not in the situation of one adult group claiming the right to set the definitions of another. We are rather trying to equip a child to *exercise* power, to hold off unequal and deeply damaging contests of power while the child is still acquiring it. It may be said that it is almost impossible to establish a clear line between legitimate nurture and oppressive control; and this is indisputably true. But the difficulty is not to be dissolved by denying its presence and complexity. It is in negotiating the risks here that we discover a good deal about our own adulthood, and the denial of the difficulty is a denial of the very realities of mature choosing.

Because of the risk and difficulty here, we are going to be very tempted by the flattened landscapes of 'consumer' choice. It fits well into a political landscape where responsibility for the interest of the other is consistently obscured. The consideration of the fate of our children is one of the few areas in which, it seems, we are still capable of being frightened back into reflection on such responsibility. Nearly everyone in our society with any direct involvement with children experiences directly and painfully the sheer *unsafety* of the child today. Half-defined terrors hide around every corner, scarring events like the Dunblane massacre leave us both terrified and helpless. But the fact that the greatest incidence of child abuse occurs in the home, or in a supposedly 'controlled' environment (sexual abuse in Children's Homes) ought to give us pause. Some damage to the corporate psyche seems to be taking place, some loss of the burden and gift of nurture, for this to be quite so prevalent. What if children need to be protected from contemporary adults, quite simply? Because contemporary adults have abandoned their role and trust? That is an absurdly extreme idea; but does it contain enough to worry us constructively?

At the end of the day, the problem goes deeper than we have been able to probe in this chapter. The reluctance to think about nurture and the learning of choice is fundamentally, I suggest, a reluctance to think about the role of *time* in the formation of identities. The style obsessions of our day help to

58

reinforce the idea that identities can be purchased and discarded; the fascination of some with virtual reality and cyberspace illustrates vividly the attractions of a post-humanist milieu in which the closed options, self-determinations and irreversible sequences of an older sense of human identity are challenged or regarded as transcended. I want to look at some of the attendance issues from other perspectives later on. But one of the points worth registering at this stage is that an incapacity to see people as *produced*, formed in their biology and psychology by the passage of time, implies a fixity in our perceptions of each other that is potentially very troubling. A world of timeless consuming egos, adopting and discarding styles of self-presentation and self-assertion, is a social as well as a philosophical shambles.

To recognise a cultural loss and a cultural crisis is (notoriously) not much of a step to solving it; but it is something. It gives a perspective from which to question public policies and debates – even though the underlying issues are not easily capable of being resolved by planning alone. At present in the United Kingdom, education is suffering a steady attrition of resources and imagination, and is at every level under pressure to give priority to narrowly functional concerns; it is treated politically as a consumer good to be marketed to parents or students. In the long run, this is bound to weaken any sense of corporate responsibility and public intelligence. It is not that responsibility isn't learned and exercised by individuals and families in continuing tradition, despite what goes on in the educational establishment; but how is the vision of the individual or family to be supported and enlarged? St Augustine's passing observation in *The City of God* [12] that the household learns its values from the city, is worth pondering, however odd it may sound to modern ears. And since our attitudes to education are only a part of the general trend towards the sovereignty of market metaphors, we have to continue to train ourselves and each other to challenge the supposed *obviousness* of such metaphors – indeed, to expose the fact that, applied to areas like education and healthcare, they are singularly bad metaphors. If we can free ourselves from at least this bit of slavery, we might be able more robustly to challenge the narrow models of choice that fuel the market metaphor.

This investigation raises some further questions about the kinds of bonds and conventions that actively pull against the sovereignty of market rhetoric, that construct the self as something other than an abstract consuming machine. It will not do to treat these problems about choice and childhood as simply arising from the faulty options of individuals: that would only be to *illustrate* the problem itself, by treating the morally interesting

[12] Augustine, *The City of God*, Book xix, chapter 16.

question as one about individuals exercising freedom in a vacuum. To say that things go wrong because free agents happen to select the wrong one of a set of possible courses of definite action is to assume that options and actions are not significantly constrained by the individual and collective past, or by the choices of others.

Take a familiar example, a relevant one in the context of this chapter. The protection of the imaginative space of childhood obviously needs a background of security, adult availability and adult consistency; a background of constantly shifting adult relationships, with the investment of energy involved in starting, sustaining and extricating oneself from relationships, doesn't, on the face of it, sound like a promising basis. The tempting conclusion is, as some enthusiastic 'communitarians' would argue, that divorce should be made more difficult in law, so as to guarantee greater stability in the family. Unfortunately (as anyone with any experience in counselling troubled couples will ruefully confirm) this is precisely what can *not* be guaranteed by multiplying legal obstacles. To make it legally harder to make a wrong choice is still to see the important factor as the individual's will: restrain that will by legal force, and all will be well, the choice will not be made. But this would be to ignore the manifold factors, interior and exterior, that can cause an option for divorce (like an option for abortion) to appear attractive. Somehow the matter has to be addressed at another level, in a wider context: what are the social supports for a marriage or other committed partnership? What level of practical assistance (from paternity leave to crèche facilities to professional advice in emergency) are readily available? And – elusive but important – what messages about fidelity, patience, the formation of persons in time, are being given out by the enveloping culture? In short, what do we, as a society, think and do about sustaining bonds of different sorts? This will not prevent a specific wrong choice, or resolve at a stroke the mess and suffering of the broken family; but without this sort of question, no real resolution is possible. We shall only compound the suffering.

Present trends in reacting to marital breakdown lay a fair bit of emphasis on the importance of *conciliation* services – that is, services which, while not necessarily aiming at the full restoration of a partnership, offer the possibility of working at and thinking through reasonable common aims for a couple separating – financial fairness, proper provision for children, and so on. This is in fact a good example of a process in which the sovereignty of individual will is appropriately challenged, so that a potentially endless spiral of competitive struggle is checked and negotiation becomes possible. In a conciliation process, everyone has to allow that their initial account of what they need or want is *revisable*; and this is at least a small part of the construction of a social environment that contains or manages conflict. But, as we have noted, it is just that kind of environment that seems to be under serious threat these days; and it is no use asking how we are to mend our losses in the area of the experience of childhood as sketched in this chapter without looking at other and wider losses, losses in respect of what I shall be calling 'charity' in our social world.

2

Charity

John Bossy's *Christianity in the West, 1400–1700* is a vivid, learned and delightful portrait of a period of major change in Church and society; and one of the many original ways that Bossy offers of measuring change is through the shift that took place in the meanings of certain words – and, indeed, to the whole way in which *meaning* itself was thought about. Following Michel Foucault, he observes that, at the earlier limit of the period he is studying, meanings are about resemblances and continuities: the universe is a vast system of cross-reference, and for something to be significant, to communicate a content, is for it to share in the 'field' of reference of something else. 'In [this] earlier universe things participated with each other, with the language which described them, and the persons who spoke of them.'[1] Thus, in the case of

[1] John Bossy, *Christianity in the West, 1400–1700* (Oxford, 1985), p. 169.

one of the words whose meaning lurches dramatically away from its earlier course, ' "Charity" in 1400 meant the state of Christian love or simple affection which one was in or out of regarding one's fellows; an occasion or body of people seeking to embrace that state; the love of God, in both directions.' By the latter end of Bossy's period, it had come to mean 'an optimistic judgement about the good intentions of others' (as in a 'charitable' interpretation of something), a benefaction for the needy (a person can now be 'dependent on charity'), or the institutional means of continuing such a benefaction (*a* charity, in the modern sense of what the Charity Commissioners concern themselves with).[2] The word has ceased to mean anything much like a *bond*, except in the weak sense in which two or more people may have 'charitable' attitudes towards each other; and the very bondedness, the continuity, between the mediaeval meanings has been practically destroyed.

Much of Bossy's book is in fact about charity in the older sense, the sense still preserved in the 'love and charity towards your neighbours' of the Book of Common Prayer. Charity is the manifestation of what Bossy calls 'the social miracle'[3] – the extraordinary processes by which sectional loyalties were from time

[2] On the history of organised charity, see Ian Williams, *The Alms Trade. Charities, Past, Present and Future* (London, 1989), esp. chapters 1 and 2.

[3] Bossy, *Christianity in the West*, chapter 4.

66

to time interrupted and overcome by a sense of integration, of belonging with an entire social body extending far beyond one's choice or one's affiliations of interest and 'natural' loyalty. In terms of institutions, the immense popularity of fraternities in the later Middle Ages witnesses to the desire to move beyond kinship loyalties and hierarchical structures towards a state of highly formalised friendship, a reciprocal and egalitarian community. 'In some cases', Bossy writes, 'the incorporation of persons of differing status was a formal object of the fraternal institution.'[4] This was cemented by common ceremonies which invariably included regular celebratory meals, but which also stressed that essential building-block of social civility, the formalising of mutually respectful and affectionate greeting. These voluntary bodies, whose primary purpose was simply social bonding outside the family structure, could and did play significant roles in controlling factional strife in (for example) Italian cities; in some areas, what we think of as the parochial system in the Church actually developed later than the fraternity system. The fraternity *was* the worshipping community, responsible for organising liturgical provision and pastoral care.[5] And in terms of *events*, 'charity' was honoured and secured by major public festivals – notably, by the end of the Middle Ages, the summer holiday of

---

[4] Ibid. p. 58.
[5] Ibid. pp. 62–3.

Corpus Christi; though there were other significant occasions on which the public renunciation or transcendence of violent rivalry was more or less obligatory. At Corpus Christi, however, the 'social miracle' was firmly and explicitly rooted in the entire history of God's dealings with the world, through the medium of the mystery plays in England and elsewhere, and in the public processions displaying the Sacrament of Christ's body. What is shown here is not only the meaning of social bondedness in relation to the act of God and the worshipping community, but – to return to the point made earlier about the very nature of meaning – the way in which that social meaning works, by a kind of 'nesting' of frames of reference within each other: the social body, the Church as Body of Christ, the sacramental presence of Christ's body in the Eucharist; a subtle crossing and recrossing of the boundaries between fields of discourse.[6]

What charity involves in this context is above all the opportunity for suspending relationships characterised by competition, rivalry. The civilities of the fraternity – greeting, meeting and eating, as Bossy nicely puts it[7] – direct energy away from competition towards the maintenance of friendly exchange; or, in

[6] Ibid. pp. 71–2; cf. the now classical study by Miri Rubin, *Corpus Christi. The Eucharist in Late Mediaeval Culture* (Cambridge, 1991).

[7] Bossy, *Christianity in the West*, p. 59.

other words, the way to 'succeed' in the context of the fraternity is to become proficient at receiving and at initiating acts that embody mutual recognition and thus mutual honour or respect. Honour itself is not here the heavily charged privilege of aristocracy that it so often is in pre-modern societies, but a kind of contracted dignity, an agreement to speak the same language and listen to the other as an equal. And in this as in other ways, Bossy's 'charity' is very like a *game*.

Games are unproductive. The point is not to make anything concrete out of the common activities agreed, but to perform the activities themselves. And while games may be competitive, the reward of competition is in the first place simply recognition as an exemplary performer (games can be won without prizes being awarded). There is certainly an element of this kind of competition in the behaviour of mediaeval fraternities or those involved in pre-modern festivals; but what needs to be emphasised is that this is not competition for limited goods, so that what one gains another loses. Since social activity outside the framework of 'charity' *is* regularly characterised by the sense of rivalry for limited goods, the festival or the fraternity comes to be a vastly important redefinition of what is involved in acquiring 'goods' at all. The material world appears as a world of scarcity – at least in the sense that no material acquisitions can be infinitely divided out. The game of 'charity' is based on the implied proposal that there are goods to be worked for that are completely different in kind from material goods, goods that exist *only in* the game, within the agreed structures of unproductive action.

We can easily overlook just how eccentric a proposal this may be. David Lodge's barbed novel of academic manners, *Changing Places*, depicts the dim English hero, Philip Swallow, trying to introduce his American hosts to a parlour game called 'Humiliation'. 'The essence of the matter', one of the Americans later reports,

> is that each person names a book which he hasn't read but assumes the others have read, and scores a point for every person who has read it. Get it? Well, Howard Ringbaum didn't. You know Howard, he has a pathological urge to succeed and a pathological fear of being thought uncultured, and this game set his two obsessions at war with each other.[8]

Manifestly a good game: the 'goods' to be won in the game are very precisely at odds with the kind of competition prevalent in the general environment. When the obnoxious Ringbaum finally gets the point, he practically ruins his academic prospects by admitting he has never read *Hamlet* (a problem for a professor of English). But this is a very extreme case, serving only to point up what is subversive about games in their 'pure' form. And the fact that organised sport has now become a major 'industry',

[8] David Lodge, *Changing Places* (London, 1975), p. 135.

70

with performers competing for colossal cash rewards (and the corruption that goes with that) is an oblique testimony to this subversive and potentially baffling element. Games, we seem to assume, are too important to leave to players, who might perform for pleasure. And the kind of politician eager to promote competitive games as a form of training for competitive economic activity, or what have you, has missed the point with impressive completeness; or perhaps has *got* the point, that games left to themselves dangerously mock and relativise other sorts of competition.

Charity is bound up with the spirit of carnival, in the sense that it challenges any assumption that we are, as human beings, committed first and foremost to victory in the battle for material goods. There is such a thing as a social good (a social miracle), accessible only by the suspension of rivalry and the equalising of honour or status. Nothing is to be won for possession – as in the simplest kind of game, where winning is immediately dissolved by starting the game all over again. Thus the 'ordinary' activity of achieving or acquiring status is shadowed by activities in which status is *assumed*, mutually granted, as a condition of play: not everything depends on competitive performance. Something is seen as prior. We could say that charity here also has to do with *conversation* – an activity that need not be productive, that presupposes mutual recognition, an activity in which 'success' is measured simply by the maintenance of the activity itself. Charity becomes visible where it is clear that certain bonds are treated as already established, not as always *to be* established; where it is assumed that the basic human position is not that of individuals uneasily making treaties with each other, but of exchanges of recognition, acknowledgements that within or alongside or against the world of calculated cooperation – and calculated non-cooperation – is a realm where the possibility and reality of exchange and common concern are agreed or given beforehand. At the most basic level, no one *decides* to start talking. In a crucially important sense, language is not an *invention*, a way of solving a problem. The very idea of a problem to be solved *assumes* language. This is why it is difficult to theorise about the origins of language and why philosophers have often come to grief trying. The myth that language is something revealed by the divine solves nothing, but it should be possible to see why it is attractive, when the alternative seems to chase its tail so frustratingly.

The forms and customs and relations that Bossy pulls together as manifestations of charity can be seen as celebrations of this sense of something prior to negotiation. But the paradox is in the entailment that these voluntary associations and designer rituals are supposed to recover or maintain contact with those aspects of the human situation that aren't chosen or designed. On the whole, the bonds or unities we do not choose are linked for us with kinship or nationality; but the trouble with *that* is that it turns so promptly into an inflated kind of individualism, with its own bloody and bitter competitiveness. But the bonds expressed or recognised in carnival and fraternity are significant because they are not grounded in *anything* contingent or local. In one sense, they are quite arbitrary, even absurd: pure play. But if you treat them as optional, as dependent on any one person's initiative or consent, the game is over. It becomes involved with what it is most supposed to be at odds with – anxieties about power. Why should I follow the rules *they* make? What are *they* trying to get *us* to do? You can't play in those circumstances.

This, incidentally, may throw some light on the difficulties we – typically – get into over the problem of 'exclusive' language, gender-specific terms for human activities seen as privileging male over female. There is a whole range of practices in language that might once have been construed as playful, occasions of charity – religion, metaphor, drama or fiction, and so on. It was claimed that they celebrated common or basic modes of recognition between human beings. But certain kinds of analysis strongly suggest – to put it mildly – that these ways of talking are in fact shaped by a non-playful interest, and encode policies and decisions that both express and reinforce the freedom and initiative of men over against women. We can't, it seems, play any longer. Self-consciousness is always fatal to play, and if we go on trying to play, ignoring the critical analysis, we are accepting as given what has now been redescribed (accurately or not) as the decision of one group against another. Charity has evaporated; or else we have recognised that it was never really there.

This is a problem we shall need to come back to later. What it highlights, though, is the difficulty of carrying on the game of charity if we suspect that it is *really* dependent on someone's or some group's choice. I said earlier that no one decides to start talking, no one decides to start playing, to initiate the non-productive, celebratory subversions that surround the supposedly serious world of material rivalry. We come to the rather bizarre position that these voluntary, arbitrary, groundless activities *cannot* be treated just as ordinary matters of choice: the assumed equality of status cannot simply be withdrawn or conceded by one agent's decision. To play at all is to deny that kind of 'freedom'. Somewhere in and around this awkward acknowledgement lies the shadow of the religious underpinning once accorded to charity, the interlocking of radical social respect with the honouring of God, the sense that the creation of a fraternity or the invention of a social ritual was not a human assertion or positing of meaning, but an attempt to feel towards and cope with a set of unchosen truths about the universe, and ultimately with the most comprehensive 'fact' of all, the *dependent* condition of the universe and everything in it. The apparent groundlessness of charity conceals a reference to the 'groundedness' of the universe – but in so doing, continues to put into critical or even comic perspective all other imaginable grounds for social cohesion, mutual recognition or allocation of status.

Bossy and Foucault hint at the directions taken as societies drift away from charity; but it is perhaps in the last quarter-century that North Atlantic society has most dramatically shown the effects of this abandonment. Remaining rituals of charity have been more and more eroded. I've mentioned already the translation of sport into industry, surrounded by sponsorship and massive economic investment. But the development of competitive sport (especially football, for some reason) as a vehicle for arbitrary violence between spectators or supporters makes the same point. In a context where what are supposed to be 'ordinary' forms of competition and status acquisition have become charged or problematic, what seems to happen is that play is loaded with the hopes and terrors of non-playful experience. When social and economic competition have become increasingly violent, some will be more systematically disadvantaged, some will become more and more incapable of letting go the compulsive, even exhilarating, struggle for position. Think of the alleged social profile of football hooligans: a certain percentage (probably not a majority) from the long-term unemployed, a further, probably larger, percentage from young or youngish wage earners, doing reasonably well for themselves. The working situation is skewed in two ways. Either there is no possibility of finding a way in to the world of serious economic acquisition and negotiation; or that world takes on an obsessive character – unsurprisingly, considering the bleakness of the alternative. The idea of a rhythm that controls competition by subversive egalitarian rituals becomes more and more inaccessible; sport becomes another tribal engagement. The surrounding environment freights economic activity with so much anxiety that the interruptions of the game seem threatening, not liberating; anxiety and violence are carried over into what is meant to be play.

But this is only to point to a vicious circle. The skewed character of work in our society is intensified all the time by the lack, the thinness or the impotence of the remaining social rituals that embody charity. In such a situation, these surviving practices that point to the social miracle bear too heavy a load, and buckle out of shape, becoming prolongations or displacements of, or compensations for the destructive-competitive activities of non-playful society. Things are not helped by the intensity of media attention: sport, from football to chess, is defined in the media as what – professional – others do. For the professional, there is a need, spoken or unspoken, not only to win within the terms of the game, but also to win in terms of the rewards that publicity can confer, the odd and fragile 'goods' that are supposed to go with celebrity. For the mass audience, this has largely ceased to be *their* ritual: it is something enacted for their entertainment, rather than an activity that might affect their own modes of behaving and of understanding themselves.

Mention of the media prompts a short digression on the rake's progress in perceptions of the British monarchy in recent decades. In a rather curious way, monarchy can act and sometimes has acted as a focus for 'charity', a ceremonial representation of social cohesion, allowing citizens to find at least a form of lateral equality as 'subjects'. This has always sat awkwardly with the facts of monarchical rule: arbitrary patronage (for example, 'the Court' as a locus of unaccountable political power) and attitudes of servility. The tension between monarch as icon and monarch as absolute executive master in, say, Tudor England or Tsarist Russia, is not very easily resolved. But the remnants of sacred eccentricity surrounding the monarch in Britain (touching for the king's evil, presenting Epiphany gifts of gold, frankincense and myrrh in the Chapel Royal or – until the rite was sanitised late in the eighteenth century – washing the feet of the poor on Maundy Thursday) preserved a trace of the idea of the monarch as representative person, whose functions had a good deal of the 'game' about them. The rot set in (from the point of view of charity or play) when monarchs started dressing habitually in military uniform, thus giving an obvious visual and imaginative priority to their role as personifying the state's supposedly legitimate violence. And as this role in turn was rapidly emptied of content, monarchy had to reinvent itself; the monarchies that survived into the twentieth century were generally those most flexible in performing this job. Part of the difficulty, though, lies in the fact that in a basically secular environment there is no easy way back to the model of the monarch as representing the sacred, the unquestionably 'given' in human affairs, the monarch as speaking for a society through the performance of symbolic acts or the receiving of sacral honours. Even the Middle Ages had not been uniformly enthusiastic about such a scheme of things: there were other and better ways of celebrating sacred bonds. It was the erosion of some of these other ways in the sixteenth century that concentrated unprecedented sacredness on monarchy (divine right was no part of the accepted wisdom of the Middle Ages). And – as with football – the concentration overloads and distorts.

What were monarchs to *do* in this colder climate? The answer, certainly in Britain since the high Victorian period, was to become an icon of ordinary secular and familial life: to be publicly what everyone is supposed to be privately. Hence the quite novel interest, from the Victorian era onwards, in the Royal *Family*. Hitherto, the royal kindred had

been a confused assortment of higher nobility, interesting (if at all) in the context of court and dynastic
intrigue; but now intrigue was to give way to the idea
of 'archetypal' family relationships. Royalty do not
so much have to do anything special as to undergo
publicly the common experiences of their subjects
(or mostly their bourgeois subjects). It is no use
blaming the mass media here for their obsessive
attention to the private lives of royalty (as rather a
lot of royal kindred have discovered in recent years).
The very *raison d'être* of royalty has come to be seen
as the living of ordinary lives in public: the claim to
privacy or the recognition of an inner life of stress,
unresolved emotion, betrayal or resentment has
great poignancy but is in painfully obvious tension
with the rationale of royal status in modern Britain.
It is true, though, that the methods and expectations
of a very sophisticated news media don't help. Tact
and collusion once helped to avoid public scandal
(think of the astonishing restraint of the British
press in the months before the abdication crisis of
1936); but this fitted with a culture of reserve and
general expectations of public decency. When the
culture changes, the media will want royalty to share
in the effects of an erosion of barriers between public
and personal; and we end up with the tragicomic
situation of an archetypal family publicly experiencing precisely what most families experience in an
increasingly exposed way – marital stress, anxiety
and depression, confusion about values and

purposes. It is a kind of nemesis of the post-Victorian royal myth.

Yet something far more archaic surfaced in 1997 with the death of Princess Diana. The images of her, the images, precisely, that had consolidated her 'iconic' status in the modern sense, often had about them an echo of sacrality – even to the sacredness of the royal touch. Her death produced an utterly unexpected outpouring of 'charity'-related activity, egalitarian rituals to purge unmanageable emotion (whose relation to the actual circumstances of the Princess's death was often pretty remote). The rest of the Royal Family was required to participate in these rituals; remarkably un-modern things were said about the need for the Queen to be present in London with her grieving people, symbolically summing up or giving voice to their sorrow, and so on. It will take a long time to get the measure of all this. It is largely true that the 'performance' of royalty – as has been so often remarked – had become a stylising of our common problems, a soap opera rather than a touchstone of common meanings. Its increasingly demystified, prosaic performance, did not stand at any useful distance from us – except at intensified ritual moments, coronations, jubilees, royal weddings. The public enactment of 'ordinary life' fails to jolt us into the recognition of bonds and identities that are funda-mental and critical, but not exactly ordinary. Yet for reasons that are far from clear, this death occasioned a sort of remystifying. The demand for the 'modern-isation' of the monarchy that was thought to arise from these events represents something of a misreading of the signs. The British public indeed showed itself unhappy with royal protocol – but not in the name of a modern and secular ideal (there was little that was remotely *republican* about the reaction); rather what was on view was a potent lament for a lost sacredness, a magical and highly personal, but equally a ritualised, focus for public loyalty. The 'lost icon' was not simply the dead princess; it was a whole mythology of social cohesion around anointed authority and mystery – ambiguous, not very articulate and not easy for either left or right in simple political terms.

II

Some of the locations of residual charity in the 1990s are surprising – not least because of that obviously residual character and because of their socially limited scope. Much of what is said and written about contemporary dance culture, for instance, makes it clear that this functions power-fully as an instrument of charity in the mediaeval sense. Journalists have been eloquent about the 'rave' as a model of un-anxious, unproductive, egali-tarian and co-operative behaviour, facilitated by certain soft drugs, particularly Ecstasy. In contrast to other kinds of celebration, we're told, especially those fuelled by alcohol, there is no endemic violence at a rave, and no atmosphere of sexual threat. This may be an implausibly utopian picture, but there is no denying its attractiveness and coherence; and by all accounts the claims about the basically non-violent character of this environment are well grounded. The recent Criminal Justice Act, by imposing panicky and heavy-handed restrictions on such activity, has produced a more active culture of political outrage than we have seen in Britain since the headier days of the poll tax protests – a testimony to the passionate *need* evidently felt for egalitarian, celebratory and non-violent assembly: for institutions of charity.

Unfortunately there are still questions to be asked. This is an environment in which there is a distinctive mixture of (yet again) tribalism (the corporate patriotism of youth) and a quest for anonymity, a cancelling of the particular, including the particularities of the acting self. We are looking at a phenomenon deeply and self-consciously anchored in the separate identity of – mostly – the under-25s, in the musical and social style of one sector of society, largely unattached in terms of family or working commitments. For all its vaunted egalitarianism, it is not easily accessible to those whose social location is different (and there is a faintly paradoxical flavour in the earnest assertion of a civic right to perpetrate large-scale noise pollution). It appeals to the rather un-rooted (not exactly the same as rootless) climate in which the young adult lives, especially in a society where only a minority of under-25s are likely to be in employment with any long-term prospects (if, indeed, they are lucky enough to be in employment at all). It isn't too difficult to see the force of the egalitarian transcendence of the rave culture, and the relative ease with which the ethos is absorbed. To become no one in particular: this is what is offered here, and offered to those who have not yet been able to shape much of an identity in other ways, in the traditional ways represented by early and lasting sexual bonding and early entry into what was once probably a lifetime's job. The structures for organising an old-fashioned identity are remoter, not very attractive, and can hardly fail to look more than ever alien and burdensome. Unemployment and general social fluidity have lifted what once looked like the self-evident pressures to 'settle down': why not extend the latency period, at least for weekends?

It has become quite common for the serious left-wing press to remark on the new politics of the under-25s, shaped by resistance to the Criminal Justice Act, and by a scattering of 'occasional' issues, notably (in Britain between 1994 and 1998) the export of veal calves and the construction of by-passes. There is a significant sense in which this is quite genuinely a politics of 'charity', in which the *style* or medium of action is at least as important as the issues involved, a style that is anti-hierarchical, aimed at short-term effect, passionate, participatory and sometimes anarchically witty. But perhaps we should think back for a moment to some of the issues discussed in the first chapter. Childhood is, amongst other things, a situation in which it is possible to learn how to choose by being protected from an enslaving bondage to choices playfully or experimentally made. Only gradually do loss and risk come into view as concomitants of choosing in the adult world. And the difficulty with a politics of charity is that it so readily ends up as a politics of extended childhood, in which there are no real negotiations to be made. It is as if the muddled erosion of ideas about childhood that I have tried to sketch has prompted this passionate effort to reclaim the space of play whose boundaries have been so consistently violated. But a refusal to learn the language of cost and ambiguity in fact lands you in a worryingly vulnerable position: others will be making decisions in another language, another mode, decisions in which you will have no share; you may be ignored, attacked, humoured, even indulged, but you will not be a participant.

This is certainly not to say that the prevailing forms of political engagement need no challenging; but it is no use, alas, simply saying that these forms are withering away. Issue-based and interest-based politics may often appear to fill the landscape for those involved, but can also mean ignoring the longer rhythms and further reaches of the situations in which issue and interest come to the fore. Thus the egalitarian innocence of dance culture takes for granted a colossal technological hinterland – the production, marketing and reproduction of music, the chemical sophistication required for the development of 'designer drugs', even the Byzantine politics of the fashion industry. How does all this *work*? What makes it possible? Whose labour, in what conditions, whose investment, whose profit? And if the answers to such questions are not completely palatable – as, in a diversified industrial economy, they probably won't be – what sort of changes are possible and how are they to be secured? Again, if we take the issue of the export of live animals in barbarous conditions, the moral dimension looks fairly clear – indeed, it is clear when stated simply in terms of disgustingly cruel practices; but the point at which labour, planning, cost and uncertainty come in is when you ask about the livelihood of a West Wales cattle farmer who is in no position to dictate or control the conditions of the industry he depends on. To say (and this would be a perfectly sensible response) that if a sufficient number of suppliers collaborated in pressing for change something might happen, is a step in the right direction. But it is a step towards the world of long-term strategy, complex economic balances and potentially frustrating nego-tiations. To refuse this move, though, is to ignore who it is who *concretely* bears the cost of significant decisions.

All this returns us to our central concern. A politics entirely based on 'charity' in the sense of egalitarian transcendence, non-competitive communion, and so on, fails to be a politics at all, because it depends on not recognising the truth that the non-charitable world habitually deals with – conflicts of interest and desire, the unavoidability of loss, the obstinacy of others. It is simply not the case that we are able instantly to recognise and welcome an identity of interest in every other we come across. We are not transparent to each other in that way. We 'learn' each other, we cope with each other, in the trials and errors, the contests and treaties of speech; which takes time, and doesn't quickly or necessarily yield communion.

But here is a clue to understanding some of our confusions about charity. Once again, there is a bit of a vicious circle in evidence: as the institutions and rituals of charity decay, as we lose a common language affirming us where we 'just are', without having to win a place, our political life fragments and corrupts. There are fewer controls on rivalry, fewer qualifications to the picture of social life as essentially or primarily conflictual. And this in turn means that the polarisation, between those who have and those who don't have the means to manage this conflict successfully, intensifies. More people are excluded from negotiating important decisions and are left with no stake in their social environment – and no language about where they unproblemati-

cally and non-negotiably belong, no system of charitable symbols. For the losers in the conflict, there is
a stark choice between an unrelieved, or practically
unrelieved, alienation, and the adoption of some
sort of charity-oriented project to take the place of
the missing political dimension. The latter is a
powerful challenge to a culture of passivity and
'victimage', and the contribution of community
politics to the felt welfare of the disadvantaged
is enormous. But it will inevitably stand not as
a moment in the wider political rhythm but as a
radical alternative to 'public' engagement; and this
has consequences whose ambivalence has to be
acknowledged.

Historically, the point of what Bossy calls charity
lies in its complementarity in respect of the negotiating and conflictual world around. Its rationale is
bound up with such a context. In one sense, of
course, charity celebrates a state that exists
supremely in its own right, a state of pure converse
on conversation, social joy. But precisely as such, it
exists beyond history and beyond what we can know,
think or say about civil society and political society.
It is 'mythical', though not in the sense of being
some kind of pure projection or aspiration. The
institution/ritual of charity tells us that to have a
language to negotiate or quarrel *in* is already to
presuppose the social miracle, the fact of linguistic
sharing. Charity uncovers the bedrock of speech:
sheer converse, the exchange of sounds in codified

patterns and the peculiar exhilaration that attaches just to that. It affirms what it is in language that is 'there' before and after argument and context – which is not self-expression (a meaningless idea outside the frame of converse) but the possibility of recognition.

III

I want to look briefly at the ways in which two very different contemporary writers have dealt with this. Ursula Le Guin, author of a number of brilliant 'alternative world' fantasies, delivered in 1986 at Bryn Mawr College a Commencement Address which has become something of a classic in some circles.[9] It deals with the tension and complementarity between what she calls the 'father tongue' and the 'mother tongue'. This is *not* a distinction between 'how men think' and 'how women think', though the address occasionally veers towards saying something a bit like this; it is meant as a distinction between modes of speech used by both men and women, although the historical and cultural situation of most women means that they are likely to be more at home than men are with the 'mother tongue'.

The 'father tongue', Le Guin suggests, is the discourse of power – not necessarily (though

[9] Ursula Le Guin, *Dancing at the Edge of the World. Thoughts on Words, Women, Places* (London, 1989), pp. 147–60.

frequently) authoritarian or oppressive, but a language designed to get things done, and, with a view to getting things done, to offer 'disinterested' analyses of situations. Thus it is inevitably a language that distances the speaker from what is spoken of; it is most itself when written rather than spoken; it does not expect an answer; 'It goes one way', and it depends on the energy that comes from *fission*, the 'forcing of a gap between Man and World'. It is the language you go to college to learn more fully. 'It isn't anybody's native tongue.'[10]

The 'mother tongue', on the other hand, is 'inaccurate, unclear, coarse, limited, banal ... repetitive ... earthbound, housebound'. It is *essentially* conversational, it always expects an answer. 'It goes two ways, many ways, an exchange, a network.'[11] Le Guin beautifully and memorably catalogues some of the idioms of this dialect:

> Good morning, hello, goodbye, have a nice day, thanks. God damn you to hell you lying cheat. Pass the soy sauce please. Oh shit. Is it grandma's own sweet pretty dear? What am I going to tell her? There there don't cry. Go to sleep now, go to sleep ... Don't go to sleep![12]

This is a language constantly ignored or belittled by speakers of the 'father tongue', regarded as

[10] Ibid. pp. 148–9.
[11] Ibid. p. 149.
[12] Ibid. p. 150.

'primitive'. But without it no one ever learns their real native tongue, the language of transformation, imagination, the conscious *art* (including house-keeping, cooking, making clothes, along with what we designate 'high' art) that makes style, pattern and beauty out of our biological existence. And without this elusive native tongue, we become incapable of telling the truth, 'telling what time of night it is'. This is very well said, and, as will be obvious, something close to this is at the heart of the argument of this chapter. I suspect, though, that there are some confusions about the distinction of dialects. I'm not convinced, for example, that the 'father tongue' is the sort of utterance that requires or expects no answer. In one sense it clearly does expect answers – responses, arguments, action. And we ought to think about the fact that most of the utterances Le Guin lists as instances of the 'mother tongue' require or expect *no* answer (what's the answer to 'Oh shit' or 'Go to sleep now'?). It's true that written, analytic language cannot be *answered* in the same way as moves in a conversation. But at least some of the discipline of the 'father tongue' is to say things in such a way that someone might be able to reorganise the material or the argument and take it in a different direction. It would be very odd to say of science, philosophy or even theology that they worked without correction, disagreement and exchange, given the actual history of such discourses.

But Le Guin's underlying point can still stand. There is (broadly) purposive talk, designed to change situations in particular ways, and which therefore opens up contests about the sorts of change looked for and who is to execute them; and there is the talk that is *designed* for nothing, that simply articulates a situation, identifies it, we could say, as a *human* situation, one that can be brought to speech. We could put it another way and say that such talk is not dominated by 'interest', by considerations of power and advantage. What matters is not victory but keeping the exchange going. This, I suppose, is the sense in which Le Guin can say that the mother tongue expects an answer: it is about maintenance, the unobtrusive and hard-to-formalise ways in which people attend to the background regularities of a shared world, and so it values bare continuation, participation in the exchange, in a way that can be baffling or infuriating for someone conditioned to the idea of verbal exchange as an exchange of information or of signals about who's in charge. Death, for example, is surrounded by clichés; many a priest engaged in a bereavement visit will have discovered the extraordinary importance of saying or allowing to be said a whole range of what might look 'objectively' like empty bromides. Some things require saying, and originality is not what's looked for.

This dimension of 'maintenance' is brought out very plainly in the second contemporary discussion I want to refer to. Charles Taylor, the Canadian political philosopher, has published an important essay on the debate in recent political thought between 'liberals' and 'communitarians' – the debate between those who (very broadly) begin with a basic conviction about societies as composed of individuals endowed with intrinsic rights and liberties that require both protection and room for fair and balanced negotiation, and those who see persons as constituted by social and communal belonging and as finding their value or dignity, perhaps even their sense of 'rights', through identification with the values of the community.[13] In his discussion, Taylor stands back a little from these questions to ask what it is that differentiates 'matters which are for me and for you, on the one hand, and those which are for us, on the other'.[14] At the simplest level, I may say, over the garden wall, 'Fine weather we're having': my neighbour and I have both been *aware* of the weather, but to begin a conversation about it is to make it something we attend to together. Such conversation is emphatically not just a putative exchange of banal or useless information: the 'information' that I and my neighbour are both enjoying the weather, not very important information anyway, could easily be

[13]   Charles   Taylor,   'Cross-Purposes: The   Liberal– Communitarian Debate', in Charles Taylor, *Philosophical Arguments* (Cambridge, Mass./London, 1995), pp. 181–203.

[14] Ibid. p. 189.

exchanged or acquired without a conversation at all. But, when we initiate a conversation, something distinctive happens:

> A conversation is not the coordination of actions of different individuals, but a common action in this strong, irreducible sense; it is *our* action. It is of a kind with – to take a more obvious example – the dance of a group or a couple, or the action of two men sawing a log. Opening a conversation is inaugurating a common action. This common action is sustained by little rituals we barely notice, such as the interjections of accord ('uh-huh') with which the nonspeaking partner punctuates the discourse of the speaker, and with rituals that surround and mediate the switch of the 'semantic turn' from one to the other [i.e. how we learn to recognize that another speaker has paused, that it's my turn].[15]

Conversation thus represents, Taylor argues, the break-through into a recognition of common goods, things we *can only* value or enjoy together. He distinguishes carefully between goods that can be, and perhaps need to be, provided collectively (welfare, law enforcement, fire protection and so on), and those that are essentially communal – that is, those cases in which the positive and participatory enjoyment of some other agent is intrinsic to my own awareness of well-being or satisfaction. And this is the foundation for a particular vision of politics, the classical 'republican' model in which citizens participate in ruling; in which government is

[15] Ibid. p. 189.

not always 'them' over against 'us'. 'The bond [of belonging in a society] resembles that of friendship, as Aristotle saw. The citizen is attached to the laws as the repository of his own and others' dignity.'[16]

This is to say, in effect, that the work of politics doesn't get done without a recognition that my good or dignity has no substance, no life, without someone else's good or dignity being involved. This is more than a contract of mutual respect, securing my position by guaranteeing somebody else's. It is an acknowledgement that someone else's welfare is actually *constitutive* of my own, in a way that extends beyond any simple relation between two individuals alone: the ideal position is one in which an indefinite number of agents perceive their welfare as including their relations to each other and their consent to and enjoyment of each other's flourishing. Which takes us back very clearly to the definitions of charity with which this chapter began: charity is about bonds that are not negotiated, not the result of balancing interests. And Taylor is claiming that conversation, friendship, attending a concert with other people or sharing a joke are in fact foundational for any political practice that is not to collapse into an endless bargaining between interests. Such bargaining, Taylor argues, is unlikely to generate 'common sentiment', shared loyalty, because the institutions of government are

[16] Ibid. p. 191; on 'republican' government, cf. pp. 200–1.

inevitably seen in such a context as arbitrators, always to be persuaded, cajoled, manipulated or even blackmailed by one interest group or another.[17] Hence the burgeoning of single-issue politics and the decline in the percentage of the US population who actually vote; not a phenomenon peculiar to the other side of the Atlantic, of course.

I've already argued that, in practice, a politics conceived of purely in terms of 'charity' is not really political: it will always tend to ignore (as I think Taylor is sometimes tempted to) the facts of radical inequality and unavoidable contests. A British writer would probably have a lot more to say about the complex relations of *class* with power, and about the struggles to secure access to certain basic goods for the disadvantaged, issues not necessarily helped by the assumption of a classical 'republican' model as a starting point; and a Marxist might observe that Taylor's society sounds impressively untroubled by problems over the control of labour and production or the management of markets. However, I believe Taylor's most significant insight stands, and is entirely congruent with what I suggested earlier. Exchanges of a game-like character, with the 'little rituals we barely notice' that go with them, are the foundation for a politics that looks beyond pure contest and the management of competing interests – that offers a

[17] Ibid., for example, p. 201 on the triumph of 'procedural' models of justice, based on 'judicial retrieval'.

kind of ground for assuming the worthwhileness of the political enterprise itself.

Some of Taylor's critics have seen in the appeal to 'common sentiment' a danger of collusion with racism, or at the very least with static and exclusive forms of nationalism.[18] Taylor is, in fact, careful to identify some of the questions that arise in connection with a strong corporate political commitment to a specific language and cultural identity (Quebec is the example he discusses at length). But it should be possible to spell out why nationalism, let alone racism, is actually at odds with his basic premise. The 'common sentiment' he invokes, like Bossy's 'social miracle', is precisely *not* the celebration of an ethnic identity. Ethnic or national or 'racial' identity is always already something publicly 'there'; which is why there is a difference between carnival or Corpus Christi and a *national* event. The latter will have some things in common with the 'charitable' festival – a suspension of 'normal' rivalries and productive activities – but the unity it invokes is in no sense miraculous. It is a celebration of certain alleged facts about language,

---

[18] An essay by Andy Lamey, 'The Contradiction in Charles Taylor's "Politics of Recognition"', *Times Literary Supplement* 5025 (23 July 1999), pp. 12–15, comments sharply on the somewhat ahistorical features of Taylor's view of distinct cultures and his reluctance to theorise about the complexities of their actual changes and interactions.

history, and (in an often disturbingly loose sense) relations of kinship, facts that are supposed to be there for examination – and are also vulnerable to being revalued in the processes of examination. Supposedly clear ethnic identities are again and again exposed as political creations, usually constructed to support a broader reading of history in the interest of a particular group. This may be a dominant group: Victorian and Edwardian imperialism liked the idea of an 'Anglo-Saxon' identity somehow shaping the destiny of the United Kingdom; myths of 'Nordic' and 'Aryan' distinctiveness had a far more malign and destructive import in the German Reich. Or the story may be told on behalf of a disadvantaged group: national identities, with 'unique' national varieties of genius, were described and defended by the subject communities of the Ottoman and Habsburg empires in nineteenth-century Europe; Wales and Ireland discovered new unities and identities in resistance to English cultural tyranny during the same period. The appeal to a common ethnic identity tries to persuade us to look to some given state of affairs – a common memory, a common speech, a common 'blood' – that will ground shared feelings and overcome tensions. But this given state of affairs, historically speaking, is normally a skilled and selective arrangement of elements that gains its solidity and definition by being deployed against other such arrangements by other groups. 'Common sentiment' is limited in advance by the limits of the common heritage being deployed, one that is ours-and-not-theirs.

I am not trying to dismiss the reality of cultural traditions in their local distinctiveness, nor denying the liberating potential of discovering a shared history or language that has been suppressed or silenced. But we need some strong suspicions in play to avoid turning such a shared experience into a matter of timeless identity or divine vocation or manifest historical destiny. When national identity is invoked in any of these ways, a decisive step is taken *away* from the social miracle. The miracle, the common sentiment, the sense of necessarily social goods bound up with an indefinite number of others, all these surface when we are *not* focussing on the question, 'What do we happen to have in common?' – looking for the answer in some identifiable state of affairs. That can easily become a question about what conditions have to be met before we can legitimately recognise each other as partners. The social miracle, charity, draws attention to recognitions or possibilities of recognition *prior* to any agreement about what we have in common, in history or race, attitude or ideology. Social joy rejoices in the surprise of recognition, not in the establishing of a spuriously objective ground for fellowship outside the present 'miracle' of converse.

To be more precise. If we are licensed to speak to each other, to recognise one another, because of common history or some form of natural kinship, we are saying that there is something beyond the social exchange, some greater, prior, independent reality whose interest and integrity will abide whether or not I actually make human contact now. The social exchange *illustrates* such a common ground, perhaps in some way reinforces it; but it doesn't *constitute* anything in itself. I recognise an other as like me in relation to some third term – the natural feature we have in common, race, class, even opinions. They are 'out there', for both of us. But Taylorian 'common sentiment' as revealed in conversation is different. I discover in the conversations of charity that what we have in common is, in one sense, simply the conversation itself; or rather, that my interest is bound up, not with the 'out there' we may both be referring to, not with the common defence of what we share, but with the continuance of the conversational relationship. And just as the conversation did not need conditions of recognition laid down in advance before it could start, so its continuation does not need assurances of sameness, recognisability, in respect of some external factor. I recognise the other as like me simply in respect of being a speaker and listener in this shared act of conversing; to break off (or to demand credentials) is to refuse the whole process, to opt out of the game, to declare that you are no longer going to recognise; and of course conversations have such moments, when you realise, with whatever degree of shock, that what you thought was happening isn't – when someone manifestly is not listening or under-standing, when you perceive your words being distorted, when you are in one way or another deprived of your conversational standing.

Obviously we are talking about a spectrum of different types of encounter. There *are* conversations stimulated or enabled by a recognition of something 'out there' to which both relate; but we recognise them as non-miraculous, reasonably predictable. There are relations that develop out of shared activity, doing the same thing alongside each other, even though the being alongside isn't intrinsic to the doing; and there are relations that develop in shared activity that is necessarily collaborative, where the along-sideness is part of what is done. Taylor's example of going to a concert in company is nicely balanced between these categories, I suspect; and there are some occasions of shared activity of the first kind that, because of circumstances, acquire a quality more like the second and third kind. Conversations between mothers in a perinatal unit are 'about' a contingent experience that happens to be shared by the participants; but it often seems to be also a kind of mutual enhancement of that experience *through* the conversation. Personal interest is *felt* as furthered by or through the other, the common experience itself only taking shape in one mind by the sharing of speech; and this might make us reflect on the ways in which the very idea of 'common experience' already presupposes something about language. There are experiences like *performing* in a concert together, a clear example of activity where the 'doing together' is wholly essential to what's done, even though the shape of the doing is externally dictated. And there are, finally, the relations of friendship, erotic partnership or committed life in community, where the conversing relation is itself the heart of the action: what is being done *is* the formation of social joy.

And Taylor's point (and mine) is that a social practice excessively dominated by one or another kind of preoccupation with the 'out there' element in relations lands us in societies trapped by relations of contest or bargaining, relations in which mutual involvement (my interest *involves* yours and yours mine) slips out of view; and these are societies which *as* societies will command diminishing trust and fidelity. The social order appears as a 'something', a mysterious and alien reality that does not succeed in convincing us that it is there *for* us, or that our interests are bound up with its. It is as if the *standard* form of relation between human agents is a temporary agreement by independent partners to do something together, something which could be done by others and done without substantially changing the identity and position of the contracting parties; while in the background is a supposedly neutral system of administration and arbitration that concerns itself with issues wider than an individual or group of individuals can cope with. Because of its role as an arbitrator or tribunal, every particular individual or interest group is likely to regard it as foreign, as needing always to be persuaded about any specific project or local concern.

IV

This picture will not be unfamiliar to those living in modern Western democracies, especially in Britain and North America. The philosophy of government on both sides of the Atlantic in the 1980s was based on a minimalist picture of the State as a mechanism for getting the sort of things done (war, economic policy) that could not be done by 'lesser' associations, and a strong commitment to 'family values' understood as the expression of kinship bonds and serving as a covert or overt metaphor for patriotic solidarity; nothing much in between was recognised as having any substance. Some commentators in Britain thought it ironic that governments who claimed to be 'rolling back the frontiers of the State' should prove in practice to be responsible for any number of extraordinary interventions in the local and the particular – educational and industrial policy and practice, environmental issues (or rather, often enough, the sidelining of local environmental concerns), even broadcasting decisions. But there is no real contradiction: the State is there precisely as an arbitrator, detached from local concerns; no legitimacy is allowed to local problem-solving, no imagination is invested in the management of conflict at this level, since everything between the State and the kinship group is at best contingent and insignificant and at worst an enemy of individual liberty (that is, the liberty to negotiate strictly on one's own behalf in the social market). Combine this – especially in the USA – with a culture often deeply preoccupied with *rights*, and the fragmentation is even more acute. My position or my interest group's position needs protecting and reinforcing from the tribunals of public order: practical politics thus rapidly becomes a matter of how these tribunals are to be persuaded to acknowledge and enforce claims. It is certainly true that this sort of concern arises from the acute vulnerability of some groups, minority and otherwise disadvantaged groups, in a diverse and increasingly mistrustful environment. But the effect of a policy of arguing claims in this way is ultimately to aggravate both the suspicions that originally prompted the search for protection and the sense that the social order in its public and comprehensive form of legality is essentially something alien.

In our present cultural climate, all this poses an enormous problem. The concentration on rights as the primary focus of political action is a response to the long and appalling history of inequity, the denial to certain groups of a voice of their own, a freedom of self-determination or self-definition. To stand against the pursuit of such freedom is to collude with oppression. The difficulty is that the pursuit of enforceable claims requires me or us, the claimants, to present ourselves as victims, and to quarry our history for suffering in a way that can isolate us further from each other, can even produce the unhappy effect of a kind of competitiveness in suffering ('Our history is more tragic than yours . . .'). The macro-political effects of this can be seen in the competing narratives of different groups in the Balkans or central Africa or the Middle East; the micro-political in the bitter and complex tensions of minority and disadvantaged groups in urban North America (what agenda can be agreed between Afro-Americans, women, Hispanics, gay men, gay women, Asians . . . ?). So much here works against the social miracle; yet there is no simple path to charity by ignoring the imbalance and injustice in our societies that generates such a pattern.

The challenge is to do with imagination: with imagining relations other than those of master and slave, advantaged and disadvantaged, and imagining a definition of my or our interest and identity that would require the presence and welfare of others with whom I was not forced constantly to struggle for precedence. The liberal project of emancipation and entitlement for those who have been deprived of voice and power, the liberal State's guarantee of positions and freedoms – all this is a matter of means rather than ends. As an end in itself, the liberal State is vacuous: at best it offers a rather inadequate

longstop in disputes about human ends conducted by
a variety of specific interest groups. Yet in securing
some possibilities for relations not skewed by
concerns about power and advantage, it is an indispensable moment. What then, though? If we could
imagine a political system that was more than
liberal, it would have to be one that actively
supported or promoted forms of social encounter
that were not wholly competitive. I suspect that the
liberal-versus-communitarian polarisation is not
actually very much help here. If the choice were
(and *whose* choice exactly would we be talking
about, anyway?) between a rights-based order in
which particular claims by groups or individuals
could be 'fairly' assessed, and a society whose
values were established by an unspoken (and
unaccountable) community consensus, the options
would be unpromising: a 'cold' fragmentation
preserved in a rather fragile state of truce or a 'warm'
community identity that absolved itself from the
difficulties of managing *real* difference and *real*
inequality. But there might be more to say if the
model we are looking to is what, following Taylor,
I've been calling 'conversational'.

Here, then, are two areas for speculation in
respect of the conversational possibilities of a
more-than-liberal society: first, how does the state
system view the arts? I am not here thinking
primarily of state subsidies for high-profile
activities that might justify such subsidies by

attracting tourist income; nor even of subsidy for experimental and innovative work. These are probably the extremes in contemporary discussion of public funding for the arts – a discussion that, on the one side, assumes the need for simple economic justification for any money spent on creative activities, and, on the other, assumes something like a moral duty on the part of the keepers of public funds to act as (indiscriminate) patrons. What I have in mind is rather the role of public funding in the support of local and collaborative projects in the arts – travelling companies, local youth orchestras, civic museums, 'residency' arrangements for writers in a particular locality, with the understanding that regular readings and discussions are part of the contract – and so on. The subsidising of such activities is a recognition of the arts as activities importantly disconnected from profit-making and importantly linked to the health and vitality of a town or region. Public subsidy entails some expectations of excellence; and this generates skills and sets standards for more informal local ventures. All in all, the message sent is that activities promoting conversation, activities strongly bound up with the notion of collective and collaborative goods, are of significance for the wider polity. They enshrine the charity without which the social world reduces simply to a relentless struggle for advantage; they create situations in which the unlimited advantage of success of one individual or even one sub-group actually undermines the whole activity in question.

Richard Hoggart's recent essay on *The Way We Live Now*[19] has a trenchant section on arts funding, with some solid practical proposals. As he says, 'The arts are to be kept up if we believe they contain works of the creative imagination of which any mature culture should be proud; and, secondarily, if we believe existing audiences could be greatly widened once we gave proper thought to how to set about it.'[20] Hoggart's focus is, rightly enough, the defence of the arts as enlarging the possible ways in which human beings see and speak of themselves, against the profit-obsessions of the new right and the ultimately patronising relativism of a certain sort of fashionable radical. Yes; but we should also, I want to suggest, think of how some of the very *processes* of art as well as its content enlarge the imagination of social belonging by insisting upon patterns of relation drastically different from those that prevail in a context where goods are competed for. And this may in turn suggest, as Hoggart himself intimates, that the ideal situation is one of partnership between public subsidy and voluntary support. If the main or sole source is public money, there are always the dangers, the twin, oppositional dangers, of passivity and complacency and of self-promotion at the expense of others. Some

[19] Richard Hoggart, *The Way We Live Now* (London, 1995).
[20] Ibid. p. 233.

kind of quite strictly matched funding secures the essential connection of the social miracles of art to the public interest of a whole state, while also building into local artistic enterprise the no less collaborative disciplines of self-financing. From both sides, some of the risks of omnipotent commercial sponsorship, chillingly detailed by Hoggart, are kept at bay.[21]

Second, and reverting unashamedly to the concerns of my first chapter, what messages are given by the educational system about the possibilities of charity? If my arguments here have been right, a good educational institution would be one in which conversation flourished – that is, one where activities were fostered that drew students away from competition as the norm. A good deal of nonsense is talked about competition as the sole guarantor of excellence; anyone who has ever been involved in the intensive work of, say, drama in a school will know something of how excellence is guaranteed by the sense of mutual accountability that characterises such work, rather than by any appeal to instincts of rivalry. To acknowledge someone's distinctive skill and require them to use it in collaboration with a larger project is an important challenge (as well as affirmation) for the individual; and the entire process is part of learning patterns of behaviour that properly pull against assumptions current in other

[21] Ibid. chapter 10 on sponsorship and its effects.

areas of the institution. Some aspects of the educational process are inevitably competitive because *selective* – the examination system being the most obvious case. But there is a dangerous barbarism in encouraging the notion that these aspects are somehow the essence of education. To have pressures pulling vigorously in different directions is a mark of both health and realism in education – at any rate, if 'realism' is defined as having something to do with the variegated realities of social life, as opposed to the realities of the job market alone.

But there's the rub: 'realism' *has* been conscripted into the service of a particular ideology – the notion that education is primarily about refining the skills necessary for an individual to succeed, and, more particularly, to succeed in an environment in which every outcome will be bitterly contested by rivals. For some complicated theological reason, this is now referred to as a 'vocational' emphasis. And, as noted in the first chapter, competitiveness *within* the institution is matched and confirmed by competitiveness *between* institutions. In order to secure a favourable placing in the league tables – in order to become 'competitive' in attracting parental and community investment – a school or college must impress on students their duty to perform 'competitively' and not to waste time. The danger is, or ought to be, clear: the danger of eroding other kinds of learning that occur through particular sorts of *process*.

A brief autobiographical note: I remember with gratitude the experience of a school play in which I took part as a teenager and which gave me, though I couldn't have said so at the time, of course, an abiding benchmark for imagining 'charity'. In a fairly academically intense environment – the Welsh municipal secondary school just before comprehensivisation – it was a salutary surprise to discover the skills – technical, electronic and mechanical – of boys from less academically successful forms in the school; or even the non-correlation between dramatic gifts and the ability to shine in A-Level English classes. Like all such enterprises in schools, it necessarily brought a shift in relations with staff involved in the production: there were the beginnings of the possibility of relating as adult to adult. And so on; a fairly common experience, but, for others as well as myself, I'm sure, a defining moment in seeing the power of something other than bargaining for advantage or running for individual victory.

What kind of priority can any of this have if educational policy is increasingly driven by 'vocational' concerns, in the strange contemporary sense of that word? The more-than-liberal society should be recognisable by a corporately and politically owned commitment to an educational pattern that has room for collaborative creation. And – to pick up a point mentioned earlier in this chapter – it is important to remember that sport, sometimes cried up as a refiner of the competitive spirit, can also and equally be a trainer of the sense of common sentiment and mutual need: paradoxically, the team that plays well in competition is one that has learned to work non-competitively within itself. But perhaps most importantly of all, this whole issue bears painfully on the question of 'moral education', an area heavily populated by muddle and cant at present. Every so often, a public figure complains that children are not being taught the difference between right and wrong; and some other public figure, probably from a certain sector of the educational establishment, will patiently explain that children are being morally educated because they are being given the chance to articulate and discuss how they actually make their decisions. More cannot be expected, apparently, since we lack a clear public moral consensus ('we live in a multi-cultural environment').

Unfortunately, however, this defensive response begs the question. There is in fact a robust cross-cultural consensus on many matters (does anyone expect a British Muslim to argue that there is nothing wrong with rape?); and there is a very clear moral orthodoxy agreed on in the teaching profession (how many educational relativists would accept that the rightness or wrongness of racism was a matter of cultural specificity?). But the most important point is what both critic and apologist fail to see: that moral education is neither the imparting of rules in a vacuum nor the discussion of how young people (think they) decide issues, but is bound up with the roles and responsibilities actually and actively learned in the corporate life of an institution. To borrow a phrase from Amitai Etzioni, moral education involves the attempt 'to *increase the awareness and analysis of the school as a set of experiences*'.[22] It is no use at all to pontificate about the need for 'values' to be communicated if the entire style and pace of an institution allow no room for understanding the experiences of learning in their diversity, or if the institution moves more and more towards a monochrome version of what learning is ('training'); if the institution sees its task as the – increasingly anxious and hurried – job of passing on quantifiable information and measurable skills at the expense of reflection on the character of its common life as educative.

There are plenty more areas in which we could think about the possibilities of charity – institutions, from the public library to the Citizens' Advice Bureau to the credit union or food cooperative, which in various ways represent the more-than-liberal vision and which require some quite complex partnerships between public and private support. But in all of them, the level of *public* investment is an

---

[22] Amitai Etzioni, *The Spirit of Community. Rights, Responsibilities and the Communitarian Agenda* (London, 1995), p. 104.

index of how far a society as a whole understands charity, how much room it leaves for people to meet and relate as something other than strangers or rivals. Legislation about rights is a worthy attempt to secure social presence for those whose voices have been stifled, but what it cannot achieve is the *felt* recognition of a common humanity granted and welcomed, which is the fruit of events of charity and disciplines of conversation. Equally, of course, it is no use simply appealing to the responsibilities that are supposed to accompany rights; this is where communitarianism of the more naive kind succeeds only in turning upside down the rights-based paradigm, failing to go beyond the question of what we can expect from or claim from each other. No claim, whether we put rights or responsibilities in the driving seat, will make sense without the prior underpinning of recognition. And recognition entails a move beyond the idea that my good, my interest, has a substantial integrity *by itself*: no project is *just* mine, wholly unique to me. I have learned from others how to think and speak my desires; I need to be heard – but that means that I must speak into, not across, the flow of another's thought and speech. And, in all this, in the thinking of what it is for me to think at all, I may gradually understand the sense in which the robust, primitive, individual self, seeking its fortune in a hostile world and fighting off its competitors, is a naive fiction. What lies beyond that understanding is a commitment to the charitable conversation that has in fact always and already included me.

Putting it slightly differently: to recognise the presence and the possibility of the social miracle involves a demythologising, even a dissolution of my picture of what a self looks like – the picture that I am encouraged to think obvious and natural by countless pressures, cultural, political, religious. At the end of the first chapter, I touched on the question of how we might come to the point of seeing our accounts of 'natural' needs and desires as revisable, capable of being *thought*, a point that becomes more and more elusive the more all areas of experience, from childhood on, are colonised by the sovereignty of images to do with marketing and purchasing. In this chapter, I have tried to show how the same question can be raised from a rather different perspective, how it is prompted by the obscuring of the 'social miracle' and the withering or marginalising of conversational models of social existence.

We return to the central problem: how is my 'self' brought into question? It seems that where charity is eroded, so is the freedom to question the self, to challenge the mythology of the atomistic system of desires confronting other such systems. Chickens and eggs, of course: we could not simply say that a decay of critical perspectives on the self *caused* the decay of 'charitable' space in social transactions, nor that the barbarising and trivialising of social experience in the acquisitive-competitive mode *caused* the corruption of our awareness of our selves. But the loss of a questioning appropriation of selfhood and the loss of so many of the institutions of charity go together; one is not going to be restored without the other. With this in mind, the second half of this book turns to look more directly at what has been damaged or abandoned in the way we imagine selves – and in particular the self's relation to its past.

3

Remorse

An internationally celebrated interviewer is engaged in a televised encounter with a recently and comprehensively disgraced politician. Perhaps, the interviewer suggests, the word that the public is waiting to hear is 'sorry'. The politician's response is inarticulate, his face registering a mixture of anger, hurt and bewilderment – as if some finer sensibility had been outraged, as if some crassly insulting remark had been made. Public power – even in disgrace – means never having to say you're sorry.

I have in mind one particular and memorable incident; but the scene and the script have become more and more familiar of late in the North Atlantic world. People are made to pay (after a fashion) for their delinquencies by an active, sophisticated and not very scrupulous news industry; they are occasionally induced to say that they regret 'errors of judgement', or the distress caused to those who trusted them. Sometimes it is possible to shift blame:

there is a flourishing market in political memoirs which attempt to deflect reproach on to cabinet colleagues, false friends or open enemies. But meanwhile, destructive and hugely costly lurches in public policy (such as the poll tax in Britain in the 1980s), or cumulative drift, waste and confusion (penal policy in Britain for a couple of decades), or a growing culture of secrecy and non-accountability in some areas of international relations (arms trading, the Iran–Contra scandal of the Reagan administration) continue to characterise the corporate ethos of political life. Whether justly or not, this sense of *unaccountable* behaviour is popularly linked with individual scandals – sexual irregularity, murky financial arrangements ('cash for questions' in the House of Commons). The corporate political culture of the USA is so riddled with corruption in the shape of immense subventions from lobbying commercial interests that it is increasingly hard to recognise any moral authority at all in what is transacted in Washington. In Britain, the defeat of the Conservative administration in the spring of 1997 reflected (among other things) a new level of furious impatience with political secrecy and evasion, sharpened by several scandals or suspected scandals in the mid-1990s, not least the handling of the Scott Report on arms dealing. People want to know, more intensely than they might have done a couple of decades ago, to whom legislators now answer.

The cynical response is that they appear to be answerable first and foremost to the imaginary public created by professional image-managers, the iconographers of the media culture. Failure is failure to sustain a visible style, a particular kind of presence; reversals of policy (over the poll tax; or, on the left, the dramatic flight from commitment to an antinuclear stance on the part of party leaders, and the continuing muddle over educational priorities and principles, or the proper role of welfare) have to do with complex assessments of gains and losses in these elusive currencies of style or presence. And a public figure involved in sexual or financial scandal survives just as long as the damage to a collective political image can be contained; sometimes this proves to be a remarkably long period. The recent confusion over President Clinton's sexual delinquencies illustrates a number of complex features in this general picture. His enemies have been perceived, accurately enough, as interested in maximal public humiliation for him rather than any kind of reparation or repentance. Public reaction has been largely dominated by a healthy measure of distaste for this strategy. The President's own public response has been to apologise, as it appears, for the hurt done to his relations with the American people, and a good deal of comment has similarly treated the whole affair in terms of injured relations and consequent trauma as between President and people. Evasion and sentimentality predominate, beautifully instanced in the significant use of the word 'inappropriate' to describe Clinton's lechery. For all the rhetoric of error and appeals for forgiveness, it still seems that the losses that matter are losses to an image with fairly clearly calculable benefits, losses in a market of starkly depersonalised and external goods. To say that one of our major cultural bereavements is *remorse* is to raise the question of whether we are still capable of seeing failure or betrayal as inner and personal wounds, injuries to a person's substance.

I suppose it is not unrelated to what some commentators lament as the loss of a sense of 'honour'. In its most robust form, in pre-modern societies, honour is a category far more solid and deep-rooted than 'reputation' in our own world, with which it might be easily confused. Honour is part of a tight mesh of perceptions and evaluations of what you do, which teaches you what you may think of yourself and expect of yourself, as well as what you may expect of others and they of you. Loss of honour may result from accepting without protest a failure on someone else's part to give you what is owed to you, or from a failure on your own part to conform to what might rightly be expected of you. And such a loss means dropping out of an entire system of exchange, of mutual perception or recognition: nobody knows how to talk to you any longer. There have been, and perhaps there still are, societies where you can die of dishonour, because there is no convention left by which you can go on being intelligibly connected with other people. You cannot reconstruct for yourself what their formalised perceptions and evaluations provided for you. Quite literally, you cannot respect yourself.

Honour has so often been bound up with arbitrary matters – kinship, race, wealth – and has had so many and so obvious paralysing and corrupting effects in societies that it has acquired an unmistakably bad name; we are generally disposed to ignore it as a moral issue. St Teresa of Avila famously castigated the honour-obsessions of sixteenth-century Spanish society, declaring more than once that the sense of honour was the one thing that had to be eradicated thoroughly in the sisters of her communities. She did so, however, on the basis of a detailed model of expectations and evaluations within the Christian community – a counter-system, with sanctions at least as powerful, not so much emptying out the notion of honour as radicalising and broadening it: our honour depends not on contingent social factors, but on our status as the 'kin' of the Son of God.[1]

It is not so easy to ignore the question if we take seriously some of the matters raised in the last chapter. Honour formalises systems of *recognition*, grounds upon which conversation can proceed. More than this, it assumes that the capacity of others to recognise me, to talk to me, is indispensable to how I perceive and experience my self. To lose some

---

[1] On this theme in St Teresa, see R. Williams, *Teresa of Avila* (London, 1991).

dimension of how I am seen and regularly responded to is to lose part of the substance of myself (and all this will be discussed at greater length in the concluding chapter). It is tempting in our environment to misunderstand this dependence on how I am seen as a sign of individual weakness, as if it were always the mark of an unhealthy lack of proper self-regard. But for cultures in which honour is significant, self-regard is learned precisely and only as a way of being-in-society, not as the individual's assertion of an abstract or pre-social identity. This is why in such cultures *shame* is both a personal and a social penalty: it is not just a particularly acute form of embarrassment, which I may brazen out or which I hope will be forgotten, but a real restriction on what I am able to think and feel about myself, as much as on what others think of me, make of me, say to me and understand about me.

A society without even residual traces of honour and shame would be a very odd one. It would have to work on the assumption that what finally secured my identity was, at the end of the day, the exercise of my will, the resources of an individual energy. The constant in my experience would be that I am always able to *choose* to construct a worthwhile picture of my existence; and in this sense I should be invulnerable to that enormous investment of my identity in connectedness with others that is typical of a society oriented towards honour. You might then expect, in a culture without a lively concept of honour, all kinds of difficulty about appealing as a moral sanction to the dangers of diminishing the solidity of the self by ignoring the perceptions of others, since the self's solidity would always be secured by the will's freedom to affirm itself. You might expect a situation in which shame was no longer any kind of regulating factor in what was thought or said about behaviour. There might be a variety of pragmatic replacements for it – the dread of embarrassment, of appearing out of step, the fear of losing public plausibility – but these would have to do with possible disadvantages, weakenings of a negotiating position in the sphere of public transactions, not with possible moral injury to the self. You would expect an immense investment of energy in strengthening the image of the willing or choosing subject, whether by a therapeutic rhetoric of 'feeling strong' in the face of adverse circumstances, or by a market environment encouraging ideas of free-floating consumer liberty and offering a range of *styles* as an aid to a creative will. You would, in short, expect an environment rather like ours in the contemporary North Atlantic world.

A confidential tape is released on which a politician can be heard arranging to cover his tracks after conniving at a criminal action designed to blacken his opponent's name. Another politician ardently denies on a Monday his involvement in a sexual or financial scandal, calculating very exactly the level of evidence likely to be available and the level of support for which he can rely on his colleagues; on Wednesday, after a new item of evidence emerges, or after his colleagues have made their own calculations about PR damage, he resigns, subsequently admitting mistakes but complaining bitterly of the malice of the news media and the disloyalty or lukewarmness of colleagues.[2] A prominent executive in a large company resigns when charges of substantial embezzlement are pending; questioned, she explains that her therapist is helping her to feel strong at this time of tension, and to acknowledge how her misdemeanours were in fact a sign of her passive acceptance of the role of a victim or dependant in the organisation. Again, large sections of the quality press are devoted to a painstaking analysis of the subtle distinctions between subcultures in the world of popular music, distinctions involving favoured brands of clothing, drinking habits, dialect. In some quarters, a fascination develops with the phenomenon of the 'cult' book or film, the formation of a small subculture. In the background of all this, though seldom articulated with any clarity, is the promise that the self can be reinvented: in practice, as often as not, this means that identities can be, if not openly purchased in every case, at least selected and constructed from the material that society leaves lying around. Those who

[2] The pattern became depressingly familiar in the last days of the administration of John Major in Britain in the mid-1990s.

have neither the image of a community to shape or make intelligible their choices, nor the purchasing and negotiating power to reconstruct themselves (styles do not come cheap) are left in an alarming state of emptiness in regard to their identity: they are more or less doomed to have identities thrust upon them, identities that simply leave them as objects of mingled fear and derision for those who can operate their choices successfully. Think of the odd process by which the young single mother has acquired the status both of a social threat and of an instance of failure in negotiating power and self-determination; or of the scarifying contempt of the young recreational drug user for the addict. When identities are constrained by this powerlessness in the market, there is not a lot left for the self-asserting will but violence, to others and to oneself in the high-risk atmosphere of hard drugs, petty crime, joy-riding, or whatever.

A culture which tolerates the loss of a sense of damage to the moral identity, the loss of shame or remorse, is bound to be one that dangerously overplays the role of the will in the construction of human persons. Because we live, in fact, in a world where choice is never the imposition of will in a vacuum – as the first chapter of this book attempted to show in a rather different context – a doctrine of the will's power and resourcefulness in constructing and maintaining identities is a doctrine that cannot but distort and obscure a whole range of facts about people's grossly unequal access to the various commodities on offer for building identities, from fashion accessories to professional counselling or analysis. And this means that illusory pictures of our identity are quite directly linked to the springs of violence among those who are dispossessed. It is no use trying to address the self-directed and other-directed violence of much urban poverty without mounting a sustained assault on the most readily available myths about the self in our culture overall. To challenge those myths is itself a necessarily political move, not just a metaphysical observation or an appeal for intellectual conversion.

We *could* say that the problem lay in the lack of an 'inner life'. But that is rather misleading, given the way we so often understand such an expression (again, this will be further discussed in the final chapter). Someone may be powerfully aware of inner images, desires, hopes, may enjoy (or endure) a complex fantasy experience, may even be intrigued, perhaps obsessed, by the analysis of motivation (they may retain a therapist and have a strong concern with 'spirituality'). Such a person could no doubt claim to have a quite well-developed 'inner life'. But all of this would be compatible with a central absence of any vital experience of being involved in or answerable to the perceptions of others; it could easily be a strategy for invulnerability. Interiority can become something appealed to as the locus of an unchallengeable authenticity ('How can I be wrong when I'm so sincere?'). Take away the props, the conditions that allow these styles of supposed self-awareness to flourish and that encourage the picture of a given individual selfhood exploring its constituent elements, and what remains to hold in position a place from which to speak, to become recognisable? An inner life conceived in terms of what I see when I engage in certain kinds of more or less structured introspection is in fact a wholly shadowy affair if it fails to take on board the self's existence in others, the other's investment in my reality. Paradoxically, the inner life as an object for individual scrutiny becomes another externalised production, deeply vulnerable to the contingencies of the material world, the degrees to which the will has access to the mechanisms of comfort and attainment. We need to think through the ways in which the regard, expectation and valuation accorded by another subject deliver a reality that could be more seriously described as 'interior' precisely because it is *not* open in all respects to the simple introspective gaze and not vulnerable to my individual circumstances. It is interior to me not because it is hidden from the other and visible to me, but because it is hidden from *me*.

This needs a lot of further discussion, and the next chapter will attempt some clarification. But the reason for approaching issues about selves and souls by way of reflecting on remorse, honour and shame is that these areas of our human experience and discourse are unintelligible except on the assumption that my past, my publicly identifiable history, the story that can be told of me, does not *belong* exclusively to me. I can set out to reorder it, to rewrite it in various ways, but I don't in fact control it. My actions have had effects and meanings I never foresaw or intended; even the meanings I *did* intend have now become involved with the speech and the story of other lives. I cannot separate out my biography as a thing in itself. But that in turn means that I cannot *absolve* myself; just as I cannot love myself truthfully without another person's love, because I cannot without deceit and corruption love a self abstracted from the vision, involvement and investment of others. If I were able to absolve myself, I should be saying that my acts and their meanings could be – as it were – reclaimed, drawn back out of their life in the lives of others and ordered by my will; and that would be a large and bold claim to a certain kind of power over those others in whom my past is still alive.

The psychopathic killer apparently unmoved by any other agent's perception of his acts is the most obvious example of this enormous energy of self-reclamation; but there are analogies nearer home for all of us. When political regimes change, in Germany in 1945, Romania in 1989, South Africa in 1991–2, it becomes quite hard to find anyone who ever supported or acted for the old order; public figures and administrators reinvent themselves, reclaiming their lives from the lives of their victims in a final and consummate assertion of their power. But the same can be seen in a domestic context. The parent or spouse who has abused other members of a family will, with apparently profound conviction, deny what has been done, or shift the blame on to their victim, thus confirming still further the destructive effects of their actions, the erosion of another person's sense of worth. Therapeutic self-discovery brings to light injuries from formative years; and to begin to be liberated from their effects, it will be necessary to challenge the person responsible to accept the effects – intended or not – of their actions or habits in the past. Refusal of this ('I don't know what you're talking about. You had a happy childhood') risks damaging the processes of healing very deeply, unless the new perception of the self is strongly reinforced by counsellors and friends. We are – painfully – learning more of this as we learn more about the phenomena of child abuse. Yet therapeutically-guided introspection itself is not always innocent. In a society increasingly dominated by the rhetoric of therapeutic self-discovery, like so much of North American culture, it is possible for therapy to become in turn a tool of denial, a way of neutralising the perspectives of others or retreating into an enclosed frame of reference in which the story of victimisation acts as a total explanation and justification for all the contours of a biography. The agonising and insoluble riddles over the authenticity of some memories of abuse, the questions raised about therapeutic techniques that predetermine what is 'recovered', make this whole area one of the darkest and most complex on the contemporary scene. And, more broadly, there can be a trivialisation of the language of hurt and victimage that serves simply to protect me from the perceptions of anyone who might be my own victim. I am allowed to think as if my presence in the life of someone else is a matter for which I now have no active responsibility; my involvement with others in the past becomes first and foremost something done *to* me, a relation in which I do not have a primarily active role. How are we to find our way to a therapy that recognises *mutual* presence, effect, investment, in a situation where therapy is so often prostituted in the service of creating or restoring a sense of solitary peace with oneself?

II

The denials and refusals of remorse represent a passionate protest against the inexorable conclusion that my past is not under my control. For all that we tend to think of the future as the unknown and uncontrollable, the fact is that the past is just as bad, or worse. George Steiner's story, 'Return No More'[3] outlines a particularly harrowing

---

[3] George Steiner, *The Deeps of the Sea and Other Fiction* (London, 1996), pp. 149–96.

encounter, at several levels, with the terror of an uncontrollable past, owned by too many contesting minds. Werner Falk is a German, returning to the village in Normandy where he was billeted as a soldier at the time of the Allied landings. He was responsible for the execution of a son of the family with whom he was lodged, but he has come back to court and marry the younger daughter. He attempts in two ways to soften the shock of his return: by describing the nightmare he endured himself in his home town of Hamburg during its fire-bombing, when he was made to shoot a woman in terminal and intolerable pain from phosphorus burns – a woman who was in fact, he believes, his sister; and by appealing to the fact that only in the nondescript quiet of the Norman village did he ever escape the shrill violence and unremitting tension with which he grew up in the Germany of the Reich. He is trying as best he can to accept his responsibility, agreeing that the 'grave' he emerged from in the peace of the Norman farm was all too promptly filled by the farmer's executed son, and that there is no reparation possible. Yet he is also looking for a language to share: he too has been hurt, literally crippled, by the continuing machinery of violence and reprisal, and now longs for some way of turning the whole history towards the light. Arguing passionately with the woman he wants to marry, he insists that renewal and reconciliation are not the simple, the trivial options.

' . . . On the contrary. It's much simpler to stiffen in silence or hate. Hate keeps warm. That's child's play. It would have been much simpler for me to die in Hamburg near the canal . . . Do you think it's easy to come back here? In Germany we don't talk about the past. We all have amnesia or perhaps someone put an iron collar around our necks so that we can't look back. That's one way of doing it. Then there's the other, the unrelenting way. Steep yourself in the remembered horrors. Build them around you like a high safe wall. Is that any less easy or dishonest?'

She lashed out 'God knows I wish the past didn't exist! I didn't ask for these memories, did I? You forced them down our throats . . . And now you come and tell us we should forget and live for the future. You're spitting on graves.'[4]

He protests: he is not asking anyone to forget, but pleading for remembrance of *all* the war's victims. ' "If you think of all the dead, of yours and of ours, it will become more bearable." '[5] Movement has to begin again; something purposive must be done.

The marriage is agreed. On the evening after the ceremony, Falk is kicked to death by youths from the local farms, including Blaise, the youngest of the family he has become so bound to. Has he simply come back too soon, as the old farmer mutters at the end of the story? Yes, but the force of this powerfully unsentimental fiction lies deeper. There will be *no* proper time for return, because Falk's narrative of redemption, resurrection, is not his alone to tell: one

[4] Ibid. p. 176.
[5] Ibid.

man's empty grave is filled by someone else, and that death in turn sets off its own consequential stories. No one, it seems, is free to develop their own personal story of healing, because a thousand small filaments unite them to those they have touched, even those they have touched indirectly. Is Falk making an illicit, an impossible claim? In one sense, yes; but he is doing so with a full, articulate awareness of the need both to acknowledge the dead and to find a common language, grounded in shared injuries to the soul's substance that are beyond reparation or explanation. If there could be a path to redemption, surely this is it.

But there is no alchemy that can be relied upon; whatever is *said*, the past remains, violently, itself, a foreign country indeed. Steiner leaves us with insoluble tensions. There is no hope without remorse – the return to the victim, the acknowledgement of what is beyond mending or recompense, the proffering of one's own pain and unfreedom not as a weapon but as a gateway into talking together (into charity?); the alternatives are as Falk depicts them, hatred or amnesia. But acknowledgement and the will to charity can guarantee nothing. Remorse is not automatically a lever to change things, least of all the past.

What Steiner points us to is the uncomfortable *powerlessness* of remorse. To acknowledge the past, the past in which I am enmeshed with countless others and which I cannot alter by my will, is entirely and unavoidably a risk, an exposure of vulnerability. When it meets hostility, refusal to understand or inability to understand, it has no sure solutions; the new conflict that may be generated will increase the sense of helpless involvement in the lives and agendas of others. Remorse, in other words, doesn't bring history to a standstill. What it offers is something quite other, and not by any means so attractive: the possibility of *thinking* history, living consciously in time. Refusing remorse is refusing to think what it is to be a subject changing according to processes and interactions outside my will: to take refuge in the mythology of the invulnerable core of free selfhood, always equipped to construct a desired identity, is effectively to say that the roots of my identity are not in time. As hinted earlier, this mythology can work in more than one way. The idea of an actively free self selecting what it is to be, is complemented by the self-as-victim, a 'true' identity overlaid by things that happen to it, but capable of being excavated and reconstructed, free of the accidental deposits of a personal history.

Remorse involves thinking and imagining my identity through the ways in which I have become part of the self-representation of others, groups or individuals; and so learning to see my (or our) present style of self-representation as open to question. It is in some degree to make *internal* to myself what I have been in the eyes of another. At the corporate level, this is, of course, a highly charged matter. If the former colonial power makes reparations to the indigenous peoples of its old territories, it will look like a confession of weakness or uncertainty about its role and standing. It will be an admission that its own account of its past is vulnerable to revision in response to what others perceive and say. It will impinge on the lives of a large community, whose sense of their worth and identity may be bound in with a particular version of their nation's past, a version in which the perception of that country by others has never played any part. The anger and dislocation this can generate has been much discussed in Britain in the last couple of decades, as the imperial account of Britain's history has been increasingly discredited and displaced in the educational system. But the process is in many ways made harder by the rhetoric that surrounds the whole question of reparation: understandably, more is demanded than bald acknowledgement; but, in emphasising the claim of the victim and the right to press for something like a restoration of the *status quo ante*, it risks its own denials of history and involvement, risks refusing a future that is actually *different* precisely because of the complex of injurious but undeniable relations that are now part of a colonised people's past. Once again, we have to do with the question of identities in *time* and the seductions of anything that looks like offering an escape from them. And a related point has to be made about the mindset of the former imperial or colonial power: no language about this is helpful or truthful that simply expects from the present-day community an acknowledgement of past crimes in terms of simple present guilt. Such ways of talking end by cheapening the currency of the language of remorse and responsibility.

But this does not alter what is most fundamentally required, which is the relinquishing of an identity placed beyond challenge or judgement, and the moving into a sense of identity that admits not simple guilt but the manifold ways in which we are real in the language and narrative of others rather than in a privately scripted and controlled story. This admission is unavoidably and painfully a loss of power; but what I have been suggesting here is that to try and conserve power in such a context is to lose moral substance and to refuse the work of historical thought. Putting it slightly differently, you could say that remorse has to do with finding the self in the other; refusing remorse amounts to defining 'real' selfhood out of both time and conversation. And such a refusal stops me understanding that what I now am has been *made*: that is, it is not fixed or obvious, not the result of a neutral, natural process, but is the deposit of choices, accidents and risks. If I am not capable of understanding this, I shall see myself as a bundle of 'natural' phenomena – instincts, desires, affinities – not open to critique, not capable of being thought through or articulated in recognisable speech. In political terms, this is the seedbed of fascism and violent xenophobia.

The 'timeless' self is, of course, much the same as the consuming self we looked at in the first chapter – the self making choices without loss and without inner consequences. Change occurs for such a self not through the slow and difficult processes of learning new ways of seeing and speaking my history, new modes of productive labour in our speech and imagination, directed towards that history which is necessarily not the possession of one subject; change is conceived either as a simple assertion of will or a capitulation to the will of another – as if change were never anything but violence. But this is also what makes for such a morally thin atmosphere in the discourse of rights touched on in the second chapter. It is worth pausing further on this tough and contentious issue. As noted earlier, to challenge the language of rights is to risk colluding with ignorance and oppression: our talking about rights has taken shape as a way of affirming what it is about human beings that cannot be negotiated away or extinguished by the claims of sectional interest. The problem arises with the possible implication that what is non-negotiable or 'essential' in human existence is primarily a set of abstract entitlements; which in turn suggests that actual historical conditions are secondary to the imperatives of meeting a cluster of timeless conditions. It is then possible to assess and condemn any specific complex of historical relations according to their failure to embody the entitlements laid down in some kind of primordial charter for human life. What comes *first*, it seems, is a self to which certain things are due.

But this sounds dangerously mythological if we are learning at all to think of selves as being formed in particular histories, particular kinds of interrelations. And if there are no primitive individuals possessed of entitlements that can in some way be enforced in the tribunals of public life, this does not mean that we are stuck without any ground or impetus for questioning what happens to prevail in any given social or political order, that we have no reason for challenging patriarchy, racism or whatever. The point is how we construe the 'essential', the aspects of human history deemed not to be vulnerable to the disasters of political history. Talking about human beings in the context of conversational relation takes it for granted that human subjects are *difficult*, complex, that understanding calls for time; if forms of relation prevail in which this difficulty is denied and other subjects are constantly being drawn into one party's agenda and definitions, there is – manifestly – no conversation in any significant sense. In consequence, no *thinking* is going on: the processes of power are still working at a pre-reflective level and neither party in the relation is engaged in specifically human activity. In plainer English, oppression is a situation where people don't talk to each other; where people don't find each other difficult. One party's language reaches out to incorporate the other's experience, which cannot speak for itself. The white supremacist who sincerely claims to understand what the black population 'really' wants; the male (psychiatrist? theologian? novelist?) who meditates uninterrupted on the essence of femininity; the fashionably radical historian passing judgement on the ethics and ideology of an earlier culture; the 'Orientalist' discussing Asian history, or the secularist discussing the Middle Ages – all these represent not an infringement of 'rights' but a failure to begin thinking, a failure to find things difficult in the characteristic way human language implies that they are difficult.

This is relevant to the concerns of this chapter because different pictures of what is 'basic' to human subjects produce different models of what is possible and appropriate in relation to the complex question of guilt and injury. If we begin from the individual with claims, an injury will be seen as an infringement of these entitlements, the abiding loss of something like moral property. To rectify the situation, someone (not necessarily the original offender) has to recognise this loss and determine what might make it good. What is in view is *reparation* – which could involve the literal restoration of property (as with aboriginal land claims in Australia or Canada, a matter of much bitter public contention), with, in its train, very often,

139

counter-claims about infringements of existing *de facto* title. When slaves are emancipated, slave-owners demand compensation; twenty-odd years of feminism, and men begin to complain of their disempowerment. What this model does *not* deliver is a sense of historical violence or dispossession as a breakdown in the possibilities of speech and thought, a failure of human self-representation in talk and in common life (in charity): something that decisively injures and changes the offender as well as the offended. The loss in question is not moral property but moral *presence* as enacted in a true conversational relation. But if we are starting from this point, what 'makes good' loss or injury will not be simply the enforcement of a claim and the resto-ration of property, but the creation of some possibility of speaking together, or thinking one's own reality through the medium of another's history, seeing oneself in the other.

The language of right and claim, when it becomes the dominant form of moral discourse in a society, may well be a factor in muting the possibility of remorse in the fullest sense. In such a context, recog-nising responsibility for the condition of a victim is to recognise liability, a potential rival claim to goods that are currently mine. I am threatened with loss; and there is inevitably a strong incentive to resist admitting to anything that would expose me to the adverse award of a tribunal. The victim is a *competitor*. But, in the perspective of convictions about interrelation and language as fundamental, remorse is the recognition of a loss already experienced by myself and the other; and the victim is a *partner* in the labour of restoring thinking and converse. What is 'due' to the victim is the freedom to share in the definition of who and what they are, to participate in the exchange of conversational presence. This is an always unfinished task, because (as was suggested earlier) each fresh moment carries its own possibilities of misstatement and misrecognition of self and other. But in risking such misapprehension (and the risk, as in Steiner's story, may be a great deal more than theoretical or verbal) the language of remorse at least avoids the stand-off that the language of rights seems to be condemned to; it does not wait for the restoration of a situation in which all entitlements are satisfied before engaging in social converse, challenge and even cooperation. *Civic* life, public argument and contest and negotiation about what might be practical and desirable goods for everyone in the manageable short term, requires the impatient and risky engagement of partners in what may be still a very imperfectly equal field. Odd as it may sound, there is a way of talking about rights that stifles this vital civic process and debate by its appeal to a kind of abstract, suprahistorical tribunal to settle the matter of reparations before any positive social future can be thought about. What tribunal could equalise the score of deaths in Northern Ireland, let alone Rwanda? What could count here as a satisfactory settling of offences or payment of debts?

There is, of course, a very fine line between this invocation of the need for civic vitality rather than abstract settlement of claims and a potentially corrupt appeal to social cohesion as an imperative that overrides the protests of a minority voice. But it may be quite important simply to recognise that there *is* such a line. The distinction between a society of vocal and sometimes quarrelsome citizens and a society of claimants arguing rival bids before a tribunal is a perfectly real one. What is essential in preventing the corruption I have spoken of is a certain scepticism about appeals to 'social cohesion', a recognition that social unity is not ever something unproblematically given or achieved. What I've called civic vitality actually assumes that such cohesion is always in formation: its shape is not yet given and could not be present in any sense without the release, the becoming-audible, of all potential civic voices. What we have to try and separate in our minds is, on the one hand, the emergence of a civic voice engaged in public debate about shared goods and the emergence of a *plaintiff's* voice, requiring satisfaction. In a society more and more preoccupied with this latter model, where being a victim is almost the essence of being a moral presence, one of the hardest tasks we face is the transition from acknowledging inequity and injury to active common labour and language.

And one of the things that makes this particularly hard is the implicit demand for victims to lose their innocence. As claimant or plaintiff, the oppressed, silenced self is simply a sign of another's guilt; the morally interesting business lies in dealing with *that*. But as an acknowledged 'civic' voice, as participant in the defining of goods, the self emerges into risk. As an agent involved with others, it lives with the possibilities of new misapprehensions and exclusions; in the terms of this book's first chapter, it becomes involved in adult choices. To settle for being primarily or essentially a victim is to say that my identity is not something for which or in which I *labour*, to treat identity as buried and static. 'Labour' entails the risks of staking my selfhood in ways vulnerable to change and to critique.

In short, the relation between oppressor/aggressor and victim, in a context where remorse is not properly available, leaves *both* in a strikingly similar position. There is a competition for moral security, for the ability to bear your own scrutiny with confidence. Aggressors can maintain security because they do not allow any other perspectives into the images that define the self except those that are securely controlled: the idea that some portion of moral substance is invested in the uncontrolled histories and discourses of others is something to be ignored or resisted. And the victim is secure as a self that has not yet been required to act, a self whose status has been determined by the acts of others; at best it is asking for the possibility of action and self-determination, at worst it is bound to the role of passive innocent, perhaps intensifying it by the refusal of anything less than total reparation – which is always inaccessible, since our history cannot simply be either unravelled or halted. Two kinds of timeless identity; two selves attempting to stand outside language and difficulty.

III

It is not too hard to put flesh on these abstractions; we have only to look at the aftermath of pretty well any major reversal or upheaval in power relations in recent history. The white South African is emerging from a culture that is – intriguingly – shaped *both* by the denials of the oppressor and the pleas of the victim. Until recently, the dominant culture of the white population was pervaded by the refusal to admit that its moral substance was in any way affected or injured by the massive structural inequity prevailing in the country. It was not unknown for defenders of the system to claim that the old Republic of South Africa approximated closely to a truly 'Athenian' democracy, a civic enterprise of egalitarian converse; though such defenders did not always note the fact that might confirm the parallel most closely and uncomfortably, the fact that both depended upon a slave economy. Within the white population, Afrikaners in particular (though not exclusively) refused to think their identity *through* thinking their relations with the non-white population – refused, therefore, to think what it was to be *African*, to be where they in fact were. The life of the township or he 'homeland' might be deplorably deprived, and the conscientious white person might give time and resources to lessening such deprivation; but it remained quite strictly immaterial to the self-perception of the dominant culture (deprivation being put down, perhaps, to the sad congenital incompetence of the 'African', or to unfortunate but in principle transitory economic contingencies). At the same time, this self-perception on the part of Afrikanerdom was significantly shaped by its own history of victimage – the 'desert wanderings' of the Great Trek, fighting off hostile tribal attacks, the struggle with the British Empire, the period of suffering and brutal discrimination at the hands of the British (concentration camps, the attempts to curtail the Afrikaans language). The internal and external battle against apartheid in the last few decades has been in significant part a battle against this deep-rooted and deeply felt myth of innocence; it has been far more than a straightforward struggle for shared political power or equitable land ownership. It has been a demand for the relinquishing of a particular kind of moral self-image – and has undoubtedly been experienced by Afrikaners precisely in these terms.

The world being the way it is, moves towards power-sharing in South Africa were prompted by pragmatic considerations as much as anything. The maintenance of white privilege by 'freezing' the great majority of the total population within the constraints of a low-wage, labour-intensive economy becomes harder and harder in a competitive, market-oriented international situation. However reluctantly, the dominant population has to begin to see its economic interest as bound up with factors in the international market beyond its control and definition. The early days of Nationalist government in South Africa were marked by a curious kind of idealism: the country might be doomed to economic stagnation, but it would be fulfilling its God-given task, wholly misunderstood by the world around, of pastoral and patriarchal care for an inferior race. This ascetic vision was effectively dead by the end of the fifties; but the implications of operating in a modern international economy took time to sink in. By the mid-eighties, the tensions were widely acknowledged within South Africa to be unsustainable. And the limited but persistent nuisance of international sanctions played some part in this process as well. But it cannot then be surprising when political change turns out to be less than straightforward; self-perceptions don't necessarily alter when economic and political constraints do. The new dispositions of power will be in many respects costly to the formerly dominant group, and this will, for some, reinforce the myth of victimage, even where this does not take the overtly patho-logical forms of militarised Afrikaner nationalism. Not all the tact and imagination of a Mandela can avoid this.

And this means that all kinds of troubling questions about the past are left unresolved. If a significant proportion of the white population remains privately wedded to the self-perceptions that reinforced apartheid, even when the structures have begun to shift, what real political conversation, what 'charity', can emerge between former masters and former slaves? How far can the native African trust the former masters, now that their behaviour is – perforce – different? Is the past really named and dealt with? Because if it isn't, the prospects for common 'civility' are poor; as noted earlier, such refusals to confront the past deny the passage of time and the reality of vulnerability. This can result in a further turn of the screw in the self-perception of the oppressed: I sense that I am seen (or half-seen) in much the same terms as before; only now this has become structurally less visible, it is also harder to call to account. Frustration threatens. And there is also the tension in the post-revolutionary situation arising from the dual need somehow to bring the guilty to judgement and to build the civic institu-tions that will cement mutual trust and help to dissolve the easy and fixed roles of oppressor and victim. It is a tension much in evidence in the workings of the Commission for Truth and Reconciliation presided over by Bishop Tutu. The establishing of the Commission was a genuine attempt to deal with the problem of naming the past without falling into the trap of insisting on legal reparation or retribution – an attempt at a massive exercise in national therapy, bringing recent history into a more honest focus. Its difficulties are painfully obvious. The Afrikaner and European communities have shown only a very limited willingness to review the stories they tell of themselves, and such confessions as have been forthcoming have often been felt to be less than completely serious precisely because they cost little in terms of public shame, let alone punishment. The good intentions of the Commission have appeared at times as having the effect of cheapening the very language of truth and reconciliation. What is more, a further shadow appeared in the 1997 hearings, over Winnie Mandela's activities. Memories of township violence are in any case easily invoked by many in the white population to show how all-pervasive evil was in the eighties (we, the white population, are not the only villains): if we are disputing the moral high ground, what about the casual and senseless butcheries of township gangs? Was Mrs Mandela indeed responsible for a reign of terror, and how far does collusion with such terror extend? The past, in other words, might be troubling to an ANC loyalist as well as to a supporter of the Nationalist Party, because it questions the innocence of the oppressed; just as the new situation, in which the ANC activist now has the responsibility for meeting or failing to meet the demands of the African population at large, is fraught with the risk of guilt and fresh division.

Thinking about South Africa in such terms does not, emphatically, mean that its situation is worse or more hopeless than elsewhere. Quite the contrary; it is just because South Africa has managed so radical a transformation with so little public violence in the immediate process, and because its new administration has shown itself capable of such moral seriousness (as reflected in the Commission's work), and because it has been characterised by extraordinary levels of public generosity and patience from former victims of oppression that it focusses so clearly the problems that remain. Even in a situation where the practical risks of serious and large-scale violence seem to have been contained, and where there is willingness to move beyond recrimination and the demand for reparation, the fears and tensions over the possibility of remorse are still immensely powerful; it remains a threat to any safe possession of a moral self-image. And my argument so far in this chapter suggests that the international culture of which the new South Africa is becoming a part will do little to resolve such anxieties. South Africa should remind us that the corporate selves of dominant and oppressed groups in a society do not simply lose their histories by the fact of structural change; they thus remain vulnerable, tense and mistrustful constructions to the extent that these histories are not thought and imagined afresh.

More painfully, we might look at the moral tangles around the state of Israel and its relations with its neighbours and minority populations. In the background, there is what is still the major moral and political trauma and outrage of the twentieth century, the attempted extermination of a community identified not only as dispensable from the point of view of a dominant group, but as positively *requiring* to be exterminated, dispensed with, for the 'health' of the wider society. How are we to think or speak about a situation that goes so far beyond the relatively simple matters of oppression or master–slave relationships? It is not possible to consider Jewish responses to the Shoah as just a very extreme version of the 'plaintiff's voice'. Again and again, the literature moves towards one or another kind of silence; beyond protest or even claim. And this in turn leaves other communities – the ones that failed to see or intervene or identify at the time of the genocide – with nothing to say. Perhaps this is actually beyond remorse in the ordinary sense: the injury to the 'moral substance' is just too deep for retrieval.

That is what we might hear in some of the passionate rhetoric of the Israeli Right: if no remorse is possible or effective, if nothing can be said that changes or moves on from the memory of outrage, the relation of Israel (understood as the moral heir of the European Jewish history of this century, and all that led up to it) to what is not Israel is unlike other political relations. Israel always remains the martyr community, facing the possibility of diabolical assault and destruction; what Israel does will always be a defence and a protest against this unchanging fact. Hence the situation in which Israel is seen by some of its vocal citizens as never involved in *merely* political negotiation, never being a political community among others in a region. We are invited into a frame of reference beyond politics, almost beyond history. The Holocaust silences some kinds of discourse, some kinds of poetics or theology – a well-worn theme in European and North American philosophy and cultural theory in the last few decades; but it also, paradoxically, establishes an incomparably radical new beginning for the settler communities in Israel, the remnant. Here is a territory of promise restored, a surface on which new meanings may be inscribed, free from any guilt or complexity attaching to the centuries of exile. For such a community, the issues around remorse, the finding of the self in the other and the painful forging of a shared world that comes out of this, are not readily accessible or intelligible.

The non-Jew can only observe from an embarrassed distance, carrying the weight of post-Holocaust silence. But the observations can be voiced, if only because so many Jewish thinkers have voiced related anxieties about what can become a solipsistic and apocalyptic vision of a world beyond politics, time and guilt. There are those, like the late Gillian Rose, who press the question back to the sources of such an apocalyptic vision: will it do, finally, to treat the Shoah as beyond *thinking*? In a brief essay on 'The Future of Auschwitz',[6] Rose challenges the two most obvious reactions that might be evoked at the site of the death camp – an identification 'in infinite pain with the victims' on the one hand, and, on the other, a tormented questioning as to whether *I* could have done this. Instead, she proposes, the question that needs to be evoked is, 'How easily could I have allowed this to be carried out?'[7] This question, according to Rose, focusses the central tragedy of the modern consciousness. Beyond the simple oppositions of innocence and guilt, victim and torturer, lies the overwhelming fact of modern politics, the militarisation and mystification of the state as an impersonal mechanism. This represents a schism between my moral awareness, my scrutiny of myself as (more or less) self-determining, self-forming, agent, and my political location as a subject involved in processes

[6] Gillian Rose, *Judaism and Modernity. Philosophical Essays* (Oxford, 1993), pp. 33–6.
[7] Ibid. pp. 35–6.

beyond my control, processes for which I can disclaim responsibility.[8]

If I understand Rose at all correctly here, she is intimating that the Holocaust is 'beyond remorse' not because it is a diabolical evil that resists analysis, or an apocalyptic break in habitual historical inter-action, but because it shows how the modern alienation between public and private goodness, law and morality, can leave us with no vocabulary for thinking and speaking about evil, guilt or tragic loss in the public, political sphere. Faced with such things, we don't know who is responsible, and are (guiltily) inclined to feel a little relieved; it can't be pinned on *us*, even if we adopt the fashionable language of corporate guilt and corporate apology.

In this most extreme outrage, the paralysis of 'ordinary' notions of remorse, the apparent impossi-bility of reparation and the exaltation of the martyr community to a place outside 'ordinary' politics in fact brings into sharp relief the basic problems of remorse as experienced in personal matters. Failure in remorse is failure to find ourselves in the other; in the context of the modern atrophy of political morality, it means the failure to recognise the moral loss to us as agents that results from the corruption and untruthfulness and barbarity of corporate life. If we

[8] Ibid. p. 36; cf. several other essays in this collection, notably 'Of Derrida's Spirit', pp. 65–87, and 'Walter Benjamin – Out of the Sources of Modern Judaism', pp. 175–210.

cannot even begin to think the memory of the
Holocaust in relation to the language of remorse, we
cannot properly identify the reality of *political* evil –
which leaves us with the unhappy gulf Rose speaks of
between the self as moral agent and the self as
political or civic subject. To put the Holocaust
outside what can be thought about is to set in stone
the division between what conscious reflective
agents do and what mysterious collectivities do. The
savage debates over whether it is right to attribute the
genocide to more or less innate historical tendencies
in the culture of Germany, whether the average
German was virtually predestined to be a 'willing
executioner', are not helped by a certain failure, on
both sides, to consider the nature of strictly political
evil, the dispositions of power and responsibility that
might concretely allow Germans or anyone else for
that matter to become, collectively, executioners.
And the use to which the militarist Israeli Right can
put the mythical and apocalyptic model of the Shoah
as a unique break in language and history should
give us some pause. It reinforces, by the bitterest
of paradoxes, the precise problem about the relation
of morality and law that produces our own (non-
Jewish European or North American) moral paralysis
on the subject. If the Holocaust somehow takes us
beyond language and politics, the actions of the
remnant community are outside law and negotiation
and the recognition of self in other, and it is no use
trying to discuss collective regional security, presup-

positions about historical rights of residence on the part of non-Jewish people, politically defensible frontiers or any kindred matters.

For Europe, the Holocaust must still be *thought* about: silence, however potent its motivation, can be an evasion here. And thinking about it should direct us precisely towards the ways in which the modern political collective moves us away from categories of shame, responsibility, even the possibility of acknowledged failure in public discourse. This is not at all to domesticate or generalise or reduce the horror of what was done to European Jewry. On the contrary: to begin to think thus is to think of the specific and local human identities extinguished in the slaughter, the identities that belonged already in and with the selfhood of specific others – the specific neighbours and fellow-citizens who colluded, actively or passively, in the outrages of the Reich. A collective and apocalyptic crime against a collective sacrificial victim allows no personal, no local mourning, no political thought (who 'allows' public decision and how?), no sense of the death of charity as the damnation of specific agents incapable of seeing themselves as agents in a public order. This has nothing to do with trying to make the Holocaust bearable or healable, to fit it into a framework where remorse can be uttered and absolution secured. Nothing softens what was said earlier about the risk and powerlessness of remorse; no one can guarantee forgiveness.

But if the very possibility of forgiveness, of some kind of morally different future that moves us away from the relations of torturer and tortured, is not wholly to disappear, remorse has to be 'released': we have to learn to *grieve appropriately*. In another of her essays,[9] Gillian Rose explores the distinction between two kinds of mourning. There is the 'political melancholy' which assumes that history is essentially tragic or catastrophic, that the enemies of human welfare are always already victorious. Revolutionary tyranny can rewrite the past: so our present efforts for or witness to justice lie always under the shadow of a possible future cancellation, even annihilation. In this perspective, the temptation is to look for a moment of Messianic or apocalyptic (and therefore violent) transformation, something going beyond the ambiguous and already corrupted process of gradual social change.[10] But, Rose insists, there is another kind of mourning which does not assume despair, and so does not drive us to the longing for violent and magical change. This is what she calls 'inaugurated' mourning,[11] grief that has its origins in the knowledge (in some particular here and now) of concretely possible fulfilments concretely threatened or lost. Such mourning depends upon investing what we perceive with an 'aura', a solidity, a position not ours,

[9] Ibid. 'Walter Benjamin – Out of the Sources of Modern Judaism', pp. 206ff.

[10] Ibid. pp. 206ff.

[11] Ibid. p. 202.

from which we may ourselves be seen. And this sense of a specific, located otherness is directly related to 'the ability to know and be known ..., to look and have one's gaze returned'[12] – and so to the 'acknowledgement of the relation of the other to herself in my relation to myself'.[13] The self-relatedness of what I perceive is its substantiality over against my presence to myself; but that self-relatedness is not a self-enclosure, but the capacity to be seen or recognised, expressed and experienced as a 'look' directed at us, as something that enables our own self-perception. This mutuality is the ground of the ability to sense loss in a particularised way. We grieve because we are aware of loss; but to understand loss is also to understand fulfilment or recognition, to have been familiar with 'knowing and being known', and so to be free of despair. There are specific things to be hoped for, which are not cancelled or annihilated because they are bound to the specificity of relations, the concrete differences that are made by one person's selfhood evolving in dependence on others. The mourning that arises in this relational particularity enables me to endure as a 'witness' to other possibilities in the face of catastrophe; even to remain open to the ironic and the humorous; it also, because it recognises that recognition between persons *happens*, allows the possibility and intelligibility of forgiveness.

[12] Ibid.
[13] Ibid.

IV

We are brought back to the central point in this chapter: remorse occurs when there is a sense of the *implication* of my self with the other (the other person, the wider moral or material environment), such that another's loss becomes – not the *same* as mine, but the cause of loss to me, specific, historical loss. If we simply said that someone else's loss 'became' mine, we should be abolishing the distance between me and the other; recognition in the other would collapse into absorption, and we should be left only with melancholy, in which all pain or tragedy is defined in terms of *my* sense of a loss of power or value. As Freud argued, mourning recognises that what is lost is different from the self, while melancholy treats all loss as the loss of something in or about *me*.[14] Melancholy is thus alien both to remorse and to forgiveness. But proper mourning *connects* the catastrophe of another with my own fate: it looks towards a potential and lost moment, or a not-fully-discerned level of belonging together, and asks for a new solidarity – which is what forgiveness is meant to create. In a sense, what matters is less the achievement of this solidarity than the asking,

[14] Freud's 'Mourning and Melancholia' is to be found in vol. XIV of the standard edition of Freud's works. For an excellent discussion of some of the issues here, see Susannah Radstone, 'Heroes for our Times: Tommy Cooper', *Soundings. A Journal of Politics and Culture*, no. 3 (1996), pp. 191–208, esp. 199–204.

because such an asking indicates *hope* and *need* for the lost connection. It makes a firm statement about the human position: that connectedness or recognition is fundamental to any position that can reasonably be called human.

Remorseful mourning does not allow me to be a hero; nor does it allow the fantasy of a new, post-revolutionary order that is 'heroic', beyond the needs expressed in mourning. It bars the way even to the exalted sentimentality of identifying with victims. When Rose describes the two obvious reactions to the Auschwitz exhibitions – identification with the sufferers on the one hand and tortured self-examination on the other – she is describing two kinds of imaginative heroism: the leap of self-abnegating compassion into the abyss of the Other's suffering, and the descent into the dramas of my own will, bravely testing and facing its frailty. She invites us to look away from both, and to see ourselves neither as victims nor as performers or perpetrators, but as suppliants, and as significantly deceived (and self-deceived) participants in a process that is distorting and impoverishing us.[15] A return to the dramas of the will risks a return to fascism with its

[15] Rose speaks (*Judaism and Modernity*, p. 36) of 'our sentimentality as modern citizens': ' . . . it is the relation between different oppositions – innocence and might, authority and force – between the inner and outer boundaries of our self-identity and lack of self-identity that turns us into strangers to ourselves as moral agents and as social actors'.

massively theorised denials of the really other and its fascination with individual and corporate heroism, the triumph of the will. In relation to the agonies of the political identity of modern Israel, this addresses uncomfortable challenges to both Jew and non-Jew. It questions the apocalyptic isolationism of a consciousness that always assumes the privilege of the victim, just as it questions the romantic inarticulacy of the guilty European consciousness. It requires attention to questions that neither is eager to ask, about what it might mean for Jewish and non-Jewish identity to need each other's interaction or negotiation. It requires – without weakening the empirically exceptional and spiritually nauseating particularity of the murder of the Jews – some language in which the two kinds of grieving involved, for Jew and non-Jew, can speak together.

Rediscovering remorse, then, has a lot to do with the capacity of a culture to leave room for the non-heroic, to celebrate the vulnerable and even the comic. It may sound very strange to associate the sense of the real otherness of a lost object or of another's suffering with the dimension of the comic: but comedy is one very important vehicle for acknowledging and dramatising human involvement in a world that is very imperfectly controlled by human planning, and in which the wills and desires of others frustrate the tyrannies of any single human ego. Comedy typically shows us different kinds of frustration that may be encountered by our planning

– the 'hostility' or at least unpredictability of the material environment, and the complexity of different agencies and strategies subverting each other. What makes this comic rather than tragic is that characters *survive*; they are not wounded to death, mortally diminished. Frustration is part of a continuing story, from which people may or may not learn; and the audience is faced with a world in which the failure of control is amenable to being thought and imagined without paralysing terror. The point at which comedy pushes hardest at its boundaries is where such terror is most audaciously evoked. We wonder a little at classifying some of Shakespeare as comedy because he plays so dangerously with terror and loss – Malvolio, Shylock, Angelo ... And perhaps at those boundaries comedy is most powerful, because it doesn't pretend that the risks are small or that the terror is a silly mistake.[16]

But comedy intimates finally that the uncontrollable environment can be the source of deliverance as much as of damnation; if it damns us, as perhaps it does with Shylock and Malvolio, this is, in dramatic terms, because we choose the distinctive hell of placing our own wills at the centre of things (the moral colouring remains incurably ambiguous, not to say offensive, and there is no way of blandly

---

[16] Radstone, 'Heroes for our Times: Tommy Cooper'; see also Mark William Roche, *Tragedy and Comedy. A Systematic Study and a Critique of Hegel* (Albany, NY, 1998), esp. pp. 303–10.

absolving Shakespeare of class and racial cruelty). Comedy is thus deeply inimical to fascism – though it is also deeply inimical to most kinds of planned reform; it enacts a conviction that what finally delivers human welfare or reconciliation is some process supremely indifferent to the images human beings construct of themselves. It isn't an easy idiom, and it is normally a very vulnerable one. Societies in which control and clearly projected images of the self are prized and guarded make comedy difficult at every level; and what tends to happen is that the comic vision splits between burlesque and satire. By burlesque, I mean simple evocations of the unexpected or embarrassing, episodes of broadly sketched absurdity: banana skins. And by satire, I mean the pointed localised depiction of abuses and self-deceptions, designed to shame or ridicule individual groups, to diminish their public 'honour', with the longer aim of making some sorts of untruthful, self-regarding behaviour more risky and unattractive.

But the very conditions that drive people to satire will also be likely to make satire itself harder and more ineffective. Satire arises when image and reality are ridiculously at odds; but this happens in cultures obsessed with the control and manipulation of images, cultures concerned to lessen the possibility of being properly 'shamed', substantially diminished by losing the regard of others. The whole strategy of public life depends, in such a context, on evading or neutralising or simply rubbishing what might be entailed in the idea of the regard of others. There comes a point where satire tips over into the tragic, where it is an enterprise doomed by its very nature and environment to frustration. Think of Jonathan Swift, the rising spiral of the satirist's fury ending in insanity.

Our century has been well endowed with situations beyond satire. This has, of course, been for diverse reasons. Genocide defies satire, since it is professedly about eliminating the uncontrolled regard of the other. The slaughter of whole communities entails the abandonment of shame. But equally there are varieties of impenetrable bureaucratic cultures that defy satire as effectively because they create and maintain a self-referential and self-justifying dialect. Thomas Merton years ago pointed to the enclosed world of military jargon in the Vietnam War ('To save the village [from the Communists], it became necessary to destroy it').[17] More recently, the records of the Iran–Contra arms deal of the Reagan administration offered an example of the same confident, untroubled, unassailable absurdity and untruth; as did the findings of the Scott Report in Britain in 1996. Both

[17] Merton's essay on 'War and the Crisis of Language' first appeared in *The Critique of War*, ed. Robert Ginsberg (Chicago, 1969), pp. 99–119, and is reprinted in Thomas Merton, *The Nonviolent Alternative* (New York, 1980), pp. 234–47.

'Irangate' and the Scott Report prompted satirical versions of the story in the media; but it was hard not to feel that these responses were somehow futile and impotent. The uninhibited British television revue, 'Spitting Image', for once produced a sophisticated and powerful moment, in a programme devoted to the Reagan presidency: after much (often tedious) broad caricature, the Iran–Contra episode was narrated 'straight' by a senior British political figure (David Steel), and introduced by the statement that what followed was impossible to satirise. It is sobering to reflect that this paralysing of satire was achieved not by totalitarianism but by the sophistication of a managerial society, confident in the 'freedom' of its communications media. The irony is that the more tightly and overtly controlled, but less sophisticated totalitarianisms of Eastern Europe produced an extraordinary crop of authentic and humane satirists, from Mikhail Bulgakov to Andrei Sinyavsky or Milan Kundera; rather as if the presence of overt risk stimulated a deeper vein of satirical critique. If you are really risking your freedom or even your life as a satirist, you'd better have something worth saying.

One thing that is often noticeable in this sort of satire is that there may be a strong tacit appeal to a common history and (I use the words advisedly) a common myth and iconography. Bulgakov's *The Master and Margarita* blends a folkloric demonology with the poignancies of classical 'realist' Russian fiction and with the evocation of a figure who haunts both Russian folklore and the Russian novel – the powerless Christ, on trial for his life. Sinyavsky's *The Makepeace Experiment* effects a similar blend of traditional themes, retelling the story of the Russian Revolution as a mixture of folklore (the magical and anarchic powers of the 'trickster', familiar from mythologies the world over, the discovery of a magical technique that goes comically and disastrously wrong) and apocalypse (the biblical and post-biblical accounts of the last days and the appearance of Antichrist – a recurrent Russian fascination, found at its most sophisticated in the 'Tale of Antichrist' by the late nineteenth-century poet and metaphysician, Vladimir Soloviev). Satire needs and utilises tradition; you could even say that satire presupposes 'charity', in the sense already defined in these pages, the common points of reference that control individual acquisition and assertion. Eastern European totalitarianism failed to suppress the satirical imagination partly because it was a governmental system imposed upon a largely *pre-modern* base, religious, agrarian, narrative-minded. If satire dies in the 'free' world, one of the incidental casualties of the end of history we hear so much about, this may have a good deal to do with the erosion in Western modernity of this kind of base, of the sense of being located in a significant universe, a folk tradition, a religious metaphysic, even one no longer carrying full intellectual conviction. But that is an issue to which we shall return. All that needs noting for the moment is the difficulty, the frustration, of satire in a cultural environment that successfully manages the images of public life in such a way that it seems as if critical scrutiny is efficiently neutralised in advance, and there are no strongly felt images and narratives to foster scepticism about what is presented and marketed. It isn't that such a culture fully *settles* with the managed images that flood it, or even that it is unaware of what is going on in the processes of management; but the resources and tools are lacking that might change perception and behaviour in the light of other pictures. There is no lively, subversive, taken-for-granted mythology that could shame someone into penitence by displaying them clearly against a generally-accepted or understood moral and imaginative backdrop. Not much is left but burlesque, usually deluding itself that it is really satire.

Some of this is related to that familiar contemporary cliché about the brevity of attention spans in the world of technical modernity. It isn't, in fact, all that reliable a cliché: examples of sustained attention are not too difficult to find (watching a football match requires level of interpretative skill, empathy and intelligence that would probably daunt us if they were presented in the abstract). But it does at least register the undoubted truth that the communication systems of the mass media *assume* more and more that interest in and analysis of particular sets of events (a scandal, a war, a famine, a policy decision) are going to be short-lived. The extraordinary phenomenon of day-long news presentations takes it for granted that information means simply the unbroken succession of unrelated complex images. The 'flickering image' of modern media communication, about which so much has been written, represents a very powerful bid to define what really counts as knowledge; and it is a bid that has little room for a sense of location, for irony, for the growth of imaginative understanding out of a vague hinterland of memories and impressions, or for the sense of a slow unfolding of the consequences of acts and choices. Where events come from and go to is not a question to which the media can afford to spend too much time on, and this helps massively to define how understanding itself is understood – which in turn makes the satirical enterprise harder. In a rapidly-moving stream of images, why should one set of images look more absurd than another?

We are being drawn back towards concerns expressed earlier about time and choice. I spoke of 'flattened landscapes' in our thinking about choice these days, a picture conditioned by seeing selves as if they were timeless desiring and deciding mechanisms; and it is the same seduction of the timeless, the abstract self that is at work in our difficulties over honour and remorse. An abstract self is one that has no life in the lives, speech and perceptions of concrete others. Once you grant that a self has such a life in the other, it ceases to be timeless, defined by its present self-disposition and self-description. Its *past* is conserved outside itself, beyond its control. And this can, if it is thought through, remind the self of how its options are conditioned or foreclosed in advance by the history of choices made, the inevitable history of loss that makes us actual and not abstract subjects. The controlled self, making its dispositions in a vacuum of supposed consumer freedom and determining the clothing in which it will appear, is a fiction, no less potent for being self-generated.[18]

So what are we to say about a self that is not a fiction, a self formed in time and in relational space, in the uncertainties of language and negotiation about what was once called the soul? All our reflections so far have been, in essence, a prologue to this question. It is one that is easily misunderstood as 'metaphysical', in a rather misleading and malign sense of that much-abused word – a question about

[18] On remorse, time and the self, several of the essays in Murray Cox (ed.), *Remorse and Reparation* (London, 1999) are enormously illuminating. See esp. Cox's introductory remarks, and the essays by Michael Borgeaud and Caroline Cox, '"The Most Dreadful Sentiment". A Sociological Commentary', pp. 135–44 (esp. pp. 137–8 on the formation of a remorseful self through socialisation), and Nancy Scheper-Hughes, 'Un-doing. Social Suffering and the Politics of Remorse', pp. 145–70 (esp. pp. 156–63 and 168–70 on the experience of the Truth and Reconciliation Commission in South Africa).

invisible essences, the things there might be in the world in addition to the material ones. Talking about the self in such a vein is in danger of being idle and pre-moral. The urgent issue is how we speak truthfully of a material life that includes among its material activities a self-representation that is ventured in the community of other speakers, a material life that somehow *represents* the duration in which it lives. And why this might be territory that is in some respects better charted by using the word 'soul' rather than simply 'self' is the question that our final chapter will try to address.

4

Lost Souls

A missionary has just returned from years in a remote part of Africa; at the airport in Philadelphia, he is met by his sister-in-law, and they discuss their anxieties (his mother is dangerously ill) as they begin their journey to join the family.

While we were talking in this way, I took the car keys from her, and on the way out of the parking lot I backed into the side of a parked car. It was somebody's brand-new Buick and it was pretty badly dented. I remember jumping out of our car like a jackrabbit. My heart was pounding and I started shouting at my sister-in-law through the closed window of our car. I was screaming something about insurance, calling the police, or whether we should drive away without letting anyone know. I was actually trembling with panic.

My sister-in-law apparently had no idea of the state I suddenly was in; I suppose I was not manifesting it in any gross way ... [S]he was relieved that I took charge in such a calm and attentive way. Fantastic!

The truth was that, inside, I, whoever I was, had disappeared into nothingness. Back in the car, after everything was on the way to being settled and after we were out of the parking lot, the thought of my mother's illness came back to me and also the thoughts of all that had gone on in Africa ...

... But it kept coming back to me in the weeks that followed. At least once a day and then more and more often I would suddenly be stopped in my tracks by the overwhelming experience that my Christianity has disappeared *because I myself had disappeared*! It was almost always connected to something minor, some personal irritation ...[1]

The missionary is clear and adamant about the difference between the loss of self so vividly described here and the loss of ego that mystics speak of. He has strong 'religious experiences', he says, in which his sense of identity disappears, but these are comparable to the loss experienced in the car park after the accident, and leave a similar residue of bewilderment and self-disgust. They have nothing to do, as far as he can see, with any entry of the self into selfless love or any such spiritual ideal. 'I didn't know ... what secret I had stumbled onto, but no one was going to talk me into believing it was something good.'[2]

What the 'secret' might be takes time to unscramble, but it appears to be something like this. Our (North Atlantic) culture fosters, even in some senses rewards, a privileging of the reactive over the

---

[1] Jacob Needleman, *Lost Christianity. A Journey of Rediscovery to the Center of Christian Experience* (New York, 1980), p. 75.

[2] Ibid. p. 77.

active in our relations with the world. We become used to the pressure of stimuli that are calculatedly and habitually addressed to the more transient kinds of emotion, hunger for rapid gratification; which also means that the frustrated emotional hunger, the desire that meets a shock, an unpredicted check, is overwhelmed with panic, the sort of panic that shuts out other habitual considerations as to how I manage my environment. The American missionary just quoted is describing an early form of road rage, and his account very reasonably suggests that the problem is less about traffic than about the inner life of drivers. But he is also suggesting that *gratified* emotion in such a general cultural environment is equally an odd and problematic relation to our circumstances, no more healthy or complete than the experience of savage frustration or shock. Whether negatively or positively, what is in focus is myself as absorbing or reacting to a *momentary* and atomised stimulus. What I have called the active element in my coping with my environment is obscured: precisely what *doesn't* come into focus here is the self as initiating, making, transforming. To pick up the language used at the end of the preceding chapter, my responses to my environment do not 'represent' the way in which I exist in time.

This needs a good deal of unpacking, of course. Momentary, reactive relation to the circumstances I am in is in fact shaped by an enormous range of factors, visible and invisible – by a personal history, by various physical constraints, by the ensemble of cultural assumptions that forms my imagination. Nothing is more fatuous here than talk about purely 'natural' desires, instincts or reactions, or talk about the postmodern self's liberty to reinvent itself from moment to moment. What I want now and how I feel now and what I am capable of 'inventing' are grounded in certain basic dispositions, limits and needs in a material constitution; but no one element in this exists without cultural mediation. We learn what we are in language and culture – even what we physically are. What I feel is structured by how I have learned to talk; what I want is what I picture to myself in the images I have learned to form from the observation of others, images that are not innocent representations of objects and goals but complex, differentiated constructions existing in potentially tense relation with the world of other subjects. To isolate the supposed reaction of a moment, to say or imply that any such felt reaction is not amenable to criticism and thought, that it is some *thing* other than the life of a linguistic process, is illusion. To put it provocatively, there is no great gulf between (complex and time-taking) reason and (innocent and instantaneous) passion: there are more and less self-aware ways of talking about passion, more and less in the way of examining how our reactions have been learned, or at the very least, how the representation of our reactions to ourselves has been learned. Thus there is a way of constructing, of talking about

174

or figuring, what's going on that is open to the questions, Why *this* reaction? Where does this sensation or response or desire belong? or, most simply, What's it (literally) *like*? – and is, as a result, capable of representing, however sketchily or inadequately, the time that has made a subject what it is. When there is no such openness, what you have is not an innocent or primitive consciousness but a fictive one – just the same image of a bearer of timeless needs and desires that we looked at so unsympathetically in earlier pages. The point is that it is no less a cultural, language-formed construct than the traditional model of a continuous and reflective self.

But if we live in a culture embarrassed by the inevitability of learning in or through time, suspicious of what seems to be a qualification or restriction of the 'natural' legitimacy of the ego's demands, this fiction will be potent and widespread. Our American missionary was simply documenting the dramatically immediate, barely conscious impact upon him of an environment privileging the reactive, atomised response to situations, an environment generative of a pervasive air of suppressed panic. What is distinctive in his account, however, is his identification of this as a loss of the *self*. I shall come back later to my own reasons for rendering this as a loss of the 'soul'. But it is clear from the missionary's story that part of what is lost is a sense of temporal context: in the reaction of emotional panic, both short-term (his mother's illness) and long-term (African experiences) concerns disappear. Nothing unusual, you may say, in panic reactions blotting out longer-term memories, a wider mental world; but what if our cultural environment increasingly expects, imagines, provides for and nourishes panic? And has no sure means of affirming or restoring the actual 'time of the self', the wider mental world? The missionary's initially puzzling comparison with his 'religious experiences' in the USA seems to indicate that an environment can deliver what feel like highly satisfactory and 'positive' states which are in fact varieties of panic reaction, ways of obliterating a timebound self under intense pressure. It would be interesting, though beyond the scope of this essay, to look into the ways in which 'religious experience' in the North Atlantic cultural milieu is regularly cultivated in such a way as to produce this kind of obliteration, even defined as what successfully delivers a sense of 'timelessness', whether through experiences of 'oceanic' absorption or through varieties of ecstatic states. This is not at all to dismiss the seriousness or significance of such states; but we might need to reflect on what exactly they mean in the broad cultural scene, how they slot into a particular view of what the most desirable conditions for the self might be.

The implication of all this is that the self excluded or occluded in the intense, reactive panic described is necessarily something involved in *narrative*; more specifically in narratives that are constantly being revised, re-edited. If my narrative is simply a cumulative story of things happening, I shall treat each event as an abstract item to be catalogued, and I shall fail to see how what happens reorders what I have been as well as shaping what I shall be. To register an experience *now* is to know that the past I can relate/narrate is now to be seen as capable of bringing me *here*, of producing *these* results; or to acquire a perspective in which the past now appears in this or that kind of analogy, this or that kind of tension, with what's said and done now, and so is changed in some measure (which is why it is not so easy to write dispassionate history, history that carries no implicit comparison with the way we live now). Every 'telling' of myself is a retelling, and the act of telling changes what can be told next time, because it is, precisely, an *act*, with consequences, like other acts, in the world and speech of others. The self lives and moves in, only in, acts of telling – in the time taken to set out and articulate a memory, the time that is a kind of representation (always partial, always skewed) of the time my material and mental life has taken, the time that has brought me here. To step aside from this kind of telling and retelling, this always shifting and growing representation of the past, is in effect to abandon thinking itself or language itself.

The process of 'making' a self by constructing a story that is always being retold is a prosaic and universal one, so much so that we habitually don't notice that it's what we are doing – hence some of the confusions and corruptions this book has attempted to outline. But if we ask what it is that brings us to an awareness of what we're doing, we need to look more closely, I suggest, at two moments that commonly heighten self-consciousness. The first of these is conflict or frustration; the second (which I will examine later) is love.

Now to speak of the experience of frustrated desire as a moment of growth is immediately to invite a moralistic misreading – the idea that conflict is a stimulus to self-development. But more than this is in question here. What Hegel called the unhappy consciousness, the subject aware of its lack of power in making the world intelligible, is not a *stimulus* to development (here's a problem, let me develop my spiritual muscles in overcoming it), but belongs to the essence of development itself. I desire peace, I desire to be at home with myself; but the edge and the energy of the desire, the *movement* involved, comes from the already experienced knowledge that I am 'irretrievably dispersed in a multiplicity of unstable feelings and changing relationships', in the words of a recent and formidably original inter-

[3] Walter Davis, *Inwardness and Existence. Subjectivity in/and Hegel, Heidegger, Marx and Freud* (Madison, Wisconsin, 1989), p. 98.

preter of Hegel, Walter Davis.[3] The self I know is the self that is not at one with itself but is moving and changing; the self is always 'in question', under criticism, a matter of thought. This is *implicitly* recognised whenever there is a gap between desire and reality – that is to say, whenever desire comes into the focus of thought, when it is delayed and denied long enough for it to be a problem. It is *explicitly* recognised at moments when that gap is created by a concrete event, a check upon or a refusing of the claim of desire (not just, as in the first instance, when there is an awareness of a process to be gone through before satisfaction can be attained). The more I reflect on this, the more I see that my desire to be (at one with, at peace with) myself is exactly what is frustrated by the very act of thinking truthfully about myself (as an historical and mutable reality); but, on the other hand, the only way in which it is possible for me to be (at one with) myself is to be reconciled to the reality of change and so of frustration – to think through a world where I exist in, and only in, that negotiating with what is not myself spells frustration to a self that is simply looking for identity or self-presence. I can only be where I 'truly' am by recognising that there is no fixed place where I am innocently and timelessly I alone and incorrupt. And the recognition of how I 'negotiate' is what gives me the material for a telling of my self.

'Subject is what it becomes because reflection shows that its being is always at issue.'[4] This particularly dense formulation by Walter Davis means that a self is only really definable *in* the act of self-questioning; reflecting on the self can't be a way of thinking about an 'item' that will stay in focus while we look at it. The act of questioning is the act in which the self is itself. Reflection, says Davis, is 'irreversible';[5] that is, reflection itself becomes the experience that the self thinks about: the questioning of the self, hesitating in its frustration, is the consolidation of selfhood that then, in turn, presents itself for thought. 'Inwardness develops not by escaping or resolving but by deepening *the conflicts that define it*.'[6] To be a conscious subject is to be involved in thinking through what it is to experience check or limit. Which is why (back to our American missionary) the unthinking, reactive position in regard to such a check or limit is exactly the sign of a loss of self or even of 'subject', in Davis's terms – and the loss too of action, transformation and real linguistic identity. It needs also to be said, though, to avoid another obvious misunderstanding, that this should not be construed so as to deny 'selfhood' to any but the most articulate or self-aware of human subjects. The understanding or thinking of frustrated desire is not primarily a conceptual exercise; it is what goes on (in the child,

[4] Ibid. p. 104.
[5] Ibid. pp. 104–5.
[6] Ibid. p. 105; my italics.

in the 'handicapped' or senile) whenever reactive emotion gives place to other responses, whenever it is possible to shift into other modes of relating to the situation – not necessarily by what we might want to define as 'reflection', but in whatever still allows acceptance or peace or the taking of a new initiative. Those with experience of the 'handicapped' adult will, as much as any parent, know what it means to discover the resource of the apparently non-reflective in coming to terms with reality.

II

If what has been so far said is true, one of the most powerful enemies of the self will always be anything that encourages us to imagine an environment without friction. George Steiner, in a notoriously provocative essay, suggested that a major part of the difference between European and American fiction lay in the 'Edenic' assumptions of the latter, shaped by a society resolved upon justice, 'a general dignity of mass status', and its concomitant yearning to eliminate what makes for tragic frustration. And in 'Proofs', a novella closely related to the themes of this essay,[7] Steiner sets up a confrontation between

[7] The essay is 'The Archives of Eden', included in George Steiner, *No Passion Spent. Essays 1978–1996* (London, 1996), pp. 266–303 ('a general dignity ... ' p. 300). The novella, originally published in 1992, appears in Steiner, *The Deeps of the Sea and Other Fiction* (London, 1996), pp. 313–69.

an old-style Italian Communist – a skilled proof-reader, literate, ironic and passionate – and a modernising Marxist priest, who argues, with no less passion, that the price of tragedy, difficulty and the art that comes from them is unbearably high. The other replies that, 'Every little step forward is made of sweat and mutiny ... No-one has ever learned or achieved anything worth having without being stretched beyond themselves, till their bones crack. "Easy does it", says America to mankind. But easy has never done it.'[8] Steiner himself admits that this may be massively wrong as an assessment of America (though he is able to point to analyses like that of Philip Rieff – and, one could add, Christopher Lasch – to bear out the diagnosis of a culture obsessed with 'escaping or resolving'); it sits badly with a patient reading of a good deal of the literature of the American South, or even of the mature Saul Bellow. But what Steiner succeeds in doing is at least to alert us to what we might look for, what we might be suspicious about, in the art of our culture (once again, 'North Atlantic' in general terms, not exclusively North American); how we might identify enemies of the self in styles and fictions that erode *difficulty*.

The American missionary we met at the beginning of this chapter is one of a number of figures (some at least semi-fictional) sketched by Joseph Needleman

[8] Steiner, *The Deeps of the Sea*, p. 349.

in a rambling and complex but very striking book on *Lost Christianity*, the second part of which is entitled 'The Lost Doctrine of the Soul'. Needleman's theme is that traditional – specifically Christian – doctrine and exhortation are meaningless in our present context so long as we have no idea of what *sense of self* such teaching is addressed to; to hear what is said in religious discourse, we must build a selfhood radically unlike what we take for granted as the modern norm of subjectivity. Hence the apparently throwaway remark quoted earlier about the ersatz loss of self that a modern subject may be able to produce through 'religious experience', as in the case of the returned missionary; religious language and discipline applied or addressed to the modern self produces something importantly different from what the language is originally about. It is this alternative sense of self that Needleman calls the 'soul'; but it is notable that he defines it in terms remarkably close to those used by the secularist Davis writing about the 'subject'. 'The mediating attention of the heart [perhaps parallel to Davis's 'reflection'] is spontaneously activated in man in the state of profound self-questioning, a state that is almost always inaccurately recognised and wrongly valued in everyday experience.'[9] Authentic religious (in this case, Christian) practice begins in the attempt to attend to the moment of self-questioning – to refuse to cover over, evade or explain the pain and

[9] Needleman, *Lost Christianity*, p. 167.

shock of whatever brings the self into question, to hold on to the difficulty before the almost inevitable descent into pathos and personal drama begins. 'The soul' is what happens in the process of such attention: 'it is a movement that begins whenever man [*sic*] experiences the psychological pain of contra-diction'.[10] But it is thus also a very vulnerable reality, since the pain of contradiction is habitually expected to be eased or removed. The point of bodily disci-pline, ascetical training, in this perspective is to provide a 'routinised', expected and accepted, experience of contradiction, so that the happening of the soul may build up steadily and consistently.[11]

But in this respect, there is a convergence with some strands of psychoanalytic thinking that insist on the character of the analytical relationship as a place for experiencing a kind of planned frustration. You may begin analysis assuming that what will happen is the learning of truths that already exist but are hidden (never yet brought to consciousness); and this learning is to be facilitated by a skilled professional who is able to give you an authoritative account of what you *really* mean, what is really going on. When 'transference' occurs, when the person being analysed makes a substantial emotional investment in the analyst, this is all about the analyst's position as the person who has something I desire. But the critical

[10] Ibid. p. 175.
[11] Ibid. chapters 8 and 9, passim.

importance of working through transference lies in the handling of the frustration, the sense of betrayal, experienced when the analyst refuses to tell me or give me what I want. My perspective, as the person undergoing analysis, is that 'the truth is out there' (to coin a phrase): there is an Other in whom is the secret that will heal me or satisfy me, that will answer to my desire in such a way that I no longer feel the pain of desiring. When the analyst refuses to gratify me, to reveal (or indeed to *become*) the answer to my desire, refuses to put an end to my pain, then and only then may I perhaps begin to understand what a self is and what it isn't. Here is an eloquent description from a practitioner, Chris Oakley:

> The encounter that is counted upon is linked to a crucial refusal, that is, the refusal by the analyst to gratify demands of the analysand. Inevitably the analysis begins with suffering … This suffering will be addressed to the Other, which is where the analyst stands, standing in for the Other … Eventually the analyst will respond and it is through this that the potentiality in the situation can emerge. This potentiality is for coming up against the realization that the Other does not exist.[12]

If the analysand's desire is met (as, of course, strictly speaking, it can't be, if the theory of the analytical

---

[12] Chris Oakley, 'Otherwise than Integrity', in Robin Cooper, Joseph Friedman and others, *Thresholds Between Philosophy and Psychoanalysis. Papers from the Philadelphia Association* (London, 1989), pp. 120–45, p. 141.

relationship is correct), this would mean that there was indeed a *given* self with specific requirements which could in principle arrive at an immanent balance, identity or fulfilment as and when the requirements are satisfied. Desire would thus become only an accidental feature of the human consciousness. But to understand the pains involved in working past transference, to understand why I *must* be 'betrayed' by the analyst refusing to meet my requirements and aspirations, is what allows me to think my 'self ' as what is coming to birth in the process of experiencing frustrated desire. My wholeness or balance is, ironically, a matter of recognising the fundamental error in the picture of a buried self whose needs can be met once they've been brought to light. Instead, I come to see that I cannot fail to be involved in incompletion; and that *no thing* completes me. My 'health' is in the thinking or sensing of how I am not at one with myself, existing as I do in time (change) and language (exchange). Were it otherwise, the self would not be something that could be thought about at all. It would disappear in the fulfilment of its supposed desire; it would be identical with itself; it would have gone beyond language and reflection. To nurture such a picture while living in a vulnerable and mobile body is a recipe for the most damaging inner dislocations and the gravest dysfunction in relating to a material world in which other perspectives are presented, 'spoken for'.

But Oakley would add that this thinking of myself becomes more and not less accessible if the analyst is able to negotiate the very seductive pressure to become 'necessary' to the analysand. 'One can be lured', writes Oakley, 'into a form of deal, and a great deal will hinge on the outcome of this. If one is engaged in fulfilling the other's desire then paradoxically one deprives the other ... If one allows oneself [as analyst] to be seduced into becoming merely the one who loves the analysand, ... [t]here will have been an abdication from the position of the Other and one will be consigned to being merely an other amongst others.'[13] Thus even the analyst's passion to understand or to heal has to be refused at a certain level if the analyst is not to become simply a presence in the imagination of the analysand, to collapse into the 'sameness' of the analysand's world instead of continuing to stand for a total *difference* that uncovers the incompleteness or fragmentedness of the analysand. And for this, as Oakley hints, the analyst must be persistently aware of his or her own frustrated desire, that desire which is not to be filled up by meeting the desire of the analysand or even by seeking to become (in self-understanding) what the analysand 'secretly' desires – that healing Other who exceeds all desiring.[14] The analyst, in short, can only *represent* the completely Other, the 'non-existent'

13 Ibid. p. 142.
14 Ibid. pp. 143–5.

point beyond desire, when he or she knows they cannot *be* that Other.

The complexities of all this are intimidating. But we might try and summarise like this. The self becomes adult and truthful in being faced with the incurable character of its desire: the world is such that no thing will bestow on the self a rounded and finished identity. Thus there is in reality no self – and no possibility of recognising what one is as a self – without the presence of the other. *But* that other must precisely *be* other – not the fulfilment of what I think I want, the answer to my lack. The therapy that releases or constructs the viable, truthful sense of self that is needed for a life without crippling misperception is a therapy that represents such otherness. And (here is a further twist of paradox) it must represent and not claim to *embody* it; if it slips into the latter, it becomes a new slavery and illusion. The claim to embody the Other says, in effect, that the Other is *here*, an answer, a gratification, a terminus of desire, so that the Other is reduced to the dimension of my lack and ceases to be Other. Thus analyst and analysand must both operate in awareness of the complete absence and difference of the Other, each refusing gratification or completion to the finite other. Each has an interest, as we might say, in the continued life of the other's desire; because as long as that remains radically open, as long as each subject sees and accepts incompleteness, each secures the truthful life of the other, blocking 'the illusion of a perfect circularity of desire', the fantasy of a static, symmetrical mutuality of gratification in which the two parties are only 'each other's other', not representations of the liberating Other who does not and cannot appear.

Psychoanalysis understood in these terms (which not all practising analysts would own or even grasp, admittedly) is not just a skilled invitation to the life-giving contradiction or frustration of desire; it works as such by doing something significantly more, by invoking the necessarily absent, non-particular ('non-existent') Other. It is a three-cornered relation, not only a dialogue, in which the presence of the absent third makes possible some kind of liberation from the net of ideas and projections that binds us into the fantasy that some specific other can supplement our lack, once and for all, and end our desire. And the absent, 'non-existent' third is manifest as the condition for a truthful recognition of my own limits, of the persistence of my incompleteness, because it is not itself *a* point of view, mirroring or competing with mine; it is not another system of desiring, any more than it is something to be fitted into the system of *my* desiring. Its otherness is radical enough to allow me to be other – to be distinctive, to be the this-and-not-that of temporal particularity. And the finite other who 'holds' this perspective does so only out of the same awareness of the permission given by the 'third' to be a finite self; if this is not so, I remain trapped.

III

I wrote earlier of *two* moments that offer a heightening of truthful self-consciousness. I am stirred into facing what I am as a voice and an agency in time when I encounter what frustrates my unexamined desire, and I can to some extent discover this by discipline, by the classic disciplines of asceticism, certainly – fasting, the contemplative refusal of images, the challenge to hopes for sexual gratification – but also by certain aspects of that odd and ambivalent modern ascesis, the analytic process. But the second moment is less amenable to 'discipline'. In a sense, it is more primitive than what we have just been discussing. It is the experience of being in love.

We'd better be precise: not simply the experience of desiring or being desired, nor an obsessional preoccupation with another, but the moment of acknowledged conviction, shared by two people, that each is accepted, given time and room, treated not as an object of desire alone but as a focus for attention and fascination. In the analytic relation, what prevents the other from dissolving in fantasies of wholeness and gratification are the 'contracted', ritualised refusals of the analyst. In falling in love, what prevents it is a complex of factors – the need to *go on* discovering the other, as well as to have the other as a listening or witnessing presence for my own self-discovery; the almost impersonal gladness that the other exists (especially at early stages of a relationship); the spontaneous (however short-lived) forgetfulness of my own interest, dignity or protection. There is plenty that is paradoxical about all this – and it is formidably easy to sentimentalise. But the truth is clearly that in the relations we designate as 'being in love', the urge for sexual grati-fication is blended with a range of other affects and concerns that enable the subject to *speak* and see himself or herself afresh. Simultaneously there may be what looks like a naive egotism, the pouring-out of feeling and memory, and an equally naive attention to and absorption in the other's difference and often the other's need.

'A kind of storytelling that makes you coherent is part of falling in love,' says A. S. Byatt towards the end of a long and wholly compelling series of conversations on women writers of fiction with the Brazilian analyst, Ignês Sodré.[15] Both partners in love long to find a way of expressing and discovering truth, because they have been given a kind of *promise*: the possibility opened up by the fact that I am not only physically desirable to another, but someone that another person wants to spend time with, is the possibility that I have a solidity and complexity that demands time to be taken in exploring or uncovering it. The promise is a promise

[15] A. S. Byatt and Ignês Sodré, *Imagining Characters. Six Conversations about Women Writers* (London, 1995), p. 246.

of my being shown to myself in ways I couldn't have realised for or by myself. In the simplest possible terms – I am *interesting*. But how and why is something I can only discover by the twofold process of listening to the other partner (who tells me what I can't tell myself, shows me the face I can't simply look at) and searching for words that will be transparent to what I am, to the reality that I can't see but am now assured is there. Being in love is – familiarly – from one point of view an intensification of the sense of *me*, and from another point of view an intensification of the sense of confrontation with what absolutely is not me. It hovers between egotism and self-denial.

It is a dangerous state and an inherently unstable one. Tilt the balance towards egotism, and the point comes at which I may want to mould or control the interest of the other. Mistrusting the other's capacity to go on being interested or attracted when faced with my mediocrity or my destructiveness, I hold things back, edit and reshape what I say. In other words, I stop discovering, because I am afraid of the open-ended and risky character of what the other is giving me. I must guarantee that this openness does not finally open out on to what in me is unacceptable or frightening. Tilt the balance towards self-denial, and my love may reach the point where I can no longer see myself as solid and complex: my worth is wholly bound up with the other, and my terror is of losing myself if I lose that other. I more and more efface my own agenda, allow myself to be invaded or exploited, offer myself as material for the other's ego to digest, submit to and (consciously or not) invite violence. The two distortions of course have much in common, and at the heart of both is the same dread of loss: loss of the other, at the simplest level, but also loss of the self that the other assures for me – whether I deal with this by reclaiming control over the picture of my self or by unconditionally offering myself to the other's will.

The mutual exposure involved in falling in love is a response to the conviction that there is, fully and unequivocally, 'room' for me in someone else's consciousness and affections. And, as Byatt goes on to say, 'this desire to be wholly contained in another mind, wholly present in a relationship, can be experienced as *dangerously* close'.[16] Sodré agrees that, 'The intense desire for closeness creates claustrophobic anxieties,'[17] and observes how certain fictions derive deep energy from working with the tensions between a longing for closeness, a longing to be possessed or encompassed, and the fear of being so encompassed that my reality slips entirely away from my will and my own proper language. Just as in the analytic relationship, the shadow arises of being *reduced* to what will satisfy another.[18] In shamelessly

[16] Ibid.
[17] Ibid.
[18] Cf. Oakley, 'Otherwise than Integrity', p. 142.

193

old-fashioned terminology, we fear becoming objects of 'lust', our significance prescribed by what is acceptable and gratifying. The fact that human beings have historically treated sexual desire as a *cultural* matter – as the subject of social patterning, imaginative transformations, even religious metaphor – reflects something of this fear; which in turn reflects that *excess* involved in what we call being in love, the more-than-desire that enables us to talk about ourselves in a new way. Certainly there is a joy or a confidence that can come from being desired – but only lastingly or securely, perhaps, if the desire opens on to more than the meeting of a need; when it has what a religious person might call a contemplative dimension, a gladness that the other is not 'used up' in gratification. And that is what gives the freedom for telling a story of oneself, even for telling truths that may not seem marketable or palatable.

This in turn (and this is Byatt's point) is vulnerable: to want to be wholly present in another's consciousness can lead to obsessive self-revelation, struggling to leave nothing unsaid, not easily distinguishable from the familiar problem of testing the limits of love by provocative or potentially unacceptable behaviour. The knife-edge is between *freedom* to tell – which allows an other *time* to listen and absorb, and accepts that who or what I am here will only emerge in this *indefinite* time of speaking and listening – and *compulsion* to tell – I must *now* find the words to deliver myself totally to the other, because if I fail in this I cannot be assured of their love. Erotic love notoriously lives on this knife-edge. When it manages to escape obsession, terror and passionate hunger as its dominant modes, it is because of that space which is more than desire; and this could be characterised as grounded in the knowledge that I can be the cause of joy to another in virtue of something more or other than the capacity to meet their needs.

Which brings us back to the same theme that our reflection on psychoanalysis opened up: to be other, to be distinctive, is more than being *someone else's other*, being what fits into another's stipulated lack. Being in love makes possible 'a kind of storytelling that makes you coherent' to the extent that it realises the odd and elusive recognition of such a dimension. In being very specifically a desired other for someone, I discover that I am more than this; I give not just gratification but joy – which is precisely what isn't planned for, what isn't the scratch for the itch, the demand met. Erotic love, when it is serious and time-taking, when it goes on generating ways of speaking, seems, like the analytical relationship, to move around the non-existent third term: I discover in erotic mutuality the self that is present neither to my own unmediated self-awareness or self-examination *nor* simply to the desiring other. The other apprehends me as not being there – *now*, definitively, finally – for them alone. If you treat the analytical relationship as the provision of saving knowledge to a diseased mind, or if you treat the erotic relationship as a means for assuring relief of tension and a determinate set of satisfactions, what is lost in both cases is that vision of the self as *not* there to be possessed, to be completed or to serve another's completion; the vision of a self that is gratuitous or contingent in respect of any other's need, anyone else's agenda, and that therefore demands time, words and patience.

In other words, what is lost is what I want to call the soul. The religious resonance is deliberate, of course, since what is under discussion is not the 'soul' of early modern philosophy, an immaterial individual substance, but something more complex – a whole way of speaking, of presenting and 'uttering' the self, that presupposes *relation* as the ground that gives the self room to exist, a relation developing in time, a relation with an agency which addresses or summons the self, but is in itself no part of the system of interacting and negotiating speakers in the world. In religious terms, this agency has been seen as the source of the self's life in such a way as to establish that any self's existence is a simple, unnecessary and gratuitous act on the part of the source. The self *is*, not because of need but because of gift. The experiences and encounters we have just been analysing bring to life in us a different kind of selfhood from that of the 'normal' competitive world because they evoke just this sense of a self that is there beyond the sphere of mutual need, and therefore not to be spoken of in terms of the plain self-presence or self-identity of an object. The secular analyst or philosopher will speak of the non-existent or absent or ideal Other (that which is other to all particular others in the world); the religious observer will ask whether such a secular discourse can finally sustain the load placed upon it. The non-existent presence is neither a willed construction nor a theoretical explanation, but a dimension within certain relations that 'shows itself', in the Wittgensteinian phrase. It belongs *within* a discourse about what is made possible in relations between persons, yet does not reduce to an account of trans-actions between two desiring egos. For any self to be free to enable another's freedom means that it must be in some way aware of the actuality, not only the possibility, of a *regard beyond desire* – and so of its own being as a proper cause of joy, as a gift.

Religious discourses handle this in diverse ways. Northern Buddhism systematically dissolves the whole idea of a substantial self by dissolving the desires and reactions that seem to give it solidity, and then affirms that on the far side of the dissolution is what you might call a paradoxical presence-in-absence for the other that is pure compassion – a love without need because it is without an active centre in the world. The Jewish and Christian traditions take seriously the fact that it is within relations that these insights come to birth, and speak of a personal agency without need or desire shaping finite and temporal agents, agents at whose centre is 'the image of God', the capacity for reflecting God's gratuitous making-possible of the life of what is other – even when this is interwoven inseparably in our lives with appropriation of and action out of a particular position and set of interests in history and society. What these religious perspectives have in common is the conviction that the historical world of negotiation between personal agents with specific interests, while it may challenge fictions about timeless interiority and independence, nonetheless does not in itself deliver the possibilities of a freedom or security for the self that will decisively break through anxiety, rivalry and exploitation. It is only something outside the world of negotiation – as we saw in chapter two – that makes possible the festal abrogation of rivalry, the social miracle. The obstinacy of an other's place or interest is a critical element in understanding what selfhood is in a finite environment; negotiation is the beginning of ethics. But it cannot be its end. The critical possibilities of convergence, equality and reciprocity – the 'ideal speech situation' beloved of some philosophers – requires a recognition of what in us is not negotiable, a common being in time, a common being as gift. And Jewish, Christian and Muslim discourses ground this in the worship of a God who can't be negotiated with, who has no interest to defend and whose creative activity is therefore pure gratuity.

IV

Why has all this become culturally so inaccessible? It is partly to do with the almost infinite corruptibility of religious discourse. Those who claim to speak in the name of God will always be dangerously (exhilaratingly) close to the claim that in their speech, their active presence, the absent God who is never an existent among others is actually present: a claim of stupendous importance in legitimating any bid for power. Here, it says, is a concrete presence that will tell you what you are. The religious ideologue may say – or seem to be saying – that it is as *his* 'other' that you will find your identity (and I do mean 'his', given the history of religious hierarchy in most human cultures); and this will effect a definitive closure on what you are entitled to say about yourself. You are required or desired to satisfy the demands mediated by religious law; that is what you are for, and all you are for.

Now this can be shown to be in various ways a distortion of the underlying logic of much of the Jewish/Christian/Muslim cluster of languages. God is gracious, gratuitous: the creation of a world *unnecessary* to God reminds us that God is not 'needy'; the liberty of God challenges any notion that God can be reduced to a simple or tangible sameness with which we negotiate as we do with the other contingent presences in our mental and physical field. The passage of our speech about God into

199

silence, the self-criticism of all doctrinal utterance in the context of contemplative worship, all this warns consistently against the ideological or hierarchical closures we have just mentioned. But the truth is that such warnings are again and again ineffectual. What the European Enlightenment revolted against was precisely the sense of having your identity and capacity prescribed by a this-worldly other that claimed other-worldly sanction, claimed a kind of identity with the disinterested perspective of God. Enlightenment protested against what seemed the *arbitrariness* of the mediators of the sacred; and it sought to deliver human beings from the slavery of being defined unilaterally by the religious Other *made concrete* in the institutions and conventions of (supposedly) revealed faith. It is one thing to say that we find our identity in relation to or in transparency to an Other outside the systems of need and desire; something else to find that your identity is prescribed, pre-scripted, by the presence and the gaze of an other who is in fact as historical and contingent as you are. It is uncomfortably like the identity of the passive object of desire in pornography; in all the different rhetorics of patriarchy which prohibit a woman's presence to and for herself; in various kinds of racist ideology.

But as the Enlightenment itself collapses under the weight of its own aspirations, it too is seen as potentially a discourse of slavery or pornography, the construction of a normative, rational subject over against sensibility, barbarity, the foreign and the physical. In its origins it had struggled to find ways of articulating what it might be that *every* contingent subject was answerable to. It wasn't first about autonomy in any simple sense but about law – the universally accessible structures and limits (moral and physical) of the world, open to observation, not mediated by the carriers of privately authorised information, power based on revelation. But its own hidden investment in certain sorts of power and enslavement was to be ruthlessly exposed, as the 'universally accessible structures' were dissolved by the various critiques of later modernity. The reasonable environment, visible to all, without mediation or revelation, appeared as a system operating and operated for the benefit of a dominant economic interest (Marxism). The evolution of the knowing subject and his self-positioning in the world of human relations was unmasked as an acting-out of non-rational instincts blindly seeking some kind of equilibrium in a world of essentially material processes (Freudianism). And these acid dissolutions were themselves in turn to be exposed as discourses of a *gendered* (male) subject, defining in advance who is going to count as a speaker worth hearing (feminism – at least as important an intellectual revolution as Freud's or Marx's). Instead of the open space of universal rationality, late modernity has inherited an overcrowded and suspicious territory where every utterance has to be examined, interrogated about the interest it serves, the agenda it (knowingly or unknowingly) encodes and the power it conceals.

Put it more schematically. The Enlightenment objected to traditional authorities on the grounds that they were the products of a contingent history. These authorities had claimed to speak for the Other in relation to which, in dependence upon which, identity was assured and reinforced in a God-directed communal and cosmic order. But if the law and rationality proposed by the Enlightenment as a true and liberating source for identity and order are themselves exposed as contingent, products of particular perspectives and interests, what remains? If law and rationality are only the tools of interest, where is there any space beyond contingency? If *every* other is contingent – that is, if it is what it is by virtue of processes that might have been otherwise – then every other is a rival, a competing interest. And from this point, the self can construe itself in a number of more or less unsatisfactory ways. It can settle for a Romantic or post-Romantic picture of a 'true' self, an 'authentic' core of undetermined will, free to discover and establish its unique moral territory. It can preserve a residue of Enlightenment universalism by seeing itself as a bearer of rights, claims that can somehow be enforced in a tribunal so as to secure a position over other comparable claimants. But both these models, and others that derive from them or reflect them, are fraught with intellectual and imaginative difficulties, some of which this book has tried to trace; they do not allow us to think through what it might be to be alive and concrete only 'in' an other, although just this thought is what our language and experience of being in time constantly invite us towards. But equally, there is a logic of sorts that steps quite beyond any classical images of a unitary self, a narrative consistency making sense of me as a speaker or an agent. The most powerful trends of *post*-modernity argue for the self as a 'site' in or on which the processes of speech, the transactions of power, the sheer mechanics of desire (understood as simple lack) play themselves out. It is interesting, if sobering, to note the current fascination in the arts, especially film and novel, with themes of *addiction* (sexual as well as narcotic): as if there were a conscious focussing on the most extreme figurations of lack, to test what language might emerge and survive in such a context.

Another way, then, of saying what is lost is to see it as the possibility of understanding what it might mean to say that I am because I am *seen* at a certain depth, or that I require a faithful presence to hear my narrative, or that I have no reality as a subject that is not also a reality for and in another subject. If there is no narrative continuity, the significance of the faithful interlocutor or observer disappears. It is worth noting too that all this has a direct relevance to how *bodies* are seen and understood. Systems of bodily convention are the substance of a culture:

gestures and practices that regulate eating, sex, even conversation, are assurances that people remain recognisable to each other, that they can in fact speak to each other, that they can be seen and heard. Not to know how to prepare or host a meal, not to know the expectations and limits that make cultural sense of sexual attraction and sexual intimacy, not to be able, as we say, to read signals, not to know how to exchange courtesies – all this is tantamount to a forgetfulness of culture itself. Impatience with what seemed arbitrary conventions, and the characteristic modern conviction that each of us has a hidden self whose authentic expression must be cultivated, have left us with a fair amount of public barbarity and chaos. Particularly in the realm of sexuality, the rapid disappearance of 'codes' has produced not a paradisal erotic liberty but a society more obsessively anxious about sex than most 'pre-modern' ones. Child abuse, professional harrassment, 'date rape' are all marks of a situation in which what we thoughtlessly call 'body language' is actually failing as a structure of communication because we have no *common* sense (and often no common sense) about sex. Not that atrocity, corruption and violence were absent from the sexual life of earlier cultures; but, if my body means what I choose it to mean and your body what *you* choose it to mean, then the fear of a contest between two alien and arbitrary sets of signification in a sexual encounter will be that much higher. Sexual trust, like any other kind of trust, like the social miracle, disappears. It is an extreme case of that typical modern dilemma – being potentially at the mercy of a contingent other who will always be suspected of maintaining their place or interest by violence.

So the body as a site for the will to impose what may be varied and transitory meanings takes over from the body as speaking a recognisable language. It is not particularly surprising that there is increasing interest in 'body art' – tattooing and piercing especially – as another sign of this prevailing understanding of the body; or that some now talk of 'sexual preference' rather than sexual desire. And the cultural anxiety this breeds is not visible only on confusions about sexual boundaries and identities; it runs much deeper. For there remains the passionate desire to *be seen*, to have one's truth not only expressed but somehow acknowledged or validated. Hence the confessional obsession of so much of the mass media, an obsession that has little or nothing to do with remorse or even with the attempt to shape a coherent narrative of movement or growth. What I have to say is the truth of my experience – commonly a bundle of aspirations, recollections and often profound pains as yet un-thought, woven into no connected story, offering little possibility for bridges and exchanges with other narratives. Even a quintessentially modern and liberal commentator like Suzanne Moore, reviewing a clutch of autobiographical books in 1997, could give vent to near-despair at the 'mountains of self-obsession and self-deception that pass for heavily marketed "honesty" these days'. She writes:

> We cannot know or be certain of anything outside ourselves; it is all just too confusing. As the grand narratives shatter into millions of smaller ones, all crying 'me, me, me', myriad voices whisper: 'I may not be a novelist but I know what I'm like'.
>
> ... It is possible to read all this as incredibly liberating, allowing a plurality of voices that have not been heard before. Or it is possible to see it as the symptom of a supreme crisis of confidence in which no one can speak for anyone outside themselves, in which everyone emotes but no one thinks any more.[19]

Our one subject, says Moore, is the subject itself; which means the subject in desperate search of an audience, unable to absolve or heal itself, hungry for therapy, yet, paradoxically (through the medium of the chat show or the uncensored memoir), making itself the object of an undifferentiated alien gaze, making itself the 'other' of anonymous corporate fantasy. There is nothing here of the discipline of absence and frustration, the putting of the self in question, that might make therapy truly therapeutic, and the problem of the day is *not* that we live in an excessively therapeutically oriented culture but that we haven't a clue what therapy might involve.

[19] Suzanne Moore, 'How was it for me?', *New Statesman* (15 August 1997), p. 44.

The American novelist and essayist, Walker Percy, noted in the early eighties a further symptom of the modern self's hunger and confusion.[20] The autonomous self is lonely: deprived of any means of finding an adequate or satisfying home in the cosmos, it tries to build bridges out of the isolated condition of both human self and human species by demonstrating that we can communicate with other species. 'Why', asks Percy, 'do people in general want to believe that chimps and dolphins and whales can speak, and why do some scientists in particular want so badly to believe that chimps can speak that they will compromise their own science?'[21] We are afraid of being alone in the cosmos as a species just as much as each of us is afraid of being alone with himself or herself. Relating this to what I have been discussing in recent pages, you could say that we are afraid of being left once and for all without an *other* of any kind to engage with. Individually, we find the possibilities of creative exchange and civility, beyond (even if not entirely without) suspicion or rivalry, slipping away from us: there are fewer and fewer conversational others, because of the dominant myths of the authentic hidden self and of the all-pervasiveness of private and competitive interest. But if there were an 'other'

[20] Walker Percy, *Lost in the Cosmos. The Last Self-Help Book* (New York, 1983).
[21] Ibid. p. 168.

for humanity itself, an other *innocent of human history* and therefore outside the human economy of violence, wouldn't we be able to feel assured that we were, after all, the object of a benign gaze, that we were heard and seen as we needed to be?

Such an other might even be sought elsewhere in the cosmos. Percy goes on to observe our interest in the possibilities of communication from extraterrestrial intelligence (not to mention the characteristically contemporary fantasy of abduction by aliens);[22] once again, the underlying agenda seems to be about loneliness. And although the alien intelligence fantasy can be (as so many films and fictions testify) the ultimate competitive threat, it can also hold out the promise of an *innocent* other. It is no accident that the two most popular and most haunting fictions of recent decades about extraterrestrials, *Close Encounters* and *ET*, represent the alien as a kind of holy child. The extraterrestrial intelligence is a voice from outside history, and so seems to offer us a way out from under history's burden; or at least a presence that will define us afresh, give us a place in some wider scheme of things where we are not trapped by what we have done and what has been done to us.

But what if neither whales nor extraterrestrials are going to step in to secure our being-at-home in the universe? Percy is concerned, as well he might be,

[22] Ibid. pp. 171–3.

with the overloading of areas of our human, inner-worldly experience as refuges for what is left of communion and conversation, as means for acquiring a clearer location in the world. In particular, we overload the whole sexual realm – 'the only mode of intercourse by which the self can be certain of its relationship with other selves – by touching and being touched, by giving or receiving pleasure, by penetrating or being penetrated'.[23] Yet this enormous loading of significance takes place at a moment when the *meanings* of the sexually engaged body have contracted in an unprecedented way to the limits of individual will and gratification. How then can sexual activity restore a sense of graciously observed presence to a self for whom the body is a surface on which arbitrary messages can be inscribed – not a medium in which or through which a coherent story is built up as part of a language shared by others? Sexual activity separated from promise and acceptance, from ordinary, prosaic fidelity, becomes one more expression of the plight of the self unable to imagine what is involved in developing an integrity over the passage of time. It is the sacrifice of the *body* – as a carrier of shared and social meaning – to the needs of an isolated and abstract subject, reduced to will and need.

These are difficult matters to write about with any plausibility, because the conservative religious

[23] Ibid. pp. 179–80.

establishment, Protestant and Catholic, has tended to react to the simultaneous trivialising and overloading of sex by a rather panic-stricken moralism, for which dissent about styles of sexual behaviour becomes the main, sometimes the only, touchstone of 'orthodoxy' or fidelity to tradition – which is simply to reproduce within the religious sphere the exact distortion and disproportion from which the secular environment suffers. It is little use trying to address this question in isolation from the broader cultural history of the modern subject. But it is within that broader history that Walker Percy sees a further and far more serious problem arising out of our misprisions about sex. In simple terms: when sex doesn't 'deliver', where do we look next?

Violence. 'The demonic spirit of the autonomous self, disappointed in all other sectors of life and in ordinary intercourse with others, is now disappointed even in the erotic, its last and best hope, and so erupts in violence.'[24] Percy is confident that this is likely to be the 'orgiastic' violence of total war; but that may seem marginally less likely now than in 1983, when he was writing (*marginally*). In the 1990s, open communal conflict seems to be the curse of societies other than the technologically sophisticated and sexually liberated. But I suspect that his analysis holds good as far as the violence of the *imagination* goes – as in the steady pushing back of

[24] Ibid. p. 190.

frontiers in what can be acceptably portrayed in film or even in print; and also in relation to the phenomena touched on at the beginning of this chapter, the rise in temperature in public passions. There is an orgiastic quality to the picturings of fictional violence, as there is to some kinds of public rage; and this is to say nothing of the rising tide of domestic violence, *and* the rising tide of rhetorical violence against certain categories of people identified as useful scapegoats – interestingly enough, often groups that are sexually nonconformist, the homosexual, the single mother. A paradox, undoubtedly: but a public in love with trivialised and overloaded sex is quick to turn on those who represent either a costly or even tragic aspect of sexual behaviour. The lone parent, apparently abandoned to the consequences of actions whose results are normally and successfully bracketed, represents an unwelcome note of risk; the homosexual's detachment from prevailing norms represents an uncomfortable relativising of the seriousness of 'ordinary' sex. I really do suspect that some of the frenzied anxiety about homosexuality arises less from moral disapproval than from the resentful sense that the homosexual is a kind of mocking *parody* of what most people assume sexual desire to be about. But that is another and a complicated question.

Returning to Walker Percy's analysis, to the idea of violence as the final assertion of a place, of being

211

there, it is clear that this means the end of any possibility of being there *for* the contemplation of some other – since the other's perspective is precisely what is negated in violence. This is what it is to lose the soul, destroying the self by destroying the other. David Mamet's play *Oleanna* was a – grossly misunderstood – attempt to reflect on this in the explosive context of the 'sex wars' of the American campus. John, the male professor in the drama, confronts Carol, a student, confused and intimidated by the whole ethos of the academic institution: his response to her, defensive, patronising, compassionate, all at once, indicates his own confusion (a confusion she has confusedly identified) about the institution he represents. He loves teaching, he claims; yet what we see of his performance and hear of his theory points to an ambiguity – a fascinated love of the *violence* of the institution (whose conventions he has mastered) along with a measure of continuing frustration and bafflement at its pressures, which he too experiences as violent. He is stuck in a Socratic method of dissolution and scepticism without a Socratic vision. John, with his anxieties over status and finance, his incoherently impatient conversations on the phone with his wife and his lawyer (constantly interrupting the supposedly pastoral situation in which he tries to counsel Carol), is a person whose soul is insecurely anchored. He can't help his collusion with all that Carol experiences as debilitating and aggressive.

When she – by a process we don't see and have to guess at – elects to respond to the institution's violence by accusing John of sexual harrassment and demeaning behaviour and language, she constructs her own style of violence, a dramatic distortion of what has happened, to which John's arguably good intentions are wholly irrelevant. Her actions have, by the end of the play, destroyed John's professional life; he explodes in a climacteric moment of real physical threat, but holds back at the last minute. Carol's final words, the conclusion of the play, are brilliantly ambiguous: 'Yes. That's right.' Is she telling John that he has now proved her right? That he has at last acted out openly the abusive and violent agenda of which she has accused him? Or, as she repeats the words, with lowered head, 'to herself ' (so the stage direction instructs), is she acknowledging the truth of his furious attack on her as a 'vicious little bitch'? Is she reverting to her position at the beginning of the play, the assumption of her innate worthlessness?[25]

Whatever the meaning of this ending, each has destroyed the other. The unutterably stupid audiences who applauded (so it's said) as John physically menaces Carol, had wholly missed the ironies already flagged in the opening scene. *Both* are helplessly unformed souls: they enforce their presence to themselves and each other by different kinds of

[25] David Mamet, *Oleanna* (New York, 1992).

violence; they diminish themselves in their negation of each other, John by his inability to listen to the full range of Carol's distress (and his repeated distraction with phone calls about his new house, his note-taking while Carol is speaking, and so on), Carol by her deliberate decision to humiliate and punish John by forcing his actions into a pattern that will require official condemnation. They are 'there' for each other only as aggressors. They are souls in hell.

Lost souls: that is ultimately what the 'lost icons' of the title point to. The skills have been lost of being present for and in an other, and what remains is mistrust and violence. It sounds odd, I suspect, to talk of a 'skill' being involved in being present for an other, a 'skill' of being seen; but there is such a thing as a habit of relinquishing controlled self-presentation; or of that attentive stillness which is somehow bound up with *being* attended to. Rilke's famous response to the 'archic statue' – 'There is no place where you go unseen:/You need to change your life' – holds something of this. To be seen: perhaps this is the foundation of any apprehension of the moral self – not, please God, in the sense of being under the all-seeing eye of a judging scrutiny, but the recognition of a life lived beyond the self-referential framework of what *I* choose or understand. This feels like loss and danger. But equally it entails that the resources for my future don't have to be found in or generated by my choice or my understanding. To put it in a deliberately question-begging way, the self that is present to itself and others without violence or anxiety, the self that might possibly be called a soul, exists in the expectation of *grace*. The disciplines touched on earlier in this chapter, the suspensions or deferrals of gratification, are, like the experience of erotic love, something to do with the expectation of grace: by deferral, by refusing what *I* conceive myself to want or need, I invite what I don't know, the 'non-existent Other'.

Souls occur when trust of a certain kind occurs, the trust implied in such an invitation of the perpetually absent Other. In the background of much of this book is the question of how our contemporary culture nurtures or fails to nurture trust. Steiner's still problematic and controversial essay on *Real Presences* identifies a deep vein of cultural dysfunction in the breaking of the 'contract' between word and world implicit in later modern and postmodern literary sensibility; and he traces a very direct connection between this and the disintegration of the self. Once words have been 'disinvested' of their involvement with the fabric of the world, the acid of deconstruction leaks into the very notion of the *speaker* of words. 'The ego is no longer itself. More precisely, it is no longer itself to itself, it is no longer available to integration.'[26] What

[26] George Steiner, *Real Presences. Is There Anything In What We Say?* (London, 1989), p. 99.

215

lies 'at the now vacant heart of consciousness' is a chaos of random others – that is, not speaking and relating others, but 'parodistic, nihilistic anti-matter'.[27] The residual self is a site where the traces of what's heard or registered lie around, where unthinking reproduction of received images takes place, where stray forces and chains of causality intersect. It is irreclaimably different from the speaker's self-image as an authorising source or a continuous presence. If there is no presence in words, there is no presence in speakers. If you can't trust the contract between word and world, speech and what it's trying to respond to, you can't trust what you may think you perceive 'within' either.

The contrasts here may be too starkly drawn, too cavalier about the degree to which the speaker is inevitably deceived about the nature of his or her interiority (Augustine was already fascinated by the inaccessibility and alienness of speaking minds to themselves); and the sense in which 'being' is capable of being uttered, the contract or covenant of word and world, has regularly been fingered over by philosophers unconvinced about neat relations between words and external objects, without a resultant nihilism. Hegel, for instance, does not describe any *contract* between language and what it is not, but seeks to trace, how, in the processes of thinking and speaking, we are drawn (if we are

[27] Ibid.

216

willing to abide the necessary moments of frustration and contradiction) into an intelligent life whose perspective is neither limitedly or exclusively mine *nor* that of 'no one in particular', and which is truthful to the extent that it transcends the perspective of any one historical agent or moment. But it would certainly be true to say that Hegel assumes a massive act of trust or faith in the historical adventure of thought-in-community; and Steiner is right to see the turn of the late modern and postmodern world as radically and newly fragmentary.

Part of Hegel's insight, however, also has to do with the more overtly political matter of how in our dealings with one another we move towards a common life, a system of *Recht* (not quite 'law', not exactly 'right', but something close to 'public rationality' as it affects behaviour, not only discourse), which all recognise as embodying their true interest. Steiner at least compels us to attend to the erosion of trust at the basis of intellectual life; but what happens when this is complemented by the erosion of trust in corporate and political life? Ours is increasingly a situation in which ordinary citizens don't (and can't) take it for granted that the institutions of society can be relied upon to work in their interest. Education, healthcare, the law, are increasingly seen as bureaucratic and incompetent systems, consuming public funds in labyrinthine administration. Cynicism about government in general spills over into cynicism about public services; and the law is an obvious target for suspicion about whose interests are being served. These alienations – well-founded or not – are far more strongly marked in the USA than in Britain, and suspicion of central government has led to reactions of an increasingly feverish and paranoid character.

'Fightings within and fears without', as the hymn puts it: I am not recognisable to (thinking, speaking) self; I am not recognisable to a non-competitive other, not seen or attended to; I cannot recognise myself, my truth or interest or welfare, in the common life. The question that presses urgently through all this is what I can then say or do that is not in some sense violent. There are of course inescapable 'violences' in all speech and action. Gillian Rose wrote of the 'violence in love' and the 'love in violence',[28] both of which we seek to avoid in an unthinking fear of risk. Love stakes a position, and so cannot help risking the displacement or damaging of another. It is never far from violence. But violence itself seeks recognition, is a rebellion against solitary withdrawal and closure; and, in appealing to otherness in that way, is obliquely connected with love's search for life in the other. But when violence is taken out of this dialectical understanding, when it becomes more and more

[28] Gillian Rose, *The Broken Middle. Out of Our Ancient Society* (Oxford, 1992), see esp. pp. 147–52.

clamant and insistent because its expectation of recognition is more and more eroded, the 'love in violence' is more and more securely imprisoned, frustrated in its residual urge towards converse. The loss of the soul becomes the loss of a *social*, not merely an individual, body.

'Where you are is where you are not,' wrote Eliot, paraphrasing St John of the Cross:[29] the recurring paradox is that our presence in the social body is only assured by the gift of a regard from outside, and that such regard is itself perceived and received only when we are dispossessed of a particular conception of presence. What has to come under judgement is the 'presence' of a single integrated system of needs and desires that is inherently violent and competitive. I become socially present when this is undermined in some degree, when the 'finished' self, justified to itself and in terms of itself, is absent; which means that to be socially present is to be present as a *soul* – as that which emerges through the disciplines of non-gratification or deferral, through love, through being seen. My presence in language, in converse and *intelligible* (that is, shared) action is grounded in an absence, the absence of the fantasy-fulfilment in which ego and object complement and 'finalise' each other (this is *for me*; I am satisfactorily myself *because of this*). And this absence is achieved in a complex set of dispossessions, sought and unsought – the 'defining

[29] T. S. Eliot, *Four Quartets* 'East Coker' (1940), pt. 3.

219

conflicts' of Walter Davis's analysis, the moment when the subject discovers that its being is 'at issue'.

But what was said earlier should alert us to the risk here of a further turn of anxiety. Being 'where you are not', being dispossessed of the clear and well-defended site that the modern ego dreams of, may be understood simply as an absorption into an endless chain of displacement – the workings of the contingent other, the other who, in fact, mirrors my own contingency and instability. And because the contingent other is an other *like me*, the shadow of rivalry is never wholly absent. That is why this chapter has returned repeatedly to the language of the non-contingent other, the other that is *sufficiently* other not to compete with me for any imaginable space, logical, psychological, material, social: the 'non-existent Other', whose absence as just another agent or presence makes possible my own exodus from the imprisoning model of presence with which I'm likely to start. And here is the basic choice, call it metaphysical, religious or even just narrative. Is the absent Other that makes possible my own saving absence and social presence simply a construct, a linguistic device to spring me from my trap and no more? It is, of course, *at least* a linguistic construct, it appears in and only in the ways in which we speak to each other, socially and 'privately'; but can it be read without remainder as a tactic to enable the soul to emerge?

Say the answer to that is Yes; the implications are not promising. If it is in some sense *my* tactic, what I do to secure my release, it is a device of precisely that will which I must displace. It risks being a self-projection, built upon a fundamentally unchallenged ego. If it is the tactic of a contingent other, how can it avoid being seen as a tactic deployed by one ego to secure a desired effect in another? We have seen the delicacy of the disciplines needed in the analytic relationship if such misunderstanding is to be checked; but on what do such disciplines rest, on what curious faith in the *validity* or legitimacy of talking like this in the first place about an identity shaped by the evoking of a significant absence? Is it ultimately the case that language is the engagement of contingent others with each other, however it may seek to limit the damage done, by means of oblique evocations of something else? Postmodernist theory itself gestures characteristically towards a non-presence that we can't help indicating – the marginal, the region of *différance*, that which surrounds speech because it is what speech both does not say and 'says' by refusing it. But in what sense this could be an Other that made anything possible is obscure: if anything, it tends to reduce the idea of social presence itself to an abstraction. The speaker is the site on which forces converge and contend: *I* am absent, not as yielding place or recognising myself in the other, but because I am the gratuitous and impotent deposit of the freezing or solidifying of one moment or aspect of the contest of forces.

The question nagging away behind all this is whether it makes sense to imagine the absent Other as somehow analogous to the giver of a gift. Hence – again – the drift in these concluding reflections towards a religious construction of the absent Other. Buddhism, which has invested so much, with such sophistication, in the language of absence, not-self and so on, insists that any actual imagining of the sheer 'that' which makes us free and lies beyond desire and self-representation will return us ultimately to the bondage of desire. It is an important and serious challenge to the insistence of the eastern Mediterranean religious traditions that, whatever the risk we have no choice but to speak at *some* point about gift or love, and therefore to recognise in the Other something like intelligence and action. Better the admitted paradox of a self-dispossessing divinity, say these traditions, better the puzzling evocations of an agency that is unqualified gift or 'bestowal' than the risk of the unqualified abstractness of the Buddhist discourse, the pointing to a wholly indeterminate There or That.

Needless to say, there is no objective way of settling the issue between these two (or any other set of) traditions. Both involve different but not unrelated forms of the disciplines of a controlled frustration of desire; both give considerable importance to *corporate* ritual practice as the context for the re-formation of the self. But what I have called the eastern Mediterranean (Jewish, Christian

222

and Muslim) discourses all give a pivotal place in their language to *gratitude* – the acknowledgement that I am acted *on* before I act or can act. The absent other in language is there-and-not-there because we are always already spoken *to*. This is expressed formally in the concept of a creation from nothing – a doctrine that establishes very plainly why the divine is not *an* other, within a system of interlocking or negotiating agencies; and why – to refer back to one of the oldest axioms in the Mediterranean religious tradition – there is no 'envy' in the divine. There is by definition nothing to compete for, so that it actually becomes possible to imagine the divine as the source of unqualified gift.

The Christian tradition in particular elaborates a bit further, in the proposals that God is, intrinsically and independently of the universe, a 'system' or pattern of agency and relation (trinity), and that God's agency is present without qualification within the material identity of one historical agent (Jesus Christ). The first of these prohibits the Christian from conceiving the otherness of the divine as in *any* way like that of one other subject in a system. The second reinforces and deepens the prohibition against seeing the divine and what is other to it as in *any* way competing for the same space (since God and the human are 'located' in exactly the same place in this particular person). Much more would need to be said about how these religious conceptualities relate to what has been addressed in this book;

my point here is only to indicate how they might be read as attempts to construct, in the light of a complex historical narrative of divine action, a resourceful language for the 'non-existent Other' which is at the foundations of speech and sociality.

Perhaps predictably, in the light of all this, the Christian tradition both represents these doctrinal notions *and* refuses to settle for any representation as exhaustive. In the early centuries of the Christian Church, there were heated debates over the correct or adequate way of articulating belief, debates that have been the object of polite wonder and not-so-polite mockery from Gibbon to the present day. Alongside these debates, however, ran a complementary development, the refining of a theology of 'denial' or 'unsaying', *apophasis*: by all means struggle to get the least misleading formula, because words do matter, and how you represent God affects what you are going to find possible for yourself and for the human community; but equally, don't mistake the words for a description of what it is like to be God, of the 'essence' of the divine. These words are not labels (strictly speaking, no words are simply labels anyway) but something more like codes of instruction, directions as to how to shape and discipline your seeing and your reacting to what's given.

And it is out of this particular balancing act that the Christian icon emerges in its full theological sense. By the eighth century of the Common Era, and in the teeth of some savage religio-political struggles, Eastern Christianity had elaborated a theory and practice of *pictorial* representation corresponding to its theory and practice of *verbal* representation. The Byzantine icon is not meant to reproduce a set of empirical data – how Christ or the saints happened to look, what heaven is supposed to be like. The famous fourteenth-century depiction of the Trinity by Andrei Rublev, the extraordinary frescoes of his teacher Feofan, the works of the 'Palaeologue Renaissance' in Constantinople with their athletic figures throwing off light as if soaked in some phosphorescent liquid – these are not an attempt to show you what God or the things of heaven look like. The Church that commissioned and used such images knew perfectly well that God and heaven – and even, in an important sense, the events of a holy life – don't 'look like' anything, and that the divine reality can't be rendered exhaustively in material terms. The image gives directions, it essays a way of bringing you into a new place and a new perception.

It does at least two preliminary things – and one central thing of some importance for the argument of this book. It shows bodily realities – the face of Christ or Mary, the portraits of saints, episodes from biblical or hagiological story – as suffused with divine action: the bodies are stylised and configured into patterns, often patterns of violent energy and often underlined by an apparently anarchic but in fact tightly worked scattering of highlights. There are no light sources outside the frame: light, pattern, significance, move *out* from a base or centre. Second, and in consequence of this, the eye is invited, or instructed, to move repeatedly *in* to this base or centre, to the sources of light. But it has many times been stressed that the *perspective* of iconic representation totally refuses anything like the convergent point of disappearance familiar in Western representational art. The 'centre' is not a distant abstract point but something at work *in* the luminous surface itself. In many instances, perspective is apparently reversed: the convergent point is the eye itself, as if the painted surface were a window into another geometrical order.[30]

But the most important feature here is what both these highly self-conscious grotesqueries are attempting to encode. The person looking at the icon is invited (instructed?) to let go of being an agent observing a motionless phenomenon: the idiom of the painting insists on its own activity, its 'bearing down' upon the beholder, shedding rather than receiving light, gathering and directing its energy rather than spreading from an invisible point of convergence. And this finds its fullest expression

[30] On inverse perspective in icons, see, for example, Leonid Ouspensky, 'The Meaning and Language of Icons' in Leonid Ouspensky and Vladimir Lossky, *The Meaning of Icons* (2nd ed. Crestwood, NY, 1982), pp. 25–49, p. 41.

in the iconographer's depiction of the eyes of Christ or the saints (no saint is ever shown in profile). As the perspective 'bears down' upon the beholder's eye, the eye of the iconic figure acts, searches, engages. The skill of looking at icons, the discipline of 'reading' them, is indeed the strange skill of letting yourself be seen, be read.

The religious icon is an evocation of the non-existent Other simply by its subversion of what we might expect in a devotional artefact. It does not work to stimulate emotion or clarify ideas or add concreteness to a process of reflection: it requires first that I take time to follow (obey) those surface movements that indicate the inner centre of illumination; then that I stand to *be* illuminated, to be the object of whatever is at work. The non-existent Other is here the absence of any imaginable or conceivable reality 'behind' the icon's surface, some further level capable of inspection: there is no normal perspectival hinterland. Or you could say that its otherness is in the fact that the icon is always a wall that confronts (at the same time as being a rather peculiar kind of window), that can't be seen from the back, and so does not occupy a space *alongside* me, does not share the dimension I inhabit. But so much of this in fact returns to the theme of the icon as what I am seen *by*: the eyes with which I must engage but cannot negotiate – because they do not hold a position like mine – occupy a dimensional point of view.

The 'lost icons' of this book have been clusters of convention and imagination, images of possible lives or modes of life, possible positions to occupy in a world that is inexorably one of time and loss. But as the discussion has developed, it has hinted more and more at a single, focal area of lost imagination – what I have called the lost soul. And *this* loss, I've suggested, is inextricably linked with the loss of what is encoded in the actual icons of Christian tradition and usage – the Other who does not compete, with whom I don't have to and can't bargain; the Other beyond violence, the regard that will not be evaded or deflected, yet has and seeks no advantage. What has been culturally lost, the sense of being educated into adult choice, the possibility (tantalisingly both political and more than political) of social miracle, active appropriation of a common good, the possibility of letting go of a possessed and defended image of the moral self, abstractly free, self-nurturing – all this will remain lost without a recovered confidence in the therapeutic Other, not 'there' for examination, for contest, even for simple consolation; so hard to say anything about without risking the corruption of the consolatory voice. But sometimes, whatever the risk, we have to force ourselves to talk, not of consolation but of hope, of what is not or cannot be lost. We *can* choose death, but we don't have to. What we are present to is neither created nor extinguished by our will. The iconic eye remains wakeful.

Index